UNIVERSITY
UNLIMITED

UNIVERSITY UNLIMITED
THE MONASH STORY

GRAEME DAVISON AND KATE MURPHY

ALLEN&UNWIN
SYDNEY·MELBOURNE·AUCKLAND·LONDON

Allen & Unwin
Sydney, Melbourne, Auckland, London

83 Alexander Street
Crows Nest NSW 2065
Australia
Phone: (61 2) 8425 0100
Fax: (61 2) 9906 2218
Email: info@allenandunwin.com
Web: www.allenandunwin.com

Cataloguing-in-Publication details are available
from the National Library of Australia
www.trove.nla.gov.au

ISBN 978 1 74237 866 4 (paperback)
ISBN 978 1 74331 056 4 (hard cover)

Internal design by Philip Campbell Design
Index by Puddingburn
Set in 10.75/15 pt Janson Text LT Std by Bookhouse, Sydney
Printed in Australia by Ligare Pty Ltd, Sydney

10 9 8 7 6 5 4 3 2 1

CONTENTS

ILLUSTRATIONS

Endpapers

Inside front cover: Menzies Building under construction, 1964, Wolfgang Sievers.
Inside back cover: Students in lecture, c. 1963, Wolfgang Sievers.

In-text images

Insert 1

Insert 2

ABBREVIATIONS

ALP	Australian Labor Party
ANU	Australian National University
AUC	Australian Universities Commission
BSM	Bates, Smart & McCutcheon
DEC	Distance Education Centre
ECOPS	Faculty of Economics and Politics
EU	Evangelical Union
HECS	Higher Education Contribution Scheme
IT	Information technology
IVF	In-vitro fertilisation
MAS	Monash Association of Students
MSA	Monash South Africa
NLF	National Liberation Front
PAC	Public Affairs Committee (of MAS)
RMIT	Royal Melbourne Institute of Technology
SRC	Students' Representative Council
TRAG	Teaching and Research Action Group
UNE	University of New England
VCG	Vice-Chancellor's Group

ACKNOWLEDGEMENTS

This book could not have been written without the generous support and assistance of many scores of people, both within the Monash community and beyond.

For occasional research assistance we wish to thank our colleague Annabelle Baldwin. Alice Davies of the School of Philosophical, Historical and International Studies assisted us with budgetary matters.

For permission to reproduce photographs we acknowledge former students David Taft, Douglas Wilkie, Pete Steedman and Peter Costello; the Sunway Group; Monash University Sunway; Advancement, Monash South Africa; Fairfax Syndication; Newspix Syndication; National Archives of Australia; University of Melbourne Special Collections; John Corker; emeritus professors Peter Darvall, Richard Larkins and Tam Sridhar; and Woods Bagot Architects. For permission to quote verse by the late Philip Martin we thank Ms Jennifer Gribble. We were unable to trace the owners of some other copyright material: anyone with information is asked to contact the publisher.

A number of present and former staff and other scholars kindly shared their own research papers, unpublished memoirs or informal recollections: Dr Arthur O'Neill, Emeritus Professor Bill Rachinger, Emeritus Professor John Crossley, Professor David Garrioch, Associate Professor Philip Mendes, Dr Cecilia Hewlett, Dr Judith Buckrich, Professor Alan Boura, Sarah Rood, Paul Rodan, Professor Jeff Giddings, David Buckingham and Catherine Harboe-Ree. We also wish to acknowledge assistance from Professor Shane Murray and Professor Claudia Terstappen of the Faculty of Art and Design.

The following people kindly agreed to be interviewed, either alone or in groups: Professor Michael Abramson, Professor Simon Adams, Associate Professor Michael Adamson, Adlina Ahmad, Dr Robin Alfredson, Dr John Arkinstall, Associate Professor Harry Ballis, Saul Bastomsky, Ron Bayly, Dr John Bennett, Emeritus Professor John Bigelow, Professor Robert Bignall, Emeritus Professor Gary Bouma, Emeritus Professor David Bradley, Emeritus Professor Johnson Bradshaw, Professor Chris Browne, Emeritus Professor Maureen Brunt, Professor Dina Burger, Professor Ed Byrne, Charmain Caroto, Crystal Chatterton, Professor Brian Cherry, Professor James Chin, Emeritus Professor Arthur Clark, Brian Corless, Professor Edwina Cornish, Hon. Peter Costello, Tim Costello, Dr David Cuthbert, Emeritus Professor Peter Darvall, Emeritus Professor Ian Davey, Emeritus Professor Ross Day, Professor Tony Dingle, Professor Peter Dixon, Professor Barry Dunstan, former chancellor Jerry Ellis, Professor Merran Evans, Professor Stephanie Fahey, Jon Faine, Emeritus Professor Solly Faine, Emeritus Professor Peter Fensham, Associate Professor Trevor Finlayson, Professor Peter Fitzpatrick, Associate Professor Kevin Foster, Dr Mary Gani, Pam and Ian Gibson, Peter Goddard, Keith Hamilton, Dr Marianne Hicks, Dr Geoffrey Hiller, Associate Professor John Hinwood, Emeritus Professor Bruce Holloway, Norman Hurrell, Uvais Ibrahim, Dr Margaret James, Associate Professor Ken Jones, Dr Viv Kelly, Lee Weng Keng, Emeritus Professor Bill Kent, Professor Walter Kirsop, Associate Professor Mike Knowles, Bruce Knox, Professor David de Kretser, Vusi Kweyama, Emeritus Professor Richard Larkins, Emeritus Professor John Legge, Lily Leong, Associate Professor Boon Leong Lan, Mike Lewenberg, Emeritus Professor Mal Logan, Emeritus Professor Dennis Lowther, Stephanie Lux, Dr Ian Mabbett, Professor Andrew Markus, Emeritus Professor Ray Martin, Lady Audrey Matheson, Dr John McDonell, Jill McLachlan, Professor Chris Messom, Lennon Mhishi, Professor Joe Monaghan, Will Moore, Petunia Mpoza, Nicolene Murdoch, Dr Dave Nadel, Professor Mahendhiran Nair, Dr Mark Ng, Associate Professor Jocelyn O'Neil, Professor Stephen Parker, Professor Leon Piterman, Gary and Kelly Pollard, Professor Robin Pollard, Emeritus Professor Ian Polmear, Emeritus Professor Bob Porter, Emeritus Professor Alan Powell, Professor Tyrone Pretorius, Emeritus Professor Marian Quartly, Shanthy Rachagan, Dr Phil Rayment, Morris Reid, former chancellor Bill Rogers, Craig Rowe, Vic Sabrinskas, Alan Scarlett, Carl Selvarajah, Emeritus Professor Gus Sinclair, Emeritus Professor Graeme Smith, Associate Professor Ralph Snyder, Cheang Kok Soon, Professor Tam Sridhar, Brian Stark, Associate Professor Bruce Steele, Professor Phillip Steele, Emeritus Professor John Swan, Professor Grahame Taylor, Neil Terrill, Eric Thorne, Phang Koon Tuck, Peter Wade, Emeritus Professor Louis Waller, Sheelaugh Walton, Ken Ward, Emeritus Professor James Warren, Hon. Dean Wells, Emeritus Professor Bruce West, Nicola Williams, David Williamson, Professor Rob Willis, Professor Sue Willis, Professor Walter Wong, Yvonne Yap, Jessica Yik and Dr Cathy Yule.

A number of others responded to our invitation to submit their written memoirs (referred to in the notes as 'submissions'): MarJo Angelico, Professor Peter Beilharz, Calvin Chow, Alan and Linda Cleeland, Chris Coney, Peter Crabb, Professor Ron Davies, Colin and Kathy De La Rue, Pamela Dooley, Michael J. Dowling, Laurie Duggan, Dr David Dunstan, Nghi Duong, Tamar Erickson, Professor Jim Falk, Diane Gardiner, Ian and Pam Gibson, Elliot Gingold, Professor Kevin Hart, Michael Headberry, Gillian Hensler, David Humphreys, Ruth Kweitel, Mark LaPirow, Tess Lee-Ack, Don Lyell, Stewart Macleod, Jared Mansfield, Dahlia Martin, Clare McCausland, Jim McGrath, Melissa McVeigh, Dr Carly Millar, Ken Mogg, Sonia Parisi, Tabatha Pettitt, Vikki Plant, Louise Price, Emeritus Professor Bill Rachinger, Emeritus Professor Merle Ricklefs, Celia Rosser, Dr Richard Scully, Sasha Shtargot, Melody Song, Leeyong Soo, Erika Stahr, Professor Roger Strasser, Associate Professor Jennifer Strauss, Karen Sutherland, Steve Timewell, Alan Wearne, Bruce C. Wearne, Stephen Wilks and Jean Youatt. Others have contacted us with stories, suggestions for sources or offers of photographs.

Inevitably, only some of these personal testimonies could be quoted in the book, but they have all contributed to the rich braid of memories that inform it. To anyone whose contribution we have inadvertently overlooked or misinterpreted we apologise. To everyone we offer our sincere thanks.

INTRODUCTION

Monash is Australia's biggest and most international university. Compared with other great universities, it is still young—just fifty years old—but its history belongs to the most momentous chapter in the 1000-year evolution of higher learning. In that half-century, universities have been transformed from academic enclaves educating small elites into comprehensive educational and research institutions serving the complex needs of entire societies. Few universities exemplify that transformation as well as Monash. Founded in 1958, at the threshold of the space age, it aspired to be modern in everything, from its starkly modernist architecture and experimental approach to learning, to its commitment to marry the humanities and sciences and orientate Australia towards Asia. Located on Melbourne's suburban frontier, it soon became Australia's first drive-in university. It was the most striking Australian example of a new kind of higher education institution, the 'multiversity'. By the late 1960s, the era of Vietnam, it was also the nation's most radical campus, popularly regarded as a hotbed of insurrection. Yet only two decades later it had enthusiastically embraced the neo-liberal Dawkins reforms and the shift towards 'the enterprise university'. Now, with students spread over six campuses and with footprints in Malaysia, South Africa, Europe and India, it is the most aggressively international Australian university. At every stage, Monash has defined itself by looking outwards rather than inwards, by embracing innovation rather than standing on tradition. To its admirers, it was 'bold' and 'buccaneering', a pacesetter for the rest of the nation; to its detractors, it could seem imperialistic, accident-prone and heedless of the lessons of experience.

Monash's founders had not aimed to overthrow tradition but to renovate it. The colonial universities had followed British custom in selecting their mottoes from classical writers. Sydney's *sidere mens eadem mutato* vowed to maintain the traditions of the old world in the new. Melbourne's *postera crescam laude* anticipated the favourable opinion of posterity. Monash would have its own motto too, but it would be English not Latin, its first council decided. Foundation Professor of Biology Jock Marshall tried to incorporate the feathered tail of a lyrebird in the university's crest. But the College of Heralds rejected the avian oddity, and the council failed to come up with an appropriate English motto. Marshall finally suggested *ancora imparo*. The words—Italian, not English or Latin—were said to be Michelangelo's, and their meaning—'I am still learning'—nicely captured the outlook of the new university. Knowledge, it suggested, was progressive, experimental and incomplete. The university would always be learning, exploring new ways of doing things, seeking new frontiers.

Fifty years on, Marshall's motto (*still* learning?) remains apposite. We approach Monash's history in that spirit of open-ended inquiry. Shortly before the university's fiftieth anniversary, in 2008, Vice-Chancellor Richard Larkins invited Graeme Davison to consider writing a new history of the university. Although some of Monash's founders, notably Louis Matheson and Robert Blackwood, had published their memoirs, and Simon Marginson had written an illuminating book on the 'remaking' of the university in the 1980s and 1990s, there was no scholarly history that encompassed the full fifty years, exploited the university's rich archives and captured the memories of the many significant individuals who had contributed to its story. Such a history, they agreed, should be critical as well as celebratory, and attentive to the relationships between the university and its society.

As trustees of funds held over from the fiftieth anniversary celebrations, a committee chaired by Professor Alistair Thomson later invited Graeme Davison and Kate Murphy to write the history together, a proposal that appealed both to the writers and to the committee. Murphy's perspective as a recent Monash doctoral graduate complemented Davison's twenty-five years as a senior academic at Monash. Because the university has supported the project financially, *University Unlimited* may be described as an official history, but in no sense is it an authorised history. From the beginning, we have been assured that the history we write will be our own, uncensored and uninhibited by official expectations. The usual disclaimer—that the views expressed are our own, not those of the university—applies. We are grateful to the members of our management committee, Al Thomson, Adam Shoemaker, Marian Quartly, Dick Selleck, Tony Dingle and Jan Getson, who have read our drafts and offered wise and perceptive advice but never attempted to direct us. Instead of a case-bound, lavishly illustrated doorstopper, we aimed at a book that would express something of the democratic Monash style—informal yet stylish, engaging yet scholarly, affordable yet elegant. We were pleased when we found a publisher, Elizabeth Weiss of Allen & Unwin, who responded sympathetically to our vision of the book and helped to give it physical form.

University Unlimited marks the fiftieth anniversary of Monash. Although it was first conceived in the approach to the anniversary of the passage of the Monash University Act in 1958, it was completed to mark the anniversary of the arrival of the first students in 1961. As we explain elsewhere, plans for the establishment of a second Victorian university had been discussed since the early 1940s. While reviewing this background, the main focus of our narrative is the fifty years from 1958 to the conclusion of the vice-chancellorship of Richard Larkins in 2008. As we write, Monash is again engaged in energetic debates about its future. While we have recounted the antecedents and context of these debates, we have not attempted to review the most recent phase of the university's history or to anticipate its outcome.

We are conscious of the trust that the university and our colleagues have reposed in us. While striving for scholarly impartiality, often revising recollections and first impressions in the light of contrary evidence, we cannot pretend to neutrality. Inevitably, our book draws on personal experience. Its narrative curve is that of Davison's own life course, as one of the generation of young Australians whose lives were transformed by the expansion of the universities. As a sixteen-year-old high school student, he gazed wonderingly into the sky when Sputnik first appeared over Melbourne in 1957, and debated C.P. Snow's essay on 'The Two Cultures'. He became an arts student at Melbourne University, the first in his family to go to university, and later taught there for twelve years. He came to Monash as a second-generation professor of history in 1982. He has never held high office, but, as a long-time deputy dean of the Arts Faculty, a member of the Waller Committee (1989) and the Arts Faculty Restructuring Committee (1998), as well as director of the Monash University London Centre (2005–07), he was often a close observer of events covered in this book and has known many of the main actors personally. Murphy is the child of first-generation university students. Her parents, both holders of Education Department studentships, were among the beneficiaries of the government largesse that underpinned the age of mass education. An undergraduate at one of Australia's sandstone universities, the University of Tasmania, she was attracted to Monash for her PhD, having already developed some sense—from across the Bass Strait—of its reputation for egalitarian unconventionality. She came to the project with little prior knowledge of the subject, unfettered, one might say, by institutional prejudices.

This book is the fruit of our shared endeavour. We each researched and drafted about half the manuscript, with Murphy concentrating her attention on student experience and Davison on the academic community. As the project developed, we pooled information, exchanged ideas and read and reviewed each other's drafts, often adding new material or suggesting new lines of inquiry, so that the book is a collaborative work. Hardly a day went by when we did not chat or exchange emails about some aspect of the book. We conducted most of the interviews together, although Murphy, who interviewed members of the South African campus in October 2010, also undertook the related archival research, as Davison did in Malaysia in March 2011. We owe a special debt to Jan Getson and Lyn Maloney of the Monash University Archives, who kindly made space available in their offices where we could install our computers, scan documents and call upon their detailed knowledge of the collections. The project simply could not have been completed as smoothly and enjoyably as it was without their everyday assistance in locating material and checking references or their enthusiastic support. We hope that this book will draw attention to the riches of the archives, which now contain a growing collection of professorial papers as well as central, faculty and departmental archives. With only modest resources, the archives staff have begun to digitise some records and make them available online. We look forward to a time when, with more resources and new-generation archival software, these wonderful collections become better known and more easily searchable.

The history of a university is a distillation of many conversations. 'University academics are professional talkers', observed Registrar Jim Butchart, who had listened, not always patiently, to many of them. No history can hope to capture more than a bucket or two from this torrent of talk. The archival record, on which we have largely relied, captures the official record of university business but misses the substance and style of the thousands of other conversations taking place in its classrooms, offices and labs. The most important things a university does lie beyond the centralised archival record—in the minds of its students, and in the lectures, publications, conference papers and activities of its members in the wider world. Even more elusive are the contributions it makes through the influence of its students. While we have attempted to describe the intellectual activities of representative individuals, and even to characterise Monash's intellectual milieu, we realise how little we have been able to capture of this important dimension of the university's history. It would require a Monash Dictionary of Biography to do justice to the many remarkable stories we have encountered but had too little space to tell.

An invaluable corrective to the limitations of the paper record, although with limitations of its own, is the oral testimony of participants. We were privileged to have long conversations with about seventy former administrative staff, academics and students, who shared their experience with extraordinary candour, humour, humility and narrative flair. Almost as many again participated in the seven discussions we arranged with present and former members of various faculties and campuses. A number of Monash 'originals', including Audrey Matheson, John Legge, John Swan and Bruce Holloway, offered their vivid recollections of the earliest phase of the university's history, although, sadly, several others, including Carl Wood, Bill Kent, Michael Clyne and Enid Campbell, died during the time we were at work. We have been able to use only a fraction of the interview material we collected in the book, but with the permission of the interviewees the digital recordings and transcripts of these conversations will become a permanent part of the university's archives, available to future researchers.

For many of our interviewees, the Monash story has been a large, sometimes the largest, project of their professional lives. It has engaged their passions and ideals as well as their ambitions. They have experienced clashes of personality and principle. We have not sought to paper over these conflicts, or the passions they stirred, for often at their heart were deeply held convictions about the nature and purpose of the university. From the beginning, Monash attracted a gallery of vivid, talented characters, whose personalities have shaped the present-day university almost as much as the policies and projects they pursued. We think that the best way to honour their contribution is to present them as personalities rather than as talking resumés.

The milieu that matters to most academics and students is not the university, which often presents itself as a remote bureaucracy, but the faculty, school or department. This is where friends are made, intellectual collaborations begin and students find encouragement, recognition and stimulus. Over the two and a half years that we have been engaged on this project, three faculties—Engineering, Law and Education—have begun historical projects, and books have also been published recently on the history of the university's campuses in Malaysia and Prato. We take heart that some parts of the Monash story that we have not had the space to tell will emerge in these publications. Those readers who are disappointed to find how little of their own department's or faculty's story appears in these pages have the remedy in their own hands: they can seek redress by commissioning faculty or departmental histories of their own.

Writing this book has reinforced our belief that the Monash story is important, not just for its own academics and students, but for the society beyond the campus. Australia is now different from what it was in 1961, partly because of the permeation of ideas, techniques and attitudes inculcated first of all on the university campuses. Opinions will vary on the success of that experiment. Some may see it as a failure, a sad descent from the days when university education was the prized possession of an elite. Others, including ourselves, will applaud universities like Monash that constantly reached outwards, even though they sometimes faltered in the attempt. Both sides will find evidence to confound, as well as confirm, their views in the following pages. History seldom delivers clear-cut, take-home lessons, and we do not offer them here. Nevertheless, in relating the story of a bold experiment in higher education, we have aspired to illuminate the future of Monash, as well as its proud, sometimes contentious and always vigorous past.

COLD BEER FOR BREAKFAST

Soon after dawn, the *Asturias* docked in Port Melbourne. During the night, while its passengers slept, the ship had slipped through the Heads, and as the sun rose over Port Phillip Bay, they came out on deck, straining for a first view of their destination. It was February 1947 and most of the ship's company were immigrants escaping the wintry austerity of a Britain still slowly recovering from war.

Louis and Audrey Matheson and their two boys were among the immigrants, although they had travelled first-class thanks to Louis's new employer, the University of Melbourne.[1] As she looked towards the wharf, Audrey recalled the afternoon just a few months earlier when Louis returned from the university to their home in Northfield on the leafy southern fringe of Birmingham. The toddlers were on the kitchen floor, playing noisily with cake tins and saucepans, and Audrey was at the table, peeling potatoes for the evening meal, when Louis burst through the door, stepped carefully through the utensils, and announced: 'We're going to Australia!'[2]

Louis was like that—'a doer', as they used to say in Huddersfield, the Yorkshire textile town where he was born. His parents were comfortable middle-class folk (Louis's father was a dentist), ambitious for their children, especially Louis, the eldest, who left home for preparatory school when he was only eight. The Mathesons were Quakers, the plain-living, hardworking, truth-telling, peace-loving religious dissenters whose influence pervaded the culture of the industrial North, and in his teens Louis had attended Bootham School, a Quaker boarding school in

Docking of MV Asturias, *Port Melbourne, 1946.*

York, famous as a nursery for scientists and reformers. By the time he arrived at Manchester University, however, he was shaking off the Quaker connection. He seldom attended Sunday meetings, and when he met and fell in love with Audrey Wood, a young civil servant, he discouraged her interest in the Society. When he graduated with first-class honours in engineering in 1932, his ambitions were already trained on an academic career. Britain, however, was slumped in the midst of the Great Depression and academic jobs were hard to come by. Three years would pass before he won a lectureship at the University of Birmingham and five before he and Audrey could afford to marry.

Over the next decade, Louis Matheson completed a PhD on the theory of structures, married, and fathered two sons. Alongside his teaching and research, he contributed vigorously to the life of his university and community. He was beginning to show an interest in university governance: his colleagues elected him to represent them on the university senate. With the coming of war, his estrangement from the Quakers became an open breach. While his younger brother followed the pacifist path, driving an ambulance in war-torn China, Louis threw his energies into the war effort. He trained army engineers and commanded an anti-aircraft battery defending Birmingham's industrial suburbs against German bombers. Yet something of the Quaker sensibility—their integrity, spirit of fearless inquiry, humility and openness—was imprinted on his character. As one of his Birmingham colleagues observed, Matheson was 'a man of culture and of the very highest character and ideals'.[3]

When peace returned, people yearned for better times. Britain's leaders were calling for a massive expansion in the supply of scientific and technical manpower, but the universities were slow to change. After a decade as a lecturer in Birmingham, Louis, now in his early thirties, was impatient to move on. After just missing out on a chair in London, he applied for the Melbourne post in civil engineering. 'He was that sort of chap', Audrey recognised. 'He didn't want to stand still . . . and the fact that the next job coming up was in Australia, we thought it was rather fun. "Let's go to Australia" . . . It didn't mean going forever.'[4]

When the Mathesons' ship berthed at Port Melbourne, one of Louis's new colleagues, Robert Blackwood, and his wife, Hazel, were on the wharf waiting to welcome them. Soon they were in Bob's car, driving down the Nepean Highway to their home in Brighton. The February sun was beating down from a cloudless sky, and the two couples relaxed in the shade, sipping cold beer. How strange, thought Audrey, to be on the other side of the world, in the middle of summer, drinking cold beer at eight o'clock in the morning! Yet there was something about the informality of the moment, and the warmth of Bob Blackwood's welcome, that made her feel immediately at home. 'We took to him at once', she remembered.

Like Louis, Bob Blackwood was a doer, an analytical man of action whose mind turned readily to questions of efficiency and productivity. A Melbourne graduate, he had joined the Dunlop Rubber company, rising to become its technical manager before the call came from his old university to help create a 'live, vital and progressive school'. Matheson quickly recognised his talent. 'He had an enviable capacity for deciding the proper course of action, in any circumstances, by stripping the problem down to essentials and refusing to be distracted by what he considered side-issues.'[5] But as they got to know each other, Matheson discovered surprising facets of his new colleague's personality and interests: he was a painter, a pianist, an insect- and shell-collector, and a keen student of archaeology and anthropology with a special interest in the cultures of Asia.[6]

The birth of a partnership. Louis Matheson (left) and Robert Blackwood, 1947.

Matheson had arrived at an auspicious moment, when the University of Melbourne was seeking to inject new vigour into its School of Engineering. New bridges, highways, dams, power stations and factory assembly lines were rolling off the drawing boards, and the profession was clamouring for new graduates. Enrolments in the School of Engineering more than doubled, from 300 in 1945 to 650 in 1950, and plans were ripening for new buildings and equipment.[7] Soon Matheson was throwing himself into the life of his new university. A photograph published in the engineering student journal *Cranks and Nuts* depicts the young professor, still wearing his Home Guard moustache, along with the conventional props of the academic—tweed jacket, horn-rimmed glasses and pipe—gazing thoughtfully into the distance.[8]

Shortly after Matheson arrived in Melbourne, a committee headed by the director of the Victorian Education Department, J.A. Seitz, proposed the creation of a technological institute based on the Melbourne Technical College. Matheson's predecessors at the University of Melbourne gave cautious support to the proposal, believing that the university's role lay in the higher sphere of degree training. But as the ambitions of the technical colleges grew larger, the university became more nervous. The foundation in 1949 of the New South Wales Institute of Technology was an ominous sign of what could be in store. A Labor government in partnership with the technical colleges, and in defiance of the University of Sydney, had combined to create a new university run on strict public service lines. According to its historian Patrick O'Farrell, its ethos—'hierarchical, distant, rule and regulation-ridden, socially conservative, respectable to the degree of scruple'—was the antithesis of the liberality and broad culture of a true university.[9] To many Victorians, it was a cautionary example of how *not* to create a new technological university.

In 1949, Matheson, now dean of engineering, made a dramatic intervention in this debate, by proposing that the technical faculties of the University of Melbourne and the fellowship diploma schools of the Melbourne Technical College should be 'fused' into a single college or institute of technology. A council, including representatives of government, industry and the two constituent institutions, would govern the new institution, but the university would remain the degree-granting body. Only by combining the resources of the two bodies, he argued, could Victoria create an institution of a scale equal to the challenges of a technological era. Ultimately, he anticipated, the new institution might require seventeen chairs and a new campus, away from the university, perhaps on the site of the Kew Mental Asylum or in the vicinity of South Carlton.[10]

Before launching his plan, Matheson had secured the support of his vice-chancellor, Sir John Medley, a humanist whose heart was in a more traditional concept of university life. If the technological faculties gained their own quarters off the crowded University of Melbourne campus, then, Medley anticipated, 'their evacuation [would provide] more room for expansion in Arts which I have no doubt would be gleefully accepted'.[11] Some of the young professor's colleagues were more cautious. They worried about associating themselves with technical school staff with lower scientific credentials and losing their social association with other university men.

In proposing a merger, Matheson had braved the potential opposition of both the technical colleges, suspicious of the university's desire for hegemony, and his fellow academics, protective of their scientific standing and anxious not to lose their links with the university. As dean, Matheson had stressed that 'the University, in its training of men, must look further than mere technical instruction. It must look to character and morals and it should keep an eye on the implications of another much abused word, "culture".'[12] He had already reorganised the school's curriculum to ensure that graduates in engineering could take an arts or science degree with only one further year of study. Geographical proximity was important if the cultural link with the university was to be maintained. 'I have always believed that the right place for the Institute was near the University, but the manifest crowding in Carlton led me to think that migration was inevitable', he explained.

Matheson had no sooner made his proposal than he realised its accomplishment was at least a decade off.

The present restrictions on building may not last so long, but I can see no prospect of their being relaxed sufficiently to allow for building on a grand scale for many years to come . . . Governments are gradually moving towards a more generous attitude to higher education and in a few years may contemplate the expenditure of several million pounds on such a venture with equanimity and even enthusiasm.[13]

He could discern the outlines of a new kind of university, attuned to the expanding needs of a technological society yet retaining the humane values, scientific rigour and research ethos of a traditional university. He had begun to think about where it should be located to exploit the educational, industrial and civic resources of the city. He had adroitly sought to transcend the political antagonisms that had previously beset the question. But he would not get the chance to realise his idea. Not yet, at any rate.

For the moment, the cards were stacked against him. In 1948, his ally Robert Blackwood resigned his chair. The general manager of Dunlop, W.A. Bartlett, had died unexpectedly and Blackwood was invited to succeed him.[14] His departure was a serious blow. 'He was full of plans for the future of his Department, and for the School as a whole, and his going leaves a gap which will be difficult to fill', Matheson admitted.[15] Soon Matheson also received an unexpected invitation: to succeed his own revered professor in the prestigious Beyer Chair of Engineering at Manchester University. It was all that the young immigrant of 1947 could have wished for. And yet he hesitated. 'May I say that I have come to my decision with great reluctance and only after anxious thought', he confessed.

> It would have been difficult to refuse an invitation to such an important chair in my old University, especially as it seems that there is much to be done there, but if conditions here had been a little more encouraging I would have done so.
>
> I have greatly enjoyed my association with this University, and could hardly ever hope for a happier place to work in. But there does not seem to be much chance the physical development which should now be taking shape in the Engineering School can be carried out in the foreseeable future. I have found it rather frustrating to have to postpone indefinitely the many plans I would have liked to put into effect in my Department.[16]

Matheson's departure, coming so soon after Blackwood's, was a blow to Melbourne. 'You will be greatly missed—not least by myself', Vice-Chancellor John Medley wrote.[17]

Shortly before he left, Matheson ran into a former Birmingham colleague, the physicist Marcus Oliphant, who had just arrived at the new Australian National University (ANU). 'Matheson, you're going in the wrong direction', he warned. 'The honeymoon period of the British universities is over, but it's only just beginning in Australia.'[18] Oliphant's optimism, Matheson believed, was premature. Perhaps one day the conditions for Australian higher education would improve, but, for the moment, the call of Manchester was stronger.

Yet the Mathesons did not leave Melbourne without a pang, recalls Audrey. 'I remember as the ship sailed down the Bay we looked longingly back at Melbourne. And [Louis] was saying how we were very happy there and it was a shame that, if he hadn't been following his own professor at his own university, we'd get back.' They would miss their Melbourne friends, 'marvellous people' like the Blackwoods. But it was the logical thing to do. Audrey was going back to her own city, where there would be grandparents, aunts and uncles ready to welcome them. And Louis, eager for a new challenge, could look forward to reorganising his old school on modern lines. 'He thought he would be very happy in Manchester', Audrey recalls, '—and he wasn't'.

ONE

AN EDUCATED DEMOCRACY

A university education is not, and certainly should not be, the perquisite of the privileged few ... We must become a more and more educated democracy if we are to raise our spiritual, intellectual and material standards.

R.G. Menzies, 1957

It is around seven thirty in the evening on 4 October 1957, and in thousands of streets and backyards Melburnians are scanning the darkening sky. Suddenly they see a tiny glowing speck, fainter than the brightest star, speeding across the horizon. All over Australia, people are star-gazing. At the Woomera Rocket Range, in South Australia, scientists peer through telescopes for a closer view, while ham radio operators across the continent tune in to the strange chirping call that signals the satellite's orbit.

For thousands of years humans had looked to the skies, plotting the cycles of stars and planets for clues to their fate. Now a new body had appeared in the firmament, not a heavenly but a human one. The announcement that Russian scientists had succeeded in launching a small satellite into an orbit around the earth excited mingled feelings of wonderment and dread in the West.[1] The achievement 'marks the beginning of a new era in discovery', the Melbourne *Age* declared. But no sooner had it saluted the Russians than it lamented the backwardness of Australia's own scientific efforts. The fact that the satellite had passed over Australia should 'help to alert authorities to our deplorable deficiencies in science and technology'.[2] 'It is not a pleasant thought that countries under Russian domination are becoming technically and scientifically ahead of us', Australia's best-known scientist, Sir Ian Clunies Ross, admitted.[3]

Students sitting for a matriculation examination, Melbourne Exhibition Building, 1957.

He was not alone in fearing that science could fall into the hands of sinister forces. A few days after the launch of Sputnik, the British government carried out the third of its atomic tests at Maralinga in South Australia, a powerful reminder to Australians of the destructive power of nuclear technology. Early in the following year, Cambridge scientist and novelist C.P. Snow argued that the academy was becoming polarised between 'two cultures': a forward-looking, optimistic scientific culture and a humanistic culture characterised by a more pessimistic, backward-looking, even tragic outlook.[4] These debates about the future of science and the universities signalled a deep ambivalence about the nature of modernity itself. Science and technology were both desirable and necessary; yet their rapid development excited acute misgivings about where, unaccompanied by more traditional ways of knowing, they might lead.

This was the moment, approaching the zenith of the postwar boom, when Monash University was founded—or, rather, considering its Sputnik-like ascent, when it was 'launched'. 'The Russians could never have imagined that the launching of Sputnik could have resulted in the founding of the Monash University', Colin Badger, Victorian Director of Adult Education, reflected a few months later.[5] Of course, he exaggerated: Sputnik had merely dramatised issues that were already ripe for decision.

For almost two decades, the Victorian government had contemplated the foundation of a second tertiary institution dedicated to the study of science and technology. After the departure of Louis Matheson in 1950, discussion rumbled on in scientific and engineering circles. In 1956, a committee chaired by Victoria's director of education, Major-General A.H. Ramsay, recommended the establishment of a university of technology but failed to decide whether it should be based on an existing institution, such as the Melbourne Technical College, or on a university with a more general range of courses. Many people wanted to locate it in a provincial city like Ballarat, Bendigo or Geelong, as a spur to industrial decentralisation.[6]

While everyone wanted more trained technologists, there was less agreement on how to train them. Matheson's successor as professor of civil engineering at the University of Melbourne, A.J. Francis, insisted on a distinction between the technologist, 'who was a man of university-type training and attitudes', and the technician, whose education was in 'operating techniques rather than on basic and applied science'. 'I am one of those who believe strongly that engineering studies are best pursued in a full university environment. There the student has the best chance, through wide contacts, to develop the breadth of outlook and sympathy that makes the full man as well as the technologist.'[7] But others scorned the idea that technologists needed the civilising influence of the humanities. 'The man of science is better and more broadly educated than he who has read only arts or law', insisted Ian Wark, chief of CSIRO's Division of Industrial Chemistry.[8] By 1956, the government was coming to believe that technology deserved a university of its own, separate from both the traditional university and 'related crafts'. While Victoria should not necessarily follow the model of the New South Wales Institute of Technology, it needed to act promptly if the state was not 'to slip behind our sister state in the realm of higher technological training'.[9]

Just as the advocates of a technological university came in sight of their goal, however, the debate suddenly took a new turn. The slow-moving caravan of technological education was quickly overtaken by a faster moving vehicle, an escalating crisis of confidence in the capacity of the Australian higher education system as a whole. The problem was not just a shortage of scientists and technologists, but a shortage of university places in every field.

The crisis had been a long time coming. In the 1940s, the postwar baby boom hit the state's primary school system with the force of a tsunami. Throughout the 1950s, the government struggled to keep up with the demand for classrooms and teachers. New primary schools and high schools, often housed in Nissen huts or makeshift portable classrooms, sprouted from muddy paddocks on the fringes of new suburbs. Hardly a week went by in the late 1950s when a new school did not open somewhere in the state. Addressing parents at the opening of a new high school in Nunawading in 1957, Education Minister John Bloomfield observed that the number of high schools in the city's eastern suburbs had grown from three to sixteen in a space of only five years.[10]

Soon the wave hit the university. The insatiable demand for university places was not a product of the baby boom alone. As education researcher Don Anderson observed, it also represented 'a revolution of expectations'. 'A significant feature of modern society is the accelerated realization by parents of the importance of education for their children.'[11] Parents denied by the Depression and war the chance to continue their education were determined that their children should not also miss out. 'We wanted to give them all the things we weren't able to have when we were growing up', one parent recalled.[12] Instead of leaving school early, like their parents, the baby boomers increasingly stayed on to complete their leaving or matriculation certificates. Between 1954 and 1961 the proportion of boys continuing to seventeen or older doubled from roughly one in ten to one in five, and among girls from one in twenty to one in ten. The proportion doubled again during the 1960s, and the gap between boys and girls began to narrow. Victorians were more likely to stay on to the end of secondary school than the children of any other state.[13]

The University of Melbourne was deluged with new applicants. Newspapers carried reports of overcrowded libraries, laboratories and lecture theatres; of tutorials being held in tin sheds, bathrooms and broom cupboards. Vice-Chancellor George Paton warned that 'education in Australia was facing its greatest crisis'. 'Despite the number of trained personnel the university was turning out each year, it could not cope with the demand from industry . . . The stage had been reached where another university was essential.'[14]

The Australian prime minister, Robert Menzies, acknowledged the crisis by appointing the chairman of the British University Grants Commission, Sir Keith Murray, to head a committee of inquiry into Australian universities. Menzies was a 'university man of the old school', with a deep, almost sentimental, affection for places of learning, and he offered the Murray Committee generous terms of reference. Even before the committee formally reported, he agreed to support its recommendation for a wholesale reform of Commonwealth funding to universities.[15] Murray reported in September 1957, only days before the launch of Sputnik dramatised the relevance of his words. He offered a far-sighted, generous and humane vision of higher education for Australia; even half a century later, many of his findings—on the integration of teaching and research, for example, and on better understanding of the Asian region—remain relevant.

Highest in his priorities was the critical shortage of university places. His advice to the Victorian government was blunt: 'The University is, in fact, bursting at its seams'. Over the next decade, the demand for undergraduate places would double, yet by 1964 the campus would already have reached its 'physical and academic limit'.[16] The university had already considered and rejected a plan to increase its capacity by hemming the Carlton campus with high-rise buildings.[17] By imposing a limit of 10 000 students on future enrolments (a ceiling already breached by 1960), it effectively passed the buck to the state and federal governments.

How was Victoria to meet the challenge? The committee considered three options: an expansion of degree-level courses at the Royal Melbourne Technical College, a separate university of technology, and a new multi-faculty university. The college was already struggling to cope with the pressure of enrolments in its diploma courses and lacked the physical and academic capacity to meet the demand for higher level technological education. A separate university of technology could not cope with the full range of students now seeking tertiary education. 'We do not think that a single faculty institution is any longer the answer to Victoria's problems', Murray concluded. There remained only the third option: a new multi-faculty university. To appease the technologists, it might begin by establishing courses in science and technology, the fields where the demand was believed to be most pressing, and later expand to include other faculties, such as the social sciences and humanities. Instead of being known as the Victorian University of Technology, it should be called, simply, the University of Victoria.[18]

By 1957, many people had begun to doubt the wisdom, as well as the practicality, of a specialised technological university. In a passage probably written by the scientist Sir Ian Clunies Ross, the Murray Committee articulated the educational philosophy behind its rejection of the technological institute model for what it sometimes called a 'fully balanced' university.

It has been becoming more and more clearly and widely recognised of recent years that the world simply cannot afford that its highly specialised professional men, technologists and scientists should not be fully educated as rounded human beings. It sometimes seems that while we have been advancing at formidable speed in our knowledge of technical matters we have been if anything falling behind in our understanding and appreciation of human values. We can handle machines and physical nature beyond the dreams of previous generations, but we handle ourselves, our families and our fellow human beings in general no better, and perhaps less well, than our fathers did before us . . . The need for the study of the humanities is therefore greater and not less than in the past.[19]

The launching of Sputnik had reinforced the conviction that science and the humanities must become partners, not rivals. 'Let us have more scientists, and more humanists', Prime Minister Menzies exhorted. 'Let the scientists be touched and informed by the humanities. Let the humanists be touched and informed by science . . . That proposition underlies the whole university idea.'[20] Exactly how Victoria's new university should integrate the 'technical' knowledge of sciences with the more 'rounded' perspective of the humanities, however, was one of the many questions left hanging by the committee. You could build a balanced university, with a full range of disciplines, but would it necessarily produce 'rounded' human beings or bridge the divide between the two cultures?

The Victorian government moved speedily to enact Murray's main recommendations. In March 1958, Education Minister John Bloomfield introduced a bill to establish Victoria's second university and named it 'Monash University', after one of Victoria's most famous sons, the engineer, military commander and administrator Sir John Monash. John Swan, a CSIRO scientist and later to be a Monash professor and deputy vice-chancellor, had suggested the name in 1956 during discussions among members of the Royal Australian Chemical Institute about the proposed technological university. In order to attract public support and funds, Swan argued, the new institution needed a more 'glamorous' title than the 'ugly' and 'cumbersome' 'University of Technology'. 'If we are to found a new University, then let us give it a name to be proud of.'[21]

Swan's suggestion lay dormant until December 1957, when his fellow chemist R.G. Gillis responded to an anonymous correspondent in the *Age* proposing to call the new university by the name of Victoria's first governor, La Trobe. 'There is much to be said for naming such an institution after a person', Gillis agreed, citing several of the great Canadian universities. 'The personal name focuses attention on personal qualities desirable in a graduate.' The name of 'Monash' was especially suitable for a university with a 'technical bias', although the great man's accomplishments were so diverse (he had graduated in arts and law as well as engineering) that its selection conveniently masked the continuing uncertainty about the kind of university it was expected to become.[22] Monash's was a familiar name in Victoria, though apparently not so familiar that everyone knew how to pronounce it. In response to a newspaper's inquiry, Sir John's daughter, Mrs Bennett, advised that the name should be pronounced with a short 'o', rather than the long 'o'—'Mohn-ash'—to which Europeans and Americans still default.[23]

As they attempted to define their vision of the new university, Monash's founders often seemed to be steering an uncertain course between narrow utilitarianism and scholarly irrelevance. While acknowledging the vocational imperatives that had created it, they yearned for the new university to be something more than a degree factory. In the back of their minds perhaps they recalled the famous words of John Henry Newman in his *Idea of a University* (1852), that a university was not 'a foundry, a mint or a treadmill' but 'an alma mater knowing her children one by one'.[24] 'The university is not a professional shop', declared Prime Minister Menzies, 'though in my day we used to identify our own by that mercantile name'. It should not be narrow or overly specialised but must 'teach and encourage the free search for truth'.[25] Victorian Liberal backbencher Robert Suggett pleaded that it was 'not a factory of learning, turning out students equipped with knowledge on a conveyor belt system; it is not, or should not be, a place of automation'.[26]

Ironically, the man John Bloomfield chose to lead the university through its first phase of development was not only an industrialist, but an expert on industrial organisation. The first chair of the university's Interim Council was 51-year-old Robert Blackwood, the former Melbourne University professor of engineering and, since 1947, general manager of the Dunlop Rubber company. The choice, according to Bloomfield, had been an almost accidental one. He had been leafing through *Who's Who* in search of another name, also beginning with 'B', when his eye fell on Blackwood's entry and his suitability for the task was immediately apparent.[27]

This story has become a part of the university's folklore. In fact, Blackwood was only the second, or even possibly the third or fourth, choice for the job. In December 1957, the *Age* revealed that the government was searching for a distinguished person to chair the university's Interim Council. Three names—Essington Lewis, the former head of BHP and tsar of wartime production; Ian Clunies Ross, the revered head of the CSIRO, and Douglas Copland, former vice-chancellor of ANU and current principal of the Australian Administrative Staff College at Mount Eliza—were said to be 'mentioned in State circles'. All were eminent Victorians whose personal distinction would bring lustre to the new university. Each embodied a dimension of its founding ideals: Lewis' industrial achievement, Clunies Ross' scientific distinction and Copland's administrative flair. As the *Age* intimated, Victorian Premier Henry Bolte had already offered the job to 'a certain gentleman'.[28] The gentleman in question, Essington Lewis, requested an outline of the chairman's duties and an estimate of the time it would require. On Christmas Eve, Bloomfield replied. Of the council's duties, the most important, he believed, was the recruitment of the university's vice-chancellor. Lewis' judgement and high standing would be invaluable in assuring prospective applicants 'that we mean business' and that the university itself would be a 'substantial and properly conducted affair'. He would also have to advise the government on a site for the university, but, since the council would have the advice of town planners and public servants, this was not likely to be 'a very time-consuming task'.[29]

Essington Lewis' fierce application to work was legendary. When he died, four years later, a simple text was found among his papers: 'I AM WORK'.[30] He gave the government's invitation 'very serious thought', but on 3 January he replied, regretfully declining the job. His time, he realised, was already heavily committed, and, while there was 'no work that I would sooner undertake', it was more work than even the man who *was* work was prepared to take on. 'The position as outlined by you and envisaged by me shows that it is a major project, and unfortunately the time factor is the major stumbling block', he decided.[31] Experience would show that Lewis' assessment of the task was correct. By declining the position he probably did the new university a favour.

The government was eager to resolve the matter, and Blackwood was appointed by the end of January. There is no record of the job being offered to either Clunies Ross or Copland.[32] Lewis' shrewd appraisal of the scale of the job may have persuaded Bloomfield to look for a younger man with more energy to give, and more reputation still to gain, than those who had already run their race. Blackwood, he explained to Bolte, could even be 'more suitable than our original choice', noting his 'reputation for hard-headed realism in financial matters'.[33]

Blackwood was indeed a rarity in 1950s Melbourne, a man who seemed to straddle the worlds of business and academia with ease. Born into an academic family, educated at Melbourne Grammar and trained as an engineer, he had risen from the research side of the Dunlop company to become its general manager. He retained strong links with the University of Melbourne, serving on its council from 1951 to 1963. When he first took the wheel at Dunlop, the quietly spoken, reflective professor may have looked, as historian Geoffrey Blainey remarked, 'like a leisurely seeker of truth who had lost his way in a rubber factory'.[34] Over the following decade, however, he led Dunlop into a period of rapid and sustained growth. The advent of mass motoring, the growth of the suburbs, and a more affluent, leisured society had generated a massive increase in the demand for the company's products, not only motor tyres, but rubber mattresses, sandshoes, tennis racquets and golf clubs. From its original

The first meeting of Monash University's Interim Council, Royal Society of Victoria, 19 June 1958. Premier Henry Bolte (centre rear) is flanked by Education Minister Bloomfield (left) and Chairman Robert Blackwood (right). Of the twenty-five members, most were industrialists and engineers; educationalist Alice Hoy, the only woman, was the sole representative of the humanities.

base in South Melbourne, the company had gradually decentralised its manufacturing plants into country towns and suburbs and risen to become the fifth-largest manufacturing company in Australia.

The membership of the Monash Interim Council reflected the government's commitment, in spite of Murray's recommendations, to a university shaped by industrial and commercial values. Victoria was in the midst of a period of vigorous industrial growth, and, as Bloomfield explained to Blackwood, Monash was expected not only to 'promote cultures and learning' but to 'supply highly trained individuals skilled in the application of advanced scientific methods to industrial processes'.[35] The council included representatives of the professions, secondary education, regional areas of the state and the University of Melbourne, but the most influential and active members were businessmen and industrialists associated with Bolte's push to 'Develop Victoria'. Blackwood's deputy was the consulting engineer and mining director Sir Walter Bassett. Of the council's twenty-five members—twenty-four men and one woman—five were professional engineers. Of the seven businessmen, five were executives of manufacturing companies, including J.R.C. Taylor of Shell Oil; William Killough, the American-born managing director of International Harvesters; Archibald Glenn, Managing Director of the company Imperial Chemical Industries; F.P. Johns, Chairman of steel fabricator Johns and Waygood; and J.W. Schulz, Project Manager of the State Electricity Commission. Michael Chamberlin, Manager of the National Trustees Company and a Catholic layman, would play an active role in discussions about the university's relationship with the churches. The government kept faith with the advocates of technological education by appointing two members of Bloomfield's 1956 committee, Ian Langlands and Malcolm Moore, while three representatives from provincial Victoria—the Geelong wool-broker F.D. Walter, E.J. Tippett of the Ballarat School of Mines and A.S. Craig of the Bendigo School of Mines—were a token acknowledgement of the government's fast-fading commitment to decentralisation. Medical education was represented by Melbourne University's professor of surgery, Maurice Ewing, and the dean of the Alfred Hospital, Rod Andrew, and secondary education by the headmaster of Blackwood's old school, Melbourne Grammar, Brian Hone, and Alice Hoy, former principal of the Secondary Teachers' College. Ron Cowan, Warden of

Bloomfield's (and Blackwood's) old university college, Trinity, represented the residential colleges.[36]

Conspicuously missing from the new council—as Melbourne University's dean of arts, Oscar Oeser, observed—were any representatives of the humanities and social sciences. Despite protests from the academy and a critical editorial in the *Age*, the government refused to redress the balance, since its size, it argued, was fixed by statute.[37] Was the omission of humanists and social scientists an oversight? Or had the government and its business supporters tacitly agreed to push on with the plan for a technological university in spite of Murray's recommendations?[38] If so, they miscalculated, for long before their appointments expired the industrialists would find themselves building a university in which students of the humanities and social sciences far outnumbered those in science and technology.

Location! Location!

The first and most challenging decision for the council of the new university was where to put it. Everyone in Victoria, it seemed, had an opinion. From the moment that the new university was announced, the minister was deluged with schemes and proposals, ranging from the ingenious to the ingenuous, and from the most visionary to the most transparently mercenary. Its final decision to locate Monash at Clayton, on the city's south-eastern fringe, came only after long and anguished discussion and the foreclosing, through political and economic pressures, of other, more attractive possibilities. In deciding where to go, Monash was also deciding what kind of university it wanted to be.

Sir Ian Clunies Ross wanted it to be located as close as possible to the centre of the city. 'Melbourne would simply have to face the problems of finding a central site', he argued. It should begin by making a careful appraisal of public land close to the city centre in places like Royal Park and the Kew Mental Hospital reserve. 'Accessibility by public transport and in reasonable travelling time was highly important.'[39] Melbourne University's professor of architecture, Brian Lewis, suggested the construction of a vertical university, along Corbusian lines, above the Flinders Street railway yards.[40] Others favoured a site close to the University of Melbourne.[41] A Parkville resident anticipated a mass exhumation to permit the location of the new campus in the Melbourne General Cemetery.[42] Melbourne University's vice-chancellor, George Paton, on the other hand, had no desire to share Parkville with another, newer university: he favoured a site somewhere in the city's industrial belt.[43]

Idealists wanted the site to be picturesque as well as convenient. The Kew Mental Hospital, a relic of dark ages in mental health but occupying a spectacular position overlooking a bend in the Yarra River, was an early favourite. The Burnley Horticultural Gardens, whose 25 acres nestled in another bend of the river, was another. 'I have worked in universities in several countries and cannot think of a finer site, not even Heidelberg, Germany', declared J.A. Dunn of Toorak.[44] The agents Goldsbrough Mort offered the historic Banyule homestead and 273 acres overlooking the Yarra in Melbourne's own Heidelberg.[45] 'It is understood that most of the great universities of the world are situated on Rivers, thus providing opportunities for boating and aquatic sports', the imaginative mayor of Keilor argued, conjuring up the romantic image of varsity lads and lasses punting along the turbid upper reaches of the Maribyrnong.[46]

A vociferous minority believed that the new university should not be in Melbourne at all. A provincial university would relieve the over-concentration of population in Melbourne, offer educational opportunities for rural youth and stimulate the economic life of its region. The first plans for a Victorian institute of technology, floated during the war, had been based on the development of existing technical institutes, including those in the state's provincial towns, such as Geelong's Gordon Institute and Ballarat's School of Mines. By 1958, as the metropolis boomed, the dream of a provincial university was fading. But its supporters were still capable of a vigorous rear-guard action. The Murray Valley Development League appealed against the 'strident capitals' to relieve 'the undergraduate choking of Sydney, Melbourne and Adelaide' in the interests of 'the many young men who wish to make the land and its problems their study'.[47]

Twenty-eight country towns and provincial cities, from Alexandra to Eaglehawk and from Queenscliff to Horsham, made bids for the new campus.[48] The Liberal government, led by a farmer and reliant on rural and provincial votes, was obliged to give them a hearing. But Bloomfield was already convinced that the university had to be in Melbourne. Rather than deliver the *coup de grâce* himself, he handed the decision to the Interim Council, urging it only to consider the need to balance development across the state.

At its first business meeting, Blackwood firmly rebutted the decentralists' case. No single centre outside Melbourne could supply more than a tiny proportion of the new university's students. Neither the government nor parents were prepared to pay the additional costs of students living away from home. It was a simple question of supply and demand: the university had to be in the largest market, and preferably close to where most of its potential customers lived. With two dissenters, A.S. Craig, Vice-Principal of the Bendigo School of Mines, and F.D. Walter, a Geelong wool-broker with links to the Gordon Institute, the Interim Council resolved that the university would be located in metropolitan Melbourne but would seek to develop unspecified links with provincial Victoria.[49]

In rejecting the provincial university, the council had also tacitly rejected another popular ideal: the residential university. The Murray Report had underlined 'the importance of residence if university life is to attain full richness' but hesitated to recommend its general adoption.[50] Australia, it recognised, was moving in a different direction, one more in line with its democratic and utilitarian ethos. Like much else in Australian life, the university was falling into a suburban mould. Three-quarters of Australian university students lived at home with their families or in lodgings, and over the following decades the proportion would increase. In later years, Monash's leaders would sometimes confess a wistful longing for a collegiate university, but already, at its birth, it was being shaped by the assumption that its students would live at home with Mum and Dad.

The turf and the fairway

To guide its decision-making, the Interim Council asked the Melbourne and Metropolitan Board of Works' chief planner, E.F. Borrie, to prepare a report on possible sites. In its landmark 1954 report on metropolitan planning, the board had noted a 'marked and increasing preference over the past fifty years for living in the south-eastern and southern suburbs' compared with the north and west. 'There is . . . every reason to conclude that this marked trend will continue', it observed.[51] In order to reach the maximum number of potential students, the new university, Borrie argued, should be located somewhere in this rapidly expanding suburban region.

An analysis of the residences of Melbourne University students showed that the optimal location for a new university to capture its potential students was in Burwood, near the junction of Canterbury and Springvale roads. As a technological university, it should also be close to industry and accessible by good public transport, criteria that pointed towards the industrial belt emerging along the Gippsland rail corridor between Oakleigh and Dandenong. And it would need to be a large, unencumbered site, at least 120 acres, preferably on Crown land in order to minimise costs of acquisition to the state government.[52]

Borrie's report drew the council's attention away from the banks of the Yarra to the suburbs. A number of attractive sites closer to the city had been ruled out by Premier Bolte's commitment not to alienate public parklands. Borrie had identified five potential sites, all broadly within the south-eastern corridor: Caulfield Racecourse, the Huntingdale and Metropolitan golf courses, Sandown Racecourse, Wattle Park and the Riversdale Golf Course. His first choice was the Caulfield Racecourse, a large expanse of under-utilised Crown land close to industry, to the Caulfield Hospital and, most critically, to good public transport. At the junction between two rail lines, and close to two trams, it was only eighteen minutes from the city. Its locational advantages were obvious, although in selecting an under-utilised racecourse Borrie may also have been influenced by the precedent set by Sydney's second university, the New South Wales Institute of Technology (later University of New South Wales), which opened in 1949 on an old racecourse at Kensington in the city's southern suburbs.[53] (The strong public service control that compromised the academic autonomy of that institution's early history may also have worked in its favour, as the chair of its first council, public service head Charles Wurth, was able to overcome the opposition of state planning officials to secure the racecourse site.)[54]

The principal tenants of Caulfield Racecourse, the Victorian Amateur Turf Club and the Melbourne Racing Club, held only twenty-two meetings a year, and, with the new Sandown Racecourse about to open, Monash was argued to have a stronger claim to occupancy. Some locals agreed with Borrie. 'As a university benefits all the people it has far greater claims than the racing fraternity, which comprises only a section of the public', Harold Luth wrote to Minister Bloomfield.[55] But it was a section of the public that included some influential people, including the premier himself, who had already stated publicly that the turf clubs, as long-term tenants, had a right to continued occupation.[56] If they were to be evicted, they would have to be compensated for the buildings and improvements they had invested in the site, which might be more than the state could afford to pay. Borrie disagreed: 'In the long run, the savings in time and fares of generations of future students in travelling to the site in preference to a cheaper but less accessible one would justify the expenditure involved'.[57] Fifty years on, it is hard to gainsay his argument.

Mindful of the problems of overcrowding that had long beset the University of Melbourne, Blackwood was determined that Monash should have plenty of room to grow. In July, he sought information from a selection of universities in Australia, Britain and Canada. Their campuses ranged in size from Manchester's 112 acres to Nottingham's 265 acres, but many, he discovered, now regretted they were not larger. In the light of his inquiries, Caulfield's 160 acres looked too small, and the cost of acquiring it, estimated at £3.7 million, too much to pay.[58] With hindsight, Blackwood may have overestimated the space requirements of a university in which the humanities and social sciences would eventually become as large as the space-hungry technical faculties. (He could hardly have imagined, however, that a day would come when the 13-acre Monash Caulfield campus would accommodate 14 000 students, more than the university's founders believed could be accommodated on the 160-acre racecourse just across the line!)

In later years, the 'loss' of Caulfield Racecourse became part of Monash folk memory. A university marooned from the railway would come to curse the sinister forces that had conspired to rob it of a prime location. According to the *Age* newspaper, the £3.7 million needed to compensate the Victorian Amateur Turf Club was the club's own estimate. The council may have erred in not examining it more closely. The City of Caulfield valued the club's land, grandstands and other buildings at about £200 000, less than a tenth of the sum of the club's estimate.[59] Even if generous allowance is made for the traditional conservatism of council valuations, and for the costs of removing the club's operations to Sandown, the compensation estimate appears to have been contrived to support a decision that was ultimately political rather than economic.

Warned off the Caulfield track, the council next turned to a 320-acre tract of land south of Huntingdale station occupied by the Metropolitan and Huntingdale golf clubs. It was less accessible than Caulfield, served by only one railway line, and ten minutes further from the city. But it was superior to any of the other sites under consideration. It offered sufficient space for the construction of a university hospital, a factor that had gained new weight in the council's deliberations since it had made an agreement with the Alfred Hospital for the provision of clinical education. The cost of compensating the clubs was estimated at a more modest £800 000. On 15 September, the council finally agreed on it. Blackwood was left to write a report for the Cabinet sub-committee assigned to consider the matter on behalf of the government.

The clubs had meanwhile signalled their determination to resist eviction. The president of Huntingdale presented a politely worded 'survey' of the issue, acknowledging the club's 'pride and self-interest', but arguing 'without bias' that, in view of the many years it took to lay out and develop a great golf course, it would be better to dispossess suburban householders than to desecrate their hallowed greens and fairways.[60] The Metropolitan Golf Club adopted a more direct approach. Club stalwart Henry Winneke, Solicitor-General and a friend of Bolte's, stormed into the premier's office. 'You call yourself a Liberal Premier', he remonstrated. 'You're a socialist of the first order . . . It's a dreadful thing to do. There's plenty of other land available—acres of it further up there in North Road—and you're going to take over clubs that fellows have put their time and money into for years—just like that.' Bolte promised to take a look at the site himself.[61] Lindsay Thompson, the only member of the Cabinet sub-committee to record his views, was also a golfer. 'It seemed a pity to destroy two of the best golf courses in Australia in one hit', he recalled. As a young man he had played social cricket matches on one of the other less highly rated sites, the Talbot Colony for Epileptics in Clayton, and admired its beautiful views towards the Dandenongs. He now encouraged its adoption as a site for the new university.[62] At the end of October, the *Age* newspaper published an 'inside' account of the council's deliberations which contained enough accurate information about the estimated costs of acquiring the various sites to elicit a public rebuke from the premier: 'If we had to pay £1 million for the site, no money would be left to start the university'.[63]

When the council met again in November, it received the disappointing but not unexpected news that Cabinet had rejected its recommendation.[64] Despite Bolte's warning, the monetary cost of acquiring the golf courses was probably not a decisive factor. The overall construction budget for the new university was about £17 million; by comparison, the difference between the £800 000 required for the golf links site and the £600 000 required to purchase the site finally chosen at Clayton was trivial. The political clout of the golf clubs was a larger factor, but even that may not have been decisive.

Step by step, Monash had been pushed away from the old rail-based heartlands of the city and further towards its suburban frontier. With hindsight, and a post–oil shock appreciation of the long-term advantage of a public transport connection, this looks like a story of myopia compounded by political cronyism. But in 1958 there were simply more votes to be lost among golfers and racegoers than to be won among potential students of the new university. And to contemporaries, especially the inner group of industrialists and technologists on the Interim Council, the loss of Caulfield and Huntingdale may have seemed no great loss at all. Perhaps they were not just being pushed away from the centre but lured, by forces now almost invisible to us, towards the suburban periphery?

The call of the suburban frontier

Long before he met the Cabinet sub-committee in November, Blackwood was attempting to open the Interim Council's mind to the advantages of sites well beyond its comfort zone. In August, after a discussion of the need to link with local industry, he 'stated his view that the Council should look to the years ahead when the industrial and residential area would extend to Stud Road; and when a University based on Blackburn Road would be centrally placed in a large area of population'. Such a campus, Blackwood continued, might be linked through a new network of north–south bus routes to the rail system at Dandenong, Box Hill and Waverley.[65] There were already members of the council who favoured a site away from the railway.[66] As the discussion proceeded, Blackwood added new potential sites to the list, some as far away as Keysborough and Burwood. Was he anticipating the government's refusal to approve the council's preferred sites? Or was he advocating a different strategy, one based on his instincts, as a forward-thinking industrialist, about where the city was heading?

In 1958, Victoria was riding the wave of an industrial boom. Under Bolte, it had taken a bold approach to the development of the state, actively seeking foreign investment, and supporting the growth of industry through state-funded housing, transport and planning policies.[67] Melbourne's old industrial base, in the inner-riverside suburbs, was being transformed by new techniques of mass production and motorised transportation. This was the age of the assembly line, the fork-lift truck, the shipboard container and the semi-trailer, new technologies that called for a new type of industrial plant located on extensive greenfield sites.[68] Between 1953 and 1963, the proportion of Melbourne's workforce employed in the outer suburbs, beyond the old industrial zone, grew from just over a quarter to just under a half. The fastest growing new industrial suburbs were concentrated in a corridor along the Gippsland railway line and Dandenong Road between Oakleigh and Dandenong. In Clayton, the number of factories grew from five in 1951 to 79 in 1960. Many of these firms, like Volkswagen (Australia), Robert Bosch (Australia) and Repco Ltd, were involved in the most buoyant sector of manufacturing: the motor car and motor parts industries. Some, like Volkswagen, were local branches of international companies recently lured to Victoria by a state government eager to attract new investment, although most were older firms relocating from outmoded plants in riverside suburbs like South Melbourne and Richmond.[69]

The industrialists on Monash's council were among the leaders of this move to the suburbs. The engineer Malcolm Moore's family company had moved one of its subsidiaries to Springvale in 1951.[70] In 1952, William Killough, the American-born head of International Harvesters, had located his company's truck plant in Dandenong alongside two other American firms, H.J. Heinz and General Motors-Holden. Peter Johns, Chairman of the steel fabricators Johns and Waygood, had built a modern plant at Sandringham in 1954.[71] In 1957, Premier Henry Bolte had opened a new £1.75 million paint factory, BALM Paints, a subsidiary of Archibald Glenn's Imperial Chemical Industries, in Dandenong Road, Clayton.[72]

And Chairman Robert Blackwood, who had overseen the move of some of Dunlop's operations to Bayswater in 1958, was also turning his mind to the relocation of its largest plant, the Montague tyre factory. In 1960, the company would purchase a 32-hectare allotment near the junction of Springvale and Wellington roads, less than a kilometre from the Monash campus, although the credit squeeze of the following year aborted the plan.

This was the new industrial frontier that had already captured the imagination of the businessmen on the Monash Interim Council. It was a landscape strikingly different from the narrow streets, crowded Victorian cottages and grimy factories of the old industrial suburbs. The new factories were low-slung structures of steel, glass and concrete set attractively amid lawns and car parks. German-born photographer Wolfgang Sievers, who photographed many of them during the 1950s and

The paint manufacturer BALM, a subsidiary of the chemical giant ICI, led by Monash council member Archibald Glenn, was among the large manufacturers to erect new laboratories and factories in Clayton in the early 1960s. Photographer Wolfgang Sievers captures the modern industrial aesthetic that also shaped the new university.

1960s, brilliantly captured the sleek functionalism that was their dominant aesthetic. To Sievers' patrons, the captains of these new industries, they represented something more: the triumphant application of scientific reason and technological skill to the organisation of everyday life. In their eyes, Monash University, located in the heart of this new industrial region, would become the intellectual powerhouse of the state's modernising thrust.

The new suburbs were a frontier of opportunity for those who worked in the factories as well as those who ran them. When the afternoon whistle blew, they drove to homes and gardens in nearby residential suburbs. North of the railway, on the rising ground towards Notting Hill and Mount Waverley, was the territory of the white-collar workforce of managers and sales staff, while to the south, on the sandy plain that stretched towards the bay, were the weatherboard cottages of the Greek, Italian and Yugoslav migrants who manned the assembly lines.[73] By the late 1950s, social scientists were visiting the new suburbs to discover how this 'affluent' working class was thinking and voting. As the suburbs matured, many of its sons and daughters, products of the new high schools and colleges already springing up along the frontier, would join the 'revolution of expectations' represented by the modern university developing in their midst.

The basis and symbol of the new suburbs was the automobile. Many of the Interim Council's members were representatives of the car industry, convinced that the automobile was the way of the future. The residents of Clayton and Waverley not only made cars but owned and drove more than people in other suburbs.[74] Everywhere were the manifestations of a new model of car-based urban development, American in origin but increasingly Australian in provenance, for which the architect Robin Boyd coined the neat but dismissive title 'Austerica'.[75] The Oakleigh Motel, the Clayton Twin Drive-In, the Pinewood and Chadstone shopping centres, the Village Green pub and Rob's Drive-In Restaurant were prominent landmarks in a drive-in landscape soon to be dominated by Australia's first drive-in university.[76]

The decision on the Monash site finally came down to a choice between two large, flat sites, both remote from public transport. In following the logic of the industrial location, the Interim Council had arrived, unsurprisingly, at a choice between two prime industrial sites.

One was a stretch of 250 acres of farmland a mile and a half south of the Huntingdale station, the other a slightly more elevated 287-acre site to the north of the Clayton station, at the intersection of the Princes Highway and Wellington Road. Its nucleus was the 160-acre site of the Talbot Colony for Epileptics, to which it was proposed that several surrounding properties would be added by compulsory purchase, including a farm, a trotting track and a wire-manufacturing company. It was closer than its rival to the industrial belt between Clayton and Dandenong but, alas, no closer to the rail. Its inaccessibility continued to worry several members of the Interim Council. Melbourne Grammar's headmaster, Brian Hone, warned that the new university had to take the overflow from the University of Melbourne. Professor Leslie Martin reminded them that the university's academic staff would depend on access to the superior laboratories and libraries in Parkville. But at last, without enthusiasm, the council plumped for the Clayton site, 'recognising the difficulties' but believing that 'they could be overcome by live and energetic development'.[77]

Monash's long search for a home was almost over. On 13 November, Henry Bolte announced that the new university would be at Clayton. Sixty orders were issued 'freezing' values on the sites that the government would compulsorily acquire.[78] To allay fears about suburban isolation, it promised to 'give consideration' to a spur line from Huntingdale, a vague promise occasionally repeated and long remembered but never kept.[79] In 1958, very few of Monash's prospective students owned a car, but in 1963, when the campus was up and running, less than a quarter of its students came to the campus by public transport.[80] 'The motor car', Blackwood later wrote, 'is increasingly becoming an adjunct to modern life. A large proportion of the students possess cars and use them to attend classes. With adequate parking more would do so.'[81]

To occupants of the site, like Matron Margaret Lang of the Talbot Colony, news of the government's decision came as 'a bombshell'. Being outside the influential circles that had warned the racing and golfing fraternities of approaching danger, they had no choice but to surrender their humble livelihoods to the common good. The proprietors of the Cyclone Wire company were said to be 'in a hole', while market gardener Reg Billings believed that his life had been 'ruined'. With tears in her eyes, Mrs O'Shea read the government's letter demanding that she leave

In 1960, Monash University stood on the very edge of the metropolis, with rows of weatherboard cottages hemming its western boundary and only a drive-in theatre, farms and orchards lying between the first Science buildings and the Dandenongs. The old trotting track, the O'Sheas' homestead—soon to become the vice-chancellor's residence—and the yet-to-be demolished Talbot Colony buildings are clearly visible.

the comfortable eighteen-room house that she and her husband had built twenty years earlier on the rise above Wellington Road.[82]

When the announcement was made, the site for the new university stood on the very edge of the suburban frontier. Matron Lang remembered when the area was nearly all farmland dotted with old pines and gum trees. 'But the growth all around us in Wellington and Blackburn Rds in the past ten years has been fantastic', she observed. 'There seemed to be new houses, shops or factories going up every month.'[83] Already, rows of weatherboard cottages hemmed the new campus's western boundary. Soon, the suburban surge would overtake and surround it, leaping across the paddocks and orchards towards the Dandenongs and the bay. One day, as Blackwood and his team had foreseen, the Clayton campus would no longer be on the fringe but close to the geographical centre of the metropolis. By then, many of the features that had influenced the decisions of its founders had changed as well. For the next twenty years, however, the names Monash and Clayton were almost synonymous.

TWO

THE MISSING PAGE

Monash has been asked to grow too fast, and do too much, too quickly with too little money for the good of its students, staff and the community.

JOCK MARSHALL, 'AN EXPATRIATE RETURNS', VESTES, 1963

In the beginning was the word. Before it became bricks and mortar, professors and students, Monash University took shape in the words of its founders. 'We are much concerned with the condition of tertiary education in Victoria', Sir Keith Murray began his confidential 1958 report to the Victorian government.[1] Melbourne University was bursting at the seams. The demand for university education was increasing more quickly than anyone had expected. Victoria urgently needed a second university.

On the last page of his report, Murray recommended that the new university should open no later than 1964 or 1965. It would take three years to find a site and appoint a vice-chancellor, and another three to recruit professors, design courses and construct the first buildings, he estimated. When they gathered for their first meeting at the Royal Society of Victoria, in June 1958, members of the Interim Council of Monash University were each given a copy of Murray's report. Mysteriously, however, the vital last page with the six-year timetable was missing. Only a year and a half later, when Leslie Martin, Chairman of the Australian Universities Commission (AUC), asked why the university was in such a rush to open, was the missing page brought to light. In the meantime, Monash had committed itself to opening not in 1964, but a full three years

Newly arrived vice-chancellor Louis Matheson (right) and registrar Frank Johnson inspect progress on the first stage of the university's building program, the Science and Engineering buildings, 1960.

earlier. The loss of those 206 words, it seemed, had fated the university
to a premature birth.[2]

How did this mishap occur? Keith Murray's report to the Victorian
government was a short typewritten document. When Martin queried
the timetable, Alex McDonell, a member of the Monash Council and
Victoria's director of education, asked his department for a copy of the
report and discovered the missing page. McDonell's son, Jack, later the first
warden of Deakin Hall, recalls his father saying that the pages of the
report had been held together with a paper clip and the vital last page was
accidentally detached before the document was copied for distribution to
the Interim Council. If only the papers had been fastened more firmly,
perhaps Monash's timetable would have been more generous.[3]

By the time the story leaked out, the university's founders could
boast that they had surpassed the expectations of their political masters,
building a new university in only three years. The revelation of the missing
page testified to their heroic achievement. There was more, however, to
Monash's accelerated timetable than just a lost document. By mid-1958,
the crisis diagnosed by Murray had worsened appreciably. Statisticians
forecast that by 1961 the number of students applying to the university
would be 1300 more than Murray had predicted, and that by 1964, when
Monash was expected to open (and the Bolte government faced an election),
the shortfall would be 3500.[4] The pressure of numbers, and perhaps of
politics, had changed the mind-set of the Interim Council. Blackwood
and his fellow businessmen, in any case, were not the types to dawdle if
they could run. After their first meeting, Blackwood had announced that
the university would give its first lectures not in 1961, but in 1960![5] 'Well,
how soon can we open, boys?' Vice-Chancellor Matheson recalled him
asking soon after he arrived.[6] As historian John Rickard later observed,
Monash, from its beginnings, was a 'university in a hurry'.[7] Haste injected
a sense of excitement and pioneering valour into the university's founding
years, but it came at a cost—in cut corners, rushed planning, confused
priorities and foreclosed choices.

Planning under pressure

'Victoria's second university must not be second-rate', architect and critic
Robin Boyd warned in March 1958. 'We have the rare and wonderful

opportunity of being able to start afresh and avoid the initial error our great-grandfathers made with the first one [University of Melbourne].' As a seasoned observer of the Melbourne architectural scene, Boyd was 'not naïve enough' to expect Monash University to become 'a triumph of the architectural art', but it might at least be a 'dignified, vital, humane community of buildings'. If so, its council had to avert the perils of short-term thinking. 'If [the university] is not a fine balance of technique and humanity from the beginning, it never will be. It cannot start on the cheap expecting to add refinement later.'[8] Monash had arrived at a moment of great expectations, when proven architectural models for a modern university campus were still relatively few. Boyd's phrase—'a fine balance of technique and humanity'—hinted at a dilemma that would continue to beset the makers of Monash: how to combine the rationality, efficiency and functionality of modernism ('technique') with the historic values and traditions of a liberal society ('humanity').

As soon as Monash's long search for a site was over, the council moved swiftly to appoint an architect to plan the campus and design the first group of buildings. A small committee surveyed the field and returned a few days later with a recommendation to appoint Melbourne's leading architectural firm, Bates, Smart & McCutcheon (BSM).[9] It was a safe, even inevitable, decision. In 1958, the principal partner of BSM, 59-year-old Osborn McCutcheon, was at the peak of his career. Since the 1930s, when he had become the firm's principal design architect, he had been a force in Melbourne architecture. As part-time director of the School of Architecture at Melbourne Technical College, he taught the young Robin Boyd, a protégé and admirer.[10] During the Second World War, he was seconded to the architectural section of the US Army Corps of Engineers, where he designed hospitals, barracks and aircraft hangars and mastered new techniques of prefabrication and modular construction. By the 1950s, he was the leading exponent of the 'moderate modernism' that was to become Melbourne's architectural signature. Two notable buildings—the 22-storey ICI building (1958), the first of Melbourne's glass towers, and the strikingly modernistic Wilson Hall at Melbourne University (1954)—established the firm's credentials.[11] When Interim Council member Archibald Glenn, Managing Director of Imperial Chemical

Industries, proposed that BSM be appointed as architects to the new university, his motion was carried unanimously.[12]

Outside the office, 'Ossie' McCutcheon was a champion yachtsman, often sailing offshore near his striking modernist home at Mount Eliza. But during January 1959 he spent less time on the water than usual, working 'under extreme pressure' to produce a first site plan of Monash University.[13] In his first report, he sought to define 'the principles and sentiments and practices of a great University', although he recognised, from the first, that high principles and deep-felt sentiments would have to contend with a tight timetable and even tighter budget. The site at Clayton was barely 'satisfactory'. It had 'little drama such as may be seen in the Berkley [sic] hills at California and the backs at Cambridge'. Monash 'must look inward and create within the boundaries its own character and feeling'. Careful planting along the perimeter and between precincts would create a series of open areas 'insulated from the noises and sounds of everyday living and from each other'.[14]

Half-consciously, McCutcheon was joining a long debate about the relationship between the city and the university. Were knowledge and learning best fostered in the cloistered calm of a semi-rural setting far from the turmoil and temptations of metropolitan life? Or was the university part of the city, drawing energy and vitality from its surroundings? Oxford and Cambridge, Princeton, Johns Hopkins and a host of small-town American colleges exemplified the pastoral ideal; the Sorbonne, the University of London and New York University exemplified the city university. Daniel Coit Gilman, founding president of the first of the modern American research universities, Johns Hopkins, expounded the American ideal of the 'campus': a community of scholars secluded from the 'distractions of modern civilization'.[15]

When journalist Geoffrey Hutton visited Monash in 1961, he noticed the village-like atmosphere around the science courtyards and remarked: 'I was given permission to call this the campus although the word does not seem to be in use'.[16] Although the word was slow to arrive, the idea was not. The words McCutcheon used to define his 'philosophy' of the university—quiet, seclusion, separation and retreat—came straight from the lexicon of romanticism. He explicitly rejected the idea that Monash might become an urban university. 'The site is in an area partly suburban and partly industrial, and cannot become integrated with active town life as are so many universities in the UK, and USA and the University of Melbourne itself.'[17]

McCutcheon envisaged the Monash campus as a 'compact' ensemble of academic buildings within a 'central pedestrian precinct'. No building should be more than six minutes' walking distance from any other. On the high, western end of the site, he arranged the faculty buildings in a semi-circle, to form an amphitheatre oriented to the site's only redeeming scenic feature: the distant view of the Dandenongs. Kindred faculties were arranged as neighbours, beginning with the social sciences and humanities and circling through medicine and the natural sciences to applied science and engineering. The large central space, the 'campus' itself, would be occupied by 'tree-studded lawns, capable of use by 8000 students' and some 'focal feature such as a lake for aesthetic satisfaction'. The university's central functions—its administration building, library, student union and great hall—closed the eastern end of the amphitheatre, nearest the Wellington Road entrance, and marked a transition from the inner sanctum of the university to the busier world outside. A line of trees, a four-lane access road and a belt of car parks marked its outer boundary. McCutcheon recognised that the demand for parking was likely to grow and feared that inadequate provision would later require the 'invasion of garden and other areas'. His estimate of 35–40 acres for parking (one car space for every four students and one for each staff member) seemed generous at the time but soon fell short of requirements. As the university grew, the car parks on its periphery steadily expanded, reinforcing the barrier between the university and the city.[18]

The main faculty buildings were concentrated at the western end of the site for practical as well as aesthetic reasons: it was quicker and cheaper to build on higher, flatter land and easier to construct a sewerage system on gravitational principles. The gently sloping eastern end was reserved for student residences and sporting fields. McCutcheon believed that the 'fully balanced university' should produce fully balanced human beings by acknowledging 'the true place and importance of extra-curricula [sic] activities'. 'Residence is essential for full and proper benefit from University training', he argued.[19] This was a wishful misinterpretation of the Murray Report, which had acknowledged the benefits of residence but doubted the willingness of Australian governments and parents to pay for it.[20] Many members of Monash's Interim Council were college men, prepared to follow their dreams. McCutcheon assumed that up to 40 per cent of Monash's estimated 8000 students would live on campus, men in the larger, northeast complex, safely separated by playing fields from the women's residences to the south. This ill-fated dream left a lasting imprint on the plan of Monash University. The negative space it created, in the form of never-to-be-built student residences, inevitably

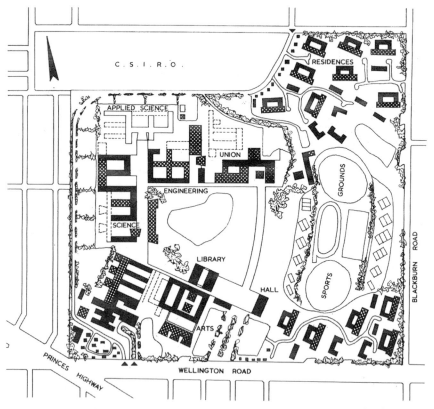

In McCutcheon's first master plan the university 'looked inwards' to a park-like campus with an ornamental lake. Faculty buildings were arranged around the circumference, like an amphitheatre, oriented to the mountains in the east, while the university's main communal buildings, the union, library and great hall, faced each other across the common space. More than one-third of the site was allocated to student residences in the expectation that 40 per cent of the university's students would live on campus.

reduced the scope for other activities, such as the proposed university hospital and the humanities and social sciences.

By the time McCutcheon drew up his master plan, American architects had given up the expectation that a university could be planned entirely from the beginning. 'Every attempt to bind [universities] to a pattern laid out in advance has failed—and ought to have failed', Harvard's Joseph Hudnut had observed in 1947.[21] McCutcheon tried to steer a prudent middle course between a flexibility that could end in chaos and a uniformity that could stifle growth. Each faculty complex was planned to allow for expansion by the addition of new modules. While there needed to be no 'rigid' adherence to a single theme, style or material, the university should exhibit a 'common denominator of character—one feeling and one philosophy of architecture'.[22] The principal buildings would be 'three-storey coupled with one and two-storey wings, and planned with quadrangles, courtyards and similar to create pleasant spaces and to further encourage quiet'. Most of the teaching and research buildings would be developed along 'very simple constructional lines, using concrete floors, brick-bearing walls carried on a simple system of pier and beam foundations', an approach that easily lent itself to the staged replication of modular forms.[23] The campus's character would be defined by the use of common materials: the dark-brown manganese bricks, grey besser blocks and white cement rendering used for all the main campus buildings, at least until the orange bricks of Roy Grounds' Blackwood Hall (1971) and the pink tones of Daryl Jackson's Gallery Building (1984) challenged the convention.

'I like building things'

Only when the physical outlines of the university had been decided did Blackwood and his fellow councillors turn to the selection of a vice-chancellor. They had clear ideas about the kind of man they wanted. He should not be over fifty, 'unless there was an outstanding man over that age'. He should have 'some academic experience in a University, together with administrative ability, training in a broad, rather than a confined discipline, energy, drive and personality'.[24] Was Blackwood already thinking, when he wrote those words, of his friend and former colleague Louis Matheson? In the decade since they had met on the wharf at Port

Melbourne and drunk cold beer on a hot February morning in 1947, both had enhanced their reputations as men of vision and energy. Blackwood had made Dunlop into one of Australia's most successful manufacturing companies. Matheson had almost completed a new engineering school for his old university in Manchester. Blackwood had urged his old friend to apply for the job, while carefully ensuring that the selection process was impeccable. Of the fifty applicants, only three were finally interviewed—Matheson; Edwin Hills, a 53-year-old geologist and chairman of Melbourne University's Professorial Board; and Phillip Law, a 47-year-old physicist, explorer and head of the Australian Antarctic Division. The decision was immediate and unanimous. Everyone was impressed by Matheson's energy, drive and executive capacity as well as his 'personal qualities and friendly approach'.[25] While he was still young, there was something in his personality—an indefinable blend of authority and ease, intellectual capacity and integrity—that instilled confidence. As one of his Manchester colleagues observed, 'he always seemed to be a Vice-Chancellor [even] when he was an Assistant Lecturer in Manchester'.[26]

Monash was lucky to get him. 'I knew they wanted you and intended to get you', his former vice-chancellor Lord Stopford confided.[27] Matheson may also have believed he was lucky to be chosen. His return to Manchester had not been as happy as he had expected. He chafed at the conservatism of some of his colleagues and had begun to look back nostalgically on his time in Melbourne. He was also doubtful about his prospects of higher office in England. 'I wouldn't have been appointed a vice-chancellor in England because I didn't belong to the right [Oxbridge] college.' More important still was the opportunity to create a new university. 'I like building things much more than running them', he later admitted.[28]

In the history of institutions, founders matter. Without the happenstance of Blackwood's appointment as chair of the Interim Council, his shrewd appreciation of a former colleague's talents and his determination to 'get him', Monash may have taken a very different course. 'Everyone looks forward to your arrival and leadership in this grand job', Blackwood wrote from Akron, Ohio, in May. 'I shall be personally very glad when you are able to take over so that I can act more as a chairman and not so much a combination of Chancellor, Vice-Chancellor, P.B. [Professorial Board], planner etc!'[29]

Over its first year Blackwood had set the council a cracking pace, but by mid-1959 the 'extreme pressure of work' was beginning to tell. Matheson's commitments in Manchester, however, prevented him from coming before early 1960, just one year from opening day.

The pace was beginning to tell on others as well. In June, McCutcheon wrote a long, confidential letter congratulating Matheson on his appointment and offering a frank assessment of the difficulties he was facing: there was not enough money, no arrangements had been made to clear the site, there were no road or sewerage plans, and there were no staff to make them. On the other hand, the university had a good interim council ('not particularly academic but very representative'), a hardworking building committee, generous help from colleagues at Melbourne University, a workable site plan and designs for the first science and engineering buildings. While trying to look on the bright side, McCutcheon was evidently uneasy about the decision to open in 1961. 'This decision', he explained, 'has been taken under pressure and in spite of our belief, upon which we have been most insistent, that no University should be planned in detail without the fullest advice and cooperation of the main executives (Vice-Chancellor and so forth) and the professorial and other staffs'. In writing so frankly, McCutcheon may have hoped to prompt Matheson either to intervene or at least to forestall later criticism of rushed decisions. Monash was being forced to grow faster and larger than McCutcheon considered desirable. 'This is a semi-tragic thing perhaps as no university of this size [over 8000 students] can hold on to the intimate and integrated form which might otherwise be so valuable', he warned.[30] Matheson was more sanguine. 'The unity of a university', he believed, 'was not a direct function of its size, but depends much more importantly on its structures'. Since Monash would be obliged to become a university of 8000 to 12 000 students, the challenge was to build it so as to 'foster an integrated life'.[31]

Early in July, Matheson and Blackwood spent a long weekend together at the Mathesons' house in Alderley Edge, Cheshire, sitting under an elm tree, reviewing the building program and the applications for the foundation professorships. Sir Walter Bassett, Blackwood's deputy, had sent a heavy package of material including McCutcheon's plans for the new science building, which they carefully dissected before offering suggestions of their own. The formal features of the complex—the long north–south back of the 'comb' devoted to central faculty and service functions, and the protruding 'teeth', representing the various departmental functions, such as lecture theatres, offices, laboratories and so on—were determined, largely, by the university's budget and timetable. Confronted with the outcome—a line of boxes without any discernible 'academic' character—the two engineers hesitated. The complex's 600-foot-long corridor, they decided, was 'not good from the psychological point of view'. Could it perhaps be broken in half to create a larger central courtyard for the pleasure of staff and students?[32] But their hesitation was only momentary. The father of architectural modernism, Le Corbusier, had defined buildings as 'machines for living'. Monash was emerging from the drawing board as a machine for learning: functional, streamlined, efficient, no-frills. 'Some sort of academic atmosphere with reasonable quiet and free—at least to some extent—of the nervous rush-and-tumble of modern city living is important', McCutcheon had suggested.[33] His clients worried that too much quiet and leisure might undermine the industrious atmosphere they saw as the genius of the new university. 'A common coffee shop for the Faculty is a good idea', Blackwood commented on the plan to colocate it with the science library, 'but here we think that this rather social activity could well be further separated from the more serious academic work'.[34] The building committee considered its chairman's suggestions but decided that there was simply no time to implement them.[35] Even the engine driver could not slow the locomotive now steaming fast towards its destination.

A few good men

Blackwood approached the founding of Monash as an industrialist: first find a suitable site, then build the factory, recruit the manager and hire the operatives. Matheson, at one with Blackwood on many things, had other priorities: Monash's biggest challenge would be finding the right people. 'There is a world shortage of university staff at present', he observed shortly after his appointment.[36] A strong leader with a preference for centralised decision-making, Matheson expected his foundation professors to exercise similar authority within their own domains. They should be excellent teachers as well as strong researchers, inspiring team leaders but good university men as well. Promising young men—the talk was always of 'good men'—with plenty of running in them were a better bet than high achievers whose best work was behind them.

The council's first appointment, 31-year-old Ron Brown as foundation professor of chemistry, advertised Monash's willingness to back youthful promise. Educated at Wesley College, the University of Melbourne and King's College London, Brown's original contributions to theoretical chemistry had won him early recognition. 'If you go back to Australia, it'll be the end of your scientific career', his English supervisor warned. But Brown was an unusually self-motivated researcher, self-taught in the theoretical principles underlying his groundbreaking research on the detection of chemical elements in space. Coming to Monash, he hoped, was a chance to build his own microwave spectrometer and, eventually, a 'respectable chemistry department'.[37]

The best British applicants were often scholarship boys, bright working-class lads whose ambition and down-to-earth manner matched the ethos of the new university. Solid-state physicist Robert Street, son of a Yorkshire miner, offered Monash an attractive new specialisation that complemented the University of Melbourne's in nuclear physics. 'He has a very pleasant personality and an uninhibited manner which should go down well with Australians', one of his referees enthused.[38] Matheson invited him over from Sheffield for an interview. The vice-chancellor designate arrived late, still dressed in cricket creams, but his 'charismatic' personality and inspiring vision of Monash's future quickly captured Street's imagination. 'Australia was unknown to us beyond the image and example Matheson was projecting', he recalled.[39]

As foundation professor of engineering, Matheson and Blackwood chose their old Melbourne colleague Kenneth Hunt. Educated at Charterhouse and Balliol College, Oxford, and with service in the Royal Engineers, Hunt was younger, more extrovert and intellectually broader than his rivals: 'an excellent sort of person to have in a University in every way', as his former vice-chancellor, Sir John Medley, observed.[40] No decision could have said more clearly that Monash intended its technologists to be educated, and not simply trained for their profession.

The chance to participate in building a new university sometimes stirred the patriotism of expatriate Australians. 'I've applied for a Melbourne chair. It's the chair of Biology at Monash University',

48-year-old Jock Marshall, a reader in
zoology at St Bartholomew's College
in London, announced to his Sydney
family. 'Academically it's a first-class
prospect in that one has a hand in
planning a department and does not
inherit the mistakes—in personnel or
equipment—of a predecessor.' Marshall
had grown up on the bushy fringes
of Sydney, where he developed a love
of native fauna. At sixteen he lost an
arm in a shooting accident, a disability
that did nothing to discourage his love
of adventure. After zoological studies
at Sydney, he was an explorer in the
New Hebrides, a student at Oxford
and a soldier in New Guinea, before
resuming his career as an evolutionary

*This picture of Professor Jock
Marshall, Australian nationalist
and professional stirrer, hung in the
bar of 'The Vicarage', as he called
his local, the Notting Hill Hotel.*

biologist in England. Marshall was a larger-than-life, contradictory
character: a mixture of the patrician and the democrat, the rugged
Australian nationalist and the Anglophile traditionalist, the scholar and
the stirrer.[41]

'On paper', Marshall thought he should get the job, and his spies
told him he was 'top of the list' but that some locals doubted he was
'temperamentally suited' to running an Australian department.[42] His
spies were well informed. 'There is no doubt that Marshall is a first-class
biologist', Blackwood admitted, but 'his personality leaves much to be
desired'.[43] Matheson recognised Marshall's faults, but also his virtues:

> It is easy to see that he can get across people and I have no doubt
> at all that his forthright and irrepressible remarks do not endear
> him to the stuffier kind of university authority. On the other
> hand he is regarded by all as a first-rate zoologist, which after all
> is the first essential, he is an Australian who wants to build a new
> university in his own country, and has problems to work on in
> connection with Australian fauna. Above all he has loyal friends

who think very highly of him and who spring to his support at any opportunity.[44]

Matheson may occasionally have questioned his generous but shrewd assessment. Marshall would often try his vice-chancellor's patience, but none of Monash's foundation professors brought as much idealism, ingenuity, passion and ebullient energy to the challenge of building the new university.

Along with the first foundation professors came the first of the university's senior academic administrators. Librarian Ernest Clark, Melbourne-born and -educated, came from the University of Malaya in Singapore, where he had built a library of 250 000 volumes from scratch. 'Melbourne is my home town and I have always wanted to return there eventually', he explained, but only 'very recent events'—the growing political tension as the dissolution of British Malaya approached—had prompted him to apply. Forthright, sometimes cantankerous, independent, cultured—he had learned Russian in order to be able to read *War and Peace* in the original language—Clark made the new library his life and adopted its staff as his family.[45]

Matheson's administrative lieutenant was Monash's first registrar, Frank Johnson. An Englishman, Johnson was educated at Balliol College, Oxford, and had served as a major in the army and an inspector of taxes in the British civil services before becoming an assistant registrar in Adelaide and later at the University of Western Australia.[46] Loyal, affable, financially adroit, though occasionally prickly, Johnson and his punctilious deputy, Jim Butchart, recruited from Sydney, became fixtures of the Monash scene, the creators, with Matheson, of the Red Book, the compendium of information and procedures which defined Monash's tradition of efficient, centralised, bureaucratic administration.

A spanner in the works

In October 1959, with only eighteen months before the first students arrived, a bombshell from Canberra stopped the university in its tracks. Instead of beginning with science and engineering, the newly formed AUC had decided Monash should begin where the need was greatest, with humanities and commerce. Behind closed doors there were dark mutterings against the committee's chairman, Sir Leslie Martin, who had always wanted, so it was said, to treat Monash as a junior college of his own University of Melbourne.[47] The AUC added further insult by reprimanding the Interim Council for proceeding to design the campus without the advice of its foundation professors.[48] This struck Blackwood as absurd. It was like saying 'You don't want to build your opera house until you have hired singers to perform in it'.[49] Some of the opera company, however, including the principal conductor, privately sympathised with the AUC's view. 'In planning buildings, unconsciously they were taking academic decisions', Matheson admitted.[50]

In October 1959, the Monash Council met with Leslie Martin, a tense encounter that Blackwood recorded as 'an epic day' in the history of the university.[51] Angry words were spoken, but by the end of the day a compromise had been reached: Monash would begin by enrolling students in all four faculties—Science, Engineering, Arts and Commerce—but the AUC would not increase its funding.[52] To accommodate the increased numbers of students and staff without encroaching on space allocated to other faculties, McCutcheon had already been obliged to raise the height of the humanities and social sciences building from three or four to seven storeys.[53]

'Here we are at Monash!'

Matheson was preparing to leave for Melbourne when news of the AUC decision arrived. After a brief tour of European universities, he spent a fortnight in the United States and Canada, where he compared notes with a Manchester friend, Tom Howarth, who was about to become the master planner of the new York University. In the United States, he investigated the prospects of financial support from firms and foundations. Some of the American industrialists who were setting up factories in Australia would be prepared to contribute, he believed.[54]

Back in Melbourne, a reluctant Mrs O'Shea had at last surrendered her large farmhouse on the Clayton campus. 'We all felt that for every reason, psychological and otherwise, we should use this house and grounds for our Vice-Chancellor's residence right from the start', Blackwood's deputy, Walter Bassett, proposed. 'It would be an inspiration to contractors and others knowing that the Vice-Chancellor was at all times in the vicinity and was prepared to be the first to live at the new University.'[55] From its very beginnings, Monash University would take shape under the watchful eye of its first vice-chancellor.

'It was a good thing it was a big house', Audrey Matheson recalls. They arrived, with their now three boys and belongings, aboard the *Willem Ruys* on 29 January 1960, almost exactly thirteen years after their first Australian landfall. 'I remember very well when we all moved into the house and my young ones were rushing up saying, "Oh, there's another room, there's another room there, how many rooms?—twenty-one!"' The family occupied the upstairs bedrooms. Louis's study doubled as his daytime office, while Registrar Frank Johnson shared the maids' rooms with his assistant.[56] Johnson drove with his family across the Nullarbor from Perth, arriving just a few days after the Mathesons and announcing his arrival with a note slipped under the door: 'Reporting for duty'. As the staff grew, the typists overflowed into the garage, forcing the Mathesons to keep their new Ford Fairlane 300 (Blackwood had vetoed Louis's request for a Jaguar or Rover) in a shed along the lane.[57]

'Here we are at Monash!' the new vice-chancellor wrote exultantly to Jock Marshall on the university's brand-new letterhead. 'Not yet fully functioning but at least making a start.'[58] Bulldozers were levelling the site in preparation for construction of the science and engineering buildings. At Matheson's suggestion, McCutcheon had sent plans for the biology wing to Marshall for comment. His reaction was explosive.[59] The building was too small, and no provision had been made for the special requirements of botany and zoology. Biology, he feared, was to become a 'Cinderella department', with botany a kind of 'sub-Cinderella' within it. Even leading physical scientists, he insisted, now recognised that 'the big and exciting advances during this half of the 20th century will probably come from the biological side'. Marshall, as expected, was being difficult, but, as time would prove, he was also right. From their modest beginnings in the shadow of chemistry and physics, the biological sciences, revolutionised by a series of momentous discoveries in genetics, biochemistry, ecology and recombinant DNA, eventually expanded to occupy most of the south-western corner of the Monash campus.[60]

In April, Marshall made a flying visit to Melbourne. The university, he discovered, 'was still a large farm. In the farmhouse lived the

The first meeting of the Monash Professorial Board, 8 November 1960, in the dining room of the vice-chancellor's residence. From left to right: Kevin Westfold (mathematics), Rod Andrew (medicine), Jock Marshall (biology), Frank Johnson (registrar), Louis Matheson (vice-chancellor), Jim Butchart (assistant registrar), Bill Scott (English), Don Cochrane (economics), Ron Brown (chemistry) and Ken Hunt (engineering). Appointed but still to arrive in Melbourne were Bob Street (physics) and John Legge (history).

Vice-Chancellor and his family. The Vice-Chancellor kept a handy stock of Wellington boots of various sizes. In some of these we ploughed through the mud.'[61] An unseasonably wet autumn had saturated the reddish clay soils, turning the campus into a giant mud heap and slowing down the construction program.[62] Just as Marshall arrived, a long trench carrying services under the main science block collapsed, adding weeks to the schedule. Nothing so defined the experience of the first inhabitants of the Clayton campus as the clay: a thick layer of glutinous mud through which they waded heroically, like soldiers on the Western Front.

In just two years, the blueprint of the university had been radically transformed. It would be much bigger than first expected, with possibly 10 000 or 12 000 students.[63] It had begun as a university with a scientific and technological bias, then it was expected to be a 'fully balanced' university that would begin with science and engineering, and only now, at the insistence of Sir Leslie Martin, had it become a university tilted towards the humanities and social sciences. The offices, lecture theatres and laboratories designed for chemists and biologists would be shared, for the time being, with historians and philosophers. And the university would have to redouble its efforts to ensure that there were enough economists, political scientists and accountants on hand to greet the students due to arrive in March 1961.

Beginning with chairs in English, history and mathematics, Monash sought senior appointments in philosophy, modern languages, economics, economic history, political science and accountancy, leaving a foundation position in psychology to a later stage.[64] Bill Scott, a 43-year-old reader in English from the University of Melbourne, with a slender publication list but a solid record of teaching and administration, beat his brilliant but more doctrinaire younger colleague Sam Goldberg to the chair of English. John Legge, a 39-year-old senior lecturer at the University of Western Australia, was a late applicant for the chair of history. 'John Legge has the academic experience, the publications, the humour, the toughness, the administrative ability and the ambition to do the sort of job that will be necessary at Monash', Oxford-based Australian Max Hartwell advised.[65] A foundation professor, Matheson believed, should be 'somewhat pioneering in temperament', a quality he shrewdly detected in Legge's new work on Indonesian history.[66] His appointment marked the first step towards Monash's long and fruitful engagement with Asia. Hector Monro, a New Zealand–born senior lecturer at Sydney, had been a journalist, librarian and prisoner of conscience during the war before writing his first book, on the philosophy of humour. 'Mr Monro', his Sydney colleague A.K. Stout observed, 'is a sound and well-read philosopher and a man of broad culture. He speaks slowly and deliberately, thinking as he goes along, and his manner suggests what I can best describe as a combination of open-mindedness with authority.' His deliberate manner, however, could be deceptive, for, as Matheson discovered, Monro could also be relied upon 'to speak fearlessly and effectively on controversial matters'.[67]

As 1960 drew to a close, the university rushed to fill the remaining vacancies. It passed over the internationally renowned but controversial

economist Colin Clark in favour of Donald Cochrane, 43-year-old dean of
the Faculty of Commerce and Economics at the University of Melbourne.
After an unsuccessful attempt to fill the chair of mathematics, Matheson
received a tentative inquiry from Kevin Westfold, a Melbourne-born
applied mathematician at the University of Sydney, who was flown down
immediately, taken to lunch at the grand Windsor Hotel, interviewed in
the afternoon and offered the chair on the spot.[68]

Perhaps the most irregular, though justifiable, appointment was of
council member Dr Rod Andrew, Dean of the Alfred Hospital Clinical
School, to the foundation deanship of the Monash Medical School. A patrician (Geelong Grammar, Toorak, Melbourne Club, lieutenant-colonel
in the AIF), Andrew was also a man of wide intellectual and artistic
interests and radical inclinations. He had already defined the progressive
philosophy, combining scientific and clinical training, that would guide
the new medical school; he was the obvious person to lead it. With Jock
Marshall, Hector Monro and others yet to come, he became an influential
voice for the progressive, secular humanism that characterised the Monash
professoriate in its early years.

This unseemly rush of last-minute local appointments had not gone
unnoticed. In Canberra and Sydney, Jock Marshall confided, people were
saying that it was 'useless for outsiders to apply because these posts were
already "sewn up" for local people who are "nice chaps" but of varying
abilities'.[69] Once again, the university's rushed timetable had narrowed its
choices. The broader contentions, however, that Monash favoured local
candidates and that the university's foundation professors were simply
'nice chaps' of mediocre ability, were not justified. By 1965, Monash had
appointed fifty professors, of whom just over half (twenty-seven) had first
graduated in Australia or New Zealand, and about one-third (sixteen)
from the University of Melbourne. To be sure, they were all chaps. The
accusation of local favouritism was more justified in 1961, when half the
appointees (seven out of fourteen) had Melbourne first degrees, than it
was five years later, when the proportion was about one-third. Monash
often went out of its way *not* to appoint Melbourne's favourite sons. Except
in the professional faculties, notably Medicine, it was rare for a Monash
professor to come to his chair without studying overseas. Most (seventeen)
of those with Australian or New Zealand first degrees had taken a higher

degree at Oxford (seven), Cambridge (four) or London (three). The Oxford connection was strongest in the humanities, the Cambridge and London connections in the sciences and social sciences. Those who were born or first graduated overseas, on the other hand, took higher degrees from a much wider range of universities, mainly in Britain, including London (six), Oxford (three), Cambridge (two), Birmingham, Liverpool, Edinburgh, Dublin and Durham. Monash professors appointed, like Robert Street, straight from overseas were in a small minority; most had a previous Australian connection.[70]

The campus and the forum

The university, according to liberals like Andrew, Marshall and Monro, was a community committed to the pursuit of rational inquiry and the free discussion of ideas. In morals, they inclined to liberalism tempered by utilitarianism, in aesthetics to modernism or eighteenth-century classicism, in religion to scepticism, in politics to the non-Marxist left. Their heroes were the intellectual giants of the European enlightenment: Isaac Newton (a seed from whose famous apple tree would be planted on the Monash campus), Jonathan Swift (whose works would form the nucleus of the Monash library's rare books collection), Charles Darwin (whose fifteen-volume collected works Marshall purchased as the foundation of his departmental library) and David Hume, John Stuart Mill and Bertrand Russell (whose writings were prominent in Monro's philosophy courses). In challenging convention, prizing experiment and originality, and believing that scientific inquiry would lead to human progress, they identified themselves with what contemporaries sometimes called 'modernism'.[71]

There was another side to the modern outlook, however. As Marshall Berman argues, the scientific impulse towards rationality, predictability and control could also fetter human creativity and freedom.[72] This was one of the tensions underlying the contemporary debate between the 'two cultures'. As a modern university campus, Monash was not only a site for such debates; it exhibited, in its very architecture, the contradictions of the modern project.

For Blackwood, the campus was a kind of factory to be designed and built, quickly and efficiently, along industrial lines. His memoir, *Monash University: The First Ten Years*, devotes almost as much space to the construction of service tunnels and the specification of concrete columns as it does to the academic functions of the university. As a fellow engineer, Matheson shared Blackwood's predilection for solutions that were rational, functional and hierarchical. The campus, they agreed, would be surrounded by a cyclone-wire fence and approached by a gatehouse manned by gatekeepers, who would direct visitors to their destinations.[73] Activity across the university would be synchronised by a master clock connected to 'slave clocks' in the various faculty buildings.[74] Porters would distribute mail to departments from a centralised mail exchange.[75] In the Union, meals would be served in two sittings, while in the faculties, uniformed tea-ladies would dispense morning and afternoon tea.[76] Academic offices would be allocated in accordance with rank: rooms with five windows for professors, four for senior lecturers, three for lecturers and two for humble teaching fellows. Secretaries would answer professors' telephones, senior lecturers would answer their own, lecturers would share a phone with a colleague, and teaching fellows would share a single phone in a common room. Students, of course, would have neither rooms nor telephones, but banks of basement lockers arrayed like those in a factory washroom.[77]

This functional modernism coexisted uneasily with the more spontaneous and collegial outlook of the liberal academics. To them, the watchwords of modernism—freedom, experience, reason—were, in the contemporary phrase, 'not so much a program, more a way of life'. Matheson shared enough of their outlook to see that the campus also had to be allowed to grow organically, in response to the desires and needs of those who inhabited it. For example, he declined to make permanent concrete pathways between buildings until the tracks worn in the muddy soil indicated the routes along which students and staff needed to travel.[78]

In October 1960, with less than five months to go before the arrival of the first students, Matheson wrote to McCutcheon: 'I am increasingly uneasy about some features of the development plan'. There was not enough room for the expansion of the medical school, the union building was too far from the centre of the campus, the administration building was not close enough to the university's 'front door' on Wellington Road, and there was simply not enough parking space for the expected influx of arts students.[79]

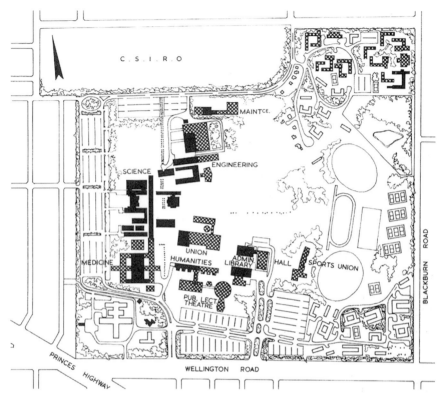

By 1963, when Monash submitted its plans for the 1964–66 triennium, the quiet centre of the campus, with its ornamental lake, had shrunk to make way for a belt of drives and car parks and the student residences had retreated to the northeast corner. The union building now faced the humanities building across the forum while the great hall, library and administration building composed a ceremonial and administrative precinct linked via a wide entrance avenue to the outside world.

The pastoral ideal of the campus as a place of quiet reflection centred on a lake and oriented to the Dandenongs was fading. First to go had been the lake, a casualty of urgent budget cuts early in 1959. By April, when council approved the first master plan, the humanities building had been pushed further north to create more car parks on the Wellington Road frontage, so losing most of what was left of its view of the ranges. The library and the administration building now faced the humanities building across a 300-metre-long rectangular space, described simply as a 'pedestrian precinct'. Towards its eastern end, in locations still to be finalised, were a 'great hall' for graduations and other ceremonies, a public lecture theatre and a 'church centre'. Each of these elements had symbolic, as well as functional, significance, and once the academics began to arrive, they began to discuss how they should be arranged.

By the end of 1960, the 'pedestrian precinct' had become 'the forum'. When it first appeared in official documents, the word was used informally: it was the forum (no quotation marks) or 'The Forum'. Soon, however, it was taken up more self-consciously. Rather than solitary scholars reflecting beside an ornamental lake, the 'forum' conjured up the appealing idea of students and professors walking together, like citizens of an ancient republic, debating the great issues of the day. The word also appeared in other collocations. Matheson referred to the 'forum-parvis' (parvis being the enclosed area outside a medieval church) to denote the forecourt of the library and to distinguish it from the 'forum/pleacherie', a planted area between the library and the administration building.[80] 'None of us knew what a pleacherie was', John Legge recalls. 'It was explained that it consisted of fruit trees planted close together and with their branches entwined. Kevin Westfold called up a picture of students with arms and legs intertwined, engaged in sexual activity under the fruit trees.'[81] In 1967, John Swan, the man who had given Monash its name, now a professor of chemistry, suggested that the space at the eastern end should be named 'Lalor Court' in honour of the hero of Eureka, Peter Lalor. The name might encourage students to practise the arts of democracy, he thought. 'I think it would be quite appropriate if Lalor Court were to become (at least at specified times) the Monash "Yarra Bank" or "Hyde Park Corner".'[82] He could not have anticipated how little encouragement the students would soon require.

Within this symbolic space, centrality became the measure of importance. Matheson considered that the student union, located at the far eastern end of the forum, was too far from the centre of action and proposed that it change places with the main library at the north-western end. Naturally, his own administration building had to be at the centre of things: he placed it next to the great hall, the ceremonial centre of the university, and closer to the Wellington Road entrance for the convenience of official visitors. Ernest Clark, however, was unhappy for his library, the true centre of the university in the eyes of humanists, to be displaced from its central position on the northern side of the forum. If it couldn't stay where it was, he asked, couldn't the union move eastwards along the forum to make room? Or perhaps humanities could shuffle a little further east to accommodate the main library on the southern side? The Professorial Board backed the librarian, but Matheson and McCutcheon insisted that there was simply no room on the south side of the forum to accommodate it, together with the towering humanities building. McCutcheon finally put his hand firmly on the plan and said: 'We need to have a tall building here'.[83] Early in 1961, the building committee had the final word: the union and administration buildings would occupy the north side of the forum; the arts, lecture theatres, public lecture theatre (later the Alexander Theatre) and library, the south side; and the eastern end would be closed by the great hall.[84]

McCutcheon had always wanted his tall building, for the symbolism as much as anything. The late 1950s was an era when glass towers had come to express the hope that scientific progress would lead to human betterment. To many Monash students of the 1960s, Monash's tower symbolised the aspirations of a new university prepared to break with tradition and offer its students a wide view of life and the world. The reason McCutcheon got his tower, however, or got such a tall one, had more to do with what Blackwood euphemistically called 'the long-term interests of ground conservation and compact operation'.[85] The simple truth was that there was no room left within the outlines of McCutcheon's master plan to accommodate the predicted 5500 arts and commerce students and staff unless they were stacked into a tall building. In August 1960, Matheson agreed that the Humanities Building should be raised to its full height, twelve storeys.[86] Monash's boldest building was a monument not to the foresight of Monash's founders so much as their myopia.

The brief to the building's architects, Eggleston, Macdonald and Secomb, mandated a modern design. Yet its form—a long, thin, multi-storey slab—was poorly adapted to the needs of a university. Its long central corridors were aesthetically dreary and uncongenial to the habits of academics, 'chronically talkative [and] sensitive to disturbance'. The only patterns of movement within the building were orthogonal (up–down and east–west) obliging its inhabitants, fortunately mostly 'healthy young

'We need to have a tall building here.' The twelve-storey Humanities Building, 1964, later to be named for Prime Minister Robert Menzies, became the most conspicuous landmark of the Monash campus.

persons', to walk long distances between outside lecture theatres and inside tutorial rooms, and from one department to another.[87]

Every hour, at the changeover of classes, the architects calculated, approximately 1675 persons would enter or leave the building within a space of ten minutes. It would take thirteen high-speed lifts or eighteen escalators to do the job. The escalators were cheaper, moved more people more quickly, took less space and cost less to maintain, or so it was said. Like other features of the modern urban landscape—the drive-in, the regional shopping centre, the highway interchange—Monash's escalators were an adaptation of Henry Ford's production line, a model of industrial organisation that programmed human activity into machine-like sequential movements.[88] While Monash's students could saunter along the forum, they had to be 're-shuffled into a different pattern' as they entered and left the Humanities Building.[89]

In Monash's early years, journalist Keith Dunstan observed that it laboured under 'an immense inferiority complex': 'a terror of becoming a mere education factory'. Located in a monolithic building in an industrial suburb, it was 'trying terribly hard to avoid the factory label'.[90] Its teachers had to work doubly hard to create a more intimate intellectual community. 'Members of the Arts Faculty', Donald Cochrane commented, 'like to take small discussion groups of 8 or 9 in their own studies, surrounded by their books and so provide a more relaxed atmosphere so essential for "Socratic" methods of teaching'. The picture of the humanist in his study, surrounded by his library, perhaps puffing on a pipe (since smoking was not yet forbidden) as he engaged in animated debate with admiring disciples was a cheerful evocation of Oxford in the antipodes.[91]

The AUC's standard lecturer's office of 100 square feet was too small, however, to accommodate a tutorial group along with the lecturer, bookshelf and desk. Matheson appealed to Leslie Martin to relax the rules. Scientists, he reminded him (Martin was a physicist) had their laboratories. Was the AUC 'so preoccupied with economy that it was prepared to prohibit the Socratic method'?[92] But the AUC was unmoved.

At last, the architect Ralph Koren, prompted by English lecturer David Bradley, devised an ingenious solution. Instead of following the AUC's standard 5-foot module, couldn't some rooms be constructed on a 4-foot module, so that arts lecturers' rooms could expand to a width of 12 feet? To provide an assortment of rooms suitable to the needs of the two faculties, offices on the north side of the corridor would have 5-foot windows, while those on the south side would be only 4 feet wide.[93] There was only one problem: now the arts lecturers' rooms, those to the north, were just a little too large. In order to meet Professor Martin's rules, rooms on the south side of the corridor were reduced by the insertion of a continuous row of cupboards. Future inhabitants of the building sometimes noticed the puzzling inequality in windows and room sizes on the north and south sides of the building,[94] but few realised its rationale, or that it represented a tiny victory for Socrates over the Canberra bureaucracy.

Inhabiting the campus

Monash had begun as words on a page. As the first stage of building neared an end, words again became important, as the university began to make the place its own, giving names and titles to its buildings and precincts. In order to 'foster public relations', the Interim Council resolved early in 1960 that 'major buildings might be named after individuals who had, *inter alia*, played an important part in the recent development of Australian universities'. Smelling a political rat, Jock Marshall urged Matheson to confer the names of 'some of the old and historic European schools on our squares, streets and walks . . . The idea may not appeal to some of the more tradesmanlike members of our brotherhood but it seems to me that it would be preferable to Bolte Avenue, Menzies Square and the gruesome like.'[95] To try to forestall such a move, the Professorial Board resolved that no 'building, square, drive or walk' should be named without its consent.[96]

A few months later, however, Chancellor Blackwood advised the board that he had sought the approval of the prime minister to give his name to the new arts building. In agreeing, Menzies had proposed the title 'Robert Menzies School of Humanities'. The professors were being consulted, but only after the event. Since the prime minister had agreed, there was no possibility of withdrawing the invitation. That the building housed social sciences as well as humanities, and that there actually was no 'School of Humanities', hardly mattered. What officialdom decided to call the building, however, did not have to be observed by the academic community. Even before Menzies arrived to open it, the building had been nicknamed, to his great amusement, the 'Ming Wing'. ('Ming', a contraction of the Scottish pronunciation of his surname, was the left's favourite nickname.) Until 2010, when the building underwent a long-overdue makeover, the official name 'Robert Menzies School of Humanities' survived archaeologically in the half-obscured signs over the southern entrance.

An unfortunate precedent had been set, but the academic community was determined to prevent its repetition. In November 1961, council approved a recommendation of its new Naming Committee, drafted by John Legge and Jock Marshall, 'that appropriate University buildings be named after a) noted pioneers and distinguished people, preferably Australians, the term "pioneer" being understood to include not only geographical explorers but persons who had pushed back the frontiers of knowledge in their own subjects, or b) benefactors'.[97] The intention was to limit the names of buildings to the honoured dead and to curb any inclination to curry favour with living politicians. For the next decade, the committee vigorously debated which famous names should be inscribed on the Monash landscape. Matheson's nomination of the Australian aviation pioneer Lawrence Hargrave for the new science–engineering library prevailed over Dean Kenneth Hunt's preference for the Victorian inventor of the thrust bearing, A.G.M. Michell. Liberal politician Alfred Deakin, wheat-breeder William Farrer and naturalist A.W. Howitt gave their names to student halls of residence, as did painter Tom Roberts, though only after Marshall, Rod Andrew and historian Geoffrey Serle promoted him over the original nominee, Arthur Streeton.[98] In 1964, Serle, a future editor of the *Australian Dictionary of Biography*, offered a long list of possible nominees, all nationalist heroes, most Victorians. 'I detest provincialism', he confessed, 'but I suppose if we don't honour the locals no-one else is likely to'.[99] In honouring locals, Monash was also honouring itself, trusting that the lustre of their deeds would add distinction to a university whose achievements were still before it.

Monash's master planner had envisaged the campus as an English park with an ornamental lake. Jock Marshall, the returning native son, had a contrasting vision: Australian bushland with a billabong. Early in 1961, he urged his professorial colleagues 'to take advantage of [Monash's] unique opportunity to plant the grounds exclusively with Australian flora'.[100]

John Stevens, landscape advisor to McCutcheon, had already begun planting the grounds with acacias, melaleucas and pittosporum in 1960.[101] Matheson encouraged the two men to consult on the program of plantings, but by mid-1961 Stevens had concluded that it was impossible to create an attractive landscape at Monash using native flora alone.[102] After a visit to the Metropolitan Golf Course, he advised the Grounds Committee that the beautiful effects achieved with native plantings in the sandy soils of Huntingdale simply could not be reproduced in the dark, water-logged clay of Clayton. He would have to work with a more limited palette of native flora unless the committee sanctioned occasional use of exotics.[103]

For Jock Marshall, a fervent nationalist, this was heresy. His commitment to native planting, his colleague Martin Canny observed, was 'an act of faith'.[104] Native plants would attract native birds and offer sanctuary for kangaroos and koalas in 'Snake Gully', the bush reserve he had created

The Menzies Building viewed from Snake Gully, 1967. Biology Professor Jock Marshall, a homecoming Australian, was determined that Monash should be Australian as well as modern, insisting that its grounds be planted exclusively with Australian native plants.

from an unsightly ditch on the north-eastern edge of the campus. It was also an act of 'retribalisation', the personal project that had brought Marshall back to Australia.[105] In the early years, his faith was sorely tested as shrubs and trees, planted by the thousands, withered in drought and drowned in the wet. When a row of Lombardy poplars appeared on the edge of the campus, Marshall organised a midnight raid to uproot them. In 1966, discouraged by progress, Matheson proposed to engage another expert, Professor Lindsay Pryor of ANU, known to favour the judicious introduction of exotics.[106] Marshall erupted. 'To appoint him would automatically change the whole philosophy of our planting, i.e. to produce a campus display that will be unique in a few decades time. This is the one way in which we have any hope of making Monash different from other provincial Australian universities.'[107] Already stricken with the cancer that would kill him, Marshall continued the fight, even lying in the back of the family station wagon as his wife drove him from Quarry Hill to meetings of the Grounds Committee. At Marshall's insistence, Matheson dropped the plan to hire Pryor and instead engaged Eltham landscape designer Gordon Ford, now regarded as one of the most formative influences on Australian native garden design.[108]

It took another two decades, and the labour of many others in draining the sub-soil, pruning dead wood and planting new varieties, for Marshall's vision to be realised. Today, tall eucalypts and groves of melaleucas soften the outlines of the Ming Wing, and over a hundred species of native birds are drawn to the campus. Marshall's act of faith, and the determination of others to maintain it, testified to the truth that great universities are not just built, but grown.

THREE

THE FIRST OF THE NEW

Having seen itself in 1960 as the first of the new universities [Monash] has succeeded, maybe, in establishing itself as the last of the old.

JOHN LEGGE, 1975

'Monash felt itself to be at the crest of a wave . . . a pioneer in a brave new educational world', one of the pioneers, historian John Legge, recalled.[1] Monash wasn't just a new university; it also aspired to be a new *kind* of university, more modern, less bound by tradition, more attuned to the aspirations of an affluent, expansive, technological society. It would democratise higher education, bringing the university within reach of a broader segment of society. It would open up new fields of knowledge and teach old disciplines in new ways. It would be more experimental, open to the lessons of experience. It would transcend the 'two cultures', humanising the technologists and making the humanists scientifically literate.

These dreams, so vivid in the minds of Monash's creators, were bound to fade, as human frailty, limited resources and conflicting visions of the good university dimmed their lustre. The pioneers, it often turned out, were fighting on more than one front, and one pioneer's vision was sometimes at odds with another's. Some sought to redeem a traditional idea of the university from a utilitarian age; others, to adapt fashionable British or American models to Australian conditions. As it finally emerged, Monash's most novel features were not always those laid down in the blueprints of its academic founders. Junior staff and students sometimes pushed professors in directions they had not anticipated. Monash has a

The tutorial, modelled here by geography lecturer Stuart Duncan in 1963, was the preferred teaching style of the new universities of the 1960s.

strong claim to be the first of Australia's new universities, but its ways of being new were not always those anticipated at the beginning.

The academic frontier

Living amid the mud and dust, clatter and clutter of a building site on the suburban frontier, Monash's first-comers were pioneers in a literal sense as well. Despite Matheson's edict that the university should have no temporary buildings, some departments were forced to improvise. The Physics Department occupied a builder's hut in the grounds of the vice-chancellor's house. On hot summer days, the hut was covered with hessian and sprayed with water to keep the occupants cool. 'We were in a large Coolgardie safe', lecturer Bill Rachinger recalled.[2] The rigours of pioneering were compensated for, however, by open fields and broad horizons. Some newcomers were escaping 'old and stodgy professors at Melbourne'.[3] 'We were pioneers', geneticist Bruce Holloway recalled, contrasting the freedom and informality of life at Clayton with the more hidebound structures of Melbourne's Parkville. Foundation Professor of Psychology Ross Day welcomed the 'freshness of the place' compared with the University of Sydney, 'old and decadent and full of myths and gods'.[4] The muddy fields of Clayton were a blank page for the pioneers to write their own story.

On the campus, as in the bush, pioneering bred an egalitarian ethos. Professors and lecturers, scientists and humanists, academics and administrators were thrown together in a face-to-face community, sharing space, ideas, facilities, shortages and frustrations. It was a fellowship of shirtsleeves and first names. Short as it was, this period lives strongly in the memories of the first-comers, a happy souvenir of a time before the university became a more impersonal corporation.

The egalitarianism was actually deceptive, for the easy relations between the university's first professors developed within an institution that, from the beginning, was as monarchical as it was democratic. Monash was very much Louis Matheson's university, the creation of a benevolent, far-sighted, consultative, energetic and eloquent autocrat. He had been the first to arrive on the campus, so everyone else was a newcomer, chosen and welcomed by him. 'I think it was one of the greatest things of my professional life to have been appointed by Louis and also to work with him', Holloway believes. 'He had a vision, no question about it.'[5] When John Legge and his family arrived on the boat from Perth, Louis and Audrey were on the wharf to greet them. A few days later, Audrey called with a bottle of sherry. How could a busy vice-chancellor justify taking the time for such gestures, some of his colleagues wondered.[6] But, as the Mathesons knew, a warm welcome could establish a life-long bond of friendship and loyalty.

'The wives of Monash University staff members, who have come from other countries or from interstate are settling into furnished homes while they "house hunt"', the *Age* reported in February 1961.[7] Even before he left London, Jock Marshall had begun making plans for the house he would build somewhere near the campus. 'If you see a large block of land on a big hill overlooking the university site, please put 2/6d deposit on it for me', he urged Blackwood.[8] The house on the hill did not materialise, but Marshall, his painter wife, Jayne, and their three children were soon happily settled in a rented farmhouse in Narre Warren, a staging post to the 110-year-old homestead they later found at Quarry Hill, near Berwick.[9]

The wives of British academics were shocked by the high prices of houses, the sense of suburban distance and the lack of a national health service. Coming from Hungary, a 'country steeped in centuries of university tradition', Marianne Bodi, wife of German lecturer Leslie Bodi, missed the cultural richness of her homeland but was excited by the prospect of becoming part of something new.[10] Many of the university's first academic recruits settled in the nearby suburbs of Mount Waverley, Glen Waverley and Notting Hill, close enough for convenience, though not in sufficient numbers to create a distinctive academic enclave.

Most of the new professors were family men whose wives were marooned in the suburbs with young children. Audrey realised: 'This is my role, to look after the wives of the people who have jobs here, who come from somewhere else, who don't have any friends and can't go out because they were tied [down with young children]'. When babies were born, she visited the mothers in hospital. At Christmas, the Mathesons hosted a children's party with balloons and donkey rides in the vice-chancellor's garden. Audrey formed a university women's group but, recalling the stuffiness of the wives' associations she had encountered elsewhere, insisted that it be run on informal, democratic lines: there would be 'no ordering

Owzat, Vice-Chancellor! Batsman Louis Matheson is stumped by a student wicket-keeper in a 1961 staff–student cricket match. Such occasions were a mark of the close, informal relations between students and academics when the university was young.

and bullying'; 'everyone should have a say in what went on'. Almost fifty years after its first meeting, she remains its much-loved president.

On Friday evenings, in the cramped dining room of the vice-chancellor's residence, the Mathesons introduced new professors and their wives to guests from Melbourne's political, business and professional worlds. 'There was no caterer anywhere near', Audrey remembers, 'and I realised very soon I would have to do all the cooking myself'. Louis sat at the head of the table carving the meat, while Audrey served the vegetables from a Magic Maid dinner wagon. The newest professor was appointed wine waiter, with instructions to ensure that everyone's glass was full. 'You can't have a decent dinner party unless you've got your glass full', Audrey insists.[11]

God-professors and their juniors

As founding vice-chancellor, Matheson had wide powers over the development of the university and its academic program. He widened them further by modifying the university's statutes to increase his executive authority, by appointing his own team of professors and administrators, and through the force of his own commanding, yet winning, personality. One of his first moves was to adopt the British practice of chairing the chief academic body, the Professorial Board, rather than following the standard Australian practice of allowing the board to elect its own chair. By placing himself at the head of the table, Matheson not only became 'totally involved in [its] decision making', but was able to influence its agenda.[12] The relationship between Matheson and 'my professors', as he liked to call them, was the linchpin of his leadership, a blend of authority and collegiality that instilled a strong *esprit de corps* among his senior colleagues. 'I adhere to the old-fashioned view that a university is as good as its professors', he observed. 'If they are good they will attract good colleagues who want to work with them and good students who want to study under their guidance.' Matheson strove to appoint 'men of proved intellectual power, imagination and integrity' and was prepared, when he couldn't find them, to leave the choice to a later day.[13] 'Better a good vacancy than a bad appointment', he would say. Once appointed, they should be left to get on with their job with as little bureaucratic or political interference as possible.[14]

But by the mid-1960s, with the university doubling in size every two or three years, the pioneering era was coming to an end. In mid-1964, the first issue of the *Monash Reporter*, 'an unofficial bulletin prepared for the information of members of staff', noted that 'while we were small it was possible, over lunch or coffee, for everyone to obtain in conversation a fair idea of the progress of events, of the thinking and planning, and of the comings and goings of colleagues . . . This', the editors ruefully admitted, 'is no longer the case'.[15] Even while talk was giving way to print, however, the university strove to cultivate a sense of community. As new staff members arrived, the *Reporter* introduced them with a brief biography, mentioning each newcomer's domestic status as well as their academic background. The campus generated a vigorous social life of its own, with chamber music, drama and singing groups, a ski club, sporting teams and a Freedom to Read Association sparked by the Bolte government's banning of Mary McCarthy's novel *The Group*.[16] At the beginning, staff and students dined together in the student Union and drank in the nearby Notting Hill Hotel. Soon, however, academic staff were demanding a social centre of their own. The Monash Club opened in 1961 but four years later still awaited a liquor licence. 'Complaints are rife about the length of time that has passed without any progress towards opening the Faculty Club bar', the *Reporter* noted at the beginning of 1965. When the bar eventually opened, the club boasted 350 members, at a time when the entire academic and technical staff of the university numbered around 450.[17] Soon, the growing numbers of sub-professorial staff, gathered around the Faculty Club bar, began to seek a larger voice in the university's affairs.

In 1962, 40-year-old historian Geoffrey Serle, the sole elected non-professorial member of the University Council, sent Matheson a copy of a paper, The Sad Case of the God-Professor. Serle had come to Monash from the University of Melbourne, where, he explained, 'the dead hand' of the university administration generated 'appalling frustration' among the middle ranks. 'The basic fault of the system is the concentration of power and responsibility in too few hands.' Professors in large departments were overworked and increasingly inefficient. Some were 'duds', but even those who were good at the time of their appointment could run out of steam. Meanwhile, some outstanding scholars refused to apply for a chair rather than 'lead a dog's life' with endless committees and no time for research.

Even at Monash, Serle feared, it might be too late for drastic reform. Something, however, could be done to curb the autocratic tendencies of the central administration and the 'god-professors' by increasing the representation of non-professorial staff, permitting non-professors to head departments and ensuring that all members of the university were better acquainted with what was going on. Rather than the 'redbrick-colonial' tradition of god-professors, it would be better to emulate the Oxbridge–American system, in which professorial rank was divorced from departmental headship.[18]

'I find myself in agreement with much of your argument', Matheson mildly replied. He had already been thinking about how the university's

Historian Geoffrey Serle (left, c. 1963), sole non-professorial member of council, contested the rule of the 'god-professor'. 'It is no use pretending the university is a community of scholars working on the basis of equality', Assistant Registrar Jim Butchart (right, c. 1960) retorted.

government should be improved, formulating the problem, as only an engineer could, mechanically: 'The trouble was to devise a governmental mechanism that will stand up to hard wear in a large university and simultaneously reduce friction to a minimum or increase participation to a maximum'. He was optimistic about the possibility of 'fundamental' reform, but sceptical of the Oxbridge–American model. 'I believe that authority and responsibility should not be far apart; decision must be illuminated by consultation, no doubt, but he who carries the responsibility must have the last word.'[19] Instead of an academic democracy, he preferred to strengthen the lines of authority by providing vice-presidents to assist the vice-chancellor, full-time deans and a smaller, elected academic board, instead of an unwieldy professorial board.[20]

Matheson's fellow administrators were even less sympathetic to Serle's manifesto. Assistant Registrar Jim Butchart, an acute observer of academic foibles ('university academics are professional talkers'), was blunt:

The days of the Anglo-Saxon Moot have gone from the community, and I think it is about time they went from the University. It is no use any longer pretending that the University is a community of scholars and teachers working on the basis of equality, rather than a hierarchical relationship (in Geoff Serle's words). This 'traditional' idea developed because such communities were not required to make the kind of decisions they now must, for they were not subjected to the kinds of pressures now experienced . . . It seems to me that these kinds of problems put us in the 20th century, and 13th century university government just won't do. The conclusion I draw is that university government now requires more formal autocracy, or if you like, that university government should be more representative.[21]

The vice-chancellor, he believed, should cease to chair the Professorial Board, and the Professorial Board and the faculties should become elected bodies, though the electorate should be confined to senior staff.

Serle's paper, later published in the Staff Association journal *Vestes*, spurred vigorous debate but little change at Monash. It was not until 1967 that a few teaching fellows were admitted as observers to faculty meetings, and their admission to departmental meetings remained at the discretion of the senior professor.

If the new university was not a face-to-face, self-governing community, what kind of institution was it? Matheson often returned to this question, measuring Monash's evolving practice against more familiar models of organisation. As an engineer, he sometimes playfully likened his university to a factory. But, while it was subject to pressures of demand and supply, the materials it handled—academics and students—were not malleable and homogeneous like those of an industrial plant. Nor was the university a military organisation. One of Matheson's senior colleagues had been a brigadier in the Royal Engineers. 'He thinks the whole place is mad', Matheson observed. 'Nobody will take any orders at all, and this, in his view, makes it impossible to run a university—and I agree with him.'[22] And nor was it a government bureaucracy, for the flow of information was poor, there was no equivalent of a free press, and the academics themselves were reluctant to delegate decisions.

Matheson was joining a debate that rumbled across university campuses throughout the world as the age of mass higher education dawned. He appreciated the issues keenly, not only because Monash was growing so quickly, but because they excited a conflict within his own personality. As an engineer and administrator, he was naturally inclined to centralised, autocratic rule. Yet, as a liberal with a deep attachment to the university idea, he wanted 'his' fellow academics to participate fully in its collective life. Through the many speeches, professional papers and memos he wrote over the decade, he attempted—perceptively, eloquently, and sometimes despairingly—to bring these ideas into harmony.

Bridging the cultures

In one of his first public statements, Matheson lamented the 'great and tragic gulf of ignorance' that was opening up between science and the humanities. 'Statesmen and administrators were becoming increasingly unable to understand what science was about, or what it could do to solve the world's problems', he explained. Finding how specialists could understand each other was 'one of the chief problems facing Monash University'.[23] Deploring the gulf between the two cultures was a common cry among academic statesmen in 1960, but there was a greater onus on a new university to bridge it.

Even before Matheson arrived at Monash, a group of interested academics from the University of Melbourne, drawn together under the auspices of the Student Christian Movement (SCM), offered a blueprint of the 'structure and function' of the new university. Their convenor, Anthony Clunies Ross, a tutor in the Department of History, was the son of the eminent scientist Sir Ian Clunies Ross, who had influenced the Murray Report's recommendation that Monash should become a 'fully balanced university'. As well as 'bridging the gulf between humanistic and scientific studies', the new university, the group argued, should give greater emphasis to the social sciences, emphasise small group discussion rather than formal lectures, and create a new collegiate structure to offset the loneliness that besets many students. Science students, they hoped, would 'unlearn the dogmatism that goes with scientific teaching', while humanities students might acquire an understanding that the sciences 'were not merely arcana revealed charismatically, but systems developed

by intellectual processes'. Their proposals were animated by a liberal
Christian vision of the university as a moral community devoted to the
advancement of knowledge, the reconciliation of science and humanity,
and the full development of the human person.[24]

Following their lead, in 1961 the Professorial Board resolved that all
science students should be obliged to take a course in the humanities and
vice versa.[25] No sooner had they enunciated this noble principle, however,
than all sorts of complications arose. Who would teach the courses? Would
the faculties yield space in their own crowded curriculum to accommodate
them? Would the requirement deter brilliant but tunnel-visioned students
from coming to Monash? In 1962, the academic community endorsed
the compulsory courses 'as an experiment' but a year later rescinded the
proposal, urging faculties to develop courses attractive enough to draw
students from other faculties on a voluntary basis.[26] Anthony Clunies
Ross, by that time a lecturer in economics, defended the idea to the
last, devising an attractive menu of 'trans-faculty' courses ranging from
'Twentieth Century Literature' and 'Marx and the Marxists' to 'The
Problem of War' and 'The Economics of Medicine'.[27]

The academic community was learning a painful lesson: the cultural
divide between first-year humanities and science students was as nothing
compared with the gulf between their professors. The pressures of
growth and the shortage of resources had quickly narrowed the scope
for experiment, forcing the university back upon traditional structures
and solutions. 'One can now see that this retreat from educational
innovation, however regrettable, was inevitable', Matheson reflected
twenty years later.[28] It was the first, but not the last, descent from the
high hopes of 1960.

Defending the cultures

Rather than bridging the cultures, most of Monash's founding professors
were busily building up their own disciplines. The university's Interim
Council had decided that its Faculty of Arts would not follow Melbourne's
example by requiring entrants to have completed a matriculation foreign
language. Registrar Frank Johnson defended the policy as a guarantee
of the essentially 'liberal' character of the first degree.[29] Humanities
academics, however, insisted their students must take at least one year

of a foreign language (or mathematics, which was regarded as a similar symbolic system) in order to graduate. Language, they argued, was an essential gateway to a culture, and in studying a foreign language students gained increased understanding of their own culture.

Soon, however, the foreign language departments, burdened with large numbers of beginners, were pressing for the reintroduction of a prerequisite. Experts on the poetry of Baudelaire baulked at drilling irregular verbs into academic conscripts. Ralph Barrell of the French Department proposed to divert the conscripts to an institute of languages staffed by language instructors and equipped with language laboratories. But was such an institute, a kind of in-house Berlitz academy, compatible with the liberal function of a university? Matheson was untroubled by the idea—'perhaps we should not be too high and mighty'[30]—but the proposal died, and for the next twenty years the language departments soldiered on, earning their bread and butter from large classes of beginners in order to support the few who progressed to more advanced literary studies. For the Faculty of Arts, the teaching of foreign languages was a symbolic issue as much as an educational one, a measure of the new university's determination to retain a link, however tenuous, with the great European tradition of *literae humaniores* ('humane letters').

Meanwhile the other culture, science, was also staking out its territory. The early 1960s was the heyday of scientific positivism, when mathematics, chemistry and physics reigned supreme. First dean of the faculty, Jock Marshall, a biologist, planned chairs in botany, geology, psychology and possibly physical anthropology. (His colleagues unanimously drew the line at geography, which joined the Faculty of Arts.)[31] His successor, mathematician Kevin Westfold, however, took a stricter view, appointing further chairs in mathematics, physics and inorganic chemistry, before finally making appointments in botany (1964) and psychology (1965).[32] Psychology was 'increasingly an experimental science', Foundation Professor Ross Day insisted. 'It is my wish in teaching the subject and developing research to stress its empirical aspects and to emphasise the role of laboratory investigation.'[33] Even so, it was not among the core laboratory subjects from which all science students were required to take a compulsory subject. Only in 1966 did Acting Dean Peter Finch propose its promotion to the inner circle. 'The time is past when one could rightly maintain that Chemistry and Physics were the only or the most important scientific disciplines . . . The study of Psychology can be pursued in a manner which by analogy with the more established disciplines, may be said, and correctly so, to be scientific.'[34] The even newer discipline of 'information science' remained outside. Instead of a chair of information science, the faculty resolved to appoint a director of the Computer Centre, perhaps in conjunction with an appropriate existing department, 'if his qualifications warranted it'.[35] In 1964, few imagined that one day, far from comprising only a small centre, information science would become an entire faculty.

The Sussex model

Monash opened in the same year as the University of Sussex, the most self-consciously new of Britain's universities. Historian Asa Briggs, later to become Sussex's second vice-chancellor, visited Australia in 1961 and outlined the philosophy of the new university in a lecture, 'The Map of Learning'. University education, he argued, was not just the passive acquisition of knowledge, but an active and personal quest for understanding. 'Being explorers ourselves in a new university . . . we wanted to make our students into explorers also.'[36] Sussex abandoned traditional faculties and departments in favour of interdisciplinary schools of social, European, Asian and African studies. Lectures were no longer compulsory, and in small tutorials teachers and students engaged in debate, experiment and discovery. Active rather than passive, intimate rather than impersonal, flexible rather than rigid, experimental rather than traditional: these were the watchwords of the Sussex model.

Matheson admired the Sussex experiment, echoing its principles in his own aspirations for Monash. 'Universities are not teaching institutions; they are learning institutions', he argued.[37]

> The details of the curriculum [were] much less important than the way in which the teaching [was] conducted and the extent to which the students were led to develop self-reliant and self-critical ways of study and thought. This could only be achieved by ensuring small-group teaching in tutorials and seminars where the student could play an active role.[38]

He urged his new Faculty of Arts to follow the Sussex model of inter-disciplinary schools.

This, it became clear, was more than his foundation professors were prepared to embrace. 'The principle of integration', insisted John Legge, 'must be balanced against the more important principle that any organisation of subjects must be based on a traditional discipline'.[39] Interdisciplinary studies were all very well if they could develop in parallel with traditional disciplines, but not at the latter's cost. The Sussex model was more suited, in any case, to a small provincial university than a large metropolitan one: after its first decade, Sussex had about 3500 students, while Monash had more than four times that number. Universities like La Trobe and Macquarie, which later embraced the Sussex model with enthusiasm, eventually reverted to a more traditional structure, as did the University of Sussex itself.

Fifteen years later, Legge felt vindicated by the outcome. Monash had avoided a possibly 'rash, gimmicky and unsuccessful experiment'. 'It has been able to seek excellence according to its own lights within a traditional framework . . . Having seen itself in 1960 as the first of the new universities, it has succeeded, maybe, in establishing itself as the last of the old.'[40] Legge's verdict has generally held sway among his contemporaries. But is it correct? Was Monash really the last of the old? Certainly, as he implies, the forces of innovation and experiment contended with equally powerful forces of tradition and resistance, especially in the traditional disciplines. The Monash Act required that the university's degrees should be established at the same standard as those of the University of Melbourne, and, for at least a generation, the academic community at Clayton struggled to emancipate itself from the question 'But what are they doing in Parkville?' There was much more to the Sussex experiment, however, than the idea of interdisciplinary schools. And there was more than one way of being new in 1960. To make Sussex the standard of newness may be to miss other important forms of academic innovation.

An inquiring attitude of mind

At its first meeting in November 1960 the Professorial Board had resolved, even before Sussex, that lectures in the new university should not be compulsory.[41] Monash was to be a university devoted to active, independent learning, not to the passive absorption of information. The tutorial and the laboratory session, rather than the lecture, would become its standard teaching modes. The spirit of innovation soon became manifest in a range of new curricula, teaching models and built structures designed to make learning more practical, more open to experiment, more based in everyday life. By bringing the world onto the campus, through the establishment of clinics and study centres, and by taking the university into the world, through fieldwork and study tours, Monash would become a distinctively 'modern' university.

Tutorials were a more familiar feature of the humanities, committed to the 'Socratic method' of learning through critical discussion, than of the sciences and technologies, where more didactic approaches usually held sway. The tutorial was already a feature of many humanities departments at the University of Melbourne; in adopting it more generally, Monash broke new ground. The Science Faculty embraced it with enthusiasm, as a means of 'promoting personal contact', explaining and reinforcing the ideas delivered in lectures, instructing students in techniques and encouraging 'an enquiring attitude of mind'. There was 'almost unanimous approval' of tutorials among science undergraduates, while academic staff recognised their value in providing 'experience in the art of self-expression'.[42]

Tutors, or 'teaching fellows', as they became known, comprised more than a quarter of Monash's academic staff in the mid-1960s, although the ratio varied across the university. In Arts and Economics and Politics it rose to one-third, with the largest complements—approaching half the academic staff—in subjects with large enrolments like English, history, politics and economics.[43] Tutorships were an admirable 'training ground for future lecturers' as well as for other careers. Future Monash professors like Bill Kent, Peter Fitzpatrick and Hugh Niall served as teaching fellows, as did opera director Elijah Moshinsky, writer Peter Corris, Reserve Bank Governor Ian Macfarlane, Victorian Treasurer Rob Jolly and political journalist Michelle Grattan. The idealism, ambition and enthusiasm injected into the life of the new university by this youthful academic proletariat would be hard to overestimate. The tutors not only acted as intermediaries between the god-professors and their students, but, as events would later prove, they could also support students against the god-professors.

Don's faculty

In Monash's emerging map of knowledge, the Faculty of Economics and Politics (ECOPS) straddled the conventional boundaries between science and the humanities, pure and applied knowledge. It was fashioned in the image of its forceful founding dean, economist Donald Cochrane. Born at the end of the Great War, Cochrane had grown up during the Great Depression and graduated from Melbourne University on the eve of the Second World War. After service in the Royal Australian Air Force, he completed a Cambridge PhD and co-authored a seminal article in the *Journal of the American Statistical Association*, one of the conceptual pillars of modern econometrics. Thereafter, he published little, quipping that further contributions could only lower his reputation. By 1960, he had spent a decade at Melbourne but was frustrated by the university's territorial jealousies and institutional inertia and, now in his early forties, saw Monash as an opportunity to build anew. To the younger Melbourne graduates who followed him to Clayton, Monash 'exuded a sense of fresh new directions'.[44]

Dark and handsome, with piercing eye and intellect, Cochrane became the most ruthlessly autocratic of Matheson's god-professors. 'He was a very strong leader—*very*', one of his first appointments, economic historian Gus Sinclair, emphasises. 'He liked to regard it [the faculty] as his own show.'[45] Among his own colleagues he was always 'Don', a convivial but rather intimidating figure in the large third-floor common room where the faculty met for morning and afternoon tea. His quick grasp of numbers and budget formulae enabled him to dominate the Committee of Deans, where the university's resources were divided. But he was less at home in the more democratic ethos of his own faculty board, preferring to outflank or outlast, rather than confront, the few brave souls like Courtney Wright and Max Teichmann who dared oppose him.

By the late 1960s, Cochrane had assembled the most impressive stable of economists in Australia. They included agricultural economist Fred Gruen, labour economist Joe Isaacs and Monash's first woman professor, Maureen Brunt. To the students of those years, however, no name, not even Cochrane's, burns as brightly in the memory as that of Keith Frearson. Born in 1922, son of a storekeeper in the Western Australian wheat belt, he enlisted in the Royal Australian Air Force and

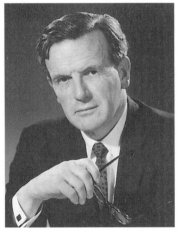

As an engineer, Matheson preferred a system of centralised academic authority, with strong professors and appointed deans. Their personalities left a deep imprint on the faculties they founded. Left to right from top, they were: David Derham (Law), Guy Manton (Arts), Kevin Westfold (Science), Richard Selby Smith (Education), Don Cochrane (ECOPS), Rod Andrew (Medicine), and Ken Hunt (Engineering).

flew Lancasters over Germany, winning a Distinguished Flying Cross, though perhaps sustaining long-lasting mental wounds. After the war, he studied economics in Perth and Cambridge, where he met the famous Keynesian economist Joan Robinson, whose ideas and friendship formed his belief in the human possibilities of economics. He returned to a lectureship at Melbourne, but when Cochrane, also an air force veteran, invited him to join the new faculty at Monash, he leapt at the chance. 'Monash became his life', Sinclair recalls. He lived like a bachelor don in Mannix College, devoting himself to his students, who idolised him for his ability to convey complex ideas lucidly and memorably, his keen sense of fun and his unselfish concern for their personal lives. He became a Monash 'character', propping up the bar at the Nott and appearing at social occasions in a dinner jacket and the red and white socks of his beloved Swans football team. In a suburban university where almost everyone was a commuter, Frearson was a resident. In behaving as though Monash was a village, he went some way towards making it one.[46]

The 1960s was the peak of the postwar boom, when Keynesian economics was ascendant. Politically astute and with strong connections in Canberra and Collins Street, Cochrane saw the growth of his faculty as 'a natural reflection of the changing character of the industrial system'. The ever-growing need of industry and government for executives, economists, market researchers, personnel managers and public servants swelled the demand for the faculty's graduates. Between 1961 and 1968, students enrolled in ECOPS rose from fifty-seven to 1400, causing it to become the largest Australian economics faculty—bigger even than the famous London School of Economics, Cochrane boasted.[47]

Like the London school, ECOPS coupled economics and politics, although the marriage was a pragmatic one designed, some of Cochrane's colleagues suspected, to satisfy his thirst for expansion rather than to integrate the disciplines. Rufus Davis, Foundation Professor of Politics (Cochrane had rejected the term 'political science'),[48] a political conservative, led a staffroom full of young radicals—Dennis Altman, Alistair Davidson, Graeme Duncan, Max Teichmann and John Playford—who reinforced Monash's reputation as a hotbed of radicalism. In Cochrane's positivist vision, quantification would drive the faculty's development. 'The Faculty considered right at the outset that the needs of management in this technological age could only be met by paying special attention to the field of quantitative analysis.'[49] In 1967, he appointed the first professor of econometrics in Australia, Alan Powell.

For bright students in tune with the mood of the times, Monash was the place to be. 'I was so proud of the place, I thought everything was terrific', Peter Dixon recalls. He was in one of the faculty's first honours classes, a talented group that included future politician Rob Jolly, banker Ian Macfarlane, management consultant George Pappas, trade union official Bob Bluer, and four economics professors: Glenn Withers, Ronald Bird, Barry Nicholls and Dixon himself. In 1967, Dixon was bold enough to ask Cochrane's advice about his future:

> I went to see the great man and put to him three problems in my life. One was that I wanted to marry a Thai woman who had been repossessed by the Thai government. The second problem was that I had no money. And the third problem was that I wanted to go to graduate school in the United States . . . He took it all quite seriously. I noticed that he took a couple of notes. He said to come back and see him tomorrow.
>
> By the time I got back to him . . . he had apparently contacted someone in Thailand and Orani had been released—he seemed to have organised some sort of bogus scholarship—and she was on her way. He told me to go and see Maureen Brunt to fix going to Harvard. Fine. Not a problem. And [as for] the problem of money—he thought he could give me a little job. Some smart-arse salesman had sold him a computer . . . He wanted me to do something with it, to prove it was a good idea. So I programmed it to do [Sir John] Hicks's Trade Cycle. It drew a picture, you see. It went down, and went up and hit the ceiling, then dropped off and came back. Anyway, it was the only thing it ever did. It was a highlight of Don's lectures for the next ten years.[50]

The first analogue computers had just appeared on the market. By later standards, they were expensive, cumbersome and slow. But Cochrane wanted his brightest students to master 'the mysteries of computers and programming'.[51] Accustomed to approving the large equipment bills of his colleagues in Science and Medicine, he relished the opportunity to acquire some expensive gadgetry of his own. Dixon, now Australia's leading economic modeller and former director of Monash's Centre for Policy Studies, was among the beneficiaries of Cochrane's academic ambition and political flair.

A new model of medical training

Cochrane's belief in the power of numbers, and in the need to test economic theory against empirical reality, reflected a key feature of the new university's academic culture. The same spirit was apparent in the eagerness of doctors, lawyers and educationists to develop new models of professional training. The common thread was an aspiration to make university education more holistic, more rigorously scientific, more grounded in experience, more attuned to the needs of an expanding society—in short, more modern. The most favoured model of education could be described, in broad terms, as the clinic: the site where student and teacher, theory and practice, were brought together to solve real-world problems. This orientation, an inversion of the ivory tower, became one of the university's most defining features, continuing to the present day.

The medical faculty set the pace. In 1959, Dean Rod Andrew persuaded the Interim Council that Monash could 'establish a medical school second to none by integrating clinical and teaching aspects from the first'. The traditional approach to medical education divided the 'pre-clinical' years of campus-based scientific education from the later years of hospital-based clinical training. This not only entailed a great deal of time-wasting travel from university to hospital, but reinforced an artificial separation between the classroom and the clinic. Andrew challenged the traditional model on both practical and humanistic grounds. The qualities of 'tolerance, humanity and insight' required of the good physician could not be instilled within a strictly scientific and vocational curriculum. Not only did the doctor's training need to be expanded to include subjects like biophysics, genetics and statistics, but it should be imparted from the first in an environment that combined the liberal education of the university and the clinical experience of the hospital.[52]

Ideally, the faculty and the hospital would become a single 'therapeutic complex' located on the same campus. McCutcheon's university master plan reserved the south-western corner of the site for a 400-bed hospital next to the medical faculty.[53] The Victorian government approved the plan, but the Hospitals and Charities Commission insisted that the university wait until the growth of the local population justified the construction of a large general hospital in the south-eastern suburbs. In the meantime, Monash medical students relied for their clinical training on the distant Alfred, Queen Victoria, Prince Henry's and Royal Children's hospitals.

Although the university hospital was some years away, Andrew had already begun to select the first professors with an eye to its realisation. Foundation Professor of Anatomy Graeme Schofield, an Oxford-educated New Zealander, seized 'the opportunity of orienting anatomical teaching so that emphasis is placed on functional aspects of the subject'.[54] David de Kretser was planning to pursue graduate studies in surgery when he joined the new department as a demonstrator in 1963. Coming after the 'traditional and moribund' teaching of anatomy at Melbourne, Schofield's approach was a revelation. 'Anatomy came alive at Monash', he recalls. Rather than just examining diagrams in a book, students were encouraged

Anatomy Professor Graeme Schofield (standing far left) with second-year anatomy examiners, 1975.

to use their own bodies as models for surface anatomy. Instead of beginning with a structure, they would begin with a case and consider how the anatomy should influence the treatment. In the process, they were not only learning a map of the body but discovering how to be a doctor.[55]

'The doctor of the future', the faculty believed, would require 'a better understanding of the scientific basis of medicine allied to knowledge of social factors in disease and the complex nature of modern society'.[56] Along with new disciplines such as biochemistry and microbiology, the university's medical curriculum incorporated studies in psychology, epidemiology and sociology. Andrew's stress on the social dimension of medicine challenged professional and political orthodoxy and anticipated the progressive health agenda of the early 1970s, including Medicare and the first community health centres.[57] In 1968, Basil Hetzel, a persuasive advocate for holistic approaches to health, was appointed to a chair of social and preventive medicine, Australia's first.

The faculty's reputation for social innovation often attracted brilliant but unconventional students. Roger Strasser, son of an Austrian immigrant, spent more of his first two years acting with the Monash Players than studying medicine. But he had not been wasting his time. He formed a new student club, Interperson, to share the communication skills he had acquired in the theatre with his fellow medical students. The club was so successful that Neil Carson, Monash's first professor of community medicine (appointed in 1975), adopted many of Strasser's ideas in designing a new unit on communication skills. Strasser later became Monash's first professor of rural health at Gippsland, while his successor as president of Interperson, Michael Abramson, became professor of social and preventive medicine.[58]

A hospital on the campus

The centrepiece of Andrew's vision, the Monash University Medical Centre, proved the hardest goal to realise. The proposed site was too small. The growth of traffic along Dandenong Road made public access difficult. Ring roads and car parks soon cut it off from the rest of the medical faculty. A teaching hospital large enough to meet the needs of the surrounding region, estimated at 1200 beds or more, required a large multistorey complex that would dwarf even the Ming Wing.[59] The university considered transferring the project to a recently rezoned site on the corner of Blackburn and Wellington roads occupied by the Clayton Twin Drive-In, but it was too far away to permit the full integration of clinical and scientific activities.[60] A planning committee, led by the brilliant but prickly professor of surgery Hugh Dudley, developed a functional brief for the project, but the state government and the Hospitals Commission repeatedly deferred action. The government's capitulation to community demands for a new hospital in Moorabbin finally dashed the faculty's hopes. Pointing to a newspaper announcement of the government's decision, Matheson addressed his disappointed medical colleagues: 'There, gentlemen, is the end of your hospital'.[61]

By the early 1970s, students were also becoming disenchanted by the gap between the faculty's ideal of clinical education and the reality. In 1972, Richard Ward, a sixth-year student at the Alfred Hospital, wrote to Louis Matheson on 'a matter of the utmost seriousness . . . the enslavement of the medical student at this university'. He was 'disturbed' by the gap between the liberal ideal of 'free learning' and the 'dogmatic traditions and theatrics of the medical system' as he experienced them in the hospital setting.[62] In September, a meeting of students at the Alfred protested against the flaws in the medical curriculum, poor communication between students and staff, and the lack of student representation on the faculty board.[63] Eager to listen, the faculty offered the students twenty-five seats on its board. Yet both Andrew and Matheson remained frustrated by the students' inability to propose specific reforms. Matheson thought he knew the cause of the malaise: it was their 'continued frustration over the campus hospital'.[64]

In April 1973, Matheson delivered an ultimatum to Premier Rupert Hamer: he should either authorise the university hospital or abandon it.[65] The government's intentions soon became clear: it planned to sell the valuable city site of the Queen Victoria Hospital to capitalise a new regional hospital on the site of an old convalescent hospital in Clayton Road, about 2 kilometres from the Clayton campus. The region would get a new 'Monash Medical Centre', but it would not be the 'Monash *University* Medical Centre' that Andrew and his colleagues had planned. 'A great vision', Matheson concluded, had been 'lost in the wastelands of political expediency'.[66]

Lawyers on the loose

Shortly after his arrival at Monash, Matheson received an urgent plea from Zelman Cowen, Dean of the Faculty of Law at the University of Melbourne. Cowen had just imposed a quota on new enrolments at Melbourne, but the demand for places and graduates continued to grow. By 1963, Melbourne would be able to accommodate only half of the 600 well-qualified students clamouring for entry.[67] Could Monash bring forward its plan to open a faculty of law in 1964, he asked. 'I have been expecting your letter, or something very like it, since I arrived', Matheson replied. But, while he sympathised with Melbourne's difficulty, Matheson had more than enough on his plate. 'At this moment we have four professors and a very muddy hole in the ground!'[68]

Deputations from the legal profession soon forced his hand. Early in 1962, Monash resolved to appoint a dean of law 'as soon as possible'.[69] Cowen had urged Matheson 'to get a first class man as Head of the School from the very beginning and to get him now'.[70] Perhaps he was already thinking of his colleague the 41-year-old professor of jurisprudence David Derham, who was duly appointed in 1963. Born into a family of lawyers, doctors and soldiers, Derham was educated at Scotch College, served with distinction in the Australian Army and married the daughter of a general before embarking on a legal career. At Oxford, he absorbed the liberal doctrines of the legal philosopher H.L.A. Hart; at Harvard, he embraced more experimental approaches to legal education.[71] 'He was deeply interested in the essential nature of legal rules', his younger colleague Louis Waller recalls, '—where they came from, how they were fashioned, and what their reach was . . . and [in] the interplay between law and morality'.[72] Derham wanted his students to study the law in conjunction with a degree in humanities or social sciences. The Monash curriculum would be designed to 'reveal the functions of law in society', not just to give graduates enough legal knowledge to practise.[73]

Like the medicos, Derham wanted to strengthen the links between theory and practice. Clayton was too far from the city to enable judges and QCs to visit on a regular basis. Instead, the law school would have to reproduce as much of the style, methods and general ambience of the law as possible. Classes would be small enough for teachers and students to dissect legal cases. In the United States, the case study had long been a feature of legal education. At the University of Melbourne, Peter Brett and Louis Waller had adopted it in their course on criminal law. They began, Waller recalls, with a sensational case of alleged cannibalism among shipwrecked sailors. 'Why begin with dullness?'[74] Derham invited them to teach the Monash course part-time, and a year later 30-year-old Waller was appointed to the Leo Cussen Chair of Law, the beginning of his long, distinguished career at Monash.

Derham designed the new law school, even sketching the arrangement of seminar rooms, offices, library and a moot court. 'A law school's undergraduate laboratory is its law library', he argued.[75] So the library should be the hub of the school, with academics' offices and classrooms arranged around it. Rather than be part of the university library it should be managed by a lawyer-librarian responsible to the Law Faculty, a dictum disputed by university librarian Ernest Clark but eventually resolved by compromise.

After only four years in the job, Derham returned to the University of Melbourne as its vice-chancellor. But he had already placed his personal imprint on the school that was to bear his name. In proposing that the law should be studied through practice as well as precept and in its social context, Derham was following a similar path to Andrew and his colleagues in Medicine. As in Medicine, the students were often quicker than their teachers to recognise the implications of the new model. In 1971, the Monash Law Students Society, supported by lecturer Peter Hanks, opened a volunteer legal referral service in a room in the Law Faculty, while other staff assisted the development of the Springvale Legal Service.[76] 'Those students who are involved have received great benefit in both a practical sense of gaining valuable legal experience and in a social sense of gaining an awareness of the grave legal and social inequities which the poor of our society must suffer', co-founder of the Springvale Legal Service Philip Slade advised Dean David Allan. 'I hope we have set a firm precedent for the introduction, in the near future, of a form of clinical education for law students.'[77] Allan supported the scheme, but the university administration, fearful that advice by half-trained law students could damage the university's reputation, was reluctant to own it officially. In 1975, Hanks and Gerry Nash introduced an elective course

The Springvale Legal Service, 1981, staffed by volunteers from the Monash Law Faculty, including Maureen Tehan (far left), Simon Smith (centre) and Maryann Noone (far right), was an expression of the faculty's interests in community law and clinical legal education.

based on clinical experience, 'Professional Practice'. The first such course in Australia, it became the foundation for what is still one of the nation's most extensive clinical legal education programs.[78]

Beyond mere practicality

To become a doctor or a lawyer you had to go to university, so Monash could adopt the clinical model without endangering the status of its degrees. Other faculties, like Engineering and Education, were nervous about appearing to be *too* practical. University-trained engineers had had to fight hard against the technical colleges to establish their credentials as the 'higher' branch of the profession. Foundation Professor Ken Hunt, a theoretical specialist on mechanism, insisted that it was 'wrong to suppose that the Monash engineering courses aim *merely* to train the student to tackle the tasks which immediately confront present-day engineers'. By acquiring a knowledge of 'basic scientific principles', Monash graduates would be equipped not just for their first job, but for a lifetime of intellectually rigorous professional practice.[79] Engineering students would enrol in a single, unified faculty, and specialise only later as mechanical, civil or electrical engineers. But personal ambition and academic specialisation soon tempered Hunt's pioneering vision. Electrical engineer Douglas Lampard was the first to break ranks, establishing his own department with its workshops and tearoom separate from the rest of the faculty. In Engineering, as elsewhere across the university, the department, rather than the faculty, became the basic unit of academic life.

As a product of the postwar education boom, Monash inevitably assumed an obligation to train the next generation of secondary teachers. In 1962, the Victorian director of education, Alex McDonell, a member of the Monash Interim Council, urged it to reject the traditional model of secondary teacher training, in which students took a bachelor's degree before completing an 'end-on' diploma of education. Only a fully integrated education course, in which students studied academic disciplines and pedagogical subjects concurrently, was satisfactory. If this model was good enough for other professions, like medicine and law, he asked, why not for education?[80] Yet the university rejected his advice. Arts professors feared that their 'rigorous' disciplines could be weakened by the 'flabbier' precepts of educational method.[81] Perhaps they also hoped to 'save' their bonded students from the clutches of the Education Department for as long as possible.

When 48-year-old Richard Selby Smith, Principal of Scotch College, was invited to the foundation chair of education in 1963, Monash had still to decide whether education should be a faculty or just a department within the Faculty of Arts.[82] Educated, like Derham, at Oxford and Harvard, Selby Smith was a moderate moderniser.[83] Education, he argued, was not a discipline in its own right, but—in words he borrowed from Harvard's recent report on graduate study in education—'a significant domain for experimental enquiry and discovery'. It would draw on a range of disciplines—psychology, philosophy, sociology, history and mathematics—linking them to 'the practical problems of actual communities'. The faculty should endeavour to provide the best research facilities for its staff, while never losing sight of 'the clinical process' through which their work was tested and applied.[84]

The new faculty grew slowly at first, but by the mid-1970s it had overtaken Law and Engineering and drawn level with Medicine. Selby Smith's blueprint was gradually filled in with professorial appointments in sociology (Peter Musgrave), psychology (Ronald Taft), science education (Peter Fensham) and history (Richard Selleck). Monash was located in a rapidly expanding suburban region, an 'actual community' ready-made for educational inquiry and clinical education. Selby Smith planned to link lecture theatres via closed-circuit television to classrooms in the nearby Monash High School, on the eastern edge of the campus, so that students could observe the educational process at work without the inconvenience of travelling.[85] With support from colleagues in psychology and paediatrics, he urged the university to establish an on-campus kindergarten for the children of university staff and as a site for clinical study of early childhood.

These were modest experiments, born of incremental, grassroots innovation rather than a comprehensive plan such as Sussex's 'New Map of Learning'. Measured against such grand designs, Monash may indeed have looked more like the last of the old universities than the first of the new. Some of its aspirations towards more holistic styles of learning, such as the attempt to bridge 'the two cultures', were stillborn, while others, such as the creation of interdisciplinary centres, progressed more slowly than Matheson, for one, may have wished.

Yet Monash had not simply transplanted Parkville to Clayton. Many of its founding academics were refugees from the older universities, determined to shake off the 'dead hand' of institutional inertia and release the spirit of innovation. They had youth on their side and the opportunity to build anew. What distinguished Monash in its founding years was its openness to experiment, its eagerness to subject academic doctrine to the tests of reason and experience, its desire to break down the walls of the academy and open itself to the world. The model of clinical professional education, first adopted in Medicine and later emulated in Law and Education, was a product of intellectual osmosis, not university policy. By the late 1960s, Monash students were often pushing their professors to practise what they preached. If Monash has a claim to be the first of the new universities, it is perhaps because it embraced the spirit of innovation, rather than adopting someone else's blueprint.

University or multiversity?

Monash had grown very fast—faster, Matheson boasted, than any university in the English-speaking world. No sooner had the university opened than Premier Henry Bolte was pushing to raise its target enrolment even higher. By the end of Matheson's vice-chancellorship, it had over 12 000 students and over 2500 staff. For Chancellor Robert Blackwood, the industrialist, universities were factories, shaped by economies of scale like any other enterprise. Turning out students was much like turning out sausages or car tyres: once you had set up the plant, the average cost decreased with each additional unit.

Among the academics, however, the benefits of growth were not nearly so obvious. In growing larger, did Monash risk losing the cohesion that had characterised its founding years? A university, they felt, should be something more than a collection of departments and faculties. It should be an academic community with a spirit of its own, not simply a soulless corporation. In thinking about the character of the university, they often harked back, consciously or unconsciously, to John Henry Newman's classic *The Idea of a University* (1852), and his vision of 'an alma mater knowing her children one by one, not a foundry, a mill or a treadmill'.[86] Monash, a brand-new, large, fast-growing, drive-in university on the fringes of a vast metropolis, seemed almost the antithesis of Newman's ideal. In 1963, Clark Kerr, President of the University of California, another similarly large, modern state university, offered a perceptive assessment of this latest stage of university development. The 'multiversity', as he called it, was a product of 'the knowledge industry'. Rather than an organism with a unified goal and structure, it was diverse, fragmented, almost anarchic: little more than a 'series of academic entrepreneurs held together by a common grievance over parking'.[87]

Louis Matheson, a captain of the knowledge industry with parking problems of his own, recognised Kerr as a kindred spirit, and his 'multiversity' as a guide to the future of his own university. He took some comfort from Kerr's belief that within the vastness of the multiversity students and academics might still experience a sense of community within their own departments or dormitories. 'Everybody knows that departments are the real functioning units of a university', Matheson observed. 'Anybody who has seen a really good department operating, with the unity of endeavour and friendly relationship that grows up between the professor and the staff and students, will realise that this is what universities are really all about.'[88] Many Monash academics would have agreed with him. Geographical isolation and the lack of social facilities on campus may even have strengthened collegial relationships. 'Thrown on our own resources for companionship and entertainment, we formed friendships which are still strong today', Brenda Niall, a long-time member of the English Department, recalled.[89] Monash, in the experience of many staff and students, was a mosaic of little communities, each with its own character and identity, rather than a community itself.

Yet many of its members longed for Monash to be something more. A true university, according to Newman, was an intellectual community, its unity symbolised by a central ceremonial building like a chapel, a great hall, a library or a refectory. To his twentieth-century Catholic descendants, the secular university was 'nothing but a collection of perpetual motion machines thrashing away in solitude'.[90] Protestants had similar misgivings, although they used different theological jargon. From the beginning, the churches had been eager to foster an ecumenical Christian presence at Monash. They had persuaded Premier Henry Bolte that the university's act should not follow the University of Melbourne's statutes by prohibiting the teaching of religion or theology. Underlying their concern was a gnawing fear of intellectual and social fragmentation. The role of religion, they argued, was somehow to integrate the university, intellectually and socially. Rather than a traditional university chapel, however, the churches sub-committee of the Interim Council proposed something more in keeping with the modern, pluralist character of the university itself: a religious centre combining an ecumenical chaplaincy centre and a 'collegiate library', presided over by an academic 'warden', whose interests spanned secular and religious subjects. 'We are of the opinion that the University has a duty to make provision for the spiritual needs of its students and that, at this stage of its development, it has an opportunity to integrate and centralise such provision in a way quite novel in Australia.'[91] To its sponsors, the centre was more a vision of how the university was to be integrated than an edifice of bricks and mortar. It would seek to 'bridge the gap between the Christian tradition and the mainly scientific ethos of the modern university', overcome 'the difficulty and danger of the separate faculties each going their own way', and bring 'the various religious groups together in the one place'.[92] That the centre was expected to 'integrate and centralise' so many dimensions of Monash's life is a symptom of the anxieties the 'multiversity' aroused in the minds of some contemporaries.

The churches volunteered to fund the chaplaincy centre, while the university was to provide the collegiate library and pay the salary of its warden. Matheson cautiously encouraged the scheme, but his fellow professors, vigilant defenders of the secular character of the university, were more reserved. Early in 1961, Matheson had turned down a request from the Catholic chaplain to celebrate Mass in a university classroom, an episode that stirred public controversy and accusations that the university was interfering with religious freedom.[93] Eventually, he promised, religious services could be held in 'proper consecrated premises'. While the Professorial Board made no objection to the chaplaincy centre, it baulked at the 'collegiate library', arguing instead for a chair in comparative religion. This was something altogether different from what its proposers had intended. Instead of a bridge between the religious and the secular, the intellectual and the pastoral, it would become a conventional academic post, studying religion 'in the normal [i.e. secular] academic framework'.[94] Faced with the professors' opposition, its supporters had no choice but to retreat, surrendering the vision of a centre mediating between the religious and the secular in favour of something more conventionally religious, an ecumenical chapel and social centre.

Progress towards the completion of the centre was slow. A proposal to incorporate it in the Union Building was rejected by its board, which suggested instead a remote location near the southwest car parks.[95] In the meantime, the chaplains, led by Reverend Job Hawkes, had created a temporary centre in the Red Cross Cottage, a relic of the old Talbot Colony, northeast of the Union Building. This accidental location turned out to be a convenient one, close to the Union and easily reached from all parts of the campus. In 1966, architect John Mockridge designed the new religious centre nearby, on the northern side of the forum. 'I have placed great emphasis on the main chapel', Mockridge observed, in explaining the form of the centre. 'It is planned as a complete circle to symbolise

Participants in a multi-faith seminar meet in the welcoming precincts of the Religious Centre, 1985.

unity and eternity, and rises high above the ambulatory and ancillary rooms which surround it, so that a dramatic release is experienced upon entering.'[96] Gradually, the circle widened to include all 'those who hold coherent religious beliefs and who wish to practise their religion and reflect upon their beliefs within the university'.[97] Its advisory committee included representatives of the various Christian denominations, Jews, both liberal and conservative, adherents of the main 'Asian religions' and, eventually, even the sceptical philosopher Hector Monro.[98]

As vice-chancellor, Matheson maintained a benign interest in the project. He hailed the laying of the foundation stone in April 1967 as 'one of the most unexpected and inspiring things that [had] happened in this University . . . a demonstration of one of the things that universities really stand for—unity in diversity'.[99] By the time it opened, in June 1968, that unity was being sorely tested, as protesting students gathered in ever-larger numbers in the forum, laying siege to Matheson's office. Even the liberal Christians whose vision of a centre bridging the disciplines, uniting the secular and the sacred, had inspired the project were disappointed in the outcome. Members of the SCM boycotted the opening ceremony, carrying placards bearing the question 'Now the bloody thing is finished what are we supposed to do with it?'[100] For Matheson, however, the opening of the Religious Centre symbolised a larger hope. 'It is a matter for rejoicing that recent developments are such that people of so many faiths have found it possible to join together to create this Centre', he declared.[101] It gave symbolic form to the conviction that the university was still, or might yet be, a community, rather than the huge, ungovernable, sorely divided multiversity of his nightmares.

FOUR

DOWN ON THE FARM

Bloody clouds and bloody rain
No bloody kerbs or bloody drains
The Student-councils' [sic] got no bloody brains
At bloody Monash.

Bob Hammond, 'Bloody Monash', 1961

Monash's first students, just 363 of them, arrived on Monday 13 March 1961. A few days earlier, Premier Henry Bolte had performed the official opening before a crowd of distinguished visitors assembled outside the newly completed Science Building. But Monash was still more of a building site than a finished campus. The students promptly dubbed it 'The Farm', a variation on Melbourne's old nickname, 'The Shop'.[1]

Journalist Geoffrey Hutton compared Monash students' entry into the unfinished university, picking their way past bulldozers and shouting to be heard above electric drills, with his own experience, half a lifetime before, of filing in to Melbourne University's imposing Gothic Revival Wilson Hall.[2] The crude conditions of the Monash site made the first students truly 'pioneers'. In the few buildings that were in operation, the clocks did not work.[3] When winter set in, Monash's clay grounds again turned to mud. One student 'felt like an explorer' splashing about the campus. Female students complained that it was useless to wear high-heeled shoes: 'There is a new fashion the Farm might set for its students—gumboots'.[4]

The community was still small enough for students from different faculties to get to know each other. The first students fondly recall rubbing shoulders with their professors and lecturers in the makeshift cafeteria,

Flour bomb fight, Farm Week, 1968.

enjoying a 'uniform spirit of pleasantness' which they believed was unique among Australian universities.[5] Memories of this golden age of academic camaraderie lived long among the first generation of Monash students, who still, fifty years later, exchange Christmas cards and gather for reunions.

They may have been coming to adulthood in the swinging sixties, but Monash's first students looked more like products of the conformist 1950s. The *Age* described them as 'quiet, sensible and unaffected'.[6] The president of the Students' Representative Council (SRC), David McConachy, played the organ at his church and grew prize orchids. John Price, later to become an active student radical, remembered that the first students 'wore sportscoats and ties and looked very respectable'.[7] Female students wore dresses and stockings. 'Melbourne University students took great pains to look as scruffy as possible, and this was one way in which we could show our difference.'[8]

The early students embraced the university's status as the 'first of the new' and, like the staff, were self-consciously aware of wanting to make a mark, both at Monash and in life. They were quick to defend Monash from criticism, proclaiming it a 'model university with infinite potential'.[9] The university was functioning so well, one candidate for the 1961 SRC elections complained, that it was difficult to prepare a critical policy platform.[10]

But change came rapidly to Monash in its first decade. Student numbers doubled in 1962, then again in 1963. By 1971, there were more than 11 000 students. As the university grew, the pleasant intimacy of its first years became more elusive. The world beyond the university was changing too. The students of the early 1960s were the first of the baby boomers, a lucky generation who still hardly knew how lucky they were.

The respectable student of the early 1960s. President of the SRC David McConachy, in 1962.

People would come to speak of 'the generation gap', a growing rift between the careful, grateful outlook of the war generation and the freer, more demanding attitude of a new generation determined, in the contemporary phrase, to 'do its own thing'. The older generation had lived by an ethic of responsibility; the young embraced a new ethic of authenticity.[11] The change manifested itself slowly, first in apparently superficial ways, such as new styles of dress, speech and popular music, later in new codes of personal and sexual behaviour, and eventually in a new, more radical politics that overflowed from the campus into the wider society.[12] By the early 1970s, Monash had become the most notorious centre of student radicalism in Australia.

A new phrase had entered the language: 'going to uni'. An older generation had sometimes talked of 'the varsity'; Americans spoke of 'going to college'; but 'uni' suggested a new kind of pathway from youth to adulthood.[13] Monash was a 'uni' from the start: more informal, more open to experiment, more resistant to privilege and tradition. The freedom entailed in 'going to uni' could be dangerous. Mishandled, it could lead to academic failure—or worse. 'You've spent three years at the uni, where you have learnt some very bad habits, like getting up late, wearing wild clothes and going to the beach in the afternoon', one penitent confessed.[14] The university became a laboratory of social change as the baby boomers began to explore the new freedoms that their parents had won for them.

Going to uni

From the beginning, people were interested to know what kinds of students Monash would attract. In the first undergraduate cohort, there were three men for every woman. Forty per cent were enrolled in Arts, about 30 per cent in Medicine, 16 per cent in Economics and Politics, 9 per cent in Science and 7 per cent in Engineering. Almost 10 per cent of the student body came from overseas, mainly from Malaya and Singapore, Hong Kong, and Borneo. Overseas students were concentrated in the technical faculties, particularly Medicine, where they made up a quarter of the first enrolment. It had taken the University of Melbourne almost a century to introduce postgraduate courses; Monash, the product of a modern, self-confident Australia, enrolled sixteen postgraduates in its first intake.[15]

The fruit of Robert Menzies' dream of 'an educated democracy', Monash was expected by some to become a university for the working class. Others feared that, founded to cope with Melbourne's overflow, it would be a university for the 'second-rate'. Some students accepted by Melbourne had chosen to go to Monash, intrigued by the prospect of entering an institution that was not 'stifled by tradition'.[16] But many came to Clayton as rejects from Melbourne or other institutions.

One of Melbourne's rejects was David Williamson, later a famous playwright, who transferred to Monash after failing third-year engineering. In one of his final exams at Melbourne, he wrote an essay about why he hated electronics: his father had been a ham radio enthusiast who constantly disappeared to the shed, causing domestic warfare. His professor spotted his talent as a writer but suggested that he would also need to make a living and arranged for him to enter Monash, where he became the sole third-year student in mechanical engineering. Although still not 'wildly interested' in his degree, it was—he says—hard to let down your lecturers when you were the only student attending 'lectures'. Under the tuition of inspirational teachers like Ron Barden and Ken Hunt, he passed.[17]

Monash students were more likely than their Melbourne counterparts to be the first in their families to go to university. But they were seldom children of the working class. Their parents were more often in sales than in the administrative, executive and managerial positions held by the parents of Melbourne students.[18] Few students at any university came from truly disadvantaged backgrounds: less than 2 per cent of school-leavers with unskilled and semi-skilled fathers went on to university, as opposed to 36 per cent of the children of professional fathers.[19] Mark LaPirow, a leader of the Democratic Labor Club at Monash in the late 1960s, recalls that

> most of the students were, in my view anyway, the children of the financially privileged. There was an expectation that upon graduation, certain employment was available; and it was a seller's market. There was an unspoken, or politically correct denial, that 'students' were an elite, but you would be blind or ignorant not to see the privilege given to us.[20]

When the social elite did arrive at Monash, it was expected to dress down, rather than give itself airs. As Stephen Wilks recalls:

One of my co-students was Tony Pratt. When I innocently asked what he planned after university, Tony, a most agreeable and modest young tycoon in the making, had a well-rehearsed reply of 'selling cardboard boxes—everybody needs 'em'. Few of us knew that his father was the wealthiest man in the state, nor would have greatly cared if we had.[21]

The life of most students was far from luxurious. A few were very poor or even homeless. Some began living in the network of service tunnels under the campus, which were warm and had power outlets that could be used for cooking.[22] University fees were not abolished until 1973, and not all students received financial assistance: in 1970, approximately 40 per cent of Monash students got by without scholarships or studentships, compared with only 25 per cent of students at Melbourne.[23] Part-time jobs were difficult to find around Clayton.

Roughly half of Monash's undergraduates were 'bonded students'—secondary teaching trainees who had entered an agreement, or 'bond', with the state Education Department. They had agreed to serve three years as teachers (or one year for women who married) in return for the payment of their fees and a modest weekly stipend. For many lower middle-class families too well-off to qualify for a Commonwealth Scholarship living allowance but too poor to support their children through university, the bond was a passport to educational opportunity. Monash entrants were more likely to be bonded than their Melbourne counterparts.[24] Vice-Chancellor Louis Matheson and his fellow professors worried about the Education Department's rigid control over subject choice and other aspects of the bonded student's life. One observer believed that the 'laissez faire attitude which is typical of most universities has never had the opportunity to develop at Monash due to the guilt complex (about missing lectures and tutorials) imposed by Studentship undergrads upon their friends'.[25] In a decade when young people increasingly aspired to 'do their own thing', 'the bond' came to be regarded as a form of industrial slavery. But without it many students would not have entered university at all.

Most of Monash's students and their parents believed that 'going to uni' was a good thing, even if they were unsure what it was good for. In 1966, the Monash University Union commissioned a group of budding documentary film-makers from the University of Melbourne's Film Society to make a short film about life on the new campus. In snatches of conversation staged in typical student haunts—the Union, the beer garden of the Nott—*Monash 66* captured something of the tensions and uncertainties of student life. Asked about the purpose of university, one young man answered that it was 'to learn', rather than only 'getting through and getting out'.[26] A well-spoken young woman rejected the idea that she and her friends were there just to snare husbands, speaking instead of self-understanding through the exchange of ideas. Like their academic leaders, students sought a middle path between getting a job and the ideals of self-discovery and intellectual development.

Adjusting to university

To many new students, the university was a strange place, offering dangerous freedoms. Some experienced great loneliness and uncertainty. Laurie Duggan was uncertain about how to *be* a university student: 'Having grown up without any notion of attending a tertiary institution it took me some time to adjust. A lower-middle/upper working-class background meant that I had an overly strong sense of correct form. It took me two years to learn to "dress down" . . .'[27]

Hanging over first-year students was the very real threat of failure. Only 57 per cent of the students who entered Monash in 1961 passed the first year (compared to 68 per cent at Melbourne). Students in the first few years suffered a 'ghastly experiment' intended to bridge the 'two cultures' which saw science students struggling through Milton and arts students through physiology or biochemistry.[28] Some of the failures and drop-outs were students who, according to available criteria, should have been outstanding. Being a 'big fish' at school was no guarantee of university success: 'He thinks maybe he was deluding himself when he sees how much more brilliant the rest of the students in his tutorial or prac. class are'.[29]

The first cohort of students found that, while academic standards were high, individual assistance was always available. The atmosphere was 'both demanding and nurturing'.[30] But as the university grew, students reported 'feelings of remoteness' in large lecture theatres.[31] Some struggled to adjust to the tutorial environment and the expectation of free, critical discussion. English Professor David Bradley trialled the serving of coffee in first-year tutorials to help ease student tensions, inspiring a series of odes to Nescafé.[32]

Some students struggled to keep up with their workload. An article by 'Sue E. Side' in the student newspaper complained about 'those damn slave-drivers at Monash. Work, study, essays, study, work, essays, on and on and on . . . Hell, I'd rather dig ditches in Siberia than put up with this torture any longer. Must think we're electronic computers or something.'[33] But not all the stresses were work-induced. As Matheson observed, 'some of our students get girl trouble, some of them get involved in religion, some in politics, some have family difficulties; the astounding thing is that any of them get through at all'.[34] By 1967, over one in ten of Monash's students had consulted a student counsellor, and demand for such services was growing faster than the university itself.[35]

Under the Colombo Plan (1950), Australian universities, including Monash, provided places for students from South and Southeast Asia. Miss Lo Siew Lin was the first Colombo Plan student to graduate from Monash, in 1965.

Monash had been founded to provide full-time education to the growing numbers of Australian school-leavers, but it soon found itself educating a wider spectrum of students with different backgrounds and expectations. Part-time students (of whom there were over 500 by 1965) were an unplanned element of student life. 'For good reasons or bad, when we started this University . . . we decided not to develop correspondence courses, evening courses or part-time courses as a question of principle', Assistant Registrar Jim Butchart later observed. Faculties had nevertheless admitted part-timers and made ad hoc adjustments to accommodate their needs. The upshot was that 'without consciously planning to be a University with any substantial part-time component, we have something like 25% of our student population who are part-time'.[36] Part-time students often felt lonely and isolated, harried and marginalised: 'There is a feeling of powerlessness and frustration because of an incessant lack of time'.[37] Mature-age students, whose numbers grew steadily after 1970, experienced similar problems in juggling work, study and family.

Adjusting to university life was perhaps hardest for the growing numbers of overseas students coming to Monash. Despite a range of welcoming activities offered by community and religious organisations, George Cally, Monash's first student counsellor, believed that Asian students experienced an 'identity formation crisis' in this unfamiliar culture. They had difficulties in managing finances, study problems, and felt isolated from their Australian peers.[38] But some foreign students prospered at Monash. In August 1964, Tharam Singh Dillon, a Colombo Plan student from Malacca, was elected president of the SRC.[39]

The drive-in university

This bloody farm's a bloody cuss
No bloody trains no bloody bus
Find no-one cares for bloody us
At bloody Monash.

BOB HAMMOND, 'BLOODY MONASH', 1961

Robert Blackwood and his Interim Council had assumed that, if they built the campus, the students would arrive. But, as opening day approached, Matheson worried about 'the various way in which our future students are likely to come here'. He wrote to the secretary of the Transport Regulation Board in July 1960, asking for new north–south bus services linking the university to the eastern suburbs. But the board was discouraging: there was no current proposal for a new bus service.[40] Meanwhile, students making their way by train from the city to Huntingdale station could either walk 3 kilometres to the campus or await the infrequent private bus.

A 1963 survey found that only about a quarter of Monash students came by public transport: the rest travelled by car, either as drivers, passengers or hitchhikers. In the opening sequence of *Monash 66*, a group of female students hitchhike along Dandenong Road when—in an ironic homage to the American road movie—they are picked up by a hip young man driving an MGA sports car. The warden of the Union Graeme Sweeney proposed official hitchhiking stands to cater for the many students who thumbed a ride to uni.[41] Steve Timewell, who attended Monash in the late 1960s, remembers hitching home to Brighton most days. 'The confidence I gained . . . enabled me to hitchhike across the US when I finished my degree.'[42]

The university was eventually obliged to take the transport problem into its own hands. In 1964, it instituted a charter service from Kew Junction, which arrived at Monash at 8.55 a.m. and departed again at 5.35 p.m. In 1966, routes from East St Kilda and South Yarra ran for several months but were withdrawn due to lack of demand. Routes from Box Hill and Blackburn were also tried, and a route from Heidelberg was well patronised. The bus service was discontinued in 1970, due to insufficient demand and a 'marked preference for private transport'. Some students actually preferred the drive-in convenience of Monash to Melbourne. 'It's better to go to Monash—you can park your car there.' The proportion of Monash people arriving by public transport steadily declined: by 1967, it was down to 15 per cent.[43] Sweeney observed that private transport fitted in with the 'unregulated life which so many students either do or would like to lead'.[44] A generation of students aspiring to 'do their own thing' left its mark in the ever-growing sea of old cars swelling the university's car parks.

Student housing

'The kind of university we are building is a new Oxford or Cambridge, not a "red-brick" second university in Melbourne', Matheson had declared in 1961.[45] In fact, Monash eschewed Oxbridge-style colleges in favour of secular student halls of residence. Only a minority of Monash's students either desired, or could afford, to live in a residential hall. But the halls became an important factor in Monash's success in attracting rural students.[46]

The first hall of residence, Deakin Hall, was not ready for occupation when the university opened. A student housing officer, Mary Baldwin, was appointed to find suitable accommodation for students in the vicinity of the university. The Monash University Act empowered the university to give, or withhold, approval for the living arrangements of its students, whether they were in lodgings, independent flats or group houses.[47] To Baldwin, who was required to inspect accommodation, this presented a huge challenge. There were very few suitable lodgings in Clayton, which was dominated by young families living in small homes. In 1964, reply-paid cards were distributed in the local area requesting offers of accommodation, but only ninety-six of the 10 000 cards were returned.[48]

It was particularly difficult to find accommodation for Asian students. Families, especially those with daughters, were reluctant to take in Asian males. The students, eager to improve their English and experience the 'Australian way of life', preferred not to be housed with 'non-Australian' (European immigrant) families.[49] Baldwin reported that landladies expected their Asian student boarders to be uniformly quiet and studious, to have no social lives, to be 'happy people' smiling all the time, to be rich, and to know how to cook.[50]

Baldwin's task was impossible. From 1963, the responsibility was passed on to students' parents to decide if lodgings were suitable. In 1965, the act was amended to remove some of the university's responsibilities for student accommodation. The university no longer stood *in loco parentis* over students' living arrangements; here, as in other matters, students were entitled to do their own thing.

Students who chose to live 'in halls' enjoyed less freedom and more support. Though no formal tutorials were held, there was close attention to the academic results of students, which often bettered those of non-halls students.[51] The halls offered a stable environment and a degree of pastoral care not available in the general university. Ken Ward, who came to Monash as manager of the northeast halls in 1969, fostered strong relationships with many of the parents, who often rang to inquire after their children.[52]

The first warden of Deakin Hall, Dr Jack McDonell of the Physics Department, sought to create a cohesive community by keeping numbers small and requiring the 200 residents to eat together. Breakfast and dinner were served to students seven days a week (and lunch on Sundays).[53] The original 'northeast halls' complex—Deakin, Howitt and Farrer halls—opened in the 1960s, and two further halls, Roberts and Richardson, in the early 1970s.

Monash rising. By 1964, the first Science, Engineering and Medicine buildings and the western section of the Menzies Building are complete. The Library and Union Building are the most recent additions. Still to appear are the Rotunda, Alexander Theatre and Great Hall.

German-born photographer Wolfgang Sievers, a graduate of the Bauhaus, captured the 'moderate modernism' of the Monash campus, the stark geometry of its first buildings thrown into relief by the shorn landscape, still almost devoid of vegetation. The Science and Engineering quadrangles, with their long corridors and replicated cuboid forms (top), contrast with the strong verticality of Eggleston, Macdonald and Secomb's Menzies Building (bottom) and the circular and rhomboidal forms of the Religious Centre (facing page, top), Rotunda and Alexander Theatre (facing page, bottom).

As a consciously modern university, Monash was eager to exploit the power of technology, a theme with a strong appeal to Sievers, whose images of engineers with their models and wind tunnels, economic statisticians with calculating machines, and language students enclosed in sound laboratories suggest a growing intimacy between men and machines.

Monash's first students, pictured here in Wolfgang Sievers' 1963 study of the Science quadrangle, wear the regulation slacks and pullovers, skirts and blouses of the era before blue jeans and long hair.

Student dining room, Deakin Hall, 1963. 'Dining together, fairly frequently, is the most significant single factor in establishing the kind of community spirit which is necessary for the success of a Hall as an educative environment', Warden Jack McDonell declared. Soon, however, set mealtimes were abandoned in favour of more flexible cafeteria arrangements.

By the early 1970s, the eastern vista along the forum was finally closed by the distinctive redbrick facade of the university's long-awaited 'great hall' (top), named for first chancellor Robert Blackwood. Vice-Chancellor Louis Matheson's desire for ceremonial grandeur prevailed against Registrar Jim Butchart's wish for a more utilitarian building suitable for holding examinations. Staff photographer Herve Alleaume captures the bold facade and spacious interior of architect Roy Grounds' design.

Faces on the campus. A terrarium maker peddles his wares at Monash's Friday market in 1969, while a staff member in the small caf (facing page) dispenses Monash's notoriously undrinkable coffee, 1971.

President David Nadel, sporting Zapata moustache and backed by Marxist heroes Engels and Lenin, solicits new members at Labor Club stall, Orientation Week 1971.

Monash's 'Shadow Vice-Chancellor' Albert Langer addresses a student meeting, 1971.

Monash's reputation as a hotbed of student radicalism attracted journalists and photographers, like student David Taft, whose candid impressions of campus life capture the ideological fervour and high drama of the day.

Jim Bacon, Monash Maoist and later premier of Tasmania, argues his case at a student meeting in 1971.

Embattled vice-chancellor Louis Matheson addresses protesting students in University Union, 31 July 1969.

Direct democracy in action. The Monash Association of Students (MAS), which supplanted the Students' Representative Council in 1968, was a radical experiment in participatory democracy. All decisions were submitted to a vote of the entire student body, thus creating the conditions for the enormous mass meetings that packed the forum.

Student discontent with the university's discipline statute climaxed in August 1969 when students cast their votes at a meeting outside university offices. (Newspix)

'Mindless madness.' Students occupying the Council Chamber, 5 August 1969. (Newspix)

Student protesters occupying the Administration Building, 1971.

At the centre of the storm. Vice-Chancellor Matheson is interviewed by the press in 1969, the height of the student 'troubles'. (Newspix)

The forum, a giant piazza in the centre of the Clayton campus, exceeded the hopes of its creators in promoting social interaction and debate.

Deakin was the first university residence in Australia to house men and women in the same building, initially on separate floors. This was a matter of expediency rather than policy. Separate wings were planned for the sexes, but the first wing of Deakin opened in 1962 to house fifty-three men and twenty-three women.[54] In 1966, the Melbourne *Herald* featured a large photograph of three girls lounging on a Deakin balcony in bikinis. This titillating image belied the experience of most male residents; a long-term resident observed that 'after a while, it's like having 50 or 60 sisters'.[55] A 'sex regulation' forbade visitors of the opposite gender after midnight, but communal breakfast the morning after proved the best deterrent for most. There were exceptions: Ward recalls disciplining a student for carpeting his walls, apparently in response to complaints about the noise he and his girlfriend made in the early hours of the morning. But McDonell reported that mixed halls presented social advantages and few disciplinary problems.[56]

The halls concept came under question in the mid-1970s. The cost of living in halls deterred students, and the opening of Roberts and Richardson halls coincided with a downturn in student demand. Perhaps, as McDonell believed, the university had never really faced up to why it had the halls and what they were to do. Halls lacked the raison d'être of a college, 'college spirit' and an academic tutorial system.[57] Students agreed. In an article called 'Deakin Hall: An Apartment House—Or Something Else', a student resident lamented the lack of a 'lively imaginative academic atmosphere'.[58]

McDonell concluded that 'the life-style of the Halls had its genesis in the sixties and was geared to the needs, conditions and social attitudes of that period'.[59] The Student Housing Office noted a marked increase in demand for 'any type of lodging with privacy and independence'.[60] Halls students began to dismantle the formality of collegiate life. At a black-tie dinner, they appeared, dressed immaculately, without shoes. Soon the custom of high table was discarded, and set mealtimes came to be replaced by an informal cafeteria style of eating. Students didn't want to be tied to mealtimes: 'They wanted to whiz in and whiz out again'.[61]

Monash's only true 'college', Mannix, named for Melbourne's long-serving Catholic archbishop Daniel Mannix, opened in 1969. The Dominican fathers who staffed the college aimed to help students to deepen their faith and to relate their studies to their religious beliefs. However, the university required that the college accept students of all racial and religious backgrounds.[62] As in halls, there was an emphasis on pastoral care. Unlike halls, Mannix offered tutorials in all subjects and adopted a formal style with academic gowns being worn at dinner.[63]

By the early 1970s, Mannix was also finding it hard to fill its rooms. Sweeney tentatively asked its master, Father L.P. Fitzgerald, whether it was time to consider admitting female students. Mixed halls were proven to be healthy, Sweeney assured him, in that 'the males become less uncouth and the females become less giggly'. Fitzgerald was open-minded but not persuaded. 'Believe it or not', he replied, 'there are young men who do not want a mixed institution'.[64] A few months later, Fitzgerald capitulated to the views of Mannix residents, who had hung a banner over the entrance: 'CO-EDUCATION FOR MANNIX COLLEGE'. The tide was running against single-sex colleges, and there was pressure from the parents of Catholic women students to offer places.[65] Mannix was 'co-ed' from 1974.

By the end of the 1960s, it was clear that the original aspiration for 40 per cent of students to live on campus was well out of reach. Even with three halls completed and plans for two colleges (Mannix and Marist) under way, residential places would account for only 12 per cent of the student population—considerably lower than at Melbourne or La Trobe.[66] Students who did not live at home mostly lived in group houses. It could be a memorable experience. Aspiring poet Alan Wearne lived in a communal house in Logie Street, Oakleigh, in 1968.

> Mess is a male student given, something plenty take near pride in, but the squalor to which this place descended still for me remains the benchmark, with jealousy, depression and madness turning it into some form of 'Will-we-get-out-of-this-alive?' psychodrama, all soundtracked by Jefferson Airplane's 'Surrealistic Pillow' and Dylan's 'John Wesley Harding'.[67]

Downtown Clayton, it had to be admitted, lacked the bohemian appeal of inner-city Carlton. Economic history student Stephen Wilks recalls that there was little interaction with the local suburban community beyond the fact that hundreds of students rented flats and share houses in Clayton, mainly south of the campus around Browns Road and lower Blackburn Road. There wasn't even a decent local shopping strip within reasonable walking distance. The only local facilities of any note were the Nott and a twin drive-in cinema with a distracting habit of screening R-rated films. Neither held out much prospect of providing a start point for an urban village to grow out of the uni.[68]

A broad education

Without a happening local 'scene', students had to make their own social life on campus. The administration expected the Union Building—completed in 1964—to become a focus for the extracurricular activities that they saw as an essential feature of university education.[69] A high-principled man who was gentlemanly and formal in style, Graeme Sweeney was appointed warden of the Union in October 1961. He had come from the University of Melbourne but soon adjusted to the 'more casual approach of Monash'.[70] For Sweeney, the role of the Union was to foster a 'broad education', creating points of contact for students from different backgrounds and supporting activities other than study.[71]

The first student clubs had made a sluggish start in 1961. 'First term seems to have been spent in expending an enormous cloud of hot air by talking of grandiose schemes and technical arrangements while the amount of activity has been nearly nil.'[72] By 1962, the year the Sports Association and Clubs and Societies Committee were formed, an estimated 50 per cent of students participated in one or more of the activities on offer.[73] Monash's first societies included the Evangelical Union (EU), the (Roman Catholic) Newman Society, the Jewish Students Society (MONJSS), the SCM, and only one political group, the Monash University Labor Club. Faculty clubs were quickly formed in ECOPS, Science, Engineering and Medicine; Arts was a slow starter. The Medical Undergraduates claimed to be the most active club in 1961, promising to 'make the halls of famed Nottinghill [sic] ring to the sounds of bawdy songs and ribaldry', but were soon rivalled by other faculty clubs such as the Law Society, formed in 1964.[74] The most popular social activities were sherry parties. Nothing was more indispensable to the Monash social scene than a plate of cheese and crackers and a bottle of Mildara Supreme Dry.[75]

The Film Club was one of the most active and the best supported of the early clubs. Judith Buckrich vividly recalled a thrilling but excruciating evening sitting between her two lovers—unbeknown to them—at a screening of Polanski's *Fearless Vampire Killers*.[76] The society's founder, Ken Mogg, was also involved in the Drama Club, which produced *Everyman* in a lecture theatre in 1961. Renamed Monash Players in 1962, the group toured country areas and performed an open-air production of *A Midsummer Night's Dream* at Melbourne's Moomba Festival in 1963, to an audience of over 5000. Later that year, the young Max Gillies played Caliban in the Players' production of *The Tempest*.[77]

Internationalism was a popular cause. Early starters included a World Government Club to combat the threat of nuclear weapons (girls were 'especially welcome'),[78] an International Club to promote understanding between Australian and overseas students, and a branch of the CIA-funded World University Service. Meanwhile, the White Protestant Society (apparently established by medical students) aimed to 'counteract the activities of the Papists, Jews, and the International Club'.[79]

The Monash Liberal Club, formed in 1962, claimed the biggest membership of any political club at Monash.[80] In the same year, the Rationalists Society called for a better road to the Notting Hill Hotel and recognition of the death of God.[81] The Monash Mining Club staked a claim on land intended for Reg Ansett's Channel 0 transmitter on Mount Dandenong, delaying building for the purposes of 'quartz prospecting'.[82]

The appearance by 1966 of the Anti-Conscription League and the Socialist Club signalled a more radical mood on campus. Organised political apathy also had its advocates, such as the Charlie Brown Associates of Monash University, formed in 1967 to foster 'greater appreciation of Charles Schulz's "Peanuts"', and the Monash Apathy Society, known for its riotous games of sog-pong (somehow involving ping-pong balls and sausages). Its membership form asked potential members' political beliefs—'Yes or No only'.[83]

Matheson and Sweeney saw students and staff as partners in the running of the Union. Sweeney believed that 'many staff members, once their student days are over, lose contact with and sympathy with, student ways of thinking and behaving'. Participation in Union activities would make them better able to understand and counsel students.[84] In the early years, academics and students often played sport together. Historian Geoff Serle played hockey, civil engineer Noel Murray coached the rugby XV, and physics lecturer Gordon Troup coached the Fencing Club. Until the mid-1970s, Wednesday afternoons were cleared of lectures for extracurricular activities, a custom known to some as the 'sports half' and to many others as 'let's go down the Nott'.

The university's planners, who had dedicated much of the site to sporting fields, would have felt vindicated by the strong participation of students in organised sport. Sports clubs (especially football and hockey) were the most popular activities on campus, and the percentage of students taking part was estimated at 25 per cent, higher than at other universities.[85] By 1966, Monash ranked with the universities of Melbourne, Sydney and Queensland in the number of sports played at intervarsity level.[86] This was in spite of the slow development of sports facilities. Sports grounds had been levelled as part of the original earth-moving, but the grass took a long time to grow.[87] Changing rooms and a first aid station were first improvised at Birch Cottage, one of the Talbot Colony's old buildings.

Chemistry Laboratory Manager Doug Ellis emerged as the presiding genius of sport at Monash. Appointed as joint deputy warden of the Union and sports administrator in 1965, Ellis was a competent and amiable administrator who encouraged all sorts of recreational pursuits, from bushwalking to badminton. He arranged for the university to purchase a large house across Blackburn Road for the use of clubs and societies. Open round the clock, seven days a week, 'Doug's Folly' was used for a variety of activities until the land was sold in the mid-1970s.[88]

The student newspaper, initially called *Chaos*, had a good deal of influence in Monash's small community. Originally edited by Ian Dudgeon and Tony Reyntjes, *Chaos* was printed weekly in 1961. It published original poems, articles, and a regular column titled 'Barnyard Banter', with jokes stolen from Melbourne University's *Speculum*.[89] Reflecting the geniality of early-1960s students, *Chaos* also celebrated staff appointments and achievements.

Chaos became *Lot's Wife* in June 1964, after editors Ross Cooper and Ross Fitzgerald were sacked by the SRC. The new editors were Tony

Schauble, John Blakeley and Damien Broderick. Broderick went on to become one of the world's foremost science fiction writers and is credited with coining the term 'virtual reality'; he was also responsible for the name *Lot's Wife*. The title was 'fraught with significance': the biblical Lot's wife 'didn't have the sense to see that she was being given a chance to escape the Bad Old Days, so she's probably still gazing in stony affection at the remains of a culture that had well and truly had its day. Our moral: Don't let this happen to you, or to Monash.'[90]

Broderick had arrived at Monash in 1962 and was well known on campus. He had very little money. 'I wore a baggy old dressing gown for a while, inherited from my grandfather', he remembered. For a year, he lived in the *Lot's Wife* office, sleeping on chairs and drinking coffee with the nightwatchmen. At age nineteen, he sold his first story to a British original fiction series and made money for baked beans and sausages by writing stories for Australian men's magazine *Man*. In his fourth year, with fellow students including Jean Bedford (the noted writer), he lived in a 'proto urban commune/collective sex'n'speed'n'hard-philosophisin' household' next to the Clayton drive-in. The house became known as 'the Vatican' (probably a play on the Notting Hill's nickname 'the Vicarage') and was renowned for its 'disgraceful' parties.[91]

Lot's shifted from letterpress hot-metal typesetting to web offset under the influence of Schauble, who went on to co-found Australia's first pop music magazine, *Go-Set*. Web offset, which had transformed student newspapers by the end of the 1960s, 'opened the floodgates to filth, corruption, fun, energy, last-minute paste-ups to fool the censors'.[92] *Lot's* soon gained a reputation for provocation and published a roll-call of future noteworthies including Elijah Moshinsky (later a celebrated international theatre director) and Peter Conrad (now a well-known Oxford literary critic).

From 1965 to 1966, *Lot's* was edited by Pete Steedman and Phillip Frazer, who took the publication in new and rebellious directions. ASIO spies were said to congregate around the *Lot's* office.[93] While a great deal of coverage was given to the Vietnam War, other matters were not overshadowed. A typical edition in 1965 contained an in-depth feature on the Dominican crisis, a double-page article on Hemingway and Kerouac, a critique of the Science Faculty as a glorified technical college, a one-act

'James Dean crossed with Elvis.' Lot's Wife *editor Pete Steedman (left) with assistant editor John Sinclair and secretary Jenny Hill, 1966.*

play about god-professors entitled 'Someone's Been Sitting on My Seat!', reviews of Hitchcock's *Marnie*, a report on the annual Australian Student Labor Federation Conference, and sports reports under the heading 'Monastic Sport'.[94] *Lot's* covered the University of Tasmania's Orr case, Aboriginal justice issues and apartheid, and published the first cartoons of Monash arts student Michael Leunig.

Oz magazine's Richard Neville described *Lot's* under Steedman and Frazer as 'the most original and exciting student paper he had ever seen'.[95] Its influence spread beyond Monash; it was read by secondary school students including David Dunstan, who went on to edit it himself in the early 1970s. But it did not please everyone. Mothers wrote to the vice-chancellor to complain about images of scantily clad females. In response to the reprimand, Steedman organised for a group of Monash staff and students to be given access to the Victoria Police collection of pornography. Sweeney, who was with the group, conceded that 'what was appearing in *Lot's Wife* was indeed tame in comparison'.[96]

Poet Laurie Duggan saw Monash as 'a little hothouse in the late 60s in an otherwise unfriendly environment' for poetry.[97] The Monash poets offered a self-conscious suburban counterpoint to the more bohemian Carlton scene centred on La Mama Theatre: poet Alan Wearne describes it as 'rather like a stand-off between two similar enough high schools'.[98] In 1967, Joachim Mauch of the Union bookshop began holding monthly poetry readings. After readings by an established poet (among them Bruce Dawe, Leon Slade, R.A. Simpson and Chris Wallace-Crabbe), the stage would be thrown open to the mainly undergraduate audience. The student poets—a mix of the eccentric, the politically grave, the flamboyant and the lovelorn, according to Wearne—included the poet and fiction writer John A. Scott and playwright John Romeril. Monash's literary moment was short-lived; by 1969, the readings had petered out. But the memories lingered. 'When a poem I am writing is rolling along well and its potential is unfolding . . . then the excitement of those Monash days can still return', Wearne recalls. 'I still regard myself as a Monash poet.'[99]

Religion in student life

Long before its radical politics hit the headlines, Monash stirred controversy for its stance on religion. In 1961, the council refused an application from its Catholic chaplain to hold Mass in a classroom during lunchtime. The council seems to have decided that, while it encouraged the discussion of religious questions on university property, the actual practice of religion was not to be allowed until the churches had realised their plans for a properly consecrated chapel or religious centre. That it had meanwhile permitted David Armstrong, a Melbourne University philosopher and avowed atheist, to address the Monash University Freethought Society on the topic 'God is evil' struck many observers as inconsistent. 'The use of lecture theatres for religious purposes commits no member of the university to anything except tolerance of the religious faith of others', protested David McKenna, President of the Newman College Students' Club.[100] It was hard, Matheson concluded, for the council to reach 'fair and liberal decisions' on controversial matters, and almost impossible on religious matters, 'which are so often characterised by the intolerance of the protagonists'.[101] But Douglas Hobson of the SCM argued that there was no difference of opinion on the matter between religious groups; if there was intolerance, it came from secularists bent on suppressing religious practice altogether.[102]

The episode confirmed a suspicion, among Catholics particularly, that Monash wished to prevent their faith from bearing on university life and experience. The Newman Society, one of the most active of the early clubs, found a 'lack of Christian consciousness' in universities: 'Christians too often completely divorce their religion from their lives as students'. The Monash branch of the SCM, which drew the more liberal Protestants, contended that 'if a student has faith he must relate it to his studies and to the university community into which God has placed him. If he has no faith he must still take the fact of faith into account.'[103] Until at least 1965, the pages of *Chaos* were more often given over to religious debate than to politics. 'This place has had so much religious talk . . . plans are under way to change the name to the Monashtry', its editors commented in 1961.[104]

The establishment of the White Protestant Society provoked a letter claiming that the religious planning of the university benefited Protestants and discriminated against Catholics: 'Consciously or unconsciously the powers-that-be at Monash University are risking a university tradition of atheism, racial prejudice, and religious intolerance'.[105] David Bradley recalls the complaints of Catholic students that the prominence of Protestant professors meant they were being subtly indoctrinated with the Protestant ethic.[106]

Large numbers of Jewish students lived within Monash's 'catchment area' in Melbourne's south-eastern suburbs. Psychologist Ron Taft estimated in the late 1960s that about one in nine Monash students was Jewish, a much higher proportion than in the general population.[107] In 1964, the University Council approved a proposal from the Hillel Foundation of Victoria for the creation of a Monash-affiliated Jewish college, but the scheme did not eventuate. However, the Jewish Students Society, formed in 1961, quickly became one of the largest clubs on campus, boasting almost 300 members by 1967.

The spirit of the early 1960s among religious students was usually cooperative and ecumenical. The Second Vatican Council of 1962–65 encouraged closer links between liberal Protestants and Catholics. At Monash, the SCM and the Newman Society jointly published the broadsheet *Wot's Life*.[108] The conservative EU, with its base in the churches of the city's outer suburban Bible Belt, was bigger than either of these liberal groups, and less accommodating.

The 1950s had been a prosperous time for the churches, seeding the growth of the student religious organisations into the early 1960s, but the aspirations of the baby-boomer generation presented a fundamental challenge to the religious, moral and political values on which the churches rested. By the late 1960s, student radicals were openly hostile to Christian students. After crusader Billy Graham's public support for the war in Vietnam, Bruce Wearne recalls Labor Club members chanting: 'Pie in the sky when you die, in the sweet bye and bye, it's a lie!' to the tune of 'Sweet By and By'.[109] Some students of faith joined the protest movement. The SCM at Monash opposed the war, becoming involved in draft resistance.[110] Monash's Christian Radical Club, which aimed to develop 'radically Biblical principles as a basis for Christian action', started as a cell of the EU and attracted Catholic nuns, SCM members, Pentecostals and other non-aligned people. But the political tensions were destructive. The club was quickly disowned by the 'central-control' of the EU Inter-Varsity Fellowship, and the SCM split, with some members joining the EU and others dropping out altogether.[111]

Student social life and larks

For full-time students in the 1960s, uni was a lifestyle. Those who travelled by public transport to Monash had little choice but to spend the day there. When they weren't in class or studying, they made their own fun. Kathy De La Rue and her friends talked away long hours drinking tea in the Philosophy Department. Sometimes, evading security staff, they climbed to the top of the unfinished, scaffolded Ming Wing to admire the view over the campus.[112]

Monash began by emulating the traditions of student life in the older universities. The first student dance, dubbed 'Farm Ferale', was hailed as the 'first step forward in Monash social life'. Dr and Mrs Matheson presided over the event, which featured a jazz band that packed the dance floor.[113] The SRC began hosting Union Nights in early 1961, with film screenings, dancing and supper.[114] The first Monash Ball, held at the Dorchester in June 1961, was an outstanding success, attracting over 300 students.[115]

But soon the editors of *Chaos* were deploring the 'apathetic response of students to organised social activities'.[116] By 1962, Union Nights had reached a 'pathetic state', following a ban on alcohol imposed after the 'wholesale carnage' of some earlier events.[117] The delay in completing the Union Building did not help matters. In 1966, an SRC representative told Sweeney that 'the label 9 to 5 University unfortunately, is painfully true'.[118]

Things had improved by the late 1960s. The 'caf' was open until 10 p.m. and often crowded with students, as was the Library foyer, a social scene in itself. The sedate student balls of the early 1960s had become much more riotous affairs. In 1969, Left, Right, In Between and Other balls were scheduled for April, but, times being what they were, the Right Ball was cancelled due to lack of demand.[119] Popular bands like the Executives, the Dream, and the Mixtures performed for hundreds of 'overlubricated' students.[120] During term, many of the era's great rock bands, such as the Master's Apprentices, Chain, and Spectrum, played outside the Union, and the Seekers performed at the campus before they became well known.[121] Off campus, students living nearby in group houses kept up a constant round of parties, still recalled years later through a haze of tobacco smoke and the lingering taste of beer, flagon red and Stones ginger wine.[122]

'Rags' are a time-honoured tradition of student life, an occasion for letting off steam, creating a spectacle and playfully mocking authority. Monash's first off-campus rag was a funeral for Adolf Hitler. A procession of about 200 cars drove slowly from Monash to Chadstone shopping centre, where the Führer was to be buried in the lawns of 3UZ radio station. After the service, he leapt from his coffin, entered the studio and interrupted the broadcast to extol the virtues of national socialism.[123]

Farm Week, Monash's answer to Melbourne University's July 'Prosh', began in 1967. The inaugural prize for the 'Hardest to Obtain' competition was awarded for the plaque from the Royal Mint on William Street; other trophies included the point posts from the Melbourne Cricket Ground. One group of students presented the organisers with a dead body in a casket, complete with hearse, a tasteless prank that the organisers decided to hush up.[124] Farm Week 1969, 'undoubtedly the worst example of student idiocy ever seen at Monash', descended into chaos and became the subject of a Professorial Board inquiry.

> For three days, the area between the Union Building and the Menzies Building was a region of constant flour fights and anyone crossing was considered fair game. Numerous visitors to the university were covered in flour and water, windows were broken, fire hoses were ruined and one unfortunate lady was rendered unconscious when struck on the head by a large water bomb dropped from the eleventh floor of the Menzies Building—this was equivalent to the impact of a brick falling from 20 ft. The total bill for damages was . . . $1340.[125]

A number of students were fined for Farm Week pranks, including third-year law/economics and politics student and future jurist 'J. Burnside', who was fined $4 for stopping the escalators in the Menzies Building.[126] From the vantage point of the university authorities, the 'lawlessness' of Farm Week and the rebellion of the political radicals had a common root in the endemic restlessness of the 1960s generation.

Consumables and stimulants

Everything so bloody dear
A bloody bob for bloody beer
And is it good—no bloody fear
At bloody Monash.

Bob Hammond, 'Bloody Monash', 1961

It was hard to get a decent bite, and even harder to get a drink, on the new Monash campus. For a while, food was cooked at a leased shop in Oakleigh and transported to the university in the same trucks used to carry waste and zoology specimens.[127] There were several food outlets on campus by the mid-1960s, but long queues and complaints about the food were common. According to an SRC survey, the majority of students felt that food at Monash was too expensive, lacking in variety and poor in nutritional value. 'A method needs to be devised to make the food more appetising . . . to abolish [the] common complaint—"this food makes me sick"', declared SRC catering representative and future politician Andrew Theophanous.[128] Particularly notorious was the caf's coffee, a milky sludge dispensed from large urns. In July 1972, when the Union Building was operating as an 'underground draft resistance centre', a motion to offer coffee to the police posted outside the campus was defeated by a student meeting on the grounds that 'one wouldn't give caf coffee to one's worst enemy'.[129]

Drinking has always been an important aspect of university culture, and Monash students were no exception. Yet there was no student bar on campus until late in the Monash story: a contributor to the problem of the 'nine to five' university. Successive state governments refused to permit the establishment of a bar in the Union, and political events at Monash in the late 1960s did little to further this cause.[130] But the Notting Hill Hotel, along with other local pubs, served well enough. Publican Kath Byer, a 'legend in her own time', dispensed kindness along with the beer and more than a few free meals to students who were broke. She 'made sure we did not make complete fools of ourselves and even drove us home when we did'.[131]

The Nott was a 'home away from (and instead of) home' for historian, novelist and political commentator Ross Fitzgerald during his time at Monash. He drank with Julian West (son of Morris), novelist Kevin Mackie, Boyd Oxlade (author of *Death in Brunswick*) and Barry Humphries. Historians Ian Turner and Brian Fitzpatrick were also regulars. Fitzgerald topped every subject in his first two years, 'propelled and energised' by alcohol. It was at the Nott that he first heard of Alcoholics Anonymous.[132]

The Nott was also where notorious *Lot's* editor Pete Steedman regularly held court, his virtuoso profanity enthralling the female arts students. David Williamson remembers attempting to 'rescue' a young woman from Steedman, who was putting the hard word on her—only to find she didn't want to be rescued.[133] Steedman brought a certain

Students in the beer garden at the Nott for end-of-term celebrations, 1971.

northern inner suburbs style to Clayton, with his black leather jacket and unkempt good looks. Arriving in 1962, he soon became known on campus for his involvement with the SRC and *Lot's Wife*, and for his frequent run-ins with the administration, particularly with Warden of the Union Graeme Sweeney. Their disagreements, Steedman said, 'came from a very simple place'.

> Graeme wanted to keep us under control, and I wanted no control, this was the first time I'd got out of control in my life . . . there was no coppers on me, there was no parents on me, there was no prefects or other jock-strappers and wankers on me, and I could do whatever I wanted.[134]

Steedman was reputedly the first student to be disciplined by the university, fined £15 for using language unbecoming to a student towards an executive officer.[135] Of twelve subjects attempted in his years at Monash, he passed only five. Steedman went on to stir up Melbourne University as editor of *Farrago* and was subsequently associated with *Go-Set*, *Rolling Stone* and other magazines. He became nationally recognised as a motorcycle-riding member of the House of Representatives for Casey (1983–84) and the head of AUSMUSIC in the 1990s.

One theory links the decline of political activity at Monash by the early 1970s to increased weed-smoking. In July 1973, Sweeney sought legal advice about whether the university would be liable for student drug use in the Union. His action was prompted by his discovery of the Monash Grass Roots Lobby, which met every Friday in the Union to smoke 'the infamous "killer weed"'. The Union Building in this period may have been a 'place apart' with its own counter-culture rules, as historian Simon Marginson had it,[136] but there were limits to Sweeney's indulgence. He was advised to take all reasonable steps to prevent drug possession and use within the Union.

Sex in the suburbs

Monash was born just as a sexual revolution was getting under way. The contraceptive pill was introduced in Australia in 1961, although it was available at first only to married women, and conservative public attitudes towards sex before marriage endured well into Monash's first years. In 1968, an 'angry' SRC president, Jim Falk, challenged an article in *Truth* which implied that free love was 'rife' at Monash.[137]

Discussions of sex and morality became a strong feature of student culture. 'New students in a university are generally told about everything during Orientation Week except those subjects that press foremost and heavily on their minds, viz., Sex, Morals and the New Student', the 1964 *Orientation Handbook* observed.[138] The SRC sponsored a series of lunchtime talks on the topic. History lecturer Geoff Bolton bravely made a case for chastity, though acknowledging its virtues were unlikely to appeal to university students. An anonymous first-year student wrote about the impossibility of living openly as a homosexual.[139] These discussions were framed in moral terms; sex and sexual orientation were not yet discussed as explicitly political issues.

Some students embraced the possibilities of sexual freedom. Leaving the Library at dusk, Ross Fitzgerald met 'sultry, dark-eyed' Janet, a first-year student, who became his first 'real love'. They made love that evening.[140] One former student has a 'vivid recollection' from the late 1960s, a time of long, full 'flower children' skirts, of a couple lying on the grass between the Ming Wing and the Union Building, 'the fellow on his back, the girl astride . . . with the skirt covering the activity'.[141]

Orientation handbooks in the 1960s listed local justices of the peace, 'for when necessity dictates a hasty marriage'.[142] Hastily or not, many Monash couples married while they were still students. Hundreds of students, graduates and staff members opted to marry in the grounds of

Miss Arts, *who comes from Berlin, but is now a naturalised Australian, is Angelica Szidat. Angelica counts most sports in her interests — and hopes to be a writer.*

Miss ECOPS *is Pauline Elfman who also wants to be a teacher. Pauline was born in Melbourne and is sport conscious, too; she skis, plays squash and tennis. She is seventeen.*

Miss Engineering *is dark-haired Julie Green from Melbourne. Julie hopes to make teaching her career. She enjoys squash, hockey and the top Winter sport: ski-ing.*

Miss International *has come to Monash all the way from Adelaide. She is Jill Evans and she wants to be a teacher. Her hobbies are squash, tennis and swimming (mostly in the Summer!).*

Miss Medicine *is another aspiring teacher. Elizabeth Page has several hobbies: baseball, tennis, dancing and amateur acting. She wants to be a teacher (no shortage of teachers soon!).*

Miss Science *is Fiona Fairweather who comes from our friendly competitor city, Sydney. Fiona is a whizz with figures (mathematical!) and wants to be a mathematician.*

'Miss Monash' finalists, 1963.

Monash. Pam and Ian Gibson, members of the first cohort of Monash students, married at the Religious Centre. Their wedding, on the Saturday before Christmas in 1968, was the last of seven to be held there that day.[143]

In the 1960s, education for women was still viewed through the prism of biological destiny. Matheson regretted the common belief that tertiary education was wasted on girls as they would 'only marry and give it all away'. But he too framed the issue in biological terms: 'To these people, I would suggest the fact that our society needs educated mothers, too'.[144] The university was dominated by male students (two to every woman), and tertiary education retained a masculine flavour that carried over into the workforce. The Careers and Appointments Office reported in 1968 that it was difficult to place girls, unless they wanted to teach.[145]

On the campus, as in the broader society, young women were seen as sexual objects. The 'belle' of Monash's first dance in 1961, 'Miss Ferale', was first-year science student Miss Barbara Woodberry; her 'most interesting aspects', according to the *Student Newspaper* (later renamed *Chaos*), 'were about 36–23–35'.[146] The annual 'Miss Monash' quest began in 1962. Miss Monash was required to be 'sophisticated, talented, vivacious, intellectual, poised, stimulating, unspoiled—in other words, SEXY'.[147] Photographs of the candidates featured annually in the student newspaper, with titles such as 'Leer Ye, Leer Ye'.[148] The Miss Monash tradition had died a quiet death by 1969, as student culture turned more serious and political, although the sexism it symbolised was more difficult to remove.

Monash had no sooner been launched than it found itself in the midst of tumultuous changes. By 1964, Matheson was already nostalgic about the students of 1961, who by 'the light of today's student fashions' seemed 'very tidy'.[149] The first students had been so respectable and respectful that student discipline seemed almost superfluous. 'Those of you who were here last year will know that we managed to get along without any elaborate code of rules', Matheson told the second intake of freshers in 1962. 'We expect students to behave reasonably and not to climb on the roofs.'[150] Discipline would not be a laughing matter by 1968. The easygoing relations between staff and students of the early years inevitably changed as Monash grew into a large multiversity. By the end of the 1960s, internal grievances had combined with broader social and political forces to turn the friendly 'Farm' into a battlefield.

FIVE

READING, RIOTING AND 'RITHMETIC

If there is a university in Australia that could disintegrate, as some of the American universities have, it would be Monash.

THE BULLETIN, 1969

By the end of its first decade, in a period marked internationally by student unrest, Monash had become the symbolic centre of Australia's revolutionary student movement. Monash's 'troubles', as they became known, began in earnest in 1967, peaked in 1968–70 and petered out around the end of 1974. During these years, 'Monash' became 'a dirty word' for many Australians.[1] In the early 1960s, the university had been defined by its confidence that it could do things differently from older institutions. Now it came under sustained attack from radical left-wing students as an agent of bourgeois repression. The Monash story in this critical period is marked by a chaotic succession of stormings and occupations of the Administration Building, known by 1970 as the 'Fortress' for its heavy security. Thousands-strong student meetings were held on the campus. Rumours circulated that the university was on the verge of anarchy, closure, or both.

Then and later, many people asked, 'Why Monash?' Was it simply an effect of media attention, as university authorities sometimes suggested? Or was it rooted in distinctive features of the student cohort, many of whom were first-generation students? Was it driven by charismatic personalities such as Albert Langer or by tactical errors on the part of the university authorities? Were the students encouraged by young,

Albert Langer, the most famous of Monash's student revolutionaries, addresses a meeting, 1971.

radical staff members? Or was it somehow related to the rapid growth of the university, from 347 students in 1961 to more than 7000 by 1967? Matters of geography were also raised: perhaps there was simply nothing else to do on this sleepy suburban campus. Some saw the large expanse of lawn outside the Union Building, which became known as the forum and was ideal for mass meetings, as a precondition for Monash becoming the leading radical university.[2]

In 1980, Vice-Chancellor Matheson remembered the first cohort of Monash students as 'a pleasant lot of young people with whom I enjoyed friendly relations'.[3] Not so the cohorts that followed; in retrospect, Matheson took on the appearance of a Lear-like figure spurned by his inexplicably rebellious 'children'. In the face of the troubles, Matheson's initial impulse was towards inquiry. Like academics worldwide, he understood the sudden upsurge of student protest as an international phenomenon with common causes and trajectories. He was influenced by the writings of John Searle, a philosopher at the University of California at Berkeley (the scene of a dramatic campus confrontation in 1964). Searle described the successful movement as uniting 'existing mistrust of authority with genuinely idealistic impulses' in order to gain widespread support from students, and then acting to undermine university authorities by provoking them into excessive reaction against students. This could lead to a crisis point at which university stakeholders, including faculty staff, demanded the sacking of the head of the university and other fundamental changes. At this stage, the university might cease to operate.[4] For Matheson, Monash's builder and custodian, these were high stakes.

The Monash soviet

Monash developed a reputation for radicalism almost as soon as it was established. The journal of the conservative National Civic Council, *News Weekly*, referred to the university as the 'Monash Soviet' and claimed there was 'more subversion per square foot than at any other Australian university'.[5] But the explosion of political agitation that cast Monash in the role of *enfant terrible* of the Australian university scene was not anticipated by the administration. As late as 1966, the warden of the Union advised the SRC on how it might address the problem of 'student apathy'.[6]

In the early 1960s, politically active students across Australia tended to be liberal reformists, acting out of a moral concern for social change through bipartisan organisations such as Student Action for Aborigines, which led the Freedom Rides into regional Australia in 1965. Campaigns were fought around such issues as capital punishment, censorship, White Australia, civil rights in the United States and apartheid in South Africa.[7] The Vietnam War and the announcement of a selective conscription system in Australia channelled student activism in more radical directions. At Monash, *Lot's Wife* began publishing articles critical of the war ahead of Melbourne University's *Farrago*.

In July 1965, Monash hosted its first 'teach-in' on the Vietnam War (the second in Australia, following one at ANU). Two thousand staff and students gathered to see anti-war campaigner Jim Cairns face off against Menzies' Minister for External Affairs Paul Hasluck. The teach-in was televised and received extensive press coverage.[8] *Lot's* noted that 'Monash has found a voice and a language that can bridge the gap between the library and the suburbs where the people who pay for the university live ... The implications of this demonstration must not be forgotten.'[9]

In 1966, Monash students were involved in demonstrations against conscription and the visit to Australia of United States president Lyndon Johnson. The SRC was forced to apologise after students on Monash's 1967 Moomba Festival float, 'Much Ado about Nothing', waved anti–Vietnam War banners and tore down Australian and American flags.[10] By the end of the decade, most students were opposed to the war. An estimated 5000 Monash students—about half the student body—marched in the first moratorium in May 1970.[11]

The radical left went beyond opposition to the war to develop a broader critique of capitalism and American imperialism. The university became a breeding ground for dissent and also its target. Radicalised students saw the university not as a 'place apart' but as a tool of capitalism which disguised its repressive nature through the myth of free thought and inquiry. Universities moulded individuals who believed they could exercise dissent but in fact could do so only within 'the usual reformist limits'.[12]

In practice, the earnest discussions of 'repressive tolerance' and political theory heard in the caf and the Nott were usually overshadowed by local issues like the power of the university to discipline students, the perennial problem of car parking, and staff monopoly of the (licensed) Faculty Club, where 'students and dogs' were not allowed.[13]

The Monash Labor Club

The Monash Labor Club moved sharply to the left following the defeat of the Australian Labor Party (ALP) in the 1966 election, which was fought on the issue of Vietnam. The election loss left many Labor Club members disillusioned with liberal democracy. Dave Nadel, President of the Monash Labor Club (1966–67), decided there was 'something wrong with Parliamentary politics'. The club 'went left', he says, 'because of the Vietnam War and conscription. And a little bit because of Berkeley.' Nadel attributes the increasing hold of Maoism on the club to a clause in its constitution that barred members of the Communist Party of Australia from joining; ironically, there was no clause banning Maoists.[14]

Matheson's problems with the Labor Club began with the arrival of Darce Cassidy at Monash in 1967.[15] Cassidy was an experienced activist and journalist who had been transferred by the ABC from Sydney to Melbourne. He developed the Labor Club's new-look agitational broadsheet, *Print*, a powerful communication tool during the years of student protest, and along with his partner, Jill, and Dave Nadel set up the first Labor Club 'headquarters' in Jasmine Street, Caulfield. The Jasmine Street commune housed most of the executive of the Labor Club and became an important focal point for its activities, including dinners and parties attended by activists from Melbourne and beyond. The house was strewn with radical literature and hummed with the sounds of traditional protest songs from the Spanish Civil War and Irish rebel refrains, as well as contemporary rock'n'roll.[16] Political debate was fuelled by alcohol and nicotine, but drugs were frowned on by the more puritan Maoist contingent, who also placed a ban on all Beatles records not long after 'Revolution' hit the airwaves.[17]

Cassidy and Nadel had met the previous year at the Australian Student Labor Federation Conference in Canberra, during which Nadel and several other Monash students were arrested at a sit-down anti-war demonstration. The arrest made the front page of the *Australian*, necessitating a fraught phone call to Nadel's 'very moderate' parents. Nadel had grown up in a lower middle-class family of German-born Jewish refugees and

attended Heidelberg High School. He arrived at Monash in 1965 as an
ALP supporter who 'hero-worshipped Jim Cairns' but soon read Marx
and moved towards a revolutionary perspective. A well-known figure on
campus, with his dark moustache, glasses and military jacket, Nadel was a
regular fixture in the small caf, talking politics over cups of strong black
tea and rolling his own cigarettes. He was eccentric and kind-hearted,
even 'saintly'. Alan Wearne recalls him taking in a young woman who
had been kicked out of home and giving her an informative lecture on
contraception. 'He had no designs on her and she still expresses her
indebtedness.'[18]

Nadel's vice-president was Albert Langer, who arrived at Monash in
1966. Langer was to gain widespread notoriety (and grudging respect in
Victorian legal circles) for his successful self-defence—at the age of just
nineteen—against criminal charges of riot, inciting a riot and obstructing
a police officer, arising from the 4 July 1968 protest at the United States
Consulate.[19] Langer arrived at Monash an ALP member but moved
towards the militant far left during 1966–67. It is often said that he was
radicalised by his arrest at the October 1966 demonstration against the
visit of President Lyndon Johnson, during which—he claimed—he was
beaten by police.[20] Langer played a strong role in determining the Maoist
slant of the Labor Club after 1967.

Langer was highly intelligent—Matheson described him as a 'brilliant
student of Mathematics'[21]—and a talented orator. Overweight, bearded
and 'with the air of a messianic rabbi', he was also—paradoxically—rather
shy.[22] He was disliked by many on the left, an antipathy containing a
measure of anti-Semitism and class envy. Langer's stepfather was Norman
Smorgon; his mother's third husband was also wealthy. As a revolutionary
communist, Langer found the Smorgon family trust fund and Toorak
home address something of a millstone around his neck. Jack McDonell,
the first warden of Deakin Hall, recalls that when Albert lived in Deakin
he was given a very nice car by his mother, which he spent a lot of time
mistreating, 'to make it look like the car of a proletarian'.[23]

The media was fascinated by Langer, picturing him as an evil
intelligence controlling events at Monash. The Monash confrontation
was presented in the press as a battle between Matheson and Langer
(once described by *News Weekly* as Monash's 'shadow Vice Chancellor').[24]

This underplayed the role of other leaders like Michael Hyde and Nadel and overplayed the commitment to Maoism among the Labor Club membership.

Poet Laurie Duggan, a 'fellow traveller' with the club (and an official member for one year), recalls that 'there was much internal debate and members and friends occupied a range of positions from slightly left of the ALP through Trotskyism to Maoism'.[25] It was, as former member Elliot Gingold recalls, a 'fairly broad church'. Gingold was never comfortable with the Maoist leadership of the organisation, describing himself variously as 'left liberal', 'follower of Che Guevara' or 'anarcho-syndicalist'.[26]

Like Matheson, the Labor Club was well attuned to international developments. The leadership consciously adopted Marxist–Leninist revolutionary strategy, assuming the role of revolutionary vanguard. They hoped to radicalise the student body through the experience of demonstrations and other direct action on local, university-centred issues relevant to student concerns.[27] Langer argued that 'police truncheons . . . [and] University disciplinary measures . . . have taught the students more about Marxist theory of the state than any amount of seminars'.[28] This style of activism was criticised by Monash's New Left group as anti-intellectual.[29]

Many Labor Club members possessed little in the way of political theory. Liz Porter recalled that much of the Labor Club debate went over her head: '[I] quickly gathered that to call someone a Trotskyite was the worst insult you could offer a person. Why, exactly, I didn't know, except that it had something to do with deserving the fate of ending up with an icepick in your head.'[30] Duggan found the 'earnestness of some of these mostly middle class people' bemusing.[31] Few of the key players were from working-class backgrounds, leaving them open to the criticism that they were driven by middle-class guilt.[32] As Philip Mendes has shown, a number of the Monash Labor Club personnel were from Jewish backgrounds, though most claimed that their Jewishness was irrelevant to their activism. Growing anti-Zionism among left-wing students saw something of a breach in the Jewish–New Left nexus by the end of 1972, as many pro-Israel Jews joined less hostile political groupings such as the Radical Zionist Alliance.[33]

Like all student activity at Monash in this period, the Labor Club was male-dominated. In the late 1960s, women's liberation had yet to

Lot's Wife *takes a satirical view of the student revolt and some of its key players, 1969.*

become prominent even on university campuses; certainly, it was largely absent from Labor Club ideology. While a few women held important positions (including Martha Campbell, who was president in 1967), women in the club were mostly relegated to 'typing, roneoing and making cups of tea, to the kitchen and the bed'.[34] Speakers at general meetings were almost always male. The media focused on the sexuality of the few female radicals, playing up their lack of make-up and their 'solemn, joyless' perversity.[35] Campbell and Kerry Langer—wife of Albert—received hate mail addressing them as sluts and bitches.

By the late 1960s, the Labor Club monopolised politics on campus, and other voices struggled to be heard. It had the largest membership of any student club at Monash: probably more than 300 at its high point. Its hold on student politics was achieved through a strong presence—along with its allies—on the Public Affairs Committee (PAC) of the Monash Association of Students (MAS), its active recruitment of 'freshers' and its control over communications. *Print* became the main source of political information on campus and a major nuisance to the administration.

The art of war

The confrontation between radical students and the administration began in 1967, in response to the awarding of an honorary degree to the Victorian premier. Sir Henry Bolte's recent sanctioning of the hanging of Ronald Ryan was 'condemned by practically everybody'.[36] *Print* claimed that Monash deans had all refused to allow the degree to be awarded in their faculty.[37] The administration evaded a clash with students by relocating the graduation ceremony to the Melbourne Town Hall, but the Labor Club organised its own anti-Bolte activities on campus. At a faux awards ceremony, a degree was awarded to Sir Henry Pig, a piglet which 'showed its great displeasure by defecating on the rostrum'. The inscription 'No pedigree for pigs', written in fertiliser on the forum lawn, was visible from the Menzies Building for months.[38]

But it was the Labor Club's decision to offer material support to the National Liberation Front (NLF) in Vietnam which swung the heat of public outrage onto Monash. While expressions of solidarity with the NLF had been an aspect of anti-war activism for some time, the decision of the Labor Club to offer it 'unspecified support', in addition to medical aid for civilians in communist-controlled areas, provoked immediate media attention and protests from the public and the Returned and Services League. What most turned public opinion against Monash, Matheson recalled, was Labor Club member Peter Price's widely reported comment that it would be 'unfortunate' if an Australian conscript was hit by an NLF bullet marked 'Monash University Labor Club'.[39]

Three students who had collected money for the NLF on campus—Langer, Hyde and William Dowling—were charged with misconduct and fined by the university. The right-wing DLP Club called a general student meeting to dissociate the student body from the Labor Club action, but their motion was lost. The meeting upheld the right of the group to collect for any cause they chose. While students stopped short of supporting the NLF, their opposition to the war inclined them to condone more radical action. Elliot Gingold, a 'fairly moderate radical', recalls:

> I did not support the Monash Labor Club when they launched their aid for the Viet Cong campaign, though I was in fact rather pleased that it suddenly made respectable the position I held of simply opposing the war . . . a lot of students now felt able to publically take what had now become a moderate position of opposing the war. The stand of the Labor club had provided us with 'left flank cover'.[40]

The public relations fallout from the NLF affair was considerable. According to one famous story, a student hitching a ride with a truck driver was asked where she studied. 'At Monash', she replied and was promptly told to get out. Bequests to Monash were cancelled, and Labor Club members received death threats.[41] The affair precipitated the passage in federal parliament of the *Defence Forces Protection Act 1967*, which made it an offence, punishable by imprisonment and/or a fine of up to $2000, to send aid to the NLF. This transformed Monash students' actions into a national political issue, to the delight of members of the Labor Club.

In 1968, public relations were further damaged by an event in which the Labor Club took no part. On Maundy Thursday, a student anarchist dressed as Christ bore a large cardboard cross through the Union, accompanied by 'Romans' with whips and a student playing 'Onward, Christian Soldiers' badly on a tuba. The group proceeded to stage a mock crucifixion. Christians, Catholics especially, were outraged, and Monash was once again condemned by the press. Police charged fourteen students with offensive behaviour; they eventually received twelve-month good behaviour bonds. The prank had no political intent, but student radicals made political capital out of the university's willingness to cooperate with the state in bringing charges against those involved.

The university's power to discipline students was the most disruptive issue driving the 'troubles', at Monash as elsewhere. It was to spark Monash's own version of Paris' 'May 1968'. In the early 1960s, the university had relied on rudimentary disciplinary provisions. When student troubles began to flare in 1967, a drafting committee led by Professor Enid Campbell began work on a revised statute. The key point of contention was the so-called 'double jeopardy' provision, which allowed the university to discipline or exclude students who were convicted of an offence off-campus.

On 15 May, the *Age* reported that Monash was considering introducing wider powers to discipline students for acts of misconduct outside the university—a claim Matheson strenuously denied. The double jeopardy issue had been bubbling since early that year, when a student had been called before the Discipline Committee to answer charges relating to a conviction for drug possession.[42] The *Age* report sparked a protest meeting of over 2000 students and Monash's first sit-in in the Administration Building, involving 400 students, on 16 May. The Campaign for University Freedom, a bipartisan coalition of members of the Labor Club, New Left and others, was set up to coordinate further activity on the issue.

The birth of MAS

The discipline fight converged with grievances about student repre-sentation in the university. The first broadsheet of the Campaign for University Freedom stated that 'we, the students, have adopted a new principle: that student-administration relations should be conducted on the basis of direct, mass student participation and negotiation, and should not be muffled, indirected and conveyed by "student leaders", SRC "experts" or whatever'.[43] Students wanted to be more directly involved in running the university. They were dissatisfied with the 'bourgeois democracy' of the SRC and resented the rigidity and authoritarianism of

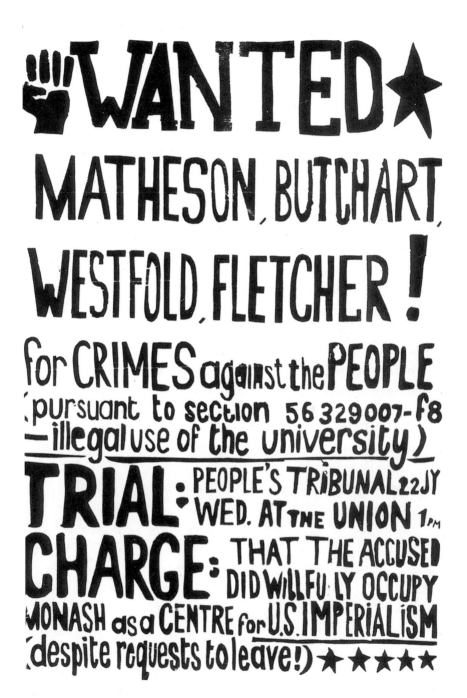

Paper warfare, late 1960s. Posters and pamphlets were weapons in the propaganda war between student radicals and university authorities during the student 'troubles' at Monash.

the administration. Matheson had been slow to recognise the importance of student representation on university boards, including the Union Board. He doubted that the 'purposes of the Union would be served by student members seeking to debate all sorts of minor items and/or speaking for the sake of hearing their own voices'.[44] This was a classic confrontation between the pragmatism of the administrator and the new politics of self-expression and personal authenticity. Students 'have begun to say that we are entitled to a voice in running this university and that if we are not given one, we are prepared to take it', declared *Print*. 'This is our university, not theirs . . . if we decide not to accept their decisions, then these decisions cannot be implemented.'[45]

In mid-1967, SRC members Jim Falk and John Price proposed an alternative system of student representation based on participatory democracy. The proposed system would comprise an administrative executive, a committee of representatives to represent students on internal matters, and a public affairs committee elected on a political basis to conduct research and present material on extra-campus matters to the student body for policy formulation. Ultimate power would lie with the student general meeting; the decisions of meetings would be binding on

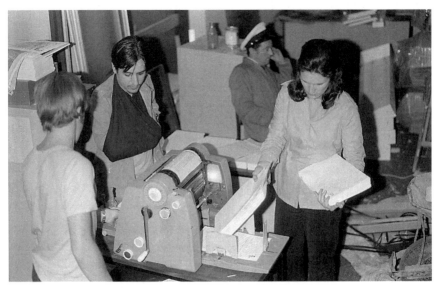

Students printing leaflets, 1971.

all elected representatives.[46] The SRC declared itself to be irrelevant and disbanded, and in June 1968 students voted to replace it with MAS, based on the Price–Falk proposals.

MAS was the only example of a system of mass democracy to be instituted in an Australian university at this time and was a critical determinant of the Monash climate in the years to come. The Labor Club evaluated MAS as an almost unqualified success. Whereas the SRC had struggled to draw nominations, MAS in its first years attracted huge numbers of nominations for the PAC. General meetings attracted large numbers (up to 5000). Critics pointed out that meetings on less contentious issues sometimes struggled to reach the required quorum of 5 per cent of the student body, but supporters argued as philosophical principle and practice that the students interested in an issue should decide that issue.[47] Jim Falk argues that, 'in its time, for what it was designed for, it was a mind-boggling success. It involved enormously increased participation and was vastly more responsive to student views than the old SRC.'[48]

Critics of the system, however, viewed MAS as a system designed to benefit the radical left at the expense of the 'ordinary' student. The DLP Club called it 'the worst form of student government yet devised by man'.[49] Their view, outlined in numerous broadsheets and in letters to the administration, was that the MAS process was open to manipulation by the few, was marred by inaccessible 'proceduralese' that stifled true debate, and was undemocratic, because not all students could attend meetings or stay to their conclusion. Furthermore, 'only radical views' were allowed.[50] The Monash University Society, formed to oppose MAS, warned that 'the intelligent, politically uncommitted student leaves the scene of the general meeting tragi-comedy disillusioned and hostile, like as not never to return'. A quorum was sometimes only achieved, it was claimed, by including lunching bystanders.[51]

Queensland Labor MP Dean Wells, a forceful character in the political scene at Monash at this time, describes MAS as a 'system of demagoguery' advantaging the radicals: 'They knew their rhetoricians were better, and thought they would sway the meetings'.[52] Matheson agreed that the system 'undoubtedly strengthened the power of the radical group to make trouble'.[53]

Year of struggle

In March 1969, the *Sun* reported that Monash was preparing for its 'year of struggle'.[54] The focus of student grievances in first semester was on car parking, an issue which some saw as bringing 'sorely needed comedy' to campus politics.[55] Despite protests from MAS and the Staff Association, the administration introduced annual parking fees of $5 for students and $10 for staff. Radicals argued that the fees were an inequitable burden on students. As Nadel said, '$5 may not sound like much . . . [but] I was living away from home on a budget of $20 per week'. Students tore down barricades and picketed the office selling parking stickers, and the Labor Club produced fake stickers that were reportedly impossible to tell from the real thing.[56]

May saw the return of the discipline issue. In June 1968, the council had passed a resolution agreeing in principle that students should not be disciplined for off-campus activities. The issue was reignited when the university amended the Status of Students Statute to allow the exclusion of a student convicted of a criminal—though not a political—offence. Matheson argued that the new clause was necessary to give the university the power to exclude convicted drug pushers and sexual offenders, but many students saw it as the reintroduction of 'double jeopardy'.[57]

A student general meeting on 6 May voted for direct action against the administration. However, motions for a sit-in and an occupation were both lost, making it unclear whether action was sanctioned or not. The meeting was adjourned to the lawn outside the Administration Building, and a number of students, led by the Labor Club, climbed into the building through a window. Acting Vice-Chancellor Professor Kevin Westfold cancelled all 3.15 lectures, probably in the hope that the meeting would be swamped by moderate students. By 3.30 p.m., approximately 6000 of Monash's 9500 students packed the area: probably the largest meeting ever held in an Australian university. They voted overwhelmingly against the offending 'double jeopardy' clauses but also voted to end the sit-in.

Negotiations over the drafting of the discipline statute broke down in July, leading Labor Club members to initiate a confrontation on Bastille Day (14 July) in which about a hundred students occupied the Administration Building.[58] The next confrontation—in early August—was a reaction to the disciplining of the students involved in the 14 July disturbance. The day before the trial of the disciplined students, MAS again voted to occupy. When the Discipline Committee (known to students as the 'Dean Machine') arrived the next morning, the building was packed, and a rally was proceeding outside. About 250 students invaded the council chamber, with journalists in tow, and the trial was adjourned. *News Weekly* ran a front-page picture of a defiant Kerry Langer slumped in the chancellor's chair, with her feet on the desk.

The *Age* editorialised that 'there is now a real danger that the mindless madness of American and European student riots is about to be re-enacted in Melbourne'. The students' 'crash-in' had taken Monash to the 'edge of violence' as students forced their way past security guards. Bolte had reportedly threatened state government intervention if Monash did not set its house in order, and the Professorial Board had given Matheson full power to 'clamp down' on student unrest.[59] On 8 August, Matheson took the dramatic step of making an address to the entire university via closed-circuit television, from an undisclosed location. Paul Francis Perry satirised the action, observing that 'perhaps he had been reading McLuhan, or perhaps he was preparing for 1984'.[60] But the sense of gravity created by the address shifted sympathy towards Matheson and the administration.[61] Speaking for about forty minutes, Matheson told the students that the disturbances had stained the reputation of their Monash degrees. The aim of the revolutionaries, he warned, was to close down the university.

Dénouement

The focus on Albert Langer became more intense in 1970 when the administration decided to exclude him from further study at Monash. While Langer's academic performance in the first three years of his course had been exceptional, he received second-class honours in his final year, probably due to his political activities and court appearances. In 1970, he applied to do a master of science preliminary course in computing and was rejected by the faculty on technical grounds. The Labor Club claimed that Langer had been excluded for political reasons, something that seemed self-evident to many. It was, says Professor of Law Louis Waller, an academic decision 'motivated by certain . . . policy considerations' and in retrospect a 'mistake'.[62] Langer, after purportedly being rejected by every university in Australia,[63] was eventually admitted to Monash's diploma of education in 1971 and went on to become a teacher.

At the end of 1969, the drafting of the Status of Students Statute had been shelved. With discipline off the radar, the administration did not anticipate the next confrontation with radical students. The occupation of the Careers and Appointments Office was intended to highlight the university's 'links with imperialism', including the use of the university as a recruiting ground for companies profiting from the Vietnam War, and the university's outreach to industry through the Monash University Scientific and Industrial Community.[64] On 29 June 1970, about fifty students took over the office and declared it an 'anti-imperialist organising centre'. The occupation lasted three days, the longest at any Australian university at that time. The occupying students produced anti-imperialist leaflets and wrote letters to large industrial firms on university letterhead.[65]

Nine students were disciplined by the university for the occupation. Two—Michael Hyde and Ralph Hadden—were expelled for life, because they had previous suspended exclusions. Five others, including Kerry Langer and Jim Bacon (later premier of Tasmania), were suspended for up to two years. Although the occupation had not been sanctioned by MAS, the 'Support the Monash 9' campaign for the reinstatement of those students attracted broad-based support.

The expulsions brought Monash to another crisis point. Debate raged about the form that direct action—if any—should take. There were public debates, mass rallies, a 'brick-in' of the Administration Building and a boycott of lectures. Leaflets circulating the university featured crossed toothbrushes as a symbol of occupation.[66] Matheson, characteristically, attempted to appeal to students using the combined forces of reason and technology: on the day of the planned occupation, his 'Limits of Protest' speech was played continually over the public address system.

In the face of an MAS vote to occupy indefinitely, Matheson agreed to hold a referendum of the whole university. A huge meeting of staff and students, estimated to include 90 per cent of those on campus that day, rejected Matheson's voting formula, which simply asked if the students should be given clemency, and instead adopted a formula offering five choices—the sentences: should stand, should have been harsher, should be reduced but still retain some exclusions, should consist of fines only, or should be remitted. The 8 October referendum was accompanied by feverish press speculation about the possibility of violence and whether the 'silent majority' would speak. Victorian Democratic Labor Party leader Frank Dowling took the opportunity to call for Matheson to be sacked.[67]

The results of the referendum were inconclusive. Of the 7620 who voted (including almost 60 per cent of the student population), about 30 per cent said that the exclusions should stand, 25 per cent voted for fines only, 15 per cent voted for some but not all exclusions to stand, and 15 per cent voted for no punishment at all. The Labor Club highlighted the fact that the majority were in favour of reducing sentences, while the *Age* interpreted the results as confirmation that most students favoured only moderate reform, proof that 'the self-appointed revolutionary elite derive their influence from nothing more than the inactivity of the student body as a whole'.[68] Council chose to interpret the referendum results as support for the status quo, announcing on 9 October that 'Council will not interfere with the penalties imposed by the Appeal Committee'.

The next day, a large MAS meeting (estimated at 5000–6000 by the Monash Labor Club, 4000 by the *Age* and 3000 by the *Sun*) called for the resignation of the council. But media attention focused on a second motion, formulated in response to the political attack from Dowling. The motion stated

> that this student general meeting . . . expresses a strong vote of confidence in the Vice-Chancellor. Whilst acknowledging that the Vice-Chancellor has not always acted wisely, this student general meeting states that in light of incredible pressure from within and without the University, he has been instrumental in keeping the University functioning. This student meeting considers that Dr. Matheson is currently the only person we would accept to run this University . . . if Dr. Matheson is removed, we will immediately consider a general strike of the University.[69]

The motion may have been less a declaration of confidence in Matheson than a rejection of calls for Monash to be placed in the hands of a tougher administrator.[70] However, Matheson had also been given a boost by a supportive petition signed by almost two-thirds of Monash's approximately 2000 staff in only five hours.[71] The Saturday papers were unanimous in their view that the outcome of the week's events was a personal victory for Matheson. The *Age* reported that Albert Langer had been jeered by other students for calling Matheson a 'bastard'.[72]

By now, it was nearly exam time. In early 1971, Matheson declared an amnesty on the disciplinary charges relating to the two October occupations, breaking the 'alternation of confrontation and subsequent disciplining that seemed to have become established'.[73]

The new guard

In the first half of the 1970s, Monash was back under control, at least in comparison to the havoc students were wreaking at La Trobe University. The introduction of the semester system in 1972 dampened political activity, as students could no longer neglect their studies until the end of the year. But Monash's 'troubles' were not yet over.

There were, says Foundation Professor of History John Legge, two waves of student action. The first, from 1967 to 1971, he views as the Australian counterpart of the student movement in Europe and America and 'political' in character. The second was directed to university matters, particularly assessment and course content.[74] Discontent first emerged in the 1971 'Smash the Exams' campaign, which encouraged students to disrupt examinations by burning papers, taking animals into exams ('200 mice, for example') or turning up drunk.[75] By the end of 1972, spurred on by the introduction of the semester system, demands grew for radical changes to assessment, including the abolition of competitive grading and staff–student control of course content. Students were sick of the academic 'assembly line' which viewed them as 'just passive cogs in the Faculty machine'.[76]

The Labor Club was not heavily involved in the second 'wave' of student action. The club had split in 1970 when Nadel formed the non-Maoist Independent Communist Caucus, and the remaining Maoist core of the Labor Club was increasingly engaged in the activities of the Worker-Student Alliance, formed in 1970, from its base at the notorious 'Bakery' in Greville Street, Prahran. By 1974, Trotskyites were the leading force on the left at Monash, through the Revolutionary Communist Club, or 'Rev Coms', the successor to Nadel's caucus. Tess Lee-Ack became the face of the Rev Coms. Lee-Ack, a PAC member of MAS who was also involved in the Women's Liberation and Gay Liberation clubs, reflected the emerging importance of identity-based politics on campus. This shift left the Maoists with little traction, as they were equivocal on the question of women's rights, and saw homosexuality as evidence of the decadence of capitalism, insisting that it didn't exist in China.[77]

The Rev Coms, influenced by the radical stance of the Victorian Secondary Teachers' Association on education policy, rejected assessment, and exams in particular, as 'serv[ing] no other purpose than to provide prospective employers with certification of certain competencies as well as evidence of a student's ability/willingness to conform to hierarchical structures and processes and submit to the discipline of the workplace'. They argued that a radical transformation in the social function of education could spur on revolutionary social change. 'We wanted to liberate education from the priorities of capitalism and make it free and accessible to all; it should enrich the lives and serve the interests of the majority of workers and the oppressed, rather than those of the minority of capitalists.'[78] Their campaign group Assessment Action attracted broad-based support. While arts students dominated, groups like the 'Dissident Physicists' were also involved. In October 1974, Monash's Medical Undergraduates Society marched through the city demanding changes to the Monash medical degree, including more contact with patients in the first three years of study.[79]

In the second half of 1974, Assessment Action led several incursions in the Administration Building, followed by an occupation that lasted eight days, the longest occupation ever to occur at Monash. The press heralded the return of old times: one headline read 'Langer's Ghost Stalks Monash'.[80] But this episode achieved something Langer never had. For the first time, police were called onto campus, at Pro Vice-Chancellor Dr John Swan's request. Seventy-six students were forcibly removed and charged with besetting a building. Matheson defended the calling of the police, telling the press that the students had held a wild party in the council chambers (a claim the students strenuously denied).[81]

Why Monash?

Other Australian universities experienced similar confrontations with students in this period, but Monash was the first to explode, inspiring activists at other institutions. What was it about Monash that made it the local home of international student activism?

Commentators then and later looked for causes in the nature of the university itself. Perhaps Monash's *newness* was fertile soil for the action of external influences—the war in Vietnam and conscription, the example of overseas protest movements? The 'lack of tradition' at Monash has been seen, by Matheson and others, as somehow destabilising its development.[82] Monash's rapid growth was also blamed for its troubles; like Berkeley in the United States, the university was held up as an example of the impersonal and alienating nature of student experience in an age of mass education.[83] 'Monash University Ltd', in the eyes of some of its students, was nothing more than a 'great big clumsy factory' producing three products: graduates, research knowledge and ideology.[84]

Others looked to explain the troubles by arguing that both staff and students at Monash were different, more inclined to revolutionary action. The *Australian* explained in 1970 that 'tradition and non-tradition' inevitably clashed at Monash due to its peculiar combination of a senior staff schooled in the traditions of established universities and a junior cohort who, 'too young for old values', sympathised more with students.[85] The Labor Club's membership included several staff members, including some who went on to be university administrators themselves, such as Ian Chubb and Marian Aveling (later Quartly). Even for those staff members not of a radical bent, unquestioned value was placed on free association and the rights of students to express their political opinions.[86]

History's Ian Turner, a founding member of the Staff Socialist Group at Monash, was among those staff members whose names became synonymous with staff radicalism. Turner recognised that Monash's emphasis on connecting theory with life (described in Chapter 3) exposed it to the risk of being perceived as subservient to the capitalist state. The university in modern industrial society, he said, faced two sets of contradictions:

> Firstly, that its intellectual tone and organisational structures are inevitably deeply affected by the dominant ideology of the society within which it operates, while it asserts a role as a centre

of free and critical inquiry, and, secondly, that its function as a provider of professional training (commonly conceived in narrow and conservative terms) conflicts with the needs of free inquiry.[87]

But, like other activist staff such as politics lecturer Max Teichmann, Turner was critical of the Labor Club's confrontational tactics and simplistic rhetoric. 'The University', he argued, 'is not a microcosm of Society, and the Administration is not a ruling class'.[88] The Labor Club in turn viewed Turner as a relic of the previous generation of radicals they sought to outdo.

How many Monash students were involved and engaged in political protest? Some, like genetics professor Bruce Holloway, have argued that 'the majority of students were not really interested'.[89] The huge turnouts for meetings suggest otherwise, at least at the height of the troubles. Activist Elliot Gingold gives a balanced assessment: 'We certainly did not have thousands of activists. But my impression was that the student body as a whole moved somewhat to the left during that period, and were certainly not as disinterested in what was going on around them as students in later times.'[90] Others have placed the radicals in the Arts Faculty and ECOPS rather than in the professional faculties, and it is true that observers like Matheson noted the 'special involvement of students of the social sciences' in the student movement.[91] But activists were busy in all the faculties; political broadsheets distributed around campus included *Spanner and Sickle* from the Engineering Socialists, *Red Atom* from Science Action and *Left Handed Lancet* from the Monash Medical Underground Revolutionary Left.

Participants believed that they were special: that Monash, as a new university, was 'a less conventional choice for bright students, so the bright students who chose it perhaps, were a little less conventional'.[92] A related theory was that students who had become radicalised at secondary school deliberately chose Monash. Certainly, from 1968 the Labor Club and other radical groups recruited in secondary schools through groups like Students in Dissent. Liz Porter arrived at Monash in 1969 already intending to join the Labor Club, 'elated' by the rumour that just to do so automatically earned you an ASIO file. The times were revolutionary, and 'Monash seemed the place to gulp it all down at once'.[93]

The making of a crisis

Monash's youthful staff and hopeful students were fertile ground for the seeds of radical praxis, but the activists alone did not make the crisis of the late 1960s. University authorities were inclined to claim that the problems at Monash were at least in part the product of intense media attention. Student protests made appealing news stories, and 'Monash', a six-letter word, fitted easily into a headline. Matheson complained that 'the press can be relied on, with pathetic single-mindedness, to report any student misdemeanour as fully as if it were an international incident'.[94] The role of the media in shaping public perceptions of Monash was significant. The public took the media's word for it that students at Monash were 'abusing their privileges' and 'wasting tax-payers' money'.[95] Arguably, the media helped to shape the tone and style of student protest and authorities' responses to that protest.

Others saw Monash's student problems as having been encouraged by problems within the administration. Matheson's tight control over university matters was experienced by students as an inflexible 'establishment'.[96] Critically, the administration played into the hands of the radicals at crucial moments, thus exacerbating student discontent. Jim Falk recalls that 'the administration, led by a rather nice but perhaps too self-confident Vice-Chancellor, made a series of strategic errors . . . which made a very bad impression on a generation seeking to reshape themselves from the shadow of their parents'.[97] Matheson's 'niceness' was itself a problem. Under pressure, his liberalism could swing suddenly to authoritarianism, perplexing students. Some observers believed that the vice-chancellor's reading of events at Monash overestimated the pressure he and the university were suffering. In 1969, John Legge wrote to a colleague that Matheson had come back from the United States with 'dramatic comparisons in mind' and had misjudged the Monash situation accordingly.[98]

The possibility of violence at Monash was often mooted in these years. The mass confrontations were inherently threatening, especially when large groups sought access—sometimes forcibly—to spaces from which students were excluded. The administration claimed on several occasions that students had used violence, but these claims related to the

News crews at Monash, 1971. Some members of the administration blamed Monash's 'troubles' on keen media attention.

'jostling' of staff members, or to destruction of property, rather than to serious assaults.

It is unlikely that Monash was ever in danger of being closed. As the Labor Club pointed out, imminent closure was only ever evoked by Matheson and subsequently taken up by the media.[99] Matheson was partly responsible for the atmosphere of crisis. His closed-circuit address to the university rivalled the student occupations for dramatic effect. For all that, it is clear that at the height of the student troubles Matheson was deeply concerned about the university's future. His addresses and letters reveal real fears about the possibility of a Berkeley or Stanford situation developing at Monash. Premier Bolte's displeasure with Monash was palpable, and he may well have used his powers to try to remove Matheson and his administration.

But the university was far from being on its knees. As Matheson himself wrote in retrospect:

> Throughout those troublesome years when, according to the press, Monash was in a state of chaos the reality was quite different. The student assault was a sort of *obbligato*, shrill and unreal, to the normal life of the university; the real themes and their development continued at a lower pitch, substantial, reliable and, in the end, triumphant.[100]

Legacies

The Monash 'troubles' petered out after the 1974 occupation: by 1975, 'student apathy' was again being lamented.[101] What was the legacy of Monash's years of radical student activity? Parking was a lost cause, but there was some modification of assessment. In the Arts Faculty, exams were abolished or their weighting reduced in favour of continuous assessment. Some provision, too, was made for students to be involved in determining course content. Changes were won in student representation on university, faculty and departmental committees; the period 'marked the change from universities being *in loco parentis* to a situation where students became much more involved in everything'.[102] But they were no longer involved in mass student meetings; the grassed area between the Menzies and the Union buildings was transformed by a series of knolls from a large open space to a disjointed one, never again to be used as a forum.

Continuous assessment and student representation came to campuses across Australia in the 1970s, and both would probably have come to Monash regardless of the years of student protest. Perhaps the important question is not how the period of student protest changed the institution, but how it shaped the students who were at Monash during this time. Many former Monash students who were only ever part of the so-called 'silent majority' were profoundly influenced by the political discussions and activism that were all around them. Elliot Gingold still meets ex-Monash students 'who apparently never got off their seats to do anything at all, but identify with the student movement of that time'.[103] The legacy of the Monash protests may be found not in the institution but in the broader culture. Students who were part of the Monash protests, either as participants or observers, have made an important mark in Australian public life as lawyers, social workers, teachers, politicians and trade union officials, as environmentalists and as feminists. Student radicals might not have brought in the socialist revolution, but they 'really changed society'.[104]

One of the sadder legacies of the troubles at Monash was their effect on its vice-chancellor. Matheson was in many ways a classic liberal: a man

'He wore himself out at Monash.' Matheson after his retirement, 1980.

basically in agreement with the prevailing organisation of society, though with a keen sense of its flaws. He believed the university, while remaining politically neutral, should draw the attention of society to 'what is wrong and what might be done by way of remedy'.[105] But he also had a strong urge towards control in what he saw as benign, modernising directions. Matheson was confounded by his encounters with students who did not play by the 'rules' of liberal reformism, who not only criticised the university he had made, but seemed to want to destroy it. By 1969, Matheson was engaged in a 'guerrilla war' against student 'wreckers'.[106] War required a martial approach, which did not come easily to the Quaker-schooled Matheson. When police were called to the campus in 1974, Matheson finally decided to retire. For him, the event represented the 'end of the idealism that had brought Monash into being'.[107]

Years earlier, Matheson had helped his sixteen-year-old son Roger to build a plywood canoe in the shed behind the vice-chancellor's residence. When it was finished, they drove to Eildon, launched the new craft into the Goulburn River and paddled downstream through its swirling, fast-moving waters to Seymour. For Matheson, the experience of leading a new university was similar to the thrills and perils of white-water canoeing:

> One has the same sense of being hurried along by events over which one has little or no control; the same knowledge that once embarked one is committed to a voyage that cannot be halted; the same feeling of navigating perilously between hazards to left and right. Above all, canoeist and vice-chancellor alike often find themselves rounding a bend and being confronted with a parting of the ways: in a few brief moments a choice has to be made upon woefully inadequate information and then one is committed to a route from which there can be no turning back.[108]

The image is revealing, not only of Matheson's confident assumption of authority—he was the helmsman of the university—but of his rueful recognition of its limits. He had steered the university through turbulent times into calmer waters. He had ridden the rapids of torrential growth, held a safe middle course against the cross-currents of university and state politics, and kept his craft afloat. (The real canoe journey had not been quite so successful: the canoe had capsized, and the two adventurers arrived at their destination soaked to the skin.)

Monash was sailing more smoothly by the mid-1970s, but the student troubles had left their mark on Louis Matheson. Louis Waller recalls that Matheson was 'very keenly hurt' by the events, which 'changed him deeply'.[109] On one occasion, Matheson went missing after an upsetting confrontation at a student meeting. When he arrived back at his office, later than expected, 'he didn't know where he'd been, he didn't know what he'd been doing'. His family believes that the events of 1967–74 contributed to the stroke he had in 1989, which left him confined to a wheelchair until his death, in 2002. Matheson, says his wife, Audrey, gave his life to Monash. 'If he did a thing, he did it with the whole of himself . . . I think he wore himself out at Monash.'[110]

LOT'S WIFE VOL XV NO. 18
AUGUST 11th, 1975

SHOCK HORROR SCOOP !! MONASH IN COMMIE VICE-CHANCELLOR BID !!

INTERLUDE: A VANISHING VICE-CHANCELLOR

As Matheson's retirement approached, his colleagues began to ponder the troubling question of his successor. Despite the conflicts of his later years, Monash remained very much Louis Matheson's university. Was anyone big enough to fill his shoes? Should anyone even try? Dean of Medicine Rod Andrew, a democrat except in his own faculty, wondered whether a rotating vice-chancellorship, like Oxford's, might be 'more consonant with the changing mores of our community'.[1] But his was an eccentric view; almost everyone else wanted a leader who combined as many of Matheson's best qualities as possible. He should be a 'distinguished and imaginative academic', 'ambitious and accomplished', a 'skilful chairman of committees', 'a person of sound judgement', a 'competent' administrator experienced in dealing with government. His wife (it was assumed that the appointee would be a man) should be 'either an asset or neutral'.[2]

In a large field, one applicant, 45-year-old John Vaizey, Professor of Economics at London's Brunel University, clearly stood out. The younger son of a Greenwich wharfinger, Vaizey had progressed from a London grammar school to Cambridge, where he took first-class honours in economics. A serious childhood illness had left him, he confessed, with a determination to pack all he could into a life he sensed (accurately, as it turned out) might be brilliant, eventful and short. During the 1950s and 1960s, he moved restlessly between appointments in Cambridge, Oxford and London, married the American-born art critic Marina Stansky, and published prolifically, not only in his main field, the economics of education, but in everything from the history of the brewing industry to the future of social democracy. A self-described socialist, he had already begun the political metamorphosis that would take him to the Conservative benches of the House of Lords.[3] In 1974, he visited the University of Adelaide, fell in love with Australia—a vision tinted with the wine and roses of the Don Dunstan era—and, when the Monash vice-chancellorship was advertised, threw his hat in the ring.

Lot's Wife *welcomes Monash's new vice-chancellor.*

To the Monash selection committee, Vaizey looked like a brilliant catch. 'He is creative, original, fertile . . . quick to pass judgement, generous, compassionate, urbane', his Cambridge contemporary Geoffrey Harcourt enthused.[4] 'An ideas rather than an organisation man', the Oxford historian Alan Bullock agreed.[5] Some of his Oxford acquaintances were more cautious. 'John doesn't suffer fools—I don't mean gladly but at all', Bill Williams, Warden of Rhodes House, confided to a member of the selection committee, Professor Robert Porter. Vaizey, the committee agreed, was their first choice, but they wanted to meet him and negotiate terms in person.[6]

In June, Vaizey flew out to Melbourne and dazzled the selection committee, now eager to recruit him. Back in his hotel, the candidate tried to reconcile his conflicting emotions: gratitude, exhaustion and anxiety, especially about his 'family situation'. He needed time to think. Back in London, he bombarded Comptroller Frank Johnson with questions. Could council member Brian Hone get Vaizey's daughter Polly into Geelong Grammar and himself into the Melbourne Club?[7] How soon would the university act on its plan to build a new vice-chancellor's residence to replace the old farmhouse where the Mathesons had lived, contentedly, for seventeen years? And what could Melbourne offer his wife, Marina, to make up for the loss of her prestigious job as art critic for the *Sunday Times*?

That a vice-chancellor's wife might be something more than a supportive consort did not at first occur to Monash's selection committee. Though eager to support her husband's aspirations, Marina Vaizey feared the prospect of becoming the chatelaine of a suburban farmhouse, dispensing tea and sympathy to professors' wives. She would like to come 'if I can find something of my own to do in Australia (pace women's lib! But I am giving up a top job and a good income)'.[8] As the Vaizeys pondered their future, Monash professors passing through London waited on the candidate, offering reassurance and seeking to gauge his inclinations. If the decision had been Vaizey's alone, Louis Matheson reported at the end of June, he would already have accepted, but 'his wife is a V.I.P. in the London art world & does not want to leave the British/U.S./European scene . . . I fear they won't come', he confided to new chancellor Richard Eggleston.[9]

Eggleston, who had taken over the search from Deputy Chancellor Ian Langlands, was eager to make a decision. The committee assured council:

A man with such imagination and so many ideas will sometimes be wrong and may sometimes be impatient with others less gifted, but the Committee believes the risk to be small and, in any event, outweighed by the advantages and distinction the appointment would gain the university.[10]

Council resolved to offer the job to Vaizey, who immediately cabled his acceptance.[11] With the long season of indecision apparently over, the Vaizeys quit London for their summer holidays, a cruise in the eastern Mediterranean.

In Melbourne, news of the appointment was greeted with enthusiasm, even incredulity. 'A "magnificent gadfly" heads for Monash', the *Age*'s London correspondent reported. Sitting in his London club, the Garrick, sipping champagne from a silver tankard, the new vice-chancellor presented a more elegant image for Monash than the 'dour engineer' Louis Matheson.[12] 'SHOCK HORROR SCOOP!! MONASH IN COMMIE VICE-CHANCELLOR BID!!' screamed the headlines in *Lot's Wife*. 'Is it possible that Monash has, at last, got something RIGHT?' After sixteen years of 'Mathesonian mediocrity', the university had chosen 'a person of character and imagination', and a socialist to boot. 'All this seems a little too good to be true.'[13] It was.

The Vaizeys returned to London at the beginning of September, 'happy' and 'refreshed',[14] but with many of their questions still unanswered. A glimmer of hope had appeared for Marina, with the rumour that British gallery director Bryan Robertson, fearful of the hostile and homophobic reaction among a section of the Melbourne artistic community, had declined the directorship of the National Gallery of Victoria. 'Marina extremely keen on job and highly qualified', Vaizey cabled Johnson. 'Please inquire soonest.' Johnson inquired, but the news was discouraging. The gallery, it appeared, had already offered the job to the runner-up, Eric Rowlison.[15]

While the Vaizeys wavered, the economic outlook in Australia was worsening. On 10 September, Johnson wrote to Vaizey, enclosing the architect's brief for the proposed new residence, estimated to cost

$150 000. 'More worrying [than the scale of expenditure]', he noted, was 'the nascent feeling amongst some of the staff, especially academic, against spending money on building a new house at a time when . . . they are facing the prospect of serious curtailment of research programmes'. Flinders University, he noted, had just scrapped plans for a vice-chancellor's residence. 'What is your reaction to these tidbits of information?'

On 15 September, Vaizey cabled: 'We have decided regretfully to stay here. Letter follows.' The fish, it seemed, had slipped the hook. By now, however, the personality Vaizey had revealed during the negotiations was causing misgivings among the committee. Eggleston acted speedily to bring the matter to a conclusion, immediately cabling his acceptance of Vaizey's resignation.[16] A week went by, and six other letters arrived discussing various aspects of the prospective appointment, before the one promised in his cable. It would be 'outrageous' to spend $150 000 on a new house, Vaizey admitted. 'I would be represented as part of a self-seeking conspiracy to feather my own nest.' Yet he and Marina were 'abandoning a way of life' and a house to which they were very attached. (A four-storey Regency terrace in Chiswick, in fact.) A residence in South Yarra was no solution 'because the whole attraction of Monash for us is the vitality and energy present on its campus'. 'I see no solution to this dilemma which does not involve unanswerable criticism from the students and the more radical staff', he concluded. Even now, though, the star candidate was loath to relinquish his antipodean idyll. Several critical passages of the typewritten letter had been altered in ink, apparently to keep the door ajar. 'I ought to carry on here' was crossed out and 'to think more carefully' inserted in the margin.[17]

On 19 September, while Eggleston was once more cabling his acceptance of Vaizey's resignation, the *Times Education Supplement* was announcing that the galloping economist was 'off to Australia'. 'People are always criticising me for being a dilettante and a gadfly and saying that I can't hold down a real job. I want to show them that it isn't true.' He rhapsodised about the 'magnificent' Monash campus, 'near the ocean, two hours' drive from the skiing', and praised the 'go-getting aggressiveness of the Australians'.[18]

Determined to prevent further embarrassment, Eggleston telephoned Vaizey on 30 September to confirm his resignation and propose a press statement. Vaizey agreed, but twenty-four hours later he had changed his mind again. His cable of 15 September was not meant as a resignation, he later explained, but more like 'going on strike' until the outstanding matters had been resolved—and he would not agree to a press statement. So the university issued a statement stating simply that Vaizey would not be taking up the appointment.[19]

The controversy rumbled on for a few days but was soon submerged in the tumult surrounding the dismissal of the Whitlam government. 'I must say that the action of Sir John Kerr and the subsequent election seem to have vindicated me in the eyes of my colleagues here totally', Vaizey confided to Bob Porter. 'Australia is now regarded as a thoroughly unreliable place!'[20] Monash also realised it may have had a lucky escape. For one brief shining moment, it had entertained a vision of Camelot in Clayton, a happy community of scholars led by a dazzling prince of intellect, with his own talented Guinevere. But when the prince turned out to be more interested in his castle than his courtiers the vision quickly faded.

By the end of the affair, Monash was further from its goal than it had been at the beginning. All it could do now was to appoint one of its reliable lieutenants, Bill Scott, to serve for a year and begin the search again. Scott was the proverbial 'safe pair of hands', a cautious, congenial senior academic who would do nothing brave and nothing foolish. Once bitten, the university would be doubly shy of a leader who dared and promised too much. Besides, by the early months of 1976, when the selection committee began its work again, the entire mood of the country had changed. Life in the university, in the new prime minister's phrase, was not meant to be easy. It would take leadership of a steadier kind to navigate the lean years ahead.

SIX

THE MULTIVERSITY

This was a farm and this is still a farm.
Only the produce differs.

PHILIP MARTIN, 'A MONASH POEM', 1986

After the excitement and disappointment of the Vaizey affair, a more sober mood settled upon the university. Everyone agreed that a 'quiet interval' was now desirable. Instead of chasing brilliant exotics with unrealistic expectations, the selection committee resolved to confine its attention to candidates with 'significant Australian experience'.[1] They still hoped to recruit an outsider, but preferably a thoroughbred stayer with a pedigree everyone respected.

In July 1976, council member Brian Hone, Headmaster of Melbourne Grammar School, briefed the committee on a visit to ANU where he had called on Professor Ray Martin. Martin was the son of Sir Leslie Martin, physicist and education advisor to the Menzies government. His career had followed a traditional path, from Scotch College to the University of Melbourne and then, in his father's footsteps, to Cambridge, where he had gained a doctorate in chemistry. In 1954, he had become a senior lecturer at the University of New South Wales and, in 1962, at just thirty-six, had been appointed first professor of inorganic chemistry

By the early 1980s, Monash's character as a 'multiversity'—large, complex and closely linked to its urban environment—was clearly imprinted on the landscape of Melbourne's south-eastern suburbs. Its character as a drive-in university is apparent in the arrested development of the university's student residences and its ever-growing border of car parks, while, to the north, the new Mulgrave bypass—the future Monash Freeway—has appeared.

at the University of Melbourne. It was there that he had first met Hone, a fellow player at Vice-Chancellor David Derham's Saturday afternoon tennis parties.[2] By the time they met again in Canberra, Martin was fifty years of age and had just completed a term as director of the Research School of Chemistry at ANU.

Hone had invited himself to morning coffee, compared notes with some of Martin's colleagues, and confirmed his impression of a quiet, charming, approachable man, a fine scientist of high integrity, not forceful or politically engaged, but capable of being 'resolute and tough' when the occasion required it. 'He will do', Hone concluded, and, after interviewing him, the selection committee, relieved to have found a sound man at last, resolved to appoint him.[3]

The Martins were happy with the vice-chancellor's residence as it was: all they asked was that an en-tout-cas tennis court be installed in the grounds.[4] Martin's vice-chancellorship, like Matheson's, would be a

Melbourne-born chemist Ray Martin brought research distinction, charm and quiet authority to the vice-chancellorship, 1977.

family affair. His wife and their children lived on campus. Rena Martin, also a scientist, picked up where Audrey Matheson—'the first lady of Monash'—had left off. She was 'a tower of strength in providing the necessary facilities to entertain people and in supporting me in every way a wife can', Martin recalled.[5] The presence of a number of senior staff from the early years, including Butchart and many foundation professors, contributed to the sense of continuity.[6]

Martin's appointment ensured stability, rather than the 'rethink of Monash' that had previously appeared desirable to some of the younger professoriate.[7] An unassuming and consensus-seeking man, he took a restrained approach to administration. His arrival coincided with the end of the golden years of university funding, which (under the guiding eye of Leslie Martin) had seen new academic vacancies, opportunities for promotion and money for new buildings, equipment and research programs. For the next decade, Commonwealth funding for higher education remained virtually stationary. Monash, alongside other universities, declared itself to be in 'steady state'.[8]

But steady did not mean static. The challenge for the university, in Martin's view, was to adapt and initiate—and not become set in its ways—within these straitened circumstances.[9] This meant supporting and promoting any initiative that advanced the university's raison d'être: scholarly excellence. Monash entered the new era in a strong position. After a decade and a half of rapid expansion, it was a high-achieving organism full of 'research-seasoned' staff.[10] The goal was to maintain this standing, reaping what had been sown in the Farm's first decade, and to secure funding sources to further strengthen Monash as a research-based university. Martin took quiet satisfaction in the steadily accumulating evidence of Monash's scientific and scholarly reputation: the numbers of its staff elected to learned academies,[11] its increasing research grant income and the steady growth of its Library's collections, which by the early 1980s had overtaken those of the University of Melbourne.

Foundation Professor of Chemistry Ron Brown believed that the smooth sailing that characterised Martin's term in office proved the effectiveness of his management style: nothing '[came] to the surface'. The true worth of his contribution might not be recognised immediately.[12] This indeed may be true. A number of important initiatives of the Martin era crystallised only after his departure. His quest for outside funding led the university towards greater engagement with the possibilities of commercialisation, and administrative reforms that took place in the Martin years established the conditions for the transformations that were to come.

Monash, in its seventeenth year when Martin took over, was no longer being 'made', but was yet to be 'remade'. Its dynamism in the Martin years came from the bottom up: from excellence in research, rather than from administrative innovation. The sense that 'nothing was happening' is partly rooted in the fact that no dominant narrative was imposed to unify the many things that *were* taking place. The university bequeathed to Martin was much more complex—as an institution and as a community—than the Monash of the early 1960s. The student *Orientation Handbook* for 1977, the beginning of the Martin era, noted that

> in no way is Monash a University. It is more a Multiversity—it is not a whole, not one world, but many. There is no one mind about Monash, about its nature, objects, aims etc. There would be few people in Monash with the same idea of what they are doing in it or trying to achieve (if anything). Don't look for a university mentality. Look at all the mentalities and then evaluate them individually. Nowhere are mentalities more apparent, formalised and distinguishable than at a Multiversity.[13]

Monash had reached a size where special effort was needed to keep lines of communication open between different sections of the university. It was increasingly difficult to maintain a sense of 'single-mindedness'.[14] Yet already the university with its many mentalities was looking beyond itself—if not yet to the world, then to the local community, industry and the market. If Matheson was largely concerned with building Monash, then Martin began the process by which it would look increasingly outwards.

The steady state

The view was not always encouraging. Universities came under increasing scrutiny by parsimonious governments and a public eager to know that its taxes were being spent usefully. The Fraser government, which had come to power after a constitutional crisis in which the campuses became a hotbed of outrage, had little reason to look upon the universities with affection. As John Legge observed, the public, too, often looked askance at 'expensive institutions, staffed by privileged people who have 26 weeks holiday a year'.[15] Government funding, whether it was measured as a proportion of government spending or in dollars per student, declined during the Fraser years. In 1978, a deluge of inquiries and government reports on higher education signalled that the golden age of government largesse was over. In Victoria, the Partridge Committee of Inquiry into Post-Secondary Education imposed a reduction in the number of students admitted to engineering and education at Monash. Universities were often compared unfavourably with colleges of advanced education, which seemed to deliver a more useful product at a lower price. Martin lamented that government policy was increasingly governed by 'the power of the purse' with little regard for the essential values and freedoms of a university.[16]

Looking inwards, the vice-chancellor also had reason for concern. Monash had grown quickly during the 1960s, recruiting the best and brightest young academics it could find. Many of its founding professors were appointed in their thirties and early forties. Twenty years later, a lot of them were still there: by 1980, almost three-quarters of the professoriate had been at Monash for a decade or more. Meanwhile, the academic proletariat of young teaching fellows, whose enthusiasm and ambition drove much of the university's culture of radical experiment, had been thinned to pay the salaries of the university's middle-aged bulge of senior lecturers. A growing proportion of university funds was swallowed up in paying for the salary increments, promotions and superannuation contributions of its tenured staff. From the late 1970s, the university's staff–student ratio began to decline until, by 1982, it was the worst in the nation.[17]

Conscious of its newer competitors and of its limited capacity to acquire new blood, Monash now began to admit, and even celebrate, its character as 'the last of the old' universities. One touchstone of its traditionalism was its reluctance to abandon its founding belief in the rule of the 'god-professor'. By the late 1970s, most Australian universities, including many of the 'sandstones', had changed their statutes to permit non-professors to be appointed heads of departments. In 1980, however, a committee headed by Professor Kevin Westfold found that the Monash tradition of professorial headship had served the university well and should continue. Monash would remain the last bastion of the academic barons.

The female academic

Most of the academic barons were, of course, male; but there were a few exceptions. In the 1970s and 1980s, Monash congratulated itself on having more women professors than any other Australian university: Maureen Brunt in economics (1966), Mollie Holman in physiology (1970), Enid Campbell in law (1967), Marie Neale in education (1970) and Jean Whyte in librarianship (1975). All had prevailed against an unwritten convention that, while women might aspire to higher education, they should not expect to reach the academic heights.

Some, like physiologist Mollie Holman, had had the advantage of academic parents (her father was an influential radiologist) and an inspiring education at Merton Hall. But her remarkable scientific talent and ambition were hers alone. After completing an MSc at Melbourne, she progressed to doctoral study at Oxford, where her pioneering research on electrical activity in smooth muscle won international attention. Attracting her from Melbourne in 1963 was regarded as a coup for the new university. She became a magnet for young researchers, an outstanding supervisor and mentor, especially to young women. In 1970, the year she gained a personal chair, she was also elected to the Australian Academy of Science, one of a handful of women to achieve the distinction.

Monash's first woman professor, Maureen Brunt, came from humbler origins. She grew up in working-class Coburg, the daughter of a self-made grocer. One day, her mother, who kept the books for the shop, overheard her husband announcing that his son would go to a private school. She insisted that Maureen should also have the chance. After three years at Coburg High School, Maureen arrived at the Presbyterian Ladies College, where, she recalls, 'I got a bit of a vision of the academic life'. To please her father, she enrolled in a commerce degree at the University of Melbourne. A quiet but determined presence among the forceful ex-servicemen who dominated honours classes in the late 1940s, Brunt was already entranced by economics. 'Nobody encouraged me', she recalls, 'it was just Economics pushing me along'. Her first-class honours thesis on the economics of retailing won her a scholarship to Harvard.

Professor Maureen Brunt, Monash's first female professor (and only the third woman to be appointed to a chair in Australia), c. 1966.

There, she remembers, for 'the first time I could have an academic conversation with women'. After stints at Melbourne, Adelaide and Harvard, she accepted an invitation to a chair at Monash, where her old Melbourne colleague Don Cochrane was dean of the new ECOPS. 'Going to Harvard gives you confidence', she later reflected. It also gave her the kudos to overcome the gender divide. America had confirmed her bent towards problems of competition and regulation, and instilled the conviction that free markets were necessary for free societies. Over the following three decades, she became an authority on the legal and economic aspects of trade practices and economic regulation. Like other academic women of her generation, she saw her rise as a combination of luck and personal determination.[18]

The successes of these stars, however, only threw into relief the general disparity between the academic opportunities of men and women. While Monash had more women professors, the proportion of women in other academic positions was lower than in the newer universities, or even at the older University of Melbourne.[19] In the era of Germaine Greer's *The Female Eunuch*, the female academic at Monash had still to be liberated. Monash—'a place of causes', as poet and English lecturer Jenny Strauss calls it—had one more cause to embrace. A self-described 'pushy female', Strauss was among those who won a first small measure of reform when the university granted paid maternity leave in 1975.[20] It was slower, however, to introduce more comprehensive measures. In 1983, after members of the Staff Association met with Martin to propose an equal opportunity program, the university announced the appointment of an Equal Opportunity Research Fellow, to investigate gender disparities in the employment and promotion of academic and general staff. In the meantime, women academics and general staff had formed an Association of Women Employees at Monash University. Over 120 women attended its first meeting, which was addressed by the newly appointed research fellow, former English lecturer Dr Gabrielle Baldwin.

Baldwin's report, completed in May 1985, presented a dismal picture. Most of Monash's women employees were concentrated in low-paid, low-status, insecure jobs. Only one in ten tenured staff members was female. While almost four-fifths of male academics were tenured, only 44 per cent of women were.[21] Men dominated the university's decision-making bodies: thirty of council's thirty-three members were male, along with 126 of the 133 standing committee members. Only on one committee did women form a majority: the Committee for People with Handicaps.[22] These patterns reflected long-ingrained practice and attitudes, but, according to Baldwin, even recent appointments to the university showed little change.[23]

By October 1986, Monash was under pressure to comply with the federal government's Affirmative Action (Equal Opportunity for Women) Act. With little time to lose, it established an Equal Opportunity Advisory Committee as a standing committee of council and appointed an equal opportunity coordinator, Dr Margaret James, who started work in February 1987. By the middle of the year, council had formally declared its intention to eliminate discrimination on the basis of race, colour or gender. It had set its course but had a long way to travel.

Pieces of the whole

At a time when knowledge was leaping disciplinary boundaries and ambitious academics were resisting the rule of the god-professors, Monash's system of academic government could easily have become a straightjacket. Happily, the university quickly evolved a new structure—the academic centre or institute—that offered an alternative avenue for academic innovation. Centres tended to focus on interdisciplinary research and graduate study, usually drew their membership from several departments or faculties, and had a flatter, more informal structure, often rotating their leadership among participants. Centres institutionalised the conversations, insights and enthusiasms that constantly bubble up in any robust and healthy academic community.

From its beginnings, Monash had leaned towards an experimental, clinical approach to teaching and research (see Chapter 3). It sought to be responsive to its external environment, translating theory into practice and refining theory in the light of experience. Centres were an organic expression of this outlook. Sometimes their sphere of influence was local, the university's immediate urban environment; more often it was national or international. Centres were more nimble, more capable of improvisation and more self-reliant than departments. Many bore the hallmark of the university's progressive, secular ethos.

Four centres had been established in Matheson's time, but by the end of Martin's there were fifteen. They included centres for research into Aboriginal affairs, migrant studies, policy studies, general and comparative literature, child studies, early human development, molecular biology and medicine, environmental studies, continuing education, laser studies, commercial law and applied legal research, and Japanese studies.

The centre idea had modest beginnings. In June 1964, following informal discussions with his colleagues in Arts and ECOPS, Foundation Professor of History John Legge proposed the foundation of a Centre of Southeast Asian Studies to coordinate postgraduate work on the region. Since his arrival, Legge had championed the development of Asian studies at Monash, and by 1964 the university had made appointments in Asian languages, politics and anthropology as well as history. At undergraduate level, he argued, Monash might aspire to cover the whole of Asia, 'from Suez to Vladivostok', but postgraduate work was necessarily more concentrated. Since Melbourne and ANU had together annexed the major fields of China, India and Japan, Monash was left with 'little room for manoeuvre'. Southeast Asia was relatively less developed, its destiny was close to Australia's interests and, coincidentally of course, it was his own field of inquiry! Most of the staff would come from the participating departments, so all that the centre required, apart from space, was a professor-director, a secretary and some money for research and scholarships.[24]

With this modest endowment, the first Monash centre was born. The idea quickly caught on. Proposals for centres of Australian and American studies received a cooler reception from Arts Dean Bill Scott, already worrying as he was about where all the professorial and secretarial salaries were coming from.[25] In ECOPS, newly arrived lecturer Colin Tatz wrote to Matheson proposing a 'Bureau of Aboriginal Affairs', 'to initiate, support, conduct and encourage investigations that may lead to a greater knowledge of the Australian Aborigines and the relations that exist or should exist between them and the rest of the Australian community'. Matheson was cautiously interested, though nervous lest Monash appear to infringe on the territory of Canberra's newly established Australian Institute for Aboriginal Studies. The agreed title of the new centre— 'Centre for Research into Aboriginal Affairs'—avoided any suggestion of an anthropological or archaeological approach.[26]

Each centre inevitably reflected the interests and commitments of its founders: in the case of the Centre of Southeast Asian Studies, of Legge, political scientist Herb Feith and its first full-time director, Jamie Mackie. All three had been drawn to Indonesia early in the post-independence period, absorbing something of the democratic aspirations of the new nation. Feith and Mackie had worked alongside Indonesians in nation-building tasks, Feith as a co-founder of Australian Volunteers Abroad. With the rise of Suharto and the coming of the Vietnam War, the focus of the centre shifted towards Indo-China, the interest of the centre's second director (1968–87), ex-American diplomat and historian of modern Cambodia David Chandler. While history and politics were paramount, the centre also engaged linguists, literary scholars, film critics, musicologists, anthropologists and educationalists. By the 1970s, it had become one of the world's leading research centres on the region, welcoming a steady stream of international visitors and producing several doctoral graduates who, like Yale's Ben Kiernan, became influential figures in the field.

Some of Monash's intellectual drive came from the talented cohort of academics whose families had fled Europe just before or after the Second World War. Their personal or family experiences of oppression, genocide, displacement and exile shaped their outlook and were registered in intellectual projects as different as sociolinguistics, law reform, peace studies and bioethics. Common to them all was a resolute resistance to all forms of discrimination and a commitment to rational, progressive, ethical reform. Herb Feith, Michael Clyne and Peter Singer, who each led one of Monash's influential centres, were all sons of Viennese Jewish families who had fled Nazi persecution in 1938. Louis Waller, whose parents had fled Poland in the same year, contributed to several centres before playing a leading role in the founding of the Australian Centre for Jewish Civilisation in 1992. Their influence as teachers, research supervisors and writers reached well beyond Australia and the academy. It would be hard to underestimate their collective contribution to the reputation of the university in the 1970s and 1980s.

Feith had originally gone to Indonesia, his biographer noted, 'to help him resolve tensions between his European and Australian self'.[27] Michael Clyne had experienced similar tensions growing up in wartime Melbourne. 'We led a rather isolated life', he recalled. 'We spoke German at home, in our first-floor flat. English was spoken in public places, including the backyard where the neighbours could hear.'[28] From his earliest years, Clyne was aware of how language shaped social experience. After graduating from the University of Melbourne, he joined the German Department at Monash in 1962 and completed the first PhD in the Faculty of Arts. Over the course of the next forty years, he became an internationally celebrated socio-linguist, publishing over 400 papers, mainly on bilingualism and language maintenance. The Centre for Migrant Studies (later the Centre for Migrant and Intercultural Studies), which he co-founded in 1974, became an energetic advocate for multiculturalism. Melbourne, 'the multilingual capital of Australia',[29] as Clyne called it, became his social laboratory: with geographer John McKay, he published a language atlas of the city and encouraged his students to investigate the rich tapestry of intercultural experience on the university's doorstep.

Many of these early centres engaged in both research and advocacy; they were 'centres for', not simply 'centres of'. 'It will not be a "do-good" organisation. Nor, I think, should it be a purely academic body', Tatz wrote about his proposed bureau.[30] Tatz was a product of yet another exodus, the emigration of white liberals from South Africa after the 1960 Sharpeville Massacre. His experience of growing up in a Jewish household, experiencing mild discrimination himself yet witnessing the deeper discrimination of apartheid, inspired a lifelong interest in the fate of 'outsiders', including Australia's most disadvantaged group, the Aborigines.[31] When he left Monash, in 1970, Elizabeth Eggleston, law lecturer and daughter of Monash chancellor Richard Eggleston, succeeded him as director of the Aboriginal Research Centre. She extended its work into issues of law, health and race relations before her premature death in 1976.[32] Only in the late 1970s did the centre get its first Indigenous directors, with the appointments of Dr Colin Bourke, an educationist (1977–81), and Dr Eve Fesl (1981–93), a linguist trained by Michael Clyne.

One of the connecting threads in Monash's evolving network of interdisciplinary centres was the conviction that social change required a critical understanding of culture. The key to understanding culture, the 1970s believed, was to have the right theory. Competing strains of Marxism, utilitarianism, feminism, Freudianism, post-structuralism and postmodernism swept the campus. 'A hundred flowers seemed to bloom', a student of that era, Peter Beilharz, recalls. 'Monash Politics was a hothouse.' Students conducted reading classes on Marx's *Capital* and a group including lecturer Alistair Davidson and Beilharz founded the journal *Thesis Eleven*. The Centre for Comparative Literature, founded by scholars in European literature in 1970, became a home for other brands of cultural theory, including post-structuralism, feminism and cultural studies. Historian Ian Turner, making his way from Marxism to democratic socialism, approached his studies of Australian popular culture in a more demotic, lighthearted style. His Ron Barassi Memorial Lecture, held in Grand Final week each year from 1966 until his sudden death in 1978, became a highlight of the campus calendar. Wearing a Richmond beanie, with a can of beer and a meat pie at his elbow, Turner insisted that the lecture was not a joke: 'I try to answer some serious social questions football raises and to pose others'.[33]

'Carn the Tiges!' Professor Ian Turner in costume for his annual Ron Barassi Memorial Lecture.

If social difference was rooted in culture, then changing the culture was the key to progressive reform. New Zealand–born Marie Neale, who became Monash's first female professor of education, in 1970, was interested in the education of 'exceptional' children, those disadvantaged because they did not live up to cultural expectations of 'normal' behaviour, either because their learning was impeded by physical or psychological disability or because they were exceptionally gifted. In 1976, through the benevolence of a Melbourne businessman, she became director of the Dinah and Henry Krongold Centre for Exceptional Children, which conducted research as well as offering a multi-disciplinary therapeutic program designed to enable children to resume regular schooling. Neale's conviction that it was possible to release 'the ingenuity inherent in everyone' was another face of the Monash ethos of progressive reform.[34] The Krongolds' gift was Monash's first notable private benefaction, inaugurating the strong philanthropic link between Melbourne's Jewish community and the university that bore the name of its most famous son.

In 1979, Monash researchers Carl Wood and Alan Trounson achieved international fame with the announcement of the first successful pregnancy by in-vitro fertilisation (IVF) in Australia, and only the second in the world. Wood had been appointed professor of obstetrics and gynaecology in 1965, when he was thirty-five, and, along with several other Monash researchers, including David de Kretser, became interested in alleviating another form of human disadvantage: infertility. Wood had envisaged the possibility of fertilising eggs 'in-vitro' outside the womb, but his team's attempts to induce a pregnancy were unsuccessful until 1978 when Trounson, an Australian animal researcher with experience at Cambridge, joined the group in what became the Centre for Early Human Development. By the early 1980s, the Monash team was 'indisputably' the world leader in the application of IVF and soon sped on to other successes, including the first birth with a donated egg and the first birth from a donated embryo. In 1985, a company, IVF Australia, was formed to commercialise the group's success in the United States. It became Monash's most successful venture in the commercialisation of its intellectual property, returning many millions of dollars to the university.[35]

Wood and Trounson were unprepared for the public controversy that followed the birth of IVF baby Candice Reed in 1980. As scientists, their attention had been on how to achieve an in-vitro pregnancy, not on the ethical and political issues it raised. Wood, a gentle, open man used to speaking his mind, did not anticipate the moral burden thrown upon him as 'the father of IVF'. The rugged Trounson took to controversy more eagerly. In July 1980, a 'widely representative' group of university and non-university people recommended that the university establish a Centre for Human Bioethics 'to carry out research on issues in human bioethics and to promote study of the ethical, social and legal problems arising out of human biological research'. To emphasise its ecumenical, interdisciplinary character, it elected a steering committee, including chemist John Swan, philosopher Peter Singer, lawyer Louis Waller, physician W.A. Walters and Dominican priest L.P. Fitzgerald. With modest seeding funds, and the secondment of Singer as director, the centre got under way early in 1981.[36]

While the centre's seminars welcomed a wide range of speakers and viewpoints, the research conducted by Singer and Research Fellow Helga Kuhse adopted an explicitly secular vantage point. It resisted the idea that 'scientists should have a completely free hand' yet believed that in 'a pluralistic and largely secular society like Australia' debate on bioethical issues should not be dominated by 'those who thought along religious lines'.[37] Born into a secular Jewish family, 34-year-old Singer had already won a reputation as the *enfant terrible* of Australian philosophy. His book *Animal Liberation* (1975) gained international attention, both as a textbook for the animal rights movement and as an example of the 'preference utilitarianism' that became the trademark of the centre's often-controversial work on a range of practical ethical issues, including fertility, disability, euthanasia and embryo experimentation. The centre rode the wave of public interest in these issues. It organised the first national conference on IVF, on 11 March 1982, the day the Victorian government announced an official inquiry into IVF chaired by law professor and Victorian law reform commissioner Louis Waller. Through its publication *Bioethics News*, later *Monash Bioethics Review*, public seminars and workshops for healthcare professionals, the Monash brand of bioethics influenced policy and debate nationally and internationally.

The impetus for the first centres was a combination of intellectual curiosity, humanitarianism and personal ambition. In proposing a new Centre of Policy Studies in 1977, ECOPS offered a more pragmatic rationale.

Financial exigency threatens the environment of creative research and stimulation within universities. The development of a new centre that would tap new sources of funds, foster a flow of research workers and unlock otherwise unavailable resources and contacts is a means by which some of the looming problems may be eased.[38]

Its first director, 34-year-old Michael Porter, an Adelaide-born, Stanford-educated economist, quickly gained a public profile. 'Sorting out the proper role of markets and governments in our economy will be an important feature of our work', he declared.[39] Porter's political links were originally on the Labor side, but his assumption that markets do things best tilted at some cherished Labor traditions.[40] He maintained that his centre was apolitical, but its advent signalled the arrival of a new phase in Monash's research culture when centres became the shop windows of an enterprise university.[41]

During the 1980s and 1990s, centres burgeoned in everything from accident research (1987) and Australian studies (1989) to women's studies (1987) and water studies (1990). Today, there are over 120 centres across the university. A history of Monash's centres would reveal the shifting foci of public concern about such issues as green chemistry (2000), global terrorism (2002), human rights (2000) and biodiversity (2007). While departments remain the steady workhorses of the university, centres are its agile racers.

Science, technology and the commercial frontier

From its beginnings, Monash was a university shaped by the promise, and potential dangers, of a scientific age. Twenty years after its foundation, the frontiers of science had advanced into realms scarcely glimpsed in 1961, such as IVF and information technology (IT), yet the moral and social challenges remained. In 1978, historian Ian Turner organised a symposium on the implications of the new technologies. The world, he predicted, was about to enter a period as significant as the Neolithic or Industrial revolutions. By 1988, at least a quarter of the Australian workforce would be made redundant by technological change. There would be no need for lecturers and librarians in this brave new world, R.D. Lansbury of administrative studies anticipated. Speaking at another conference, on computers and the law, Professor Chris Weeramantry pondered the dismal prospect that those displaced by machines might turn to socially damaging activities, even possibly bringing about the end of civilisation.[42]

Already, Monash was experiencing some of the untoward effects of technological change, in an epidemic of repetitive strain injury among secretarial staff following the introduction of word-processors. Back in 1961, when the university ordered its first computer, a Ferranti Sirius, housed in a garage-like building attached to the science wing, nobody could have envisaged how quickly computers would transform the university. Cliff Bellamy, who was appointed director of the Monash Computer Centre in 1964, saw his empire grow into one of the university's largest and most costly departments.

In 1968, Chris Wallace became Monash's first professor of computer science, a discipline that developed into a department and then a whole faculty. By the early 1980s, relationships between the Computer Centre, which serviced the needs of students and staff, and the new Department of Information Science had become tangled. Ray Martin appointed Kevin Westfold to chair a formal review of the place of computer science in the university and, despite some doubters, backed his report, which recommended the allocation of increased resources and the reclassification of computer science as a high-technology discipline.[43]

Science and technology were at the centre of Monash's first moves towards entrepreneurial fundraising. Martin was optimistic about Monash's potential to secure its future by way of the application of its research through commercialisation and consultancy. Changeable government policies and inadequate funding were greater threats to academic excellence and university autonomy, in his eyes, than engagement with the corporate sector. The hard alternatives were either 'for research to haemorrhage slowly or to get out into the marketplace and aggressively develop a strong and independent flow of research funds'.[44]

Martin had already created a Monash Special Research Fund to support research and fund other activities such as the Monash University Creche, the Clinical Legal Education program and the new Japanese Studies Centre. By the end of his term, the fund was generating about $1 million a year.[45] In 1983, a Monash University Foundation was established from funds accumulated by the Finance Committee in the university's early

Commercialising research. Computer Centre Director Dr Cliff Bellamy explaining the workings of the MONET local area network, designed to serve the needs of the university but with commercial exploitation in mind. International rights were sold to a Sydney-based firm in 1984.

years. Together with funds from alumni, industry and the public, these resources were designed to secure a measure of independence from government funding.

Monash had come to Clayton in the expectation that its science and technology would thrive through links with the surrounding industrial area. Louis Matheson's hopes of promoting such connections through a Monash University Scientific and Industrial Community were scuttled in the early 1970s by student protests against the university's links with the 'military-industrial complex'.[46] In the early 1980s, Martin renewed the vision, opening up contacts with the local industrial research laboratories of BHP, Telecom and the CSIRO. In 1983–84 he joined Ron Brown on a tour of the United Kingdom to inspect science parks and other forms of research collaboration with private companies. Their report recommended the establishment of an Office of Innovation and Liaison, headed from 1985 by experienced technical consultant Bill Algar.

The university also created its own high-tech consulting company, Montech, to 'enhance the University's image as a centre of pure and applied scientific research'.[47] Based on the University of New South Wales' successful Unisearch, the company opened an office on a site adjacent to the campus on Blackburn Road. The company survived into the early twenty-first century, but never thrived. 'Nobody in the University knew what they wanted to do with Montech', one of its directors, Bruce Holloway, reflects.[48]

Martin worked hard to reassure those academics uncomfortable with the researcher-as-entrepreneur paradigm. To allay concern, he introduced a funding formula by which the money raised by marketable research was shared between the unit that generated it and the university as a whole. The sale of Ed Cherry's invention to reduce distortion in high-fidelity sound equipment paid for the Library's acquisition of a rare collection of seventeenth- and eighteenth-century French booksellers' catalogues. Cherry was pleased with this outcome, but some harder-nosed technologists, like Dean of Engineering Lance Endersbee, resented the diversion of their faculty's commercial earnings.[49]

By the mid-1980s, Monash could tell some encouraging stories about the commercialisation of its research. Monash IVF, spun off into IVF Australia, opened its first clinic in New York in 1985. Circadian Pharmaceuticals was working to turn physiologist Roger Short's research on melatonin into a remedy for jetlag. A team from the Centre for Molecular Biology and Medicine under the direction of Tony Linnane patented a blood test for detecting the early stages of bowel and stomach cancer. Engineer Owen Potter developed a new method of drying fluid coal, and the Computer Centre created an inexpensive local area network, MONET, which was being marketed to the world. By attuning the university to the commercial potential of its research, Martin had taken the first steps along the path towards self-reliance.

Community engagement and the arts

As Monash looked to industry and the market, it was also reaching out to its more immediate community. The question of the university's relationship with the suburbs that surrounded it had been in the minds of Monash people since the beginning. Were they a cultural wasteland above which it should rise, or should the university think of itself as part of the future of the neighbourhood growing around it? Equally important was the question of how Monash was viewed by its neighbours. Sports Administrator Doug Ellis worried that 'we have not won the hearts and minds of our surrounding communities to the desired extent that they think of Monash as *their* University'.[50]

In 1980, Martin established an Advisory Committee on Community Liaison to examine ways to broaden links with the surrounding suburbs.

Reaching out to the community. Vice-Chancellor Ray Martin opening the University of the Third Age at Monash, 1985 (Director of the Centre for Continuing Education, Dr Jack McDonell, seated on right).

Monash had already forged cultural and recreational links with its neighbours in Oakleigh, Waverley, Springvale and other municipalities through the Robert Blackwood Hall, Alexander Theatre and the recently established Arts and Crafts Centre. The university supported activities such as the photographic exhibition 'Oakleigh: Portrait of the New Society', opened by Martin in March 1981 and featuring the photography of geographer Herve Alleaume. Other connections were forged as Monash staff became involved in local activities such as the Oakleigh and District Historical Society and the Clayton Arts Council.[51]

Open Day, which had begun in 1967, grew steadily more popular. In the context of public discussions about the relevance of universities to the broader community, Open Day presented an opportunity to showcase some of the more tangible fruits of scholarly work. Computer-related displays were popular—Open Day 1977 featured a computer that played tunes and a gestefax copying machine—as were children's activities and childhood-related research projects, such as the Education Faculty's work on the effect of television on children.[52]

The visual arts were an important aspect of the vision of Monash as a community hub nurtured by Matheson and enthusiastically maintained by Martin, himself a lover of the visual arts. Selected works from the Monash art collection (established in 1961) were exhibited in a gallery in the Menzies Building from the mid-1970s, and the Department of Visual Arts mounted a number of innovative small exhibitions. At the instigation of Professor of Visual Arts Patrick McCaughey, the Martins, the painter Peggy Shaw (wife of Monash Professor of History A.G.L. Shaw) and others worked towards the establishment of a more permanent gallery space, envisaged as a community drawcard similar to the Heide and Banyule galleries.[53] Built as part of the new Multidisciplinary Centre designed by Daryl Jackson and unveiled in 1987, the new gallery was the first to be purpose-built for an Australian university.

Martin's vice-chancellorship also provided the context for one of Monash's most notable creative endeavours, Celia Rosser's banksias project. The self-taught Rosser was appointed as faculty artist in science in 1970, and in 1974—as university botanical artist—began work on a series of botanical paintings depicting every known species of banksia. Rosser recalls that 'we thought there would be no more than sixty', but the number soon rose to seventy-six. *The Banksias* took twenty-five years to complete, 'longer than I had envisaged', and is considered one of the twentieth century's great botanical artworks.[54] Rosser's work, says Professor Bruce Holloway (who appointed her), 'will live on when a lot of the other research achievements of Monash have been forgotten'.[55]

Public use of university facilities was at an all-time high by 1985. In that year, the residential halls, the Arts and Crafts Centre and the Centre for Continuing Education (1973) catered to more than 12 000 members of the public. Members of the community used the facilities of the Sports and Recreation Centre (including the new Doug Ellis swimming pool) and took craft courses at Monash's popular summer school. The Blackwood Hall and Alexander Theatre were the main providers of music, theatre, dance and other performances for the eastern suburbs: each had annual audiences nearing 90 000 and were heavily booked by community groups.[56]

University Botanical Artist Celia Rosser with Vice-Chancellor Ray Martin at the launch of the exhibition of The Banksias *series, 1988.*

Blackwood Hall hosted the acclaimed ABC Monash Series of classical concerts. In March 1985, the Melbourne Symphony Orchestra became the first Australian orchestra to be played live on international airwaves, direct from Monash.[57]

Yet Matheson's vision of Monash as a thriving creative hub for the south-eastern suburbs remained out of reach. The cultural offerings of Blackwood Hall and the Alex were largely imported mainstream productions, rather than products of the university itself. The Alex specialised in children's entertainment, which underwrote its other activities. More avant-garde performances and student productions did not pay.[58] Monash's geographical disadvantages, too, ensured that the development of a vigorous Monash theatre 'scene'—or a night life of any sort—proved elusive. It simply wasn't possible to turn 'Clayton Road into Lygon Street'.[59]

Open to talent

At the same time that Monash was opening itself to the community and the market, it was also welcoming new types of students. While numbers remained stationary, the character of the student body was changing. By 1986, almost half were female, up from a quarter in 1961.[60] Women were more visible in student affairs, editing and contributing to *Lot's Wife* and running for MAS positions. More of them were now mature-age students who elected to study part-time to meet family and work commitments. Serious and well organised, they brought a maturity of outlook that subtly changed the tenor of class discussion. The student body as a whole was older: by 1976, 13.5 per cent of students were over twenty-five, up from 5.5 per cent in 1970. By 1980, one-third were part-timers.[61]

In 1974, the university introduced an Early Leavers Scheme to encourage the entry of applicants who had not completed the Higher School Certificate and had left school five years or more previously. The scheme was very popular with women, who found the experience of study both emancipating and unsettling. Going to uni had created 'radical changes' in her outlook, one woman reported. She now viewed those close to her more critically: 'Husband a businessman, friends are Liberal . . . Creating rift with husband . . . I'm looking for something more'.[62] Husbands often resented their wives returning to study. Occasionally, examinations had to be held in secret locations because husbands threatened violence if they attended. Husbands' fears may not have been ungrounded: some staff members, it was said, developed sexual liaisons with unhappily married mature-age students, convinced that they were 'saving' them.[63]

Monash's students were also becoming ethnically more diverse. Between 1970 and 1984, the proportion of first-year students who were Australian-born fell from 84 to 68 per cent. Nearly a quarter were Asian-born. In engineering, Asian-born students made up 54 per cent of the first-year intake.[64] In 1982, Dean of Engineering Lance Endersbee persuaded council to impose a quota on the number of first-year international students in his faculty, stirring spirited opposition across the university that led to a reversal of the decision. Endersbee remained unrepentant. While he was proud of the Asian students in his faculty, they were taking the places and career opportunities of the Australian students whose parents' taxes paid for the university.[65]

The 1974 decision of the Whitlam government to abolish student fees was expected to widen educational opportunity. By 1980, it was clear that it had done little or nothing to improve the representation of women, migrants, Indigenous Australians, older people, and rural and lower-socioeconomic students. At both Melbourne and Monash, students from independent schools were over-represented, although Monash had slightly larger proportions of students from state schools and rural backgrounds. The abolition of fees, it seemed, had simply transferred funds from the average taxpayer to 'a student body drawn to a great extent from the more affluent sections of society'.[66]

However, in perhaps the most profound area of social disadvantage, Indigenous Australia, Monash did make some significant progress. The Monash Orientation Scheme for Aborigines offered Indigenous students over the age of twenty-one a year of preparation for university study. Those who completed the program successfully were guaranteed a first-year place at Monash (initially in the faculties of Law and Arts) and ongoing support.

Professor Merle Ricklefs was the main driving force. Soon after arriving at Monash in 1980, he consulted Aboriginal studies' Colin Bourke about how to increase the lamentably low numbers of Aboriginal graduates from Australian universities, then estimated at no more than ten to fifteen across the whole nation. 'Perhaps I could make a contribution to the country and, even more importantly, to some of its most disadvantaged citizens', he thought. An American-born historian of Indonesia, Ricklefs was inspired by his 'personal opposition to racism in all its forms and fruits'.[67]

What was needed, Bourke advised, was a bridging program: something that had not been attempted at an Australian university. Ricklefs and Eve Fesl—who succeeded Bourke—lobbied the university and consulted with Aboriginal leaders. They sought inspiration from programs developed elsewhere, particularly in Canada. Initial funding was secured from the Department of Education and Youth Affairs and the Department of Aboriginal Affairs. The first nine students—four women and five men, drawn from all mainland states and the Northern Territory—began in 1984.[68]

The first director of the scheme, Associate Professor Isaac Brown, was born on the Cobourg Peninsula and attended schools in the Northern Territory before becoming a teacher and lecturer in speech pathology at Lincoln Institute of Health Sciences. 'He turned out to be an utterly brilliant Director', Ricklefs recalled.

Access unlimited. Isaac Brown (second from right) and Minister for Aboriginal Affairs Gerry Hand (second from left) talking with Monash Orientation Scheme for Aborigines students in 1988.

> He was articulate and urbane, with the kind of middle-class accent and personal style that reassured nervous university and government people. He was of Iwaidja and Torres Strait Islander descent and thus impeccably acceptable to Aboriginal students. He had succeeded in his studies in the mainstream white world without in any way denying his Aboriginality. When selecting students, he looked for reasonable educational achievement . . . but above all he looked for what he called 'stickability', a quality exemplified in his own life history.[69]

Recognising that Aboriginal students faced a disadvantage in university courses that required a degree of (white) cultural knowledge, the orientation scheme curriculum imparted skills that would stand Indigenous students in good stead in the marketplace, while retaining a 'strong Aboriginal flavour'.[70] By 1987, there were thirty-four Aboriginal students enrolled at Monash, and an external review had praised the scheme as a 'programme of national significance'.[71] By the time Ricklefs left, in 1993, the program had eleven members of staff and had produced a dozen graduates. 'We had, in other words, roughly doubled the number of Aboriginal university graduates in the country.'[72]

The radical moderates

A steady-state university in a time that 'wasn't meant to be easy' produced a sea-change in the outlook of the broader student body. Student culture was more restrained and less politically charged than in the late 1960s, a contrast that, as student Stephen Wilks observes, tended to leave it undeservedly in the shade. 'The sixties decade was so mesmerizing it is often assumed to be a yardstick for all other eras. It shouldn't be. The sixties were exceptional. It almost seems that we of the late seventies need to apologise for not extending the previous decade . . .'[73] The economic climate and lean employment market lent a new urgency to study. The cover of the 1980 *Student Resource Book* featured a lecturer declaring, 'We're educating you for life!', to which a student responds, 'It's a polite way of saying we'll never get a job'.[74] The pressure not only to pass but to pass well enough to compete in the job market may have inspired an increasing demand for student counselling by the early 1980s.

While the student mood had grown more serious, Monash still seemed a rarefied and radical world to students from conservative backgrounds like Tim and Peter Costello. The brothers grew up in suburban Blackburn in a middle-class, church-going family (their father, a teacher at Carey Grammar, was a Baptist lay preacher). Everybody they knew voted Liberal. When Tim arrived in 1973 at Monash, where radical students were still trying to incite revolution, he experienced 'a real culture shock'. 'You sensed', he says, 'that there are all these new worlds that you could discover . . . and from my background if you sailed out into those rapids you didn't know if you were going to be completely lost . . . !' He found a 'shelter from this whole storm' in the EU, becoming its president in 1976.[75]

For the godly, the challenges and temptations of campus life were many. Sexuality had become a more strident feature of student culture and politics, and the Gay Society was one of the most active groups. Costello recalls that a debate on the topic 'Is sex more interesting than politics?' ended with a couple publicly copulating. It 'was sort of like a world of almost Greek or Roman hedonism!' The small caf was 'heavy with dope', and the Nott was reportedly the second biggest beer-seller in Victoria in 1979. Farm Week was banned in 1984 after students bombarded lecture theatres with eggs, flour and manure, harassed motorists on the corner of Dandenong and Wellington roads, and stole a pirate statue from the Caribbean Gardens at Rowville.[76]

Younger brother Peter Costello arrived at Clayton in 1975 to study arts/law. He 'could have got in to Melbourne', but Monash was closer to home, and his uncle, a federal court judge, spoke highly of its Law School. Like his brother, Peter found the world of student politics bizarre and confronting. There were ongoing protests over assessment practices and students collecting money for the Palestinian Liberation Organisation. 'I thought, this is all pretty weird.' He stuck close to his brother and the EU for a while but was soon drawn to respond to what he saw as a ubiquitous, uncritical embrace of Marxist ideology on campus. He was also troubled by the left's hostility to Israel. At the time, he recalls, he was neither Labor nor Liberal but 'probably more Left wing than I am today'. But as an anti-Marxist in undergraduate politics he was in the minority. 'I was more or less in revolt against the status quo.'[77]

In 1976, Peter Costello stood for the PAC on a non-aligned platform, promising to moderate the extremism of previous student leaders. With the support of Christian and Jewish students, Liberals, and right-wing Labor Party supporters, he defeated candidates from the left. 'It was kind of like the Left against everybody in my time.' The left lost support over the Israel question at Monash, where the Jewish Students Society was one of the largest groups on campus.

In August 1976, Prime Minister Fraser visited the campus to open the Krongold Centre. Several hundred students protesting against Fraser and his government gathered outside the Alexander Theatre, and a brick was thrown as Fraser entered, shattering a glass door. After a failed attempt by police to clear a path for his exit, Fraser was confined in a small office for his own safety. Costello, with friend Michael Kroger (the president of the Monash Liberal Club), was caught between the protestors and police. It was a defining moment for him. 'I was no particular supporter of Fraser's but I was down there saying, "You know, look he's the Prime

Minister for heaven's sake . . . protest against him by all means but don't bash him up!"'

Costello became a vocal defender of free speech on the campus. The left argued that because students lacked the power to influence decision-making they should use the only avenue available to them—protest—to restrict the free speech of the powerful. For Costello, this was outrageous. If MAS did not allow all members of society to speak freely, it would forfeit its right to exclude the police from the university.[78] Fraser returned to Monash in 1978 to deliver the first Menzies Lecture. The establishment of this annual lecture, initiated by the Liberal Club, signalled a new era of student politics in which conservative students challenged the ascendency of the left.

Costello, in the striped jumper he wore every day and with his hair a little long at the collar, became a well-known figure on campus. He played in one of the few premierships the Monash Blues footy team ever won and was popular with women and men alike. 'It was said . . . that I was always well received by the gay community because I was quite

Big man on campus. MAS chairman Peter Costello in his office, 1976.

good looking!' Facing mass student meetings stood him in good stead
in his later career. 'It was good for parliament because it didn't matter
how rowdy the parliament was, I could always yell over them and I learnt
that at Monash.'

While still only in his second year, Costello was elected chairman
of MAS with an overwhelming majority. At the age of twenty, he had
his own office (complete with secretary), was having cocktails at the
vice-chancellor's house, running a budget and sitting on the Union
Board. For him, 'it was a pretty big world'. He was on campus all day,
'doing politics', working part-time in the bookshop, then studying until
the Library closed, at 9 p.m. He subsisted on sausages and bacon at the
Nott. In his office one day, he was confronted by fellow student and
anarchist Robert 'Red' Bingham, who 'started bashing me up'. The *Age*
ran a photograph of a grimacing Costello in bed, with his arm in a sling,
boosting his romantic image as a martyr for political moderation.

The young Costello was not opposed to compulsory student unionism.
Arriving at university, he said in 1977, was 'the first exciting step across
the threshold of union membership'. As an 'educational institution', he
argued, the student union was quite different in nature from a trade union.
Since everyone used its facilities, everyone should pay the membership
fee. MAS was a 'closer parallel of a trade union', because its members
were entitled to vote and stand for election. Only with the Australian
Union of Students, over which students had little control, did he draw
the line.[79] With Costello at the helm of MAS, Monash became a focal
point of the struggle against the domination of the Australian Union of
Students by the hard left.

Despite his friendship with Kroger, Costello was close to members of
Young Labor's right faction, especially Michael Danby. He occasionally
met the Australian Council of Trade Unions' president Bob Hawke, who
was keen to recruit him.[80] In 1978, Costello became the president of
Social Democratic Students, which coordinated social democrat clubs on
Australian campuses. All this, as well as an *Age* article in which Costello
identified himself as 'moderate ALP', fanned the rumour that Costello
was a signed-up member of Young Labor. Kroger and the Young Liberals,
meanwhile, saw him as one of them. Costello cultivated, and probably
enjoyed, the mystery that surrounded his political leanings.

In class, Costello encountered a range of views, some of which he rejected. His politics lecturer presented Marxism not as a theory but as 'the truth'. Ron McCallum taught him industrial law at the height of the arbitration period and was 'horrified' when in later years Costello advocated the deregulation of labour markets. Being on council was also 'a big part' of Costello's education. There, he met James McNeill from BHP, Chancellor Dick Eggleston, and Kay Patterson, who subsequently became his political colleague in Canberra. He 'learnt more about budgets from doing the MAS budget and presenting it to the council than in any of my lectures and that's one skill that really did come in handy'.

Despite the conservative turn in student politics, the media continued to play up Monash's radical reputation. When the Prince of Wales came to receive an honorary doctor of laws, in April 1981, they portrayed the modest crowd of 400 or 500 mostly well-wishers as a mindless, screaming mob. British prime minister Margaret Thatcher's visit to Monash aroused similar expectations. A crowd of around 300 protesters gathered, but the only signs of violence were 'three unspent tomatoes . . . a skyrocket (fired fifteen minutes after Mrs Thatcher's departure), and a pigeon's egg that fell out of a tree'.[81]

But while spectacular demonstrations were fewer and further between by the 1980s, and MAS—the official organ of Monash students—quiescent, beneath the smooth surface of the Martin years some students were engaged in activities that equalled the academic work taking place in centres for long-term social significance. For Jon Faine—now a well-known ABC radio presenter—and his friends in Monash's Socialist Lawyers group, MAS politics was not the main event. He and his classmates, including members of the influential Feminist Lawyers, were at the forefront of the emerging alternative law scene.

Faine, the son of Monash professor of microbiology Solly Faine, had arrived at Monash in 1975 as an arts/law student and spent 'the most miserable year of my life' attempting to adjust to uni.[82] Law seemed to have no connection to his world, and he was slow to make friends and awkward with girls. Instead of studying, Faine played frisbee and pool and got stoned in the caf. He missed Campbell McComas' famous 1976 law lecture hoax[83] because he thought, 'Why the fuck would you want to spend your lunchtime going to a lecture from an Oxford Professor?'

But in his fourth year, Faine and his housemates found their rented home was up for auction. He went to the Tenants Union Legal Service and found some of his Monash classmates volunteering to help the long queues of people: single mothers and others on the margins of society. A new realisation 'hit me like this ton of bricks'. The point of the law was to 'learn how to use it to help those people'. He returned the following week, as a volunteer, and every week thereafter. He enrolled in the Law School's clinical program and became involved in the community legal centre movement, meeting people who were 'using the law in an activist way'. With friend Bryce Menzies, Faine started a campaign nicknamed the 'High Court Fan Club', which established a free legal centre in a tent outside the new High Court building, opened by the Queen in 1980 amid celebrations that cost more than the annual budget for legal aid for Australia.

For Faine, Monash was not a 'steady' or quiet place but 'buzzing', especially in contrast to Melbourne, where legal student activism was practically non-existent. The involvement of Monash students in the legal centre movement is not as well known as Peter Costello's story. But it left an enduring public legacy. The Feminist Lawyers group, formed at Monash by law students Bebe Loff, Julia Pullen and others, was crucial to the establishment of the Women's Legal Service in Victoria. Monash law graduates from this extraordinary period include the current Supreme Court chief justice, the County Court chief judge, the chief magistrate and the chief coroner in Victoria.

'Buzzing' Monash may have been, but in January 1987 Vice-Chancellor Martin happily returned to what he still considered his 'natural habitat', the research laboratory. The tennis courts behind the vice-chancellor's residence had had plenty of use over his ten years in the job. Bashing a ball around the court had been 'a wonderful way to unwind from all the trials and tribulations of that very challenging job'.[84] He had ended his term on a high note, the university's twenty-fifth anniversary. The Duke of Edinburgh launched a week-long festival of events and gave a stirring, if characteristically acerbic, oration. There was positive news, too, for the university's researchers had won a 20 per cent increase in grants from the Australian Research Grants Committee.[85]

While his had not been an era for big dreams or endeavours, Martin had led the university through a period of necessary consolidation, maintaining the prestige and vitality achieved by Matheson. Monash was now viewed as a leader in medicine and law, with further strengths in Southeast Asian studies, chemistry, physics and computing. There had been some new buildings, such as the Multidisciplinary Centre and the Physiology and Microbiology buildings. If the university was not yet reaching out beyond Australia, it had established more sustained external relationships with industry and the surrounding community. Though nobody yet knew it, Australian universities would soon be running a fast race on a bumpy track. A decade of stability under Martin meant that Monash was ready to match the form of its more experienced competitors while retaining some of its youthful speed and vitality.

SEVEN

MERGERS AND ACQUISITIONS

I don't believe Monash will grow very much more in terms of student numbers.
MAL LOGAN, *AUSTRALIAN*, 15 JANUARY 1986

'Higher education in Australia is becalmed', a professor glumly observed in 1980.[1] Static enrolments, ageing academics and shrinking government funding presented a dismal scene. As a young university, Monash felt the loss of momentum more keenly than most. Without a fresh injection of vision, talent and resources, the first of the new universities could succumb to a premature old age, its leaders began to fear. They had little inkling of the storm that was about to descend on them. By the end of the decade, Monash was running before 'a cyclone of change' on a course that even its captain could not plot with certainty.[2] The wind—the rush of reforms to higher education initiated by the Hawke government—had been generated by the most profound upheaval in Australia's economy and politics since the 1950s. But the university that emerged from the storm also bore the strong imprint of its helmsman, Monash's fourth vice-chancellor, Mal Logan.

Logan was a leader in a very different mould from his predecessors. Vice-chancellors Matheson, Scott and Martin were born into upper middle-class families, attended elite city schools and studied at leading British universities. Logan was the first Monash vice-chancellor to be educated in government schools and to graduate from a rural university college. He spent half a decade teaching in high schools and teachers'

Vice-Chancellor Mal Logan (second from left) and Chairman of Chisholm Council Paul Ramler shake hands on the 1989 merger. Chisholm Director Geoffrey Vaughan (right) looks pensive and General Manager Peter Wade (left) attends to the paperwork.

colleges before his first university appointment and was in his mid-thirties before completing a doctorate. A boy from the bush who had come up the hard way, he was as convinced of the value of university education as he was critical of the social inequality in which it was embedded.

From his Calvinist forebears, Logan had learned that schooling was the way to social salvation.[3] His Highlander grandparents arrived in New South Wales in the 1860s, lured, like many others, by the yeoman dream of free selection. 'They never acquired any land', Mal recalls, 'and, except for two brothers, none ever left the Hunter Valley'. The second generation, Mal's uncles, battled on as drovers, rouseabouts, fence-menders and slaughtermen. The eldest, Jack, perished on the Somme; only in the early 1920s did the youngest, Mal's father, Alan, take the first step out of rural poverty by becoming a primary teacher.

Malcolm Ian Logan was born in 1931, in the midst of the Great Depression. When he was about two years old, his parents separated. He has no memory of his mother and was never to see her again. Along with his brother, he remained in the care of his father, who became both parent and teacher. 'He was a gentle man, dedicated completely to Noel and me', he recalls. 'He saw education as everything . . . a typical Scottish sort of thing. Education was the way you lifted yourself up a little bit.' From Moonan Flat, 'a very lonely, isolated little village', where he attended his father's one-teacher school, the family moved to Moore Creek, so that Mal could attend the well-regarded Tamworth High School. Through his teens, he cycled back and forth each day, rain or shine, from Moore Creek to Tamworth, a round trip of 14 miles. 'Our lives revolved around half-yearly and yearly examinations, all very formal and rigorous, with results being posted alongside names in descending order for each subject on school noticeboards.' It was an austere life, framed by the demands of school, lightened only by the possibility of social uplift.

As the leaving honours exams approached, Logan's academic interests became more defined. The brilliant multi-coloured chalk maps of his geography teacher Col Sullivan stimulated an interest in how the world was structured in space and time. Why were some parts of the world so much poorer than others? How can you lift people from poverty to plenty, he wondered. Later on, he became captivated by the writings of the Annales historians, students of the long sweep of history. 'The big-picture stuff always interested me; I've never been much interested in detail', he admits. When the leaving honours results appeared in the Tamworth paper, he had done well enough to win a teacher studentship at the University of New England (UNE). A good, safe career for his father, teaching looked as though it would be good enough for him too.

Boarding in a 'cold and dreary' hotel on the outskirts of town, Logan remembers his years in Armidale without affection. But the University of Sydney, where he completed an honours year and joined the fierce debates of the Labor Club, widened his horizons. Riding buses through the Riverina, he gathered data for his honours thesis, a study of irrigation in the Murray Valley. After graduating, he moved to Forbes High School in the far west of New South Wales, joining a group of fellow teaching conscripts, all young single men, living in the local pub, drinking too much, longing to escape. 'You can do better than this', an inspector advised him, paving his way to a lectureship at the local teachers' college in Armidale. Soon he was back in Sydney, married to Toni, a fellow teacher, and lecturing at the Sydney Teachers' College until, in 1959, he became a lecturer in geography at Sydney University.

Logan might well have felt satisfied to arrive in one of Australia's leading universities. He had congenial colleagues, able students and scope to develop his interests in urban geography. But the university was beset by tribal and factional antagonisms. 'It is difficult to imagine a better place to observe the follies, the successes and the tragedies of academic life than Australia's oldest university', he later reflected.[4] In 1967, he left Australia to become a professor at the University of Wisconsin, 'never intending to return'.[5] With over 30 000 undergraduates and an outstanding graduate research school, Wisconsin confounded the elitist assumptions of the Australian sandstone universities, proving that democratic access could be combined with research excellence. Logan came to regard Wisconsin as an ideal to be emulated in his homeland. He also found the academic community in Madison stimulating, although, as the political passions generated by the Vietnam War spilt onto the campus, the attractions of the United States began to fade. By the late 1960s, with teargas canisters exploding in library stacks and national guardsmen lining the corridors outside lecture theatres, the campus became a battlefield. He was on a visiting appointment at the University of Ibadan in Nigeria when a

The big-picture man, 1992. Vice-Chancellor Mal Logan, a geographer with wide horizons, made Monash into Australia's largest and most entrepreneurial university.

call came from Australia seeking his interest in a chair at Monash. To the Logans, now with a young daughter, Australia began to look more attractive. Tiny Armidale and 'stifling' Sydney had also sought him out, but Monash was new and its foundation professor of geography, Basil Johnson, had built a strong department. So Monash, they decided, it would be.

'I had never aimed to become a vice-chancellor', Logan admits. 'I just crept into it.'[6] Rather than working his way up the academic ladder, he came to the post largely through intellectual and political conviction, a dawning awareness of the importance of higher education in the 'big picture' of regional development. During the 1970s, he had begun to ponder Australia's perilous position as a small, highly protected, industrial country in the midst of a rapidly changing Asian region. Experience working at the Organisation for Economic Co-operation and Development reinforced his conviction that the nation urgently needed to lift its educational game if it was to survive in an increasingly competitive world.[7] Only in the early 1980s, however, when he was appointed by the Hawke government to the Universities Council and became a part-time pro vice-chancellor at Monash, did he seriously turn his mind to the possibility of leading the university.

A strategy for the future

The Monash Council had already begun to plan for more challenging times. In 1985, with Ray Martin's vice-chancellorship coming to an end, a committee chaired by council member and BHP chief executive James McNeill proposed major reforms to the top administration of the university. Even before the selection of a new vice-chancellor, however, McNeill began to overhaul its financial administration.

'Universities are likely to be constrained financially for the foreseeable future', he believed. 'We should aim to greatly increase our funding from non-government sources.' The old position of comptroller should become 'deputy principal and business manager' with a mandate to diversify the university's funding sources.[8] McNeill had someone in mind for the position. Probably nobody in Victoria knew more about the intricacies of university finance than 42-year-old Peter Wade. After taking a first-class honours degree in economics, Wade had joined the Victorian Treasury. There, under long-time secretary Eric Coates, he had managed the flow of government funds to universities, dealing almost daily with their senior financial officers. By his mid-thirties, Wade was deputy secretary, but when the Cain government created a new Office of Management and Budget he moved sideways into the Ministry of Transport. One day, McNeill invited himself for a cup of tea. 'I've come to convince you to come to Monash University', he explained. Wade wanted to stay in Melbourne, where his wife, Jan, was president of the Equal Opportunity Board and an aspiring Liberal politician, and the opportunity to be involved in universities again was appealing. So he signed on, expecting to stay five years at most.[9]

Monash, he soon discovered, was 'down in the dumps'. Its buildings were wearing out. Its financial systems were rudimentary. Unspent government funds were stored like beans in jam jars. Nobody knew exactly how much money the university had until the accounts had been audited. Monash, he decided, needed to manage its resources like a business, budgeting its expenditures in advance and investing surplus funds to yield the best return. Under Wade's leadership, Monash became the first Australian university to publish its budget. By investing unspent government funds, it seeded the Monash Foundation. It turned under-utilised land on the eastern side of Blackburn Road into the Monash Science Park and commercialised Monash's pioneering research on IVF. Wade became a vital part of the university's top management, a deft, decisive and ever-resourceful participant in all its major decisions. 'An idea only remained a good idea when you had the resources to do it', he believed. In the years ahead he would supply much of the detail of Logan's big picture.[10]

McNeill's report, delivered to council in August 1985, echoed many of the recommendations of Sir Alexander Jarratt's landmark report of the same year on university administration in Britain. A modern vice-chancellor, Jarratt argued, should be a corporate leader with a mandate for strategic leadership, not just an eminent academic.[11] Logan had shared his views with McNeill, even lending him a copy of Jarratt's report.[12] The next Monash vice-chancellor, McNeill proposed, should be spared 'much of the day to day routine' to devote himself to 'development and planning'. Logan, whose appointment as deputy vice-chancellor had been extended to the end of Martin's term, could hardly have written a more congenial job description himself.[13]

Even so, his appointment was not a foregone conclusion. All five of the short-listed candidates were outstanding academics with distinguished service beyond the university. All had served in senior academic adminis-trative positions, as deans, directors or deputy vice-chancellors. The most strongly favoured—Law Professor Louis Waller; director of ANU's John

Curtin Institute of Medical Research, Robert Porter; and Logan—were state high school boys who exemplified Monash's meritocratic ethos.

It was Logan's combination of strategic vision and political skill that finally told in his favour. 'Professor Logan is a leader', his friend Maurie Daly enthused, noting his 'active and penetrating mind' and his ability to win the confidence of diverse groups of people. 'He focuses on the central questions and handles consideration of them with authority', Arts Dean John Legge agreed. His would be 'a firm guiding hand who would represent us well in Canberra and Spring Street'.[14] At the interviews, staff representative Peter Darvall recalls, Logan outshone his rivals. 'As smooth as silk', he was 'Mr Charisma', exuding the larrikin charm and big-picture vision that became the hallmarks of his leadership.[15]

The choice was confirmed by the knowledge that Logan was already the university's planner-in-chief. 'Perhaps we should be beginning to put together, for our own internal use, a paper which addresses some issues relevant to the medium-term future of the university', he had proposed in April 1985. 'An excellent suggestion', Martin had replied.[16] With help from statistical officer Peter Beilby, Logan gathered data on the demand for tertiary education, both undergraduate and graduate, research funding, faculty loads and staffing. As a geographer, he was sizing up the 'opportunities and constraints' of the university's location at the 'geographical centre' of the metropolitan area.[17]

In the 1960s, Monash stood on the edge of the metropolis. Now, almost as many Melburnians lived beyond the campus, in the car-based suburbs to the south and east, as in the railway suburbs to the north and west. Monash's founders expected that as the suburbs grew, middle-class jobs and households would follow, reinforcing the university's locational advantage. But the economic changes unleashed by the floating of the Australian dollar and the lowering of protective tariffs had undermined that benign pattern of development. By 1984, Nissan, Clayton's largest industrial employer, was threatening to close its car manufacturing plant, and Logan's friend, Minister for Industry John Button, was devising a plan to rescue the car industry. The new industries of the 1980s and 1990s were in finance and IT. And instead of a cream brick-veneer house in the suburbs, the professional middle classes were moving back to trendy inner-city terraces.

'Monash is a young institution when compared with some other tertiary institutions', Logan observed.[18] But, as he knew very well, that impression was misleading. In the 1960s and 1970s, Monash's vitality had sprung from the youth of its academic staff. Boy-wonder professors led lecturers and tutors barely older than their students. By the mid-1980s, however, the university was demographically older than many of its more venerable rivals. Its professors, no longer young, were still well short of retirement. More than half of its academics were senior lecturers, most of them at the top of the scale and unlikely to go higher. So, just when they were expected to become more 'productive', 'pro-active' and 'entrepreneurial', the university's academic staff were becoming older, more inflexible and more expensive. Even worse, Terry Hore of the Higher Education Advisory and Research Unit forecast that the trend would not be reversed until the end of the century.[19]

Monash's strategic challenges, Logan believed, required 'the creation within the institution of a planning climate'.[20] Soon after taking up his position, he created a small planning group within his own office and invited everyone, including the entire professoriate, to offer advice.[21] Planning, he insisted, should be a 'bottom-up' as well as 'top-down' process. Dozens of submissions arrived in the vice-chancellor's mail. But what came up from the bottom was evidently less exciting than what Logan was learning from his friends at the top. 'The main disappointment I felt after reading all the replies was that we are a fairly introspective community', he wearily observed.[22] The fruit of Logan's inquiries, *Monash University: A Strategy for the Future*, shrewdly foresaw many of the themes of the Dawkins Green Paper released just a few weeks later. It was the first and last comprehensive planning exercise of the Logan era. It fulfilled its primary purpose, warning the academic community of the changes on the way. But in the torrent of changes that ensued, planning was quickly submerged by politics.

The Dawkins Revolution

As an ALP insider, Logan was privy to the intense debates within the Hawke Cabinet about the future of higher education. One afternoon in the early 1980s, he shared a drink at the Windsor Hotel with his friend John Button and Shadow Minister for Education John Dawkins.[23]

A rebel son of the Western Australian establishment, Dawkins went to an agricultural college, became a student radical, married an Aboriginal woman and dabbled in the Fremantle Football Club before entering politics. He abandoned his youthful Marxism to become a forceful advocate of micro-economic reform. In the Hawke government's first terms, he served successfully as minister for finance and minister for trade; but, after the 1987 election, when he succeeded Susan Ryan, the last defender of state-funded, free higher education, as minister for education, the way was clear for the most radical overhaul of the universities since the Murray Report.

From the beginning, Dawkins bypassed the Higher Education Council, dominated by the sandstone universities, and relied for advice on an informal group of sympathetic vice-chancellors and directors. Within the 'Purple Circle', as it became known, Logan was one of Dawkins' most trusted advisors.[24] Today Logan downplays the influence of the circle, which met infrequently and was only advisory.[25] Among critical Monash colleagues, however, his strong support for Dawkins sometimes raised a troubling question: was the vice-chancellor the minister's man or theirs?

The scope of the minister's ambitions soon became apparent. A senior bureaucrat recalls a meeting soon after the election when Dawkins invited his staff to list the characteristics of the higher education system on a whiteboard. Obediently, they wrote: no fees, government funding, binary divide between universities and colleges, limited places for overseas students, and so on. 'Now list the opposite of these in the second column', he directed. So they wrote: full fees, competitive funding, a unified higher education system, liberal entry for international students. Unless they could think of compelling objections, these dot-points became the new policy. The old Marxist had abandoned his socialism, but not his predilection for dialectic.[26]

The Dawkins Revolution, as it soon became known, was launched in an atmosphere of crisis. 'We live in a complex world characterised by increasing uncertainty and volatility . . . Our ability to deal effectively and equitably with change will depend in part on developments in our national higher education system', the 1987 Green Paper on Higher Education began.[27] Dawkins left no doubt about the identity of his foes or his determination to defeat them.

In 1989, Minister John Dawkins spoke at Monash's newly acquired Gippsland campus, the result of the most unlikely of all the academic mergers, he declared.

> Unless the universities, and particularly the older ones amongst them, shake off their ingrained resistance to change and can belie their image as ossified bodies incapable of adaptation, then the opportunities associated with the changes now needed in the higher education sector will simply pass them by . . . It will be the innovative, more dynamic institutions—colleges and institutes such as RMIT—who will reap the benefits of the 'New Age'.[28]

The message was clear: embrace the government's new priorities or suffer the consequences. Political and financial journalists—university graduates, almost to a man—cheered him on, denouncing the 'cosy traditionalism' and 'sheltered complacency' of their old academic stamping grounds.[29] 'The game is now up', a senior bureaucrat declared, as if he had unmasked a criminal conspiracy.[30]

Mal Logan shared many of these views. The universities, he had come to believe, were like 'medieval enclaves'. Microcosms of the protected

Australian economy, they needed to be opened up to the bracing influence of competition. 'Just as the tariff had to go, and the Australian dollar had to float, so the universities had to [change]', he argued.[31] In a statement to the *Herald* newspaper (not published at the time), he welcomed the minister's statement.

> My personal view is that the easiest way to change an institution is with the help of an outside stimulus. If the Dawkins changes are seen in this light then they could have a positive impact on Australian education. There are also fears that higher education will suffer from more direct Ministerial control. A counter argument is that education can get its case across more effectively if it is dealing directly with a Minister who is closer to government economic policy making. In turn the Minister is more accountable for his actions than he was when a statutory authority set the scene.[32]

If a university was close to the minister, so much the better for that university, one might infer.

As a member of the Purple Circle and vice-chancellor of one of Australia's largest universities, Logan was both an architect and a client of the new regime. He shared its managerialist assumptions and spoke its language. When he addressed the university's students as 'customers', his colleagues as 'workers' and its friends as 'stakeholders', when he demanded that the university 'produce' students with 'skills appropriate for the labour market' and exhorted his colleagues to become more 'flexible' and 'entrepreneurial', and when he deplored their inclination to 'introspection' and urged them to look outwards, he was both playing to his political allies and setting an internal agenda.[33]

While adopting the 'new-speak' of national competitiveness, however, Logan retained enough of the 'old-speak' of collegiality and academic excellence to persuade fellow academics that, at heart, he remained one of them. While 'moving ahead', Monash would 'preserve those fundamental values which we share with all great universities' and defend 'the right to pursue curiosity-led research'.[34] According to circumstances, he could be the prophet of the new order, laying down the law, or a loyal defender of the old, holding the philistines at bay. Like his predecessors, Logan recognised that the university was ultimately a servant of its society. Matheson, reflecting the priorities of an industrial society, had sometimes likened Monash to a factory. Logan imagined it as a multi-national corporation adapting to the ever-changing forms of a post-industrial, global society.

Everything in Australia, including higher education, was now subject to the logic of comparative advantage.[35] Dawkins required each institution to define its place in the educational marketplace. History and geography had favoured the University of Melbourne over its young rival in Clayton. So long as Monash attempted to follow in Melbourne's path, Logan reasoned, it was bound to play second fiddle. Only if it changed the tune or played a different instrument could it find its own destiny. It should not be 'simply a clone of another place', but 'lively and vigorous', 'ready to take risks'.[36] 'The challenge', General Manager Peter Wade believed, 'was for Monash to be Monash'.[37] It needed to break out of its suburban isolation by finding new locations—in downtown Melbourne, in regional Victoria and abroad, especially in Asia. Globalisation was shaking institutions free from their geographical moorings. Instead of inviting the world to come to it, Monash would go out to meet the world. By cooperating with the great forces of the age, instead of resisting them, it would become a university unlimited by location or tradition.

The orchestra plays and the dance begins

Dawkins had challenged the 'binary divide' between universities and colleges of advanced education, but even he could not have imagined how quickly it would collapse.[38] 'Along came the Dawkins reforms—bang!—and we were into full-on, high-energy educational geo-politics!' Dean of Engineering Peter Darvall recalls.[39] The Green Paper had given a green light to mergers but regarded them as only one type of structural reform. In November 1987, rumours began to circulate of a plan by the Victorian Institute of Post-Secondary Education to rationalise Victoria's higher education sector. Director Ron Cullen proposed to excise sections of the various institutions and combine them with others to create a more integrated system. The plan attracted scant support among either the universities or the colleges, each eager to preserve their integrity. It was 'long on spurious arguments and short on serious rationale', Logan observed.[40] But, along with the Dawkins Green Paper, it spurred the institutions into action. 'It is clear that the orchestra has started playing the waltz and the process of selecting partners has begun', Logan wrote to Cullen early in February.[41] 'There was a frenetic and uncoordinated jockeying for position within the Victorian tertiary education sector', with everyone determined not to be 'left out in the cold', he explained to his deans.[42] Hardly a day went by when he did not get a call from the principal of another institution looking for a partner. Everyone, it seemed, was playing the field while postponing the moment of commitment. In the academic mating game, it was better to be considered flighty or promiscuous than left on the shelf.

Logan's first response to the idea of mergers had been cautious. He avoided the words 'merger' and 'amalgamation': Monash might be interested in some 'loose co-operative arrangement' with another institution, but its own 'identity and integrity' were 'non-negotiable'.[43] By early February, however, deans were pondering a range of possible relationships, from a loose affiliation to a 'fully-integrated University of California-style multi-campus model'.[44] As the ambitions of its rivals seemed to grow, so did Monash's determination to match them. The University of Melbourne, Logan reported, intended to merge with the College of Pharmacy and the Melbourne College of Education, while La Trobe was courting Bendigo Institute. All three universities were wooing the School of Physiotherapy at Lincoln Institute. The deans came, 'somewhat reluctantly', to the view that 'Monash was likely to "lose out" unless it took quick positive steps to counter the growing strength of competing institutions, particularly the University of Melbourne and RMIT'. Rather than taking 'small bites', such as Victoria College's Rusden campus or the College of the Arts, Monash should take a 'bolder approach', by combining with Chisholm Institute at Caulfield and even Swinburne Technical College to form 'a major technology-based university in the eastern region of Melbourne'.[45] Logan issued a press statement floating the idea of a grand federation of all the universities and colleges south of the Yarra.[46]

'An increase in size', Logan argued, 'would have definite advantages, with more opportunities for pursuing new developments and greater flexibility in the allocation of resources'.[47] Monash could also reap the financial largesse that Canberra was expected to bestow on those who fell in with its policies. The mania to merge, Logan later insisted, had developed only in response to the challenge from Monash's rivals, especially the University of Melbourne. But while Melbourne's intended acquisitions were modest and close to its Parkville home, Logan aimed to absorb institutions that together almost equalled Monash in size and encompassed half the metropolis. 'We had a bit of a map of Melbourne in mind, with Monash owning everything south of the river', he recalled.[48]

Over the early months of 1988, the enthusiasm of Logan and his colleagues for a big merger waxed and waned. Education, Engineering, Medicine and Science seemed most ardent at first, while Arts, ECOPS and Law were more wary.[49] Encouraged to widen their horizons, however, the deans soon began to size up which neighbours offered the richest pickings for their own faculties. Chisholm Institute, the nearest and largest of the colleges, was on almost everyone's shopping list. So was the Rusden campus of Victoria College, just across Blackburn Road, although the deans of Arts and Law also coveted that college's headquarters, the former vice-regal residence Stonnington. A palace in Toorak would make an attractive headquarters for the university administration or a prestigious outpost of the Law School. Engineering's Peter Darvall, on the other hand, considered Swinburne, with its sound Engineering Department, a richer prize.[50]

In less than a month, Logan had persuaded his colleagues to embrace his 'bold' vision of a 'greater Monash'. At every step, he assured them, Monash's academic standing and institutional autonomy would be preserved. No forward step would be taken without first establishing a line of retreat.[51] New partners would have to come in on Monash's terms. His approach to each issue, colleagues noted, was usually indirect, throwing out hints and suggestions, yet seldom revealing his ultimate objective.[52] One by one, he convinced the deans, the Academic Board and the council to embark on the most radical adventure in the university's history. As Darvall recalls, Logan was a great persuader:

> Oh, he was brilliant in persuading every faction within the university that he was absolutely in tune with their needs and desires. 'Ah yes, we'll do something about that': I can remember he said that a hundred times. And the Academic Board went: 'Oh yes,

we're going to do something about that'. With a significant little nod of his head, and everyone would think: 'Oh my God, Mal's right onto it, you know'.[53]

While Logan painted the big picture, his lieutenants filled in the detail. If they faltered, the vice-chancellor took command himself, conceding ground to his critics without losing face, since his own position had never been clearly defined. While the band was still playing and the partners were still gazing lovingly into each other's eyes, nobody was bothered, but once the parties were committed, many of the doubts and difficulties swept aside during the courtship returned to haunt them.

By early March, Chisholm Institute had emerged as Monash's most favoured partner.[54] Founded in 1922 as the Caulfield Technical School, Chisholm had gradually evolved from a trade-training institution, offering courses in carpentry and blacksmithing, to a comprehensive college offering degrees and diplomas in business, computing, engineering and psychology. Caulfield Institute, as it became, had only recently merged, after difficult negotiations, with the State College of Victoria at Frankston to create Chisholm Institute, with a student body almost half that of Monash itself.[55] Its director, Geoff Vaughan, had arrived only three years earlier from the Pharmacy College. An imposing figure, with the square jaw, rugged build and direct manner of a former rugby international, he established an immediate rapport with Logan. They shared an irreverent attitude to academic tradition, a conviction that the day of the big university had come, and, as one of Vaughan's close colleagues noted, 'a pretty healthy love of alcohol'.[56] Strategically, Vaughan saw no advantage in merging with other colleges of advanced education, like Swinburne and Victoria, or in attempting to go it alone. Soon after becoming director in 1986, he had invited Logan to speak at a graduation ceremony. 'Thereafter', Vaughan recalled, 'we were good mates'. When the orchestra struck up at the beginning of 1988 and the search for partners began, Chisholm and Monash, just 10 kilometres apart along Dandenong Road, seemed made for each other. 'It wasn't too far after that Mal and I got together', he remembered. 'I [said] there is no choice for Chisholm but Monash.'[57]

Discussions between Logan and his close colleagues had advanced quickly during the early months of 1988. By June, when deans consulted their colleagues, it became clear that not everyone was dancing to the vice-chancellor's tune. Why are we doing this? What is the academic rationale, people asked. Across all faculties there was a worry, expressed with varying levels of vehemence, that a merger with Chisholm would 'dilute standards' or 'debase the currency' of the Monash degree. Chisholm academics had inferior academic qualifications, with a lower proportion of PhDs, and its students entered at much lower scores than their Monash counterparts. Peter Darvall produced a table showing that his colleagues published refereed articles at roughly four times the rate of the Chisholm engineers.[58] Mechanical engineer Professor Ray Jarvis 'agonised many days' before speaking up: 'I believe we cannot embrace Chisholm without being contaminated by mediocrity'.[59] Darvall was torn between loyalty to his faculty and to his fellow deans. 'I am mindful of your urgings about leadership, about long-term vision, and about cabinet solidarity', he wrote to Logan. 'The consensus is for it [the merger], but I would urge you to make haste slowly. As one of my colleagues put it, "before marriage there should be a long courtship".'[60]

If they could not avoid merging, the engineers and economists hoped at least to differentiate their product from the supposedly inferior Chisholm brand.[61] Gus Sinclair, Dean of ECOPS, a cautious, quietly spoken economic historian, offered a sober assessment: 'The balance of educational advantage [from the merger] probably becomes positive only well into the future'.[62]

In the 1960s, ECOPS had established a strong reputation as a training ground for economists, public servants and business professionals. By the 1980s, however, the rising demand for graduates in management, marketing and accounting had already changed the complexion of the faculty. Its interests now overlapped with one of the largest and most successful parts of Chisholm Institute, the David Syme School of Business, which had won a strong reputation for courses closely matched to the needs of business. Many of its staff had come from the business world and combined their work as teachers with part-time consultancy.

At first sight, ECOPS, with its strengths in economics and econo-metrics, and the David Syme School, with its connections in the business world, were possible partners. In fact, no other two sections of the merging institutions displayed quite the same degree of mutual contempt and loathing. By Monash standards, the academic members of the David Syme School were underqualified. 'It is the difference in the quality of the staff of the two institutions which is the main difficulty of amalgamation', Sinclair advised Logan. In any merged entity, he argued, the David Syme School had to be 'made subject to the Faculty of Economics and Politics'.[63] The assumption of superiority drew cries of indignation from the other end of Dandenong Road. The David Syme School, its forceful director, Peter Chandler, insisted, had 'very high standing in the markets that it serves . . . We place emphasis on professional experience as well as qualifications'.[64] The real-world ethos of Caulfield produced graduates better suited to the needs of business than the ivory tower at Clayton. How could you take seriously a faculty of business with only seven PhDs, Clayton protested. How could you take seriously a business school with *more* than seven PhDs, Caulfield retorted.[65]

Faced with this impasse, Logan made a tactical retreat, renouncing the idea of a grand amalgamation in favour of a loose federation.[66] But while retreating publicly, the parties continued negotiations informally in a so-called 'kitchen cabinet'. Participants' recollections differ on who belonged to the group (Logan, Vaughan and his deputy, John White, later John Hay, sometimes Chisholm Council chair Paul Ramler and Peter Wade), on where and when it met (Logan's house on Sunday mornings, lunch during the week, Vaughan's office in the evening), and on what was on the agenda. Everyone agrees that discussion ranged widely, no minutes were kept, and alcohol was consumed.[67] Keeping things informal until agreement was reached was very much Logan's style. Meanwhile, newly appointed deputy vice-chancellor John Hay, Logan's 'minister for mergers', was handed the task of implementation.

Hay, formerly professor of English at the University of Western Australia, had become dean of arts in 1987. Self-assured, eloquent and determined, he was obviously a man on the way up. In giving him the merger portfolio, Logan had set him a stiff assignment. 'It could not be done through federation', Hay insisted. 'My view was to have all faculties answerable to deans, with some being single-campus and others being multi-campus faculties.'[68] Through 1989 and 1990, he pushed and prodded reluctant departments into a new template of cross-campus faculties. The programs of computing scattered across the two campuses and four

The Chisholm merger precipitated a
protracted territorial struggle between
Monash's Faculty of Economics, led
by Dean Gus Sinclair (pictured top
left, with colleague Alan Fels), and
Chisholm's David Syme School of
Business, led by Director Peter Chandler
(top right, pictured with Marketing
Director John Miller), in which Deputy
Vice-Chancellor John Hay (below right),
Logan's 'minister for mergers', sought
a settlement.

faculties were merged into a new Faculty of Computing and Information
Technology, a move that 'reflected the age that we live in'.[69] Chisholm's
small programs in literature, sociology and politics joined the Faculty of
Arts, along with the Department of Politics, which fled the now-embattled
ECOPS.[70] A proposal to split the enlarged Arts Faculty in two, to create
faculties of Arts and of Social and Behavioural Sciences, was dropped in the
face of almost unanimous opposition. When all the most obvious matches
had been made, Hay lumped the 'loose-ends'—a miscellany of applied
programs mainly from Chisholm—into a new Faculty of Professional
Studies.[71] Some of the partners were refugees, fleeing the embrace of
less congenial partners: nursing from Medicine, for example. Others,

like social work and librarianship, were sacrificial lambs, offered up by Arts to maintain its disciplinary integrity.[72] But, as just about everyone recognised, Professional Studies was a shotgun marriage designed to give an air of respectability to a union that nobody expected to last. It didn't.

The biggest hurdles to the merger remained the deep-seated conflicts in Engineering and Business/Economics. Hay decided to rush one fence and skirt the other. Despite his private reservations, Engineering Dean Peter Darvall had publicly supported the merger. Once the Academic Board approved the agreement a second time, he had little choice but to push it through, even though two-thirds of his colleagues, according to an informal poll, remained strongly opposed.[73] An anonymous handbill headed 'Engineering Dean Turns Quisling' circulated in the faculty. It was 'pretty hard to take', Darvall admits, 'but the University had decided and there was no option but to go ahead'.[74]

The gulf between the David Syme School and ECOPS seemed unbridgeable. A working party eventually recommended that they continue as separate faculties for at least three years in the hope that, 'with the passage of time, goodwill and mutual respect, a more effective measure of academic integration' would be achieved.[75] It seemed the only thing to do, but the continuance of two parallel Monash faculties, each offering their wares to the same market, seemed likely only to widen the rift. 'Just as two ice-cream sellers on the beach move to positions next to each other in the middle of the beach, the two faculties' offerings will move towards each other', econometrician Max King predicted. 'Duplication will increase and in the longer run Monash's reputation will decline.'[76] Unspoken was the fear that Syme might turn out to have the brightest umbrella and the most popular flavours. In retrospect, Hay considered it a defeat. 'I should have run together ECOPS and the Syme Business School then and there.'[77] It took another two years, and dented the reputation of another deputy vice-chancellor, before the two faculties merged.

As the wedding day approached, some of the excitement of the betrothal had ebbed away, lost in the endless wrangling about territory and status. Geoff Vaughan had backed the merger from the beginning, but as the negotiations neared a conclusion he worried that Chisholm could be 'dragged into the University as an angry and disillusioned partner'. He was already looking back nostalgically to the rosy beginnings of the romance.

'Our "Kitchen Cabinet" meetings did a lot to get the venture started, it is a pity we haven't continued with them', he sighed. Now, it seemed, 'everything that Monash does is right and everything that Chisholm does is wrong'.[78] Nevertheless, he won some significant concessions. Despite howls of indignation from Clayton, the heads of the largest Chisholm programs were made 'acting professors'.

Vaughan's own future role, however, remained unclear. As former director of an institution almost half as large as Monash, he was entitled to a university-wide job 'with teeth in it'. As deputy vice-chancellor (administration), he proposed that his responsibilities should include personnel, industrial relations, budget resources, information systems and the various campuses. 'I can feel in advance that [this] arrangement will cause a shock at Monash', he acknowledged.[79] In fact, the shock was to be Vaughan's. Logan had departed on an overseas trip, leaving John Hay in charge. The university's senior administrative structure had been settled only recently and it was not a good idea to change it, he explained. Vaughan's future role might include 'such major issues' as student accommodation, parking and inter-campus organisation.[80] The unpalatable truth, as Logan later admitted, was that 'there was room for only one vice-chancellor', and none of his lieutenants was going to give anything away.[81] Later, Vaughan was made deputy vice-chancellor (research) but soon departed for a senior administrative position in Canberra. For his Chisholm colleagues, however, there was no escape: they were now irrevocably part of 'the greater Monash'.

A place in the country

The merger mania produced some odd couples, none stranger than the alliance between Monash University and the Gippsland Institute of Advanced Education. Even Minister John Dawkins considered it 'the least likely' match of all.[82] About a hundred kilometres down the Princes Highway from Clayton, the institute's campus sat amid rose gardens, green paddocks and grazing kangaroos. To the north were the billowing smokestacks of the Hazelwood power station; to the south, the rolling hills and eucalypt forests of the Strzelecki Ranges. Monash had only a tenuous symbolic link with its poorer country cousin: Sir John Monash, after whom the university was named, was also the first chairman of the

Monash Gippsland's binishell, designed by architect Dr Dante Bini and installed in December 1979, was as much a local landmark as the smokestacks of the Hazelwood Power Station. It provided a venue for graduation ceremonies, exams, and sporting and social activities.

State Electricity Commission, whose apprentices attended the Yallourn Technical College, parent of the Gippsland Institute.

In the 1950s and 1960s, when brown-coal electricity drove the state's industrial expansion, the tech prospered. When the town was swallowed by the mine, it moved to a new site at Newborough, and in 1972 an Institute of Advanced Education, offering a wider range of tertiary courses, opened on a new site at Churchill. When the courtship with Monash began, in 1988, two-thirds of Gippsland's students were in external studies, more than half of them actually living in the suburbs of Melbourne. Every four weeks, hundreds of them descended on the Churchill campus for weekend schools where eager students finally put faces to the handwriting and voices of their instructors. In the memories of former staff, these were halcyon days. They recall the sea of gleaming windscreens in the campus car parks, the village of tents and caravans pitched on the tennis courts, the crush of customers in the cafeteria and the unquenchable enthusiasm of students still reading, discussing and running their experiments far into the night.[83]

External studies, or 'distance education', as it was becoming known, was one of the pillars of the Dawkins Revolution. 'External studies provides a convenient form of education for people who, for reasons such as distance, family responsibilities and the demands of full-time employment, find it difficult to attend on-campus courses', the Green Paper declared. At present, however, distance education in Australia was an inefficient cottage industry with too many providers, too much duplication and 'mediocre' standards. In order to achieve economies of scale, the nation's forty-eight distance education providers needed to be reduced to no more than ten, and perhaps as few as six.[84]

Monash's claims as a distance educator were thin, at best. But a big-picture vice-chancellor attuned to Dawkins' goals was loath to miss out on the educational bonanza. Monash had the educational goods, and it wanted at least a share in the new distribution system. The hot favourite to become a Victorian distance education centre (DEC) was Deakin University. As the state's first regional university, in 1975, Deakin had specialised in distance education. Monash registrar Tony Pritchard had come from Deakin with a strong interest in distance education, and it looked at first as though Deakin and Monash might jointly bid for a DEC. But Deakin vice-chancellor Malcolm Skilbeck had other ideas. He envisaged an enlarged regional university, led by Deakin, unifying the various regional colleges in Bendigo, Ballarat, Gippsland and Warrnambool. The 'Country and Western University', as it became known, excited little enthusiasm among regional rivals more jealous of each other than they were even of the metropolitan universities. Before Dawkins, Monash and Gippsland had already been exploring the possibility of an affiliation. In July 1988, Pritchard advised Logan that while a formal merger with Gippsland or Bendigo (the other contender) might not be welcome, a looser form of affiliation preserving 'something of their regional character', such as a 'University College' of Monash, might be 'broadly acceptable'.[85]

When the courtship with Deakin was called off, Monash's chances of getting into the distance education business receded. It could make an alliance with Gippsland, but only if Dawkins agreed to give Victoria an extra DEC. For Gippsland, the choices were even starker. 'We'd worked out that the economic boom that would make the La Trobe Valley into the Ruhr of Australia was not going to happen', former community services officer Murray Homes recalled. 'We knew . . . that we were facing economic decline and the only way the college could operate was to protect its distance education operation.'[86] In any alliance with Deakin, Gippsland was likely to lose out. The Monash brand name was better than Deakin's. And Clayton, after all, was closer than Deakin's campus on the far side of Geelong.[87]

Everyone was hedging bets. Monash didn't want to get into bed with Gippsland until it knew who would get the DECs. Tom Kennedy, Director of the Gippsland Institute, a cautious Scot, had his own reasons for delay. As a former deputy director of Chisholm, he had witnessed the forced merger of Caulfield and Frankston and found it 'a pretty

Mal Logan (seated, left) and Gippsland Institute Director Tom Kennedy sign merger documents under the watchful eye of Registrar Tony Pritchard (right), whose interest in distance education primed the marriage, and Gippsland Institute Council Secretary Jenny Hill, 1989.

unpleasant experience'.[88] It was better to take things slowly, and win some concessions along the way, than to rush in like Geoff Vaughan and be sorry afterwards. He knew that affiliation would not be the end of the road, but going slowly allowed time to bring colleagues along.

Logan had led the discussions leading up to the formal agreement. He gave interviews on local radio and schmoozed politicians. 'Mal is a very good people persuader', Kennedy noted.[89] The big-picture man seemed to understand the role of the regional community. Once the deal was done and the detailed negotiations began, however, he handed over to his lieutenants, who wasted no time in letting Gippsland know where it stood in 'the greater Monash'. The 'spurious rhetoric of local identity and separateness' was soon dropped.[90] Kennedy's hope of becoming a 'Deputy Vice-Chancellor and Chief Executive Officer of the University College' was dashed. 'We weren't going to have any princelings running campuses', John Hay insisted.[91] Academic programs would become responsible to deans of the various faculties, rather than to their local heads. It would become, as Logan insisted, 'an indivisible whole. It will speak with one voice'.[92]

In challenging the binary divide, Dawkins had hoped that the universities would absorb the real-world orientation of the colleges, while the colleges would emulate the research culture of the universities. In reality, size, location and academic status had tipped the power balance away from the bush campus. At Churchill, people began to notice the slights, conscious or unintended, of the people from 'Monash Central'. 'You're those correspondence school chappies, aren't you?' a Clayton economist greeted his new Gippsland colleagues.[93] Gippslanders always seemed to be adjusting themselves to the expectations of their big brother up the road. Why did meetings always begin at nine at Clayton and at eleven at Churchill? Yet, as the realists noted, in the brutal mating game set off by the Dawkins reforms, it was perhaps better to be married to a rich husband, however neglectful and unfeeling he might be, than to be left lamenting on the shelf.[94]

Looking from the other end of the Princes Highway, and with the benefit of hindsight, Gippsland remained the strangest of the mergers. Logan had pursued it in order to get into the distance education business. Yet just as the merger was being sealed, the world of distance education was about to be transformed beyond recognition. The old regime of mailed-out readers, cyclostyled notes, telephone calls and weekend schools would become as antiquated as quills and blackboards. In Britain, the Open University was utilising radio and television to bring lectures into the nation's living rooms. Monash would soon take the lead in founding Australia's own Open University, Open Learning Australia. Gippsland would play an under-acknowledged role in setting it up before being dealt out of a game it had once regarded as its own.[95]

The academics revolt

In embracing the Dawkins reforms, Logan hoped to carry the academic community with him, and the first decisions were ratified by the Academic Board and council almost without dissent. By the early 1990s, with its compass set, the university might have been expected to enter calmer waters. Within the academic community, however, there had never been much enthusiasm for the Dawkins reforms. In corridors and common rooms, there were mutterings about the new managerial style of the university, with its logos and glossy brochures, resentful rumours about senior executive salary packages, company cars and overseas junkets, and disdainful comments about the new corporate language. The mergers reinforced a feeling that the university's administration was becoming divorced from the academic community. The old Monash feared that, in marrying down, it would lose status. The former colleges worried that their distinctive identities would be lost.

Only when the consequences of the mergers percolated to the labora-tory and the classroom did the academic community finally stir into action. In March 1991, thirty-nine members of the Chemistry Department, one of the university's original research powerhouses, wrote to Logan protesting the impact of recent moves to centralise the distribution of research funds. The funds available for the small projects on which many researchers depended had been drastically reduced. When their complaint was unanswered, a member of the department, Dr Keith Murray, wrote to the *Age* raising the alarm.[96] Peter Wade remonstrated with Murray's head of department, Professor Ron Brown, for not keeping him in line. Brown's colleagues were furious. The funding shortfall had come in the wake of an unpopular reclassification of general staff by John Hay, whose expertise in literary criticism did not qualify him, the scientists argued, for assessing the skills of technicians and lab assistants. A number of small grievances had coalesced into a more general malaise. 'There has been an unprecedented loss of morale at Monash', the aggrieved academics began. 'This drop of morale is largely a consequence of the perception that the administration treats academics with contempt.'[97]

In April, an informal protest group, the Teaching and Research Action Group (TRAG), called a lunchtime meeting. Its leaders were Monash veterans, senior academics who had joined the university when it was young.[98] Mathematician Joe Monaghan had studied at Cambridge and done research in California before coming to Monash in 1968. Twenty years later, when he became a professor, Monash was already in the midst of the mergers. 'I would like to think you are going to support me in everything I am doing in the future', he remembers his vice-chancellor saying. Logan was arguing that Monash had to get bigger if it was not to be damaged. Monaghan was not convinced: 'Why do you have to be big? Does this mean that the University of Western Australia is going to disappear? Does this mean that Caltech is not large enough?' The implications of the mergers dawned only when the deed had been done. 'I didn't realise what was happening until we were in the midst of it.' Without thinking much about the consequences, he decided to speak up. 'Are you the suicidal professor?' he recalls an acquaintance calling out as he crossed the campus.[99]

Encouraged by the success of their April meeting, TRAG organised a petition to the Academic Board and announced a general protest meeting in Blackwood Hall for 3 June. 'Instead of being treated as a community of scholars, we are now regarded as mere employees', its manifesto declared. It circulated a list of draft resolutions 'deploring the general direction' of the university and 'condemning' the management of the senior administration, singling out Logan, Wade and Hay. On 10 May, Logan met its leaders in his office. He seemed nervous, like a rabbit surrounded by foxes, Monaghan recalls. Under pressure, he distanced himself from the 'unfortunate' style of his principal lieutenants.[100] Sidelining Hay, he got two of his deans, Bob Porter and Robert Pargetter, to negotiate with the protesters. They pledged to consult with the academic community and to give advance notice of important issues to the Academic Board.[101] In return, TRAG's leaders agreed to delete the names of the chief culprits from its motion condemning the central administration.

A few days later, almost 400 indignant academics crowded Blackwood Hall. Neither 'revolutionaries nor political activists', they had lost faith in an administration that seemed deaf to their pleas. Chemist Ian Bayly, a Monash veteran of twenty years, had been proud when the university made him a doctor of science in 1974. But now, he lamented, that pride had 'evaporated'. Psychologist Bill Webster felt alienated from a 'dictatorial, secretive and aloof' administration. Why had TRAG agreed to amend the motion condemning the university administration, asked economist Ross Parish. 'You named the villains in the original motion and now, because they have been nice to you, you have deleted them.'[102] Between the academics and the administration—'the Castle' as it was collectively known—a gulf had opened up.

The depth of discontent shook Logan. 'It had me worried for a time', he later admitted. Hay, benched by his leader after taking the brunt of the criticism, was clearly distressed.[103] In mid-June, the Academic Board resolved to appoint a committee of inquiry chaired by one of the university's most respected figures, Professor Louis Waller, to report on its research administration. The committee, supported now by Logan and his lieutenants, beat a retreat from the centralised and 'strategic' approach to 'research management' embodied in the Research Management Committee and its successor, the Vice-Chancellors' Research Advisory Committee. Designed originally as a means of promoting Monash's success in bids for cooperative research centres and other large-scale research, these committees had become, as Deputy Vice-Chancellor Vaughan noted, 'a high-powered group whose purpose was to advise the vice-chancellor on research policy matters'.[104] Their membership, skewed towards 'big' science, and their adoption of funding formulae favouring large teams over individual researchers had sparked the grassroots revolt. The concession was enough to take the wind from behind the protest movement.

The Waller Committee issued its own manifesto. 'Research and teaching—the discovery of knowledge and the imparting of knowledge— are the prime functions of the University', it began. 'All fields of knowledge represented within the University are entitled to parity of esteem.' The university had a responsibility to 'create a collegial environment' that honoured these principles.[105] A deputy vice-chancellor (research), who should be an active researcher, would become responsible for promoting research across the university, but the 'high-powered' central research committee would be replaced by a Committee of Associate Deans (Research) (CADRES) appointed by, and responsible to, the faculties. Rather than centralising research management, Waller brought it closer to the lab bench and the library.

The belief in the indivisibility of teaching and research had a troubling corollary: that those who taught but did not carry out research (not all of them former college of advanced education staff) should now have the 'opportunity' to do so. This expectation engendered much grief and frustration over the following decade as 'research mentors' prodded teaching stalwarts to become productive researchers. Logan appeared before the committee, preaching his ideal, an American-style research graduate school, but admitted it was unreachable in an institution where any appearance of intellectual elitism excited old antagonisms. 'It . . . would have created a climate in which first-class and second-class citizens co-existed and this was exactly what he was anxious to avoid.'[106] It was a telling admission. Logan had hoped to create a new Monash, combining democratic access with research excellence. In pursuing the first, he may have jeopardised the second.

The last waltz

Two years after the release of the Dawkins Green Paper, the season of frenzied merger negotiations was coming to an end. The band was playing the last waltz, and most of the dancers had paired off. Monash had pledged itself to Chisholm and Gippsland. After a brief flirtation, it had suspended its courtship with Victoria College, which had then paired up with Deakin, leaving the fate of its Rusden campus still in the balance. Only a few lonely hearts were still waiting, with mounting anxiety, for a suitable partner. Then Logan received an urgent phone call from Minister John Dawkins: 'We've got to do something with Pharmacy, no-one will take it'.[107]

When the mergers began, no couple had seemed better suited than the College of Pharmacy and its neighbour, the University of Melbourne. With only 420 students, the college was well below the threshold Dawkins had set for an institution to stand alone. Since its foundation, in 1882, under the auspices of the Pharmaceutical Society of Victoria, it had won a strong reputation in the local profession. In 1960, it had moved to attractive modern premises in Royal Parade, close to the University of Melbourne. It had conferred its own degrees since 1981 and, under a dynamic principal, Geoff Vaughan, developed a strong research program. Everything—proximity, educational mission, student base, research potential—suggested that Pharmacy and the University of Melbourne were a perfect match.[108]

An engagement between the Parkville neighbours had been expected for so long, however, that the proposal only stirred up memories of past rejections. Since 1878, the parties had begun and broken off negotiations no fewer than six times. At the heart of the difficulty was the disdain of the medicos, who thought of themselves as scientists and gentlemen, towards the pharmacists, whom one senior Melbourne medical academic dismissed as 'second-rate shopkeepers'.[109] Between the Pharmacy College and the University of Melbourne there was barely a kilometre of leafy boulevard, but almost a century and a half of professional resentment.

Director of the Victorian Post-Secondary Education Commission Ron Cullen had included a merger between the two institutions in his blueprint for the Victorian higher education system. But neither the university nor the college was eager to merge. 'If the Victorian College of Pharmacy wished to amalgamate with my University we would be proud to receive the College but I see absolutely no reason why it needs to', Vice-Chancellor David Penington declared.[110] As everyone else partnered up, the college eventually realised that it would not be allowed to remain single. In August 1989, its council named its terms for a merger with Melbourne: the college would become a separate faculty of the university, reporting directly to the University Council. The university countered by proposing it become a school within an enlarged and renamed faculty of medicine and dentistry. Various suggestions for the title of the enlarged faculty were batted back and forth. The university rejected 'faculty of health sciences'; the College rejected 'faculty of medicine, dentistry and health sciences'. If they lost their name, the pharmacists feared, everything else, including their property, substantial reserves and historical link to the Pharmaceutical Society, could be lost as well. The university, on the other hand, was in no hurry to meet their demands. After all, the pharmacists had nowhere else to go.

Or so everyone thought. Exactly who made the first approach is not clear. Monash later maintained that it came from the college, but only after negotiations with Melbourne had broken down. But on 6 June 1990, more than two months before the formal cessation of talks with Melbourne, Logan wrote confidentially to the director of the Pharmacy College, Tom Watson, outlining a possible merger. Geoff Vaughan, the former director of the Pharmacy College who had brought Chisholm to Monash, was in the background quietly encouraging the talks. The blueprint was the Gippsland merger: first, affiliation as a college, to be followed by a full amalgamation, with the college retaining its identity as a faculty and its own advisory council. Peter Wade found a way over one of the main hurdles to a merger—the need to compensate the Pharmaceutical Society for the college's Parkville site and buildings. Because the college was incorporated as a company, a merger could be arranged by simply changing its structure to represent the interests of the new partners. With these assurances, the college moved quickly to break off talks with Melbourne, and by October the two institutions had signed the heads of an agreement.

To the pharmacists, Logan was a white knight galloping to the rescue in the nick of time. But to many onlookers there was something brazenly opportunistic about Monash's intervention. Mergers were supposed to observe the principle of contiguity, but Monash appeared to have disregarded it in annexing a little bit of Parkville. In justification, it advanced new principles of its own: that Monash was entitled to a share of the professional schools and that its presence would add value to the Parkville 'knowledge precinct'. The college, it insisted somewhat implausibly, had 'never considered itself to be contiguous with the University of Melbourne'.[111]

Events were moving in a direction that neither Spring Street nor Canberra had anticipated. Unless Monash proposed to move the Pharmacy College to Clayton, the Victorian minister for education, Barry Pullen, objected, the merger made no sense. He offered to support a case for special federal funds to enable it to buy out the Pharmaceutical Society. Logan was outraged. If the rumours of a $2 million offer were correct, he protested, it amounted to a 'disgraceful waste of public funds'.[112] Both the college and the society preferred to go to Monash but could not ignore the financial implications. Logan urgently requested Peter Wade to devise a counter-offer: in return for a long lease of the Parkville site, Monash would offer the society $100 000 a year rent and access to prime space in the Monash Science Park.[113]

It was enough to seal the deal. There were congratulations all round. The pharmacists had avoided a shotgun marriage with the Melbourne medical faculty. Monash had acquired a new professional faculty and an address on Royal Parade. Defeating the old rival, Melbourne, only added to the jubilation. 'There was a bit of sticking it up them, yes absolutely', Logan agrees.[114]

After the ball

The mergers were the most enduring legacy of the Logan era. The big-picture man had become the vice-chancellor of the nation's largest university, with campuses stretching from the shady precincts of Royal Parade to the cow paddocks and power stations of Gippsland. From playing second fiddle in Victoria, Monash had become the conductor of the biggest band in the land. Determined their university wouldn't be a 'clone' of the University of Melbourne, Logan and his lieutenants had created something quite different: Australia's first mega-university.

Logan had come to the vice-chancellorship as a planner. But the university he left was a product of 'full-on, high-energy educational geo-politics' rather than deliberative planning. More than any other Australian vice-chancellor, Logan was in tune with the Hawke government's vision of higher education, but having the ear of the minister had not enabled him to transcend the territorial skirmishing and political opportunism that finally shaped the post-Dawkins educational landscape. 'They [the mergers] worried the hell out of me', he now admits. At the time, he had promised that 'the educational gains are likely to come quickly and the political gains will position the University well for a long time to come'. After two decades, he is not so sure. The jury, he concedes, is still out on his grand experiment.[115]

He is not alone. Tom Kennedy, in retirement, still wondered whether he was right to commit his Gippsland Institute to an unequal marriage with a large metropolitan university.[116] Some of his former colleagues would vote tomorrow to restore the binary system, ruing the loss of the vocational orientation and strong community ties of the old college. In Parkville, members of the Pharmacy College long viewed the merger as a hostile takeover, even though Monash had come along only when the engagement to Melbourne was broken off. 'You mention merger, and it's like Pavlov's dog—they hear the sound of chain-saws', said one observer in 1995.[117] Vaughan became a Monash deputy vice-chancellor but locked horns with Hay (about the size of their respective offices, among other matters) and resigned to become head of the federal Therapeutic Goods Administration. A few months later, Hay also resigned, to become vice-chancellor of Deakin University, where, after its merger with Victoria College, he inherited Stonnington, the mansion in Toorak that had taken his fancy in 1988.

'I think Mal wanted size at any cost', Peter Darvall reflects. 'You'll never win the status game with Melbourne and Sydney, but if you're the biggest they've got to listen to you.'[118] Size brought educational benefits as well as political clout. The aggregation of resources delivered economies of scale and, over time, the flexibility to expand and innovate. A university of 30 000 students like Wisconsin could deliver high-quality undergraduate education to the many, and excellent postgraduate research opportunities to the few. But Wisconsin had grown organically over a century or more; could a university cobbled together from disparate parts, unified by little more than proximity and mutual survival, achieve the same result? In order to innovate, it was necessary to be able to liberate the university's resource base, turn old assets to new uses, sack redundant staff and sell off surplus property. Peter Wade had shown that Monash could get better returns from some of its assets by managing them more effectively. But not all the assets in Monash's portfolio were tradeable or blue chip. The colleges were funded at a lower rate per student than the old Monash, so the economies of scale had to be sufficient to offset the reduction of per capita income. 'It was always going to be a levelling down, but it was a question of how far down', Darvall shrewdly observes. For the former colleges, of course, it may have been a levelling up. Gippsland was able to survive within 'the greater Monash' when it might have sunk alone. In a commercial merger, it was easy for the entrepreneur to sell off assets or sack employees, but, as Monash was to discover, a public university could not simply close a campus or sack tenured academics at will.

Logan the geographer envisioned his empire extending along an east–west corridor from the centre of Melbourne through the south-eastern suburbs to Gippsland. By acquiring new campuses at Caulfield and Parkville, Monash redressed some of the disadvantages of its 'isolated' Clayton location. But geography alone was a treacherous guide to academic compatibility. Academic neighbours were not necessarily bound to become good friends. In the rush to merge, Monash had overridden deep differences between the cultures of the partners. It assumed too readily that you could blend academic cultures by simply knocking heads together. The assumption was that self-interest reinforced by a measure of coercion would quickly dissolve the archaic cultures of the binary system. Estimates varied about how long it would take: a decade, perhaps two, or even more. Today, none of the participants are revising their estimates downwards. 'It was so bloody difficult to bring together that we never used it [the amalgamation] as an instrument for institutional change', Logan admitted.[119]

'To merge is to change', two experienced observers of the Australian academic scene noted in 1988, 'and there is no such thing as painless social change'.[120] The pain and conflict engendered by the mergers lingered long after the crisis was over. Logan realised that in attacking the binary divide he was challenging values that went deeper than self-interest and loyalties that extended far beyond the campus. In the last resort, many Monash academics were closer to their fellow chemists or historians on the other side of the world than to their colleagues on the other side of the campus. When the challenge came, their instinct was to fight, and, if they lost, either to leave the university or to retreat within it. Joe Monaghan had led the revolt of the staff group TRAG, but when the revolt petered out he decided to resist no longer. 'I would protect myself as well as possible from university administration. I would make myself a castle, it would have a moat around it, with a portcullis, and I would get inside and do my research work.'[121] The mergers may have raised as many walls as they brought down. Inside his castle, Monaghan patiently investigated the behaviour of liquids, theoretical work that has illuminated problems as diverse as the formation of galaxies and ancient tsunamis, inspired applications in movie-making and surgery, and won Monaghan election to the Australian Academy of Science.

Monash old-timers mourned the university they thought they had lost. But not everything they mourned was a casualty of the mergers alone. The best antidote to nostalgia is to imagine what Monash might have been *without* the mergers. At a time when the middle classes were moving back to the inner city, it could have been marooned in a dying industrial suburb. When its academic workforce was ageing, it may have had limited capacity to renew itself. Probably, whatever gains came from the mergers could have been realised by taking on fewer partners. When was an institution big enough to achieve economies of scale? When did it become so big that it lost focus? Logan had always argued that the mergers would not be successful if they came at a cost to Monash's research standing.[122] In the short-term, the balance sheet was probably negative. By the early 1990s, Monash had slipped down the league tables for research; only after the new century had dawned did it begin to rise again.

In time, the culture of Monash *did* change. New academic recruits now have looser ties to particular campuses and programs. The post-merger university has forged alliances between traditional disciplines and applied studies. New programs like international studies are now taught over several campuses. And while the flow of people between campuses may still be slender, the electronic traffic grows exponentially. How many of these changes came about because of the mergers is open to debate. The mergers had come just as the entire culture of the university was about to change. 'Multi-campus institutions place a premium on communications', two observers noted in 1988.[123] They could hardly have known how completely the campus-based world of learning would be revolutionised by developments in digital communications over the following decade. The greater Monash had no sooner arrived than the global university came into view.

EIGHT

THE GREATER MONASH

Monash giantism is not a hormonal imbalance and not an end in itself.

PETER DARVALL, 1994

'The "greater" Monash University is now widely viewed as the success story of the national restructuring of higher education', Vice-Chancellor Mal Logan claimed in 1990.[1] The phrase 'the Greater Monash', originally coined during the Gippsland merger, soon appeared with capitals to denote the ever-growing sphere of Monash's educational empire. It had some interesting antecedents. English politician Charles Dilke had called the British Empire at its zenith 'Greater Britain'. 'Greater Monash' conveyed a similar sense of global vision, chauvinistic pride and vaulting ambition. It could provoke resentment among its rivals and ridicule even among its friends. The story that there was a sign at the Victorian border saying 'Welcome to Monash' was absurd, but only because Greater Monash extended well beyond state borders and because the university's marketing people hadn't erected it yet.

Not everyone, even among Monash's leaders, believed that bigger was necessarily better. 'Monash giantism is not a hormonal imbalance', Peter Darvall observed, 'and not an end in itself'.[2] It was justified only insofar as it furthered the university's primary purposes: teaching and research. Even so, to Logan and his contemporaries, expansion had a seductive appeal. Pioneering new frontiers was something seemingly coded into their university's DNA. During the 1980s and early 1990s, Monash expanded, rather like the British Empire, by swallowing up previously

Through its partnership with Sunway College in Kuala Lumpur, Monash took the first steps towards a program of international expansion that increasingly defined its mission.

independent institutes and colleges ('the mergers'). Soon, it also began to
grow by internal expansion, adding new disciplines to old faculties. And
finally, it began to establish new campuses (colonies) of its own, some
in Victoria, some beyond Australia, some even in cyberspace. Chapter 7
described the first phase in the development of the Greater Monash; this
chapter examines the second.

Thinking bigger

One effect of the Dawkins Revolution was to make everyone start to think
bigger. By tearing down the protective barriers between institutions, it
changed how universities thought about themselves and their place in
society. According to the neo-liberal doctrine of the reformers, this was a
healthy development: it released the pent-up entrepreneurial talents of the
academic community. Monash after the mergers looked very different from
the old Monash; it was not only bigger, but the pecking order between
faculties had changed, along with their budgetary size. There were not
only new faculties, like Pharmacy, and merged ones, like Business and
Economics, but even those apparently immune from the effects of the
mergers, like Medicine, extended their ambitions.

When Bob Porter returned from ANU to become dean of medicine,
in 1989, morale in the faculty was low, and its competitive performance
was declining. A government inquiry into medical education, the Doherty
Report of 1988, had recommended major changes in the way doctors and
other health professionals were trained. Some of its emphases—on early
clinical experience, active learning and engagement with the healthcare
system—had been anticipated by Rod Andrew's blueprint for the Monash
faculty in the early 1960s, but the faculty had since lost ground, and Porter
had to begin the reform process all over again. In May 1989, he proposed
'a radical revision of the curriculum' that would incorporate a 'scientific
and humanitarian approach, self-education and a critical evaluation of
knowledge and practice'. Students would be selected through interviews
as well as Higher School Certificate results. The faculty also began to
increase its territorial ambitions. 'We aim to broaden the base of the
Faculty and extend the range of activities from medicine to a series of
allied health areas', Porter promised.[3]

Logan and his lieutenants, 1993. From left, seated, Deputy Vice-Chancellor Robert Pargetter, Pro Vice-Chancellor Leo West, Deputy Vice-Chancellor Ian Chubb, Vice-Chancellor Mal Logan, General Manager Peter Wade, Deputy Vice-Chancellor Peter Darvall; standing, Vice-Chancellor's Advisor Elizabeth Anderson, Marketing Manager Gary Neat.

This was easier said than done. Monash had lost a bidding war with La Trobe for the previously independent Lincoln Institute of Health Sciences, which taught courses in physiotherapy, occupational therapy and speech therapy. An attempt to get a second program in physiotherapy was thwarted by Melbourne. As a result of the mergers with Gippsland and Chisholm, Monash inherited two schools of nursing, which refused, however, to join a faculty run by doctors. The task of winning them over, Porter reflected, 'would have daunted Henry Kissinger'.[4] Porter acquired a program to train ambulance officers and developed courses in rural health and forensic medicine. It took almost a decade, two more reforming deans of medicine and a shift in the culture of the faculty for Porter's blueprint to be realised. His successor, Nick Saunders, made even more 'radical' changes to the curriculum and integrated nursing, physiotherapy and occupational therapy into a successful new health sciences campus at Frankston. 'We are much more than a Faculty of Medicine', he declared in 1999.[5] Today, the Faculty of Medicine, Nursing and Health Sciences, with over 10 000 full- and part-time students, is the second largest in the university.

A field of dreams

In the 1990s, as the professional middle classes retreated to the inner city, Monash returned to the suburban frontier with a fresh mission. Clayton was built on the educational aspirations of a newly affluent middle class; Berwick, Monash's newest campus, aimed to redress the educational disadvantage of the suburban working class.

Berwick was once a picturesque, self-consciously English village on the outskirts of Melbourne. Motorists driving to Gippsland noticed the air of refinement visible in the colonial buildings and half-timbered shops along its main street, its plantations of deciduous trees, and the spacious grounds of its fashionable girls boarding school, St Margaret's. It even had its own lord of the manor, Baron Casey of Berwick, former Australian minister for external affairs, whose country seat, Edrington, looked down towards the airfield where the Caseys, keen aviators, landed their private plane.

By the 1990s, Melbourne's sprawl had caught up with the village. Blue-collar workers, subcontractors and service employees migrating eastwards from Dandenong through Hallam and Narre Warren peopled a land of sweeping drives and cul-de-sacs, brick-veneer mansions, triple garages and tiny backyards. Eager for material progress, they were the so-called 'aspirationals' whose votes swung state and national elections. Monash graduate Jane Turner (BA 1988) satirised their 'lifestyle' in her TV comedy *Kath and Kim*. Over the decade, the population of the region (Berwick, Cranbourne and Pakenham) was forecast to almost treble, from 90 500 to 242 000. Many were young people, but the proportion actually undertaking higher education was the lowest in the metropolis.[6]

Liberal member of the House of Representatives for La Trobe, Bob Charles, backed by a local committee, campaigned for Berwick to get its own university campus. In September 1990, Logan requested between $5.5 million and $6 million from the Commonwealth to construct a 'multi-purpose building' in a 'cooperative arrangement' with the Dandenong TAFE on its site at Berwick. The aim was modest: to offer first-year 'feeder' courses articulating to Monash's other campuses.[7] A year later, as it was signing off on the mergers, the Victorian government urged the university to think bigger. 'A higher education development in the area is a key State priority', Acting Director of the Victorian Post-Secondary Education Commission Ian Allen reminded Logan.[8] An election in which the marginal seats of Berwick, Cranbourne and Pakenham would be crucial was just a year away. Logan's response was enthusiastic. Instead of a modest shared 'facility', Monash offered to build its own campus 'linking higher education provision for that area to the existing campuses of Monash University'. In the geographer's mind, Berwick was becoming a link in the chain of Monash campuses stretching from Parkville to Churchill. An ideal 70-acre site was available next door to the TAFE site, between the railway and the projected freeway, on land annexed from the Casey airfield; the government, he suggested, should acquire it at once.[9]

Early in 1992, a working group under new deputy vice-chancellor Robert Pargetter began planning the new campus. Pargetter had arrived at Monash as professor of philosophy in 1989 but soon became dean of arts, where his Falstaffian presence made an immediate impression. He was, everyone agreed, 'a character': large, jolly, informal and very clever. At fifteen, he had watched his father, a heavily built man, die suddenly from a heart attack as he washed the family car. According to his friend and fellow philosopher John Bigelow, he realised that his own life might be short and resolved not to waste a moment of it.[10] As dean, he inherited a large office lined with bookshelves. But his personal library was small: why own books, when you can always borrow them, he reasoned. So he called up the university librarian and borrowed a very large quantity of duplicate copies, filling his shelves in no particular order. Unknowing visitors departed dazzled by his encyclopaedic erudition.

Pargetter impressed Logan with his strategic acuity and keen nego-tiating skills. When Geoff Vaughan resigned, Pargetter took his place, inheriting the Berwick portfolio. From the beginning, the campus caught his imagination. A former schoolteacher, he had a keen understanding of the difficulties young people faced in making the transition from school to university. And living on the suburban fringe—he tended a kennel of labradors at Lower Plenty—sparked his interest in improving its access to higher education.

Before the project got under way, local politics threatened to derail it. The City of Dandenong, backed by local Labor members of parliament, pushed for an urban location, like the redeveloped Dandenong Market. Monash insisted that it should be Berwick or nothing. Dandenong was too close to Clayton.[11] Education Minister Tom Roper hesitated. It was important not to rush the decision, he argued; 'otherwise we could end up with another La Trobe or Monash which, in hindsight, were put in the wrong places'.[12] Only on the eve of the 1992 election did he finally announce his decision. 'WE GET THE UNI!' the *Berwick Journal* trumpeted.[13] Days later, Liberal Jeff Kennett swept to power, capturing a belt of Labor-held seats including Berwick and Cranbourne.[14] In December, after yet another review, the new education minister, Haddon Storey, confirmed that Berwick would get its uni.[15]

Berwick was a field of dreams. Someone had only to build it, the dreamers imagined, and the eager students would come. A ministerial working party predicted it would have over 10 000 students by 2011, four-fifths of them from the surrounding region, and 40 per cent coming by public transport.[16] Even before the first concrete had been poured, however, Logan began to worry. The state might provide the site, and the Commonwealth the $11 million to build it, but where would the students come from? If they came from one of Monash's other campuses, then the university was simply adding to its costs without increasing its income.[17] Either the government, state or federal, would have to fund additional places, or the field could remain embarrassingly empty. Logan pleaded with the state government for 200 state-funded places to kick off the project. When Canberra refused a request for more capital funds, suggesting 'a more modest development', Monash was forced back to the drawing board.[18]

The Gippsland pro vice-chancellor, Lauchlan Chipman, a lateral-thinking philosopher, came up with a new plan. Instead of a collection of separate campuses, with a student load attached to each, Monash should see itself as a single university with multiple access points. Berwick would then become one 'component of an integrated Network of campuses in the eastern half of the State'.[19] The postmodern logic of the scheme was clear: in a world where people and information moved freely, why should the university be shackled to the campus? Exactly how the east–west 'axis' of campuses contributed to the 'course delivery system' as a whole was less clear. Would students travel from campus to campus, or migrate from one to another? Would staff hot-desk on several campuses, or remain on one while telecommuting to the others?

Technology, everyone believed, was the answer. According to the architects' brief, the campus should 'promote the image of the University as a leader in educational technology' and 'provide a central networking point for the distance-mode communications network of the university'.[20] Woods Bagot responded with an airy pavilion topped by a 50-metre communications tower and flanked by a capsized cuboid lecture theatre: a visual joke about the overthrow of the old learning paradigm by the new, perhaps?[21] Inside, academics worked in clusters behind transparent walls to encourage more networking and hot-desked to accommodate the flow of day-trippers. The Monash director of IT, Cliff Bellamy, explained how sunrise technologies—interactive television, electronic mail, desktop video-conferencing and computer-assisted learning—would transform the learning experience of students. 'No way can we teach that way', some academics objected. 'Please can we start in second semester 1995?' others implored.[22] Instead of a traditional library of books and journals, a 'virtual library' would offer a 'universal window' onto the huge array of information accessed electronically through networked databases.[23] It was a glimpse into a brave new educational world, although only some of its features were actually within reach. Pargetter, the philosopher with no books, saw it as 'a type of half-way house' between the old academic order and the new.[24]

In the meantime, however, the campus needed customers of its own. 'It is crucial that a degree unique to Berwick be a major component of the initiative, in order to attract students specifically to that campus', the staff argued.[25] Instead of meeting the latent demand among locals for standard Monash courses, the campus now planned a suite of 'niche' courses in communications, electronic commerce, tourism and IT, designed to attract students from everywhere. 'I foresee Berwick developing into a very high calibre elite campus with one of the best groups of students in the university', Pargetter enthused.[26] But most locals passed it by, preferring to drive on to the academic supermarket at Clayton than to choose from the limited menu at the Berwick boutique.

Opening day was chaotic. The weather was hot, the toilets became blocked, and cows from the adjoining paddocks strayed onto the freeway. There weren't enough chairs, so staff carried them from room to room. Of the one hundred students in the first intake, only about one-third lived locally. 'They were a really outstanding group of young people with a pioneering spirit', Campus Coordinator Jill McLachlan recalls.[27] Like Clayton's pioneers forty-five years earlier, they thrived on the rigours of building a new academic community. The first academics were a mixed bunch of idealists, eccentrics and academic vagabonds. With so many part-timers, the administrative staff, especially the two 'motherly' women on the reception desk, became guides and counsellors to everyone, befriending the lonely, finding homes for the homeless, consoling the lovelorn and taking the sick to hospital. International students arriving at Berwick from Singapore and Hong Kong were unprepared for the bucolic scene that awaited them. 'I've been out to look at the university and, did you know, there's nothing there', one puzzled newcomer reported. Pargetter waived the amenities fee because there weren't any.[28]

Soon, however, the students organised activities of their own. The annual ball was their idea. McLachlan recalls driving drunken students home in a mini-bus and sweeping out the vomit and condoms afterwards. In many ways, she reflects, it was more like a high school than a university.[29] It didn't suit everyone, but many found its intimate scale a welcome alternative to the anonymity of the bigger campuses. Its planners had imagined a futuristic campus located in cyberspace and linked by the new digital technologies to the Greater Monash. What they unwittingly created was a semi-rural college with old-fashioned virtues of informality and friendliness.

'I'm not quite certain why we went to Berwick', Logan confessed years later.[30] His confusion is understandable, for the only constant in the university's thinking was the campus itself. Pressed upon the university as a price of the mergers, Berwick was expected to redress social disadvantage on the suburban fringe. Logan hoped it would unite his ad hoc empire of south-eastern campuses. Economic exigency gave it a new identity as a prototype for Monash's advance into the world of

A brush with royalty. HRH Prince Charles leaves Monash after being awarded an honorary doctor of laws, April 1981. A crowd of 'jeering, mindless students', estimated by the press at around 1000 to 2000 and by 'Monash riot watchers' at no more than 500, greeted his appearance on campus.

By the 1970s, many of Monash's still-youthful academic pioneers had won scientific laurels. Physiologist Mollie Holman won wide regard for her pioneering work on smooth muscle and as a mentor for other women scientists. Geneticist Bruce Holloway, pictured here with technician Linda Newman, investigated the characteristics of the bacterium Pseudomonas and later contributed to the development of biotechnology in Australia. Mathematician Andrew Prentice, seen here with student Kerry Hourigan, advanced controversial theories about the nature of the solar system, later confirmed by the observations of NASA scientists. Chemistry's Ron Brown and his team successfully synthesised the biological molecule HNC in the laboratory.

Professor Mollie Holman.

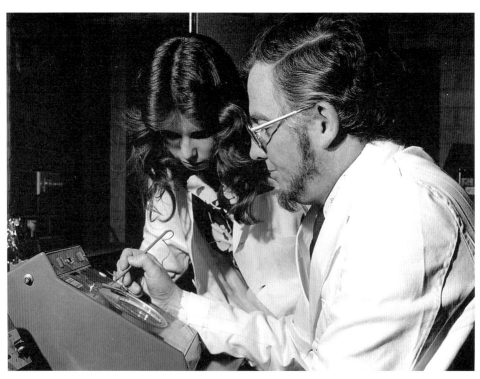

Laboratory technician Linda Newman assisting Professor Bruce Holloway, 1975.

Student Kerry Hourigan (left) and Dr Andrew Prentice checking findings, 1977.

Chemistry professor Ron Brown demonstrates how his team successfully produced the biological molecule hydrogen isocyanide (HNC).

Historian John Legge (right), pictured with director of the Centre of Southeast Asian Studies, Jamie Mackie, and former deputy prime minister of Indonesia, Dr Sudjarwo Tjondronegoro, in 1971, pioneered Monash's long engagement with the region.

In the 1970s and 1980s, the spirit of intellectual innovation flourished through the creation of centres crossing disciplines and focusing the energies of academics across the university on a range of contemporary issues.

The Centre for Research into Aboriginal Affairs, founded at the initiative of political scientist Colin Tatz in 1964, was later headed by Colin Bourke (far left), with (left to right) Victorian Aboriginal representative Reg Blow, Minister for Aboriginal Affairs Ian Viner, Vice-Chancellor Ray Martin and Professor Louis Waller. Now the Monash Indigenous Centre, it is one of the university's oldest academic centres.

Linguist Michael Clyne, a child of Austrian refugees, became the leader of the Centre for Migrant Studies and a vigorous advocate of multiculturalism. He is pictured here in 1978 (far left) with (from left) former Whitlam government minister for immigration, Al Grassby, famous for his colourful ties, geographer John Mackay and Senior Lecturer in Education Dr Gilbert Best.

In the 1970s, Monash became famous as a leader in IVF. Top: A team led by gynaecologist Professor Carl Wood (right), including Associate Professor John Leeton (left) and Dr Alex Lopata (centre), became the second in the world to successfully deliver a baby by IVF and was soon the world leader. The ethical dilemmas posed by the new techniques prompted the university to found a Centre for Human Bioethics led by philosophers Professor Peter Singer and Dr Helga Kuhse, pictured below, whose often radical ideas on fertility, disability, euthanasia and embryo experimentation stirred public debate.

Under the vigorous leadership of Professor Tony Linnane (second from right), researchers at Monash's Centre for Molecular Biology and Medicine, including (from left) Sangkot Marzuki, Phillip Nagley and Bruce Lukins, made important discoveries in the understanding of antibodies, including medical applications of the protein interferon.

After years of lobbying by staff and students, the Centre for Women's Studies was launched in 1987. Left to right: Pauline Nestor (English), Anne Edwards, Jan van Bommel, Ulla Svenson (all from sociology) and Alba Romano (classical studies) discuss plans for the centre's courses.

Set amid the paddocks and power stations of the Latrobe Valley, the former Gippsland Institute of Advanced Education became Monash's first rural campus.

Caulfield, the largest of Monash's new campuses, was home to the former Chisholm Institute, with a history stretching back to the foundation of the Caulfield Technical College in the 1920s.

Scenes of the Greater Monash. The Dawkins revolution in higher education transformed Monash from a single-campus university in Clayton to a mega-university with sites as dispersed as Parkville and Gippsland, Tuscany and Kuala Lumpur.

With its communication tower and tilted lecture theatres, the campus at Berwick on Melbourne's south-eastern fringe symbolised Monash's bid to command the new frontier of technologically driven global education.

Just twenty minutes from Florence, the Monash Prato Centre occupies the sixteenth-century Palazzo Vai in the heart of the medieval textile town, and is the university's academic base in western Europe.

Monash Sunway, the university's largest international campus, occupies a corner of the vast real-estate, retail and entertainment complex created by Chinese-Malaysian entrepreneur Jeffrey Cheah on a tract of rehabilitated mining land on the southern perimeter of Kuala Lumpur. The nucleus of the complex, identifiable by the towers and wooded area in the centre of the picture, comprises the Sunway Lagoon theme park, Pyramid shopping mall, and two multistorey resort hotels. Sunway University, formerly Sunway College, is at centre-left and the new Monash Sunway campus is in the lower left corner.

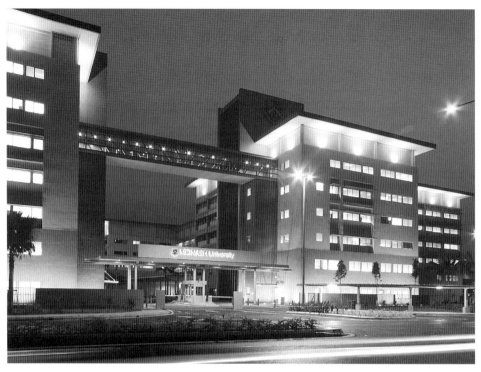

Linked by an overhead walkway, the Monash Sunway campus (right) adjoins the Tan Sri Jeffrey Cheah School of Medicine.

Students at work in the Monash Sunway 'Learning Commons'. Founded to provide higher education for Malaysia's Chinese community, the campus now attracts students from other ethnic groups and from other countries in Southeast Asia.

The entrance to Monash's South Africa campus.

Student volunteers prepare lunch at Monash South Africa's 'Saturday School' for underprivileged schoolchildren from the nearby Zandspruit informal settlement.

Still waiting. Students queue for the bus to Monash Clayton at Huntingdale Railway Station. (Newspix/Eugene Hyland)

The virtual university. Economics/law student Evelyn Young listens to downloaded lectures at her local café. (Craig Sillitoe/Fairfax Syndication)

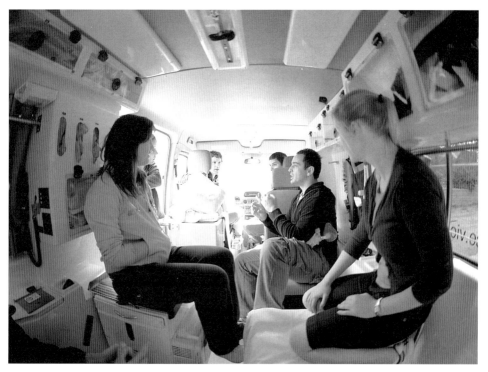

Bachelor of Emergency Health (Paramedic) students at Peninsula Campus. In the 1990s, the Faculty of Medicine and Health Sciences expanded its offerings into a range of allied health professions.

Monash in the city. The Parkville campus, home to Monash University's Faculty of Pharmacy and Pharmaceutical Sciences.

Under Vice-Chancellor Richard Larkins, Monash students were urged to equip themselves not just for their chosen profession, but 'for a fairer, more peaceful, more tolerant world'. Here, students Tina Thorburn (left) and Rachelle Adamowicz visit the Silwanendlala Ubuntu Farmers Association farming collective in Buffelspruit, South Africa, as part of a field studies course in regional sustainability run by the School of Geography and Environmental Science, 2011.

Berwick campus, 1998. Located between the Princes Highway (top right corner) and the Gippsland railway, on the site of the old Casey airfield, Monash's Berwick campus was a bold gesture of confidence in the cyber-university, symbolised by its tilted lecture theatres and communications tower.

digital education. But it was only by becoming more exclusive, a boutique for a suite of distinctive academic programs, that it was able to overcome the disadvantages of its small size and remote location. Five years after opening, it remained small, with just 1320 students, two-thirds female, most drawn from outside the region. The connection with TAFE, the original rationale for the campus, had withered, along with the regional focus.[31] A field of dreams, it was born of a belief that in a suburb devoid of higher education the students would simply come.

Its supporters are still dreaming. A later vice-chancellor considered plans to 'anchor' the campus with new residential or commercial developments. But the land had been acquired through compulsory purchase and could be used only for public purposes. Today, a new science high school occupies the northern end of the site, a multi-disciplinary health centre is under construction, and the campus will soon offer a new suite of undergraduate courses.[32] Its location, close to rail and freeway in a growth corridor, is a long-term asset. One day, surely, the dream will come true.

Beyond the campus

Beyond the suburbs lay a new educational frontier. In challenging the old educational order, Dawkins had also breached the limits of the conventional campus. In an era of fast electronic communication, social mobility and flexible production, he argued, higher education no longer needed to observe a fixed timetable of lectures, tutorials, lab sessions and exams. Thanks to radio, television, satellites, computers and the worldwide web, students could learn without the barriers imposed by tiresome university admission procedures, high fees, work and family commitments, travel constraints and inflexible academic timetables. 'Flexible delivery' and 'the open campus' became watchwords of a new era. In the 1970s, the bookish prime minister Gough Whitlam decreed that every Australian child should have a desk and a lamp. In 1992, Treasurer John Dawkins promised higher education to 'every Australian with access to a television and a letter-box'.[33] By the time these dreams were realised, the postbox and the television screen were giving way to the laptop and the internet.

Mal Logan was among the first Australian vice-chancellors to recognise that openness and flexibility would define the new higher education system. At first, only a small number of accredited DECs would be permitted to enter this new land of educational opportunity: acquiring a DEC was one of the prime motives for Monash's merger with Gippsland. By 1990, however, it was clear that new technologies and pedagogies would quickly make the old models of distance education obsolete. 'The explosive development of the information technologies enables higher education to be, to a large extent, freed from location and time constraints', the Higher Education Council observed in 1990. Monash had bought a horse and cart just as the automobile was about to appear.

In January 1990, Monash registrar Tony Pritchard wrote to Professor Robert Smith, Chairman of the National Board of Employment, Education and Training, proposing a feasibility study for a new body, the Open Learning Authority of Australia. Within the unified national system of higher education, the authority would act like a bank, enabling the exchange of credits from one institution to another. The scheme was based on a Canadian model, British Columbia's Open Learning Institute.

There was more to the initiative than immediately met the eye. Pritchard and Smith already knew each other well—they had met five years earlier at the Open Learning Centre in Vancouver, when Smith was vice-chancellor of the University of British Columbia and Pritchard was registrar of Deakin University. Smith, a geographer, and Logan had been mates since their days as students at UNE, and their paths had often crossed over the years.[34] Both were members of Dawkins' 'Purple Circle'. In January 1990, Smith became vice-chancellor of UNE, Australia's leading provider of distance education. 'I am seeking your support for the proposal', Pritchard explained, 'both because of your personal interest and expertise in this area, and because of the importance of your new University to the project'. In proposing the new authority, Logan and Smith were moving to annex the newest frontier of educational opportunity.

Logan's lieutenant, Tony Pritchard, had arrived at Monash in 1985 from Deakin University, where, as foundation registrar, he had seen it become the nation's second-largest distance education provider. Born into a churchy middle-class family, Pritchard taught science in public and private schools before becoming registrar of the Guroka Teachers' College in Papua New Guinea in 1970. New Guinea appealed to his sense of adventure, idealism and curiosity about other cultures, qualities he carried into his later career.[35] After ten years at Deakin, he was restless, and Logan, expected to be Monash's next vice-chancellor, encouraged him to apply for the job just vacated by the long-serving Jim Butchart. Pritchard rejected the traditional conception of the registrar's role—'a super-clerk maintaining an efficient bureaucracy'. He aspired to become (in the jargon of the day) a 'pro-active' agent of the 'greater Monash' in Australia and abroad.[36]

Well before the feasibility study was completed, in December 1990, Monash and UNE had positioned themselves to lead the new authority.[37] Pritchard recruited a Deakin colleague, Gavin Moodie, an expert on distance education, to lead the project. By October, Moodie had begun to build a consortium based on the Monash–UNE partnership to create a range of televised first-year courses.[38] Monash had already conducted a pilot study, 'Broadcast Learning', in partnership with the Australian Broadcasting Commission. The relationship was not always a harmonious one—'the ABC's organization is as opaque as the university's', Moodie complained—but by bringing the national broadcaster into the consortium Monash had stolen a march on its rivals.[39]

Within the gentlemanly counsels of the Australian Vice-Chancellors' Committee, Monash's ambitions had ruffled a few feathers. The entrepreneurial approach of Dawkins and Logan often sowed jealousy and resentment. Several potential partners, including Curtin and the University of Sydney, withdrew rather than submit to the hegemony of Monash and UNE.[40] Even after the contract had been won the tensions continued, with the Commonwealth requiring Monash to take on new partners and UNE complaining that it had been relegated to a backseat.[41] To allay resentment, Logan moved the headquarters of the project from the Monash campus to the city and changed its name from the Open Learning Authority to the less imposing Open Learning Agency.[42]

Trials of the first televised courses elicited more than 25 000 inquiries, with 2500 potential students purchasing study materials. Anticipating the government's decision to extend the scheme, Monash entered into discussions with the University of Queensland to create the 'University of Australia'. While Monash would run its television operations, Queensland would run the print arm. As Pritchard observed, the joint venture offered Monash a number of advantages, linking its interests in new technologies, TAFE transfer and internationalisation and its 'high-tech' Berwick campus.[43] Its old partners in the Television Open Learning consortium, however, were less enthusiastic. Anger at Monash's betrayal was exceeded only by resentment of Queensland's jumped-up arrogance.[44]

Logan met their annoyance with his customary mix of charm, bluff and chutzpah. Perhaps Monash wouldn't go in with Queensland, after all, he hinted. In mid-1992, however, the other partners launched a counter-bid under the title 'University Partnerships Limited'. The leaders included Charles Sturt University, UNE and Deakin, with support from five other universities. Government bureaucrats attempted unsuccessfully to mediate between the two bidders. Monash was unwilling to share control with a committee of sometimes divided institutions. Its brinkmanship paid off. In September 1992, Minister Peter Baldwin advised that the contract for the Open Learning Initiative had been awarded 'in principle' to Monash.

An impression remained that Monash had been favoured by its friends in Canberra. Even so, it took some months of negotiation before 'in principle' approval was translated into a firm contract.[45] Meanwhile, the future of 'open learning' was also changing. By the early 1990s,

Dawkins' original vision—'putting higher education on television'—was rapidly being overtaken by more flexible forms of learning based on the personal computer and satellite communication.

In 1993, the American scientist Robert Metcalfe, inventor of the Ethernet, promulgated a new law: the value of a network increases exponentially with the numbers of users. While broadcasting remained the basis of open learning, the university that controlled the studio commanded the field. But in the new era of distributed networks, learning would range far beyond the ability of any single institution to anticipate or control. In his 1992 paper Laying the Foundations of an Electronic University, Logan forecast a three-stage process in which electronic communication would progressively take over administrative functions, then simple communications such as library access and electronic mail, and finally sophisticated educational applications, such as computer-managed learning.[46] For the time being, televised 'off-the-shelf' courses offered a valuable avenue into open learning, but in winning the struggle to control them Monash had acquired nothing more than a precarious toehold in a terrain of ever-changing and multiplying possibilities.

A new frontier in Asia

In the 1960s, Australia discovered Asia. In the minds of the first generation of Monash academics, it was the new frontier, an exotic yet troubled region that stirred their curiosity, conscience and political commitment. Monash had proportionally more Asian students than any other Australian university. Its Centre of Southeast Asian Studies (founded in 1964) attracted some of Australia's leading experts on the region.

Logan, who had worked in Asia himself, regarded Monash's reputation in Asian studies as one of its outstanding strengths. Yet, within a short time, many of the stalwarts of the university's Asian programs had come to feel marginalised. Policy-makers in Canberra were questioning the old models of Western aid and development, with their attendant problems of inefficiency and corruption. Their gaze shifted from the politically troubled and aid-dependent countries like Indonesia, Vietnam and Cambodia—the main focus of Monash's Centre of Southeast Asian Studies—to the so-called 'tiger economies' of Singapore, Taiwan, South Korea and Hong Kong, which had successfully applied the lessons of free trade and market liberalisation. Markets not aid, competition not cooperation, seemed to be the way of the future.

As he sensed the winds of change blowing through the Canberra bureaucracy, Logan began to worry that Monash had not set its sails to catch them. In September 1987, he proposed the creation of a new institute of modern Asian studies to study the countries of the Pacific Rim. While respecting the Centre of Southeast Asian Studies, its approach, he believed, 'was a very limited one guided, quite correctly, by their linguistic skills and interest in a particular locality'. Monash had strengths in the study of Japan, China, Korea, Hong Kong and Singapore that were not being effectively harnessed. Rather than a traditional scholarly orientation, the institute would have a 'business bias'. It would aim to make Australians more 'Asia-literate'. It would offer short courses and non-award programs oriented to the needs of Australian businessmen seeking to open up new markets in Asia.[47] As Logan admitted, the institute, later renamed Monash Asia Institute, was partly a profile-raising exercise, designed to enable Monash to occupy 'a market niche we should try to exploit'. Not everyone welcomed its arrival. Two years later, its interim director noted 'the feeling of uneasiness held by a number of members of staff working in the area of Southeast Asia who had difficulty in accepting that the situation has changed'.[48]

In Canberra as well as Clayton, traditional attitudes towards Asia, including Australia's stance on educational engagement with the region, were coming under challenge. In the era of the Colombo Plan, Australia accepted an ethical responsibility 'to share access' to its educational riches with poor countries of the region. By the mid-1980s, however, market realists urged a more pragmatic view. 'Education should be regarded as an export industry in which institutions are encouraged to compete for students and funds', one report urged.[49] Australia should charge full fees to international students. Their critics warned it would only be a matter of time before domestic students were paying too. The debate raged through 1985, with Education Minister Susan Ryan reluctantly giving ground to the market reformers led by Trade Minister John Dawkins.[50]

When Dawkins became education minister, in 1987, he immediately signalled the shift in policy. 'There is an international demand for competitively priced, high-quality Australian higher education courses', his Green Paper announced.[51] Nowhere was this demand stronger than in Malaysia, the largest contributor by far to the inflow of international students to Australia. The reasons for its dominance were distinctive and historical. From its beginnings, in the revolt against British rule, Malaysia was shaped by the relationship between the Malay (Bumiputera) majority, who held political power, and the Chinese and Indian minorities, who commanded large parts of the economy.[52] Under the New Economic Policy, adopted in 1971, government contracts and jobs were reserved largely for Bumiputera, as were places in the state-funded universities. The bottled-up ambition of the ethnic Chinese was not easily suppressed, however. Those families who could afford to do so sent their children abroad for higher education, many to Australia. By 1983, Chinese Malaysians comprised around three-quarters of Monash's 2500 overseas students.

As the Malaysian economy boomed through the late 1970s, the divisions inherent in the New Economic Policy began to break down. The old sources of wealth, based on foreign-owned rubber, tin and palm oil industries, were eclipsed by new businesses based on oil, manufacturing, property and construction. The capital, Kuala Lumpur, grew within a generation to a city of more than seven million, its suburbs extending far into the neighbouring province of Selangor. Efforts to stimulate entrepreneurship among the Malay population stalled, and Chinese entrepreneurs increasingly circumvented the restrictions of the New Economic Policy by forging alliances with Bumiputera bankers, businessmen and politicians.[53]

In the mid-1980s, the overheated Malaysian economy experienced a sudden jolt. The Mahathir government sought to staunch the outflow of Chinese wealth and talent by encouraging the growth of private colleges, often in partnership with British or Australian institutions. Chinese families struggling to support their children at overseas universities welcomed the prospect of accessing a 'world-class' education, backed by well-regarded international universities, on their home soil. The educational crisis in Malaysia presented a golden opportunity for universities like Monash to 'franchise' their product to a receptive overseas market. None was quicker to recognise it than Monash's own Malaysian alumni.

Monash in Wonderland

In 1987, Registrar Tony Pritchard received an unexpected visit from one of the university's first international students. K.Y. Chin had studied economics at Clayton in the early 1960s, returned to Malaysia, and was now an assistant to Jeffrey Cheah, whose Sungei Wei Group had recently opened a private college on the southern fringes of Kuala Lumpur. Chin was interested in exploring an arrangement ('twinning') to enable students at the local Sunway College to take the first year or two of a Monash degree in Kuala Lumpur before completing their studies in Melbourne. 'I liked him immediately', Pritchard recalled. 'He explained what twinning was, and how it worked. It seemed to me that this could well be an opportunity for Monash.'[54]

Early in September, Pritchard led a small Monash delegation to Sunway. He approached the negotiations warily, determined not to compromise Monash's entry standards or commercial returns. 'Sunway's attitude is really an example of a different way of doing business—European vs Asian', he warned. 'They expect to bargain.'[55] Profit, however, was by no means the prime motive in the minds of the prospective partner. 'Sunway College', Chin explained, 'is the jewel in the Sungei Wei Group crown, a 14-year-old dream of Jeffrey Cheah, our founder, to be able to contribute to the development of education in Malaysia'.[56]

Like Chin, Cheah was one of the first generation of Malaysian students in Australia. A shy village boy from Pusing, near Ipoh, he studied accounting at Footscray Institute in the 1960s, sitting at the back of the class, hardly daring to look his lecturer in the eye.[57] Back in Malaysia, he worked in the office of a motor assembly plant until one day he spotted an unusual business opportunity. From a British tin-mining company he purchased the lease on 350 kilometres of despoiled, and apparently useless, mining land at Bandar Sunway, about 20 kilometres south of Kuala Lumpur. Over the following two decades, Cheah transformed this wasteland into a post-industrial wonderland and multiplied his investment of 100 000 Malaysian ringgits into a business empire worth 700 million ringgits.

Phang Koon Tuck, presently the executive director of Monash Sunway, joined Cheah in the early 1980s as a mining engineer and oversaw the extraction of the last deposits of tin. When the bottom fell out of the market in 1981, they turned to quarrying, plundering the site for limestone road metal, then to constructing the roads themselves. Scarred and pockmarked, the old mine site now resembled a moonscape. But it had

'Education brings out the best in people.' Malaysian entrepreneur Jeffrey Cheah, creator of a multi-billion-ringgit real-estate, hotel, entertainment and educational empire, became Monash's first international partner.

one redeeming virtue: location. Bandar Sunway lay strategically between the city and the airport, directly in the path of Kuala Lumpur's suburban advance. Having half-destroyed the place, Cheah then set about restoring it. In Hawaii and South Africa, he learned how to rehabilitate despoiled mining land. He drained it, dried it out, compacted it and replanted it with lush tropical vegetation. By the mid-1980s, the first houses and apartment blocks appeared.[58] A giant crater, half a kilometre wide, was transformed into a theme park, complete with lakes, waterfalls, jungles and an artificial surf beach. On its rim perched two towering tourist hotels, the Pyramid shopping mall and the five-storey Sunway College. For a town built on sludge, the college was a prime asset, boosting its social status and contributing to the company's residential, retail and service businesses.

But it was something more. An astute entrepreneur, Tan Sri Jeffrey Cheah is also a moralist and philanthropist. 'I believe in upholding traditional Asian family values', he says, invoking one of Prime Minister Mahathir's slogans. He runs his company paternally, with his wife and children occupying key positions. On weekends, he drives his Ferrari to the mall and walks around looking for specks of litter. His theme park delivers only wholesome family fun, and he avoids shady businesses such as casinos because, as he observes, 'it ruins a lot of lives'. The cornerstone of his philosophy, tirelessly expounded to his employees, is a belief in the transformative power of education. 'I like to see young people being educated', he exclaims. 'Education brings out the best in people.'

By September 1987, Monash's initial reservations about the twinning program with Sunway had receded. The university's high reputation in

Malaysia promised a strong flow of enrolments, perhaps as many as 1000 students a year, to offset the anticipated decline of full-fee Malaysian students in Australia. From the pages of the *New Straits Times*, a beaming Vice-Chancellor Logan assured prospective students: 'The only thing that separates Sunway College and Monash University is 6000 kilometres'.[59] Sunway's commercial strength and Monash's academic standards seemed to guarantee the scheme's success.[60] Students would have to meet the usual Australian academic entry standards, and there would be 'no discrimination on the basis of sex, race, colour or religion'.[61] The partners had been eager to introduce the first courses in economics, engineering, science and law as early as 1988, but a year later the program was still getting established.[62]

Monash's first tentative steps into Asia coincided with the last steps towards the merger with Chisholm Institute. While Pritchard was courting Jeffrey Cheah, Geoff Vaughan, Director of Chisholm Institute, and the director of its David Syme Business School, Peter Chandler, were being wooed by another Monash alumnus, the executive vice-chairman of Malaysian Strategic Consultancy, Michael Yeoh. A 1973 economics graduate, Yeoh was an influential networker between the Mahathir government and the Chinese business community. In September 1989, he drafted a 'joint venture agreement' for the David Syme Business School to offer its bachelor of business degree in Kuala Lumpur. After completion of the study program, supervised by the school, students would be awarded Monash University degrees. Unlike the Sunway program, the scheme contained no requirements about entry standards, residence in Australia, course design and approval by Monash academics.[63] At a time when Clayton was accusing Caulfield of debasing academic standards, the deal had the potential to derail the whole merger. Logan requested Vaughan to defer consideration of the scheme. His advisors were not so polite: it was time to pull the David Syme people into line. 'They cannot be permitted to go off on these independent frolics.'[64]

Pritchard was anxious at first that the link between the Malaysian Strategic Consultancy and Syme Business School might imperil the Sunway partnership, but by early 1990 he began to warm to it. 'I think it is important for us to diversify our interests in Malaysia . . . Monash . . . is big enough to associate itself with more than one twinning partner.' News of the second twinning partnership did temporarily 'upset' Jeffrey

Cheah, but Pritchard sought to reassure him with an undertaking to expand courses in computing and commerce on Sunway's new campus, due to open in 1991.[65]

In June 1991, a large party of council members, senior staff and their wives flew to Kuala Lumpur to officiate at Monash's first graduation ceremony outside Australia. To Clayton academics, angry with the mergers and anxious about academic standards, this junket, as it was often described, showed how far the administration had lost touch with the rest of the university. But Logan understood the importance of such gestures in Malaysia. A few months later, when Mahathir floated the possibility of allowing foreign universities to establish private colleges in Malaysia, Monash, 'an entrepreneurial university with a strong involvement in overseas programs', was well positioned to take up the opportunity.[66]

Monash had been considering the idea of an offshore campus for some time. It surveyed opportunities in Thailand and Indonesia, but neither offered the same combination of commercial and strategic opportunities as Malaysia. Mahathir's speech elicited a flood of offers from potential Malaysian partners. A wealthy Chinese businessman, Dr Foo Wan Kien, offered to build a new campus on land to be donated by the Sultan of Perak in the southern city of Ipoh. Dato M.S. Tan, currently in partnership with Taylor's College, proposed a Monash campus in association with the foundation of an exclusive secondary school in Kuala Lumpur.[67] Wary of the ambitions of other Australian universities, particularly Sydney, Monash was eager to consolidate its position in Malaysia, setting out its 'vision' for 'Universiti Monash Malaysia' in an expansive prospectus.

> The vision . . . is for a complete campus of Monash University, Australia, offering a broad range of undergraduate, graduate and research programs of relevance to Malaysia. The language of instruction will be English. The campus will be a truly international university, involving a partnership of Australian and Malaysian scholars, teachers and researchers.[68]

Among the prospective partners, Sunway at first appeared to be no more than 'a remote possibility'. It was more interested in further twinning arrangements and 'would take some persuasion to contemplate a Monash-only venture'.[69] It was also pursuing a possible partnership with the University of Nottingham. Over the following months, however, the advantages of the Monash–Sunway link became more apparent. Ipoh was too far from the main market for students, and none of Monash's other suitors had Sunway's financial strength or academic experience. Nottingham wanted its own campus from the outset, something Sunway could not provide. 'There was never any doubt in my mind that if we were going to do anything in Kuala Lumpur, it would be with Jeffrey Cheah', Logan later affirmed.[70] With hindsight, the partnership may have seemed foreordained, although the record suggests a more tentative courtship.

After many visits and dinners, with accompanying gifts, singsongs, honours and greetings, the partners finally signed a memorandum of understanding in June 1994. Monash University Sunway Campus would share the premises of Sunway College at Bandar Sunway until it attracted the 800 students required to build its own campus. Sunway would provide the resources, including staff, buildings and equipment, while Monash would supply a resident campus director and take responsibility for curriculum examinations and academic standards.[71] The campus was to be wholly owned by Sunway, but Monash would receive a royalty on every student and could acquire equity over time.

For the partners, the benefits of the alliance were largely intangible. Sunway gained the prestige and portability of the Monash degree. 'It will be a marketing advantage to be able to use the Monash name', Michael Yeoh assured his colleagues in the David Syme Business School.[72] Monash had first sought to go offshore to offset the possible loss of income from Malaysian students in Australia. But the Malaysian campus was also a symbol of the Greater Monash, unbound by constraints of geography and responsive to the promise of a globalising world. 'As the boundaries between the countries in our region begin to be lowered, especially by the movement of people, a truly international university like Monash should not be geographically bound to Australia. A campus in Asia is a natural outcome.'[73] Engagement on the new campus would inspire new forms of teaching and learning and open opportunities for cross-cultural research.[74]

The vision also posed some tantalising questions. Could Monash stay true to its core academic values in a country where religious and political expression was constrained, and where public universities were subject to racial quotas and compulsory religious teaching? Could the university guarantee that its Malaysian campus offered degrees of equal standard when it paid its staff much less than their Australian counterparts? Leo West, who succeeded Tony Pritchard as Logan's international emissary, insisted that, as a private university, Monash was exempt from the government's controls over public universities. If there were any suggestion of imposing ethnic quotas, for example, the university would simply walk away from the venture.[75]

As his retirement approached, Logan was eager to see his vision realised. 'I would be very pleased if we could bring our plans to fruition before the end of the year', he wrote to Cheah at the beginning of 1996.[76] For a moment, in the middle of 1995, a cloud had passed across the horizon when rumours reached Monash that Sunway was still pursuing the relationship with Nottingham. Logan enlisted the help of his friend John Dawkins, now retired from parliament, to lobby in Kuala Lumpur.[77] But, despite his representations, the Malaysian government continued to delay the decision. Each side, it seemed, was waiting for firm evidence of the other's intentions. It was not until 1997, shortly after Logan had retired, that the Malaysian government gave its approval and the final decision to open the campus was made. Logan had gazed into the promised land, Monash's first overseas campus. He, more than anyone, was the architect of the Greater Monash, but it was his successor, David Robinson, who finally built it.

NINE

THE EDUCATIONAL SUPERMARKET

Students must be seen as contributors to the advancement of Monash, in addition to their role as education consumers.

THE MONASH STUDENT PLAN: UNIFIED AND LOCALISED, JUNE 1998

In the 1990s, the children of the baby boomers arrived at Monash. Like their parents, they came hoping to 'do their own thing'. One young man planned to grow his hair and get an earring. University was 'where you can do all the things your fascist school told you were wrong, immoral or destructive'.[1] At university, your teachers and parents would no longer be standing over you. You wouldn't have to answer to anyone. But, while university still promised a kind of liberation, it was a freedom that no longer came for free. The baby boomers were the lucky beneficiaries of Gough Whitlam's decision to abolish university fees; their children were the first generation to experience the user-pays university.

The end of free education, heralded by the introduction of the Higher Education Contribution Scheme (HECS), in 1989, coincided with the onset of economic recession and an uncertain labour market. Fewer students received government support or grants, making them more reliant on paid work. They were effectively part-time students, splitting their week between work and study, with less time to spend on campus or in extracurricular activities. A revolution in IT would soon alter teaching, learning and study habits forever. Universities were changing, and Monash changed more than most.

A student hastens through the Campus Centre, formerly the Union Building, while others lounge between classes. (Photograph: Erin Jonasson/Fairfax Syndication)

A new generation goes to uni

Under the Unified National System, more people were going to university than ever before. Between 1989 and 2000, enrolments in Australian universities grew by close to 60 per cent. Young people had a 47 per cent probability of attending university at some stage in their lives, a high figure relative to comparable countries.[2] A degree had increasingly become a prerequisite for employment in a society where paper credentials trumped experience. Some of those enrolling at university were there because they had looked for a job and couldn't find it. In the 1960s, a degree was a golden path to success; in the 1990s, it might not even get you an interview. The old dream of an educated democracy was coming true, but the dream had lost some of its lustre.

Monash's student population grew by about one-third in the decade after 1991, from 32 800 to 46 000, roughly in line with the growth of the Australian university population as a whole. The proportion of international students more than doubled, from 8.9 per cent in 1991 to 21.2 per cent in 2001, giving Monash the largest slice of Australia's international student market, 10 per cent. Those born overseas grew from 22 to 40 per cent, almost half of them from Southeast Asia.[3] Women, a small minority in 1961, now outnumbered men. In 1990, the Labor government's paper *A Fair Chance for All* had charged universities to better reflect Australian society. But higher education remained a largely middle-class affair. Two-thirds of Monash students had fathers in professional and managerial occupations, and a disproportionate number—over a third—came from private schools. Those from lower socioeconomic families (11.2 per cent) were below the national average, and their share was no better at the end of the decade than it was at the beginning.[4]

Clayton, now a little city of over 16 000 students, remained the hub of the Greater Monash. *Lot's Wife* warned newcomers that they could be 'swallowed up in the whole mess, ignored by thousands, and trod on by an impersonal administration'.[5] Some students certainly did find its size alienating. One who found her way from the more intimate Berwick campus 'decided then and there that this shithole of cliquey groups and cold stone buildings was not for me'.[6] But others found the bustle of the campus intoxicating.

For school-leavers, getting to uni was like the release of a pressure valve. 'Year 12 is the be-all and end-all', one newcomer confessed.[7] Educators worried that students sometimes couldn't see beyond it. Too many arrived with 'the notion that first year university is slack and that life on campus is one continuous party'. Without teachers pushing them, they struggled to adjust to independent learning. 'Transition is becoming more difficult than ever', a Monash conference on the topic heard in 1995. As many as four students out of ten fared worse in their first year of university than they had in Year 12.[8] Monash responded to the concern with a range of initiatives, including teaching fellowships to enable secondary teachers to get a taste of university teaching and an enhancement program to enable high-achieving Year 12s to complete a first-year subject at school.

The mergers had doubled Monash's student population, from 15 894 to 32 800, turning many who had never intended to become university students into potential graduates. According to the university's leaders, the mergers benefited students by offering greater choice of courses and modes of study. Like an educational supermarket, the Greater Monash stocked more brands, and you could access them more conveniently. Through Gippsland's DEC you could study in your own home, and a university-wide credit transfer system enabled you to move easily between campuses and courses. No student, Logan promised, would be disadvantaged. The 'hassle of amalgamations' had only one objective: to improve educational opportunity for young people in the eastern half of the state.[9]

Many of the customers, however, were not so convinced. 'Nothing in the history of higher education has ever indicated that creating a monster university is any more efficient', one of them declared.[10] Would course standards and educational facilities get worse? You might get more choices, but were there the resources to provide them? The results of lower public investment in education were already in evidence. Parking at Clayton was 'disgusting', and the understaffed Library so stretched that student volunteers had to be recruited to reshelve books. Classes were full to bursting (*'Is this a tute or a lecture?'*).[11] Was the big university spread too thinly?

Clayton students feared that their degrees had lost prestige by their association with the former colleges. 'The credibility once gained by getting a Monash Degree is destroyed now that meat axe itinerant farmers' kids who study Applied Sheep Docking at Gippsland can get a Degree from Monash', a correspondent in *Lot's Wife* complained.[12]

The 'farmers' kids' at Gippsland were not much happier to be associated with the academic snobs at Clayton. The transition from a university college to full university status in 1993 threatened Gippsland's community character and independence. Its students lost representation on decision-making bodies as the campus was subjected to Monash's 'archaic' regulations. Students complained that the promised benefits of being sucked into the 'Monash Megalith' had not come their way. Lecturers were harder to find 'as they race off to get research brownie points'. The new thirteen-week semester took away the customary 'swot vac'.[13] Saddest of all, they lost the 'weekend schools', so long a feature of Gippsland's distance education program. 'It is hard enough to study via distance', one student observed, 'but when there is no mixing with the lecturers and other students there is really a great sense of isolation and lack of direction'.[14]

Some Clayton students hoped the mergers might actually democratise student life, through the adoption of a new, student-led 'Greater Monash University Union' that would give students more control over the provision of services and the spending of their amenities fee. But the idea proved difficult to achieve. Each of the merged institutions had its own union, with its own regulations, employment practices and the like. A cross-campus federation of student organisations was formed in 1994 but died soon afterwards. It was easier to create one big university than one big student union.

Students as customers

In a series of bipartisan changes in higher education policy, Australia's universities were being refashioned along market lines. The first breach in the walls of the free, state-funded university came in 1986 with the introduction of a $250 Higher Education Administration Charge. A more substantial change occurred three years later with the adoption of HECS, under which undergraduate students repaid a proportion of the costs of their education after graduation. The final step came with the introduction of up-front fees, first on some postgraduate courses, later on undergraduate courses. As students were gradually transformed into customers, so their relationship with the university changed from a semi-feudal to a commercial one. The objective, according to the West Review of Higher Education Financing and Policy (1998), was to be demand-driven, or 'student-centred'.

Monash strove to be 'responsive to the needs of our client base'.[15] This meant tailoring teaching programs, professional upgrading and full-fee courses to the market. Monash's first priority, according to *Strategy for the Future* (1995), was excellence in teaching, a goal now pursued with a mixture of carrot-and-stick mechanisms, including the vice-chancellor's awards for teaching excellence and a standardised system of student teaching evaluation, Monquest. Teaching performance was given more weight in selection and promotion. Already under the pressure of deteriorating staff–student ratios, academics were now urged to publish more, since funding was linked to research performance, and to teach better. Old-timers lamented the loss of collegiality, a euphemism for a less pressured life.

Some students disbelieved the university's claims to be student-focused. In the mid-1990s, arts student Clare McCausland wore a badge proclaiming 'I'm a student, not a customer'. She deplored the practice of giving subjects 'sexy' titles simply to attract enrolments.[16] Once students were called customers, however, they soon began to act accordingly. One of the most common complaints heard by the student union was that students were not 'getting their money's worth for HECS'.[17] They looked more critically at the standard of services and facilities. 'Monash had a great reputation', notes Ruth Kweitel, a mature-age student at Caulfield, 'however I was very disappointed at the poor facilities'. When the printers in the IT Department repeatedly broke down, she fired off a letter of complaint asking for her fees to be refunded. 'A week later all the printers were replaced with laser printers. Each time I entered the IT department I was always offered a cup of tea.'[18] By the end of the decade, the 'student-as-client' idea was ingrained. 'I realise you are a busy man running a large business', a student wrote to the vice-chancellor, 'but as a client of that business please seek a solution to the problem of the Student Union'.[19]

Monash students protest against user-pays education outside the university offices, 1988. HECS was introduced in 1989, heralding the end of free higher education.

International students

The customers who paid most were fee-paying students from overseas. As paying customers rather than beneficiaries of Australia's international aid program, they were entitled to a different kind of service. In 1992, the Monash Overseas Student Service became the Monash University International Student Service, a change meant to convey that students were no longer here 'because of the Australian government welfare program for third world countries' but were paying their own way.[20] 'Overseas' denoted an Australian orientation, while 'international' conveyed mutuality. The service picked up new students at the airport, took them shopping on Saturdays and provided an international student lounge as well as other welfare services. It worked closely with international student services at Caulfield, Peninsula (the former Frankston campus of Chisholm Institute) and Gippsland, offering O-Week activities such as campus tours, barbeques and camps.

The commonest malaise among international students was homesickness. It was expensive to phone home, and old-fashioned letter-writing remained common. Coming cold into an Australian university could induce culture shock. Malaysian student Lui Tat Meng was intimidated by talkative 'Aussies' and almost as alienated by Australian-born Chinese, the 'bananas' as he called them—'yellow on the outside, white on the inside'. 'At first my reaction was "They're Chinese too" and yet they're so different.' Chinese student Shian K. Cheng was shocked by the behaviour at a toga party organised as part of orientation activities. 'Beer was all over the floor. People were dancing wildly. It was a real eye-opener.'[21] The international student lounge provided a refuge where students could relax or read foreign newspapers. It was so well patronised that students often had to sit on the floor.[22]

Monash aspired to become an international university where students from many lands shared classes and exchanged ideas. But the concentration of international students in some courses and on some campuses, notably Caulfield, provoked concern. Roberts Hall had become the residence of choice for international students, in part because locals regarded shy or conscientious internationals as 'no fun'. For locals, failing a subject or two was 'no big deal', but when parents were paying high fees to send you to university the implications of too much fun could be severe.[23]

The stereotype of the 'conscientious Asian student' was a subtle form of racism. International Student Grievance Weeks at Clayton and Caulfield in 1992 and 1993 exposed more overt forms, including rudeness on the part of both academics and general staff. Surveys carried out among international students revealed a 'deep and wide-ranging level of discontent'. All students were 'increasingly assessing their education from the vantage point of consumers', and international students, who paid more, were justifiably more critical than others. Among the common grievances were high student–teacher ratios, boring lecturers, unapproachable tutors, overcrowded lecture theatres, broken escalators and inadequate provision of computers and photocopiers. Before Logan decided to internationalise, he should have provided better services at home, one student suggested. 'Why do we pay so much and receive so little in return?' 'Overseas students', another concluded, 'are nothing but milking cows for Monash'.[24]

Most international students depended on support from middle-class, but not wealthy, families who struggled on lower than Australian salaries to pay higher than Australian tuition fees. 'I was amazed that an international student doing the same course as me paid four times more than local students, not to mention living costs', Calvin Chow, a local student of Malaysian background, observes. He knows of one student who was supported by his mother, who sold nasi lemak, a traditional Malaysian dish, at only A$1 or A$2 a plate.[25] Having paid their university fees, many international students were left with too little to pay accommodation and living expenses. If, for any reason, the flow of funds from home dwindled or dried up, they could be left destitute. Some, unable to find work during the recession, were obliged to return home. Others worked up to forty hours a week, longer than the legal limit. In 1994, after representations from the Monash University International Student Service and the Malaysian Law Students Association, the university created a loans fund specifically for international students.

Learner-earners

The typical Monash student of the 1990s was a learner-earner, dividing the week between paid work and study. Under HECS, students borrowed the fees for their education from the government, accumulating a debt to be paid off when they got a job with a salary high enough to afford the modest repayments. Meanwhile, they worked to support themselves while they studied. Only a tiny number of students (less than 2 per cent in 1990, and only 0.3 per cent in 1998) came on a scholarship.[26] And only a quarter came from families poor enough to qualify for an Austudy allowance, a meagre dole apparently set, one student noted, 'by a grandchild of Ebenezer Scrooge'.[27] Students came, usually, from well-to-do households, with tastes formed by their baby-boomer parents. So they worked not just to survive, but to buy the clothes, concert tickets, restaurant meals, airfares and electronic gadgets that had become their expectation. The ostentatious frugality of the 1970s was definitely not their style.

In many countries, going to university meant leaving home. In the 1960s and 1970s, when many Monash students were on generous scholarships, they could afford to live in halls or group houses. But it was hard to assert personal independence while you were obliged, as almost two-thirds of first- and second-year students were in the 1990s, to live at home with your parents.[28] 'I can't stand being at home therefore I don't study as much as I'd like to', one Monash student lamented. 'I go out . . . to avoid seeing my parents.'[29] This pattern of dependence grew stronger over the decade. About half of Monash students depended on parents for financial support in 1990; by 1996, it was 55 per cent.[30] The pressure to work increased steadily too. In 1984, the average Australian undergraduate worked five hours a week during semester. By 2001, Clayton students worked an average of 18.4 hours.[31] This meant an 'insane juggling of study and work', which for arts student Vikki Plant included begging her friends to add her walkman to the collections placed on lecterns to record lectures she could not attend.[32] Many Monash students graduated having totted up more hours at the checkout or the McDonald's counter than in the lab or the library.

Campus life

Most Monash students were enrolled 'full-time', but few learner-earners spent a five-day week on campus. Many fitted their study around their work commitments and skipped classes when they couldn't. A crowded life made it harder to read widely, or sometimes at all. Fewer students had the leisure to engage in extracurricular activities. Pessimists began to wonder whether the students' connection with the university had become so attenuated that 'campus life' in the old sense was dead.

Yet trends towards disengagement and alienation can easily be overstated. The Host Scheme, which had been operating since the 1970s, offered campus tours, barbeques and camps to new students on all campuses except Parkville. Its continuing popularity suggested that many students entered university intending to embrace all aspects of the experience. For some, the campus remained a home away from home. McCausland and her German-studying friends took to 'hanging out' on the orange vinyl couches on the third floor of the Menzies Building. 'There'd often be a handful of people there who you'd know well or a little.'[33] Friends came to know each other's timetables and where to find each other. In a pre-mobile era, some arranged to meet by posting notes on noticeboards in the Union Building. Within the seemingly anonymous spaces of the Clayton campus, students created their own little communities, gathering wherever they could, around Library tables, in the Union, in the sports centre or in the many little groups who lunched in the forum on sunny days.

Students sign up to clubs and societies at Orientation Week, 1990.

An enthusiastic minority still centred their lives around the campus and student life. As Melissa McVeigh was about to begin at Monash in 1991, one of her mother's friends advised her to 'get involved in every aspect of university life'. 'And that is what I did', she recalls. Through the Host Scheme, she was introduced to the Monash Players, spending much of her spare time around the old Student Theatre rooms. She directed her own plays and took a turn as leader of the Host Scheme. Soon she gravitated into the crowd running *Lot's Wife*, where she fell in love with the editor, 'a cool guy' who later became her husband. She spent virtually every day on campus, usually arriving at ten in the morning and leaving only at ten at night. When deadlines approached, the group would sometimes stay up all night laying out the paper. In her recollection, her intersecting circle of friends—actors, student journalists and politicians—were 'one big social community'.[34]

Students confronted by Clayton's scale were likely to feel more at home on one of Monash's smaller Victorian campuses. Pamela Dooley, who enrolled as a mature-age student on the Peninsula campus in 1994, found it 'a very pleasant place, open, lots of nature, small, friendly, not intimidating at all', in contrast to the 'intimidating' Clayton campus, where she later completed her degree. Yet the contrast was misleading in some ways, for, as Dooley discovered, 'studying at Peninsula was a lot more lonely because there wasn't anywhere for older students to gather', unlike Clayton, which provided a mature-age lounge.[35] A bigger campus could offer more options, socially as well as educationally.

As the Clayton and Caulfield campuses became bigger and more diverse, so did the number and range of clubs and societies. Alongside the various Christian societies, there were now Islamic, Bahai, Buddhist and New Age groups. Clayton offered the broad base to support specialised faculty and discipline societies, like the Mechanical Engineering and German societies, whereas clubs on the smaller campuses tended to be more recreational in character, such as Peninsula's Waterski Club, Gippsland's Aerobics Club and Parkville's Home Brew Club.

Predictions of the demise of campus culture were sharpened by the threat from state and Commonwealth governments to curb the power of student unions. Since the nineteenth century, with the foundation of the Oxford Union as a self-governing student society offering opportunities for social activity and political discussion across the university, the Union had been a foundation of student life in British and Australian universities. John Monash, an eighteen-year-old engineering student, was among the founders of the Melbourne University Union, in 1884.[36] Its character had about as much in common with a trade union as the Melbourne Club had with the Trades Hall. Even in the 1970s, the high point of student radicalism, the Union continued largely as a self-governing service organisation, providing meals and other services to students.

In the 1990s, however, when consumer choice trumped self-government, the student unions became the target of reformers, including former Monash student politician Peter Costello. Their main grievance was the use of compulsory student fees to subsidise 'political' activities. They were inspired by memories of such overtly political gestures as Monash students' support for the NLF, but the Victorian government's *Tertiary Education (Amendment) Act 1994* prohibited the use of student fees for a much wider range of 'political' activities, such as representation of student interests, welfare, women's officers, education committees, newspapers and political clubs. The Labor government stepped in to provide funding to prop up these activities, but the prospect of federal legislation to make student union membership voluntary loomed through the 1990s, especially after the election of the Coalition government in 1996.

Old grievances may have motivated the reformers, but their cause won support from many students, whose relationship with the university had become a tenuous commercial one. In a world where you expected to pay only for what you got, it made little sense to have to pay for services you might never use, even if it was for the common good. In response to the Victorian act, the student associations were separated from the Union. MAS became the Monash Student Association incorporating the Monash Student Board, the International Students Service and the Mature Age and Part-Time Students Associations. But, while services and representation became separate functions, students now formed a majority of the Union Board, which was chaired for the first time by a student, Monash Student Association president Lorien Devitt.

From factory to supermarket

'Apathy is the norm of this decade', the 1990 *Orientation Handbook* lamented.[37] Apathy is the perennial complaint of campus activists, but the 1990s sometimes seemed to set new benchmarks for political disengagement. Student Tabatha Pettitt recalls seeing pictures of the protests of the 1960s and 1970s. 'We didn't seem to have the time in my day—there was too much work and we all knew that we had huge HECS debts coming up.'[38] At Clayton, student general meetings were often dissolved for lack of the required quorum. Editors of the Gippsland student newspaper *The Oxalian* wrote with a tinge of exasperation: 'Monash Gippsland students have all the fire of a half cold cup of tea'.[39] A mature-age student was shocked by her first impressions of the Peninsula campus: 'I was expecting a hotbed of student activism, but people seemed to be there to study rather than make political waves'.[40]

Observers debated the source of the malaise. Was it an effect of the Dawkins reforms, which had turned the university into a degree factory? The 1990 *Orientation Handbook* depicted the Menzies Building with smoking chimneys on the roof. 'Like it or not', students were on 'a production line' where they would be moulded into 'products of the brave new corporate Monash'.[41] But this was dated rhetoric, straight out of the 1960s. Students in the 1990s were not imprisoned in a factory but shopping in a giant educational supermarket. If they had cause for complaint, it wasn't that the production line was relentless but that the checkout queues were too long and some of the products weren't on the shelves. Students certainly had grievances in the 1990s, although they were not always perceived as political. And even when they were, it was harder to mobilise learner-earners, with their flexible timetables and fleeting appearances on campus, than in the days when full-time students could afford to take an afternoon off for a demo.

There were still students who wanted 'more from university life than just books and degrees' as Sasha Shtargot of the Monash Greens recalls.[42] But the big surges of political activism were sporadic contrasts to the prevailing climate of student conservatism. The end of free university education generated a strong, if short-lived, wave of activism. 'Monash is burning', the cover of the 1989 *Orientation Handbook* shouted, before admitting that it 'wasn't exactly'. A campaign against HECS brought a taste of the old Monash, with a two-day occupation of the Administration Building. But the protests died almost as quickly as they erupted. Seven years later, the introduction of voluntary student unionism legislation attracted over 1300 students to a mass general meeting, a crowd so large that Lorien Devitt at first thought 'this can't be right'.[43] But once the law was passed, indignation quickly faded. A year later, a rally against up-front fees attracted only about fifty protestors. An activist appealed vainly to his peers: 'Vietnam is over but it's not like we don't have anything to fight for'.[44]

After voluntary student unionism, the hottest issue of the decade was the introduction of up-front fees for domestic undergraduates. In April 1997, while the Academic Board debated the issue, 400 students attended a rally outside the Administration Building and held a mock funeral to mark the death of public education. More protestors arrived by bus from Gippsland, Berwick, Caulfield and Peninsula for a vigil during the later council meeting. Council deferred its decision but later approved up-front fees at a meeting during the semester break. On this occasion, the issue did not die at once. Protestors continued to camp outside the building, symbolically 'reclaiming' the university. They lounged on the 'patio' area outside, playing music and dancing to combat the Clayton chill. It was a valiant gesture, but the hundreds who attended this and other similar campaigns paled beside the thousands who had packed the forum twenty years earlier. 'The majority of students treat University as a means to an end', a student explained. 'They treat it as a business transaction. They come to study ... so they can be more employable. Political awareness and activism are things of the past.'[45]

Apathy could easily shift to downright hostility. The ideological convergence between the main political parties created a degree of cynicism towards student politicians, who were seen by some onlookers as careerists and opportunists. 'At the centre of Monash political life is the hack', a correspondent to *Lot's Wife* observed. 'Apparatchiks of no fixed ideological address, hacks see student politics as a convenient pitstop

On the way to the Lodge. Student politics in the 1990s increasingly centred on the two major parties. Here, Liberal and Labor representatives battle it out in Orientation Week, 1990.

on their way to the Lodge.'[46] It was no wonder the majority of students were apathetic when campus politicians seemed to spend much of their time abusing each other in venomous columns and letters. Students didn't 'give a shit about whether Gav hates Boc or Brad hates everybody', one reader exclaimed.[47] Antagonisms between the few participants seemed to grow fiercer as everyone else became more apathetic. Only 12.5 per cent of students voted in MAS's 1995 elections, but the contest was one of the bitterest on record, with candidates circulating 'dirt sheets' on each other. Many politically engaged students avoided party politics altogether, devoting their energies to clubs like Community Involvement and the World Action Group, or environmental campaigns about mining in Kakadu or the proposed damming of the Franklin River.

Second-wave feminism, the movement that swept the campuses in the 1970s, had peaked but not declined. Being a feminist, according to a Caulfield student, was 'about as en vogue as a Jeff Kennett haircut',[48] but if it was not voguish, neither was it passé. Monash had a flourishing network of feminist clubs, like the Women's Studies Club and the Feminist Legal Issues Collective. The Arts Faculty's Women's Studies Centre, founded in 1987 after years of lobbying by staff and students, generated a range of successful courses. Growing feminist activism coincided with increased concern about the security of women on campus. In 1989, a Campaign Against Violence Collective was established in response to cases of rape on the campus. Continued reports of sexual assaults, including rapes, generated demands for better security and lighting. Despite some gains, women's groups continued to have to justify their role, sometimes against boorish opposition. In 1990, a battle within MAS's PAC descended into farce when male members of the Liberal Club invaded the women's room at Clayton.

Cutting loose

'You're at university. You can say "sex" as loud and as often as you want', the 1991 *Orientation Handbook* exhorted. Going to university in the 1990s was a serious business. Jobs were fewer. Students seemed intent on getting their degrees and getting out. The world also seemed a riskier place. While hitching to Monash was still an option (the hitching posts survived), students, especially women, were warier about accepting lifts from strangers. But, for all that, students were still students, and they found time to 'cut loose'. If student handbooks now contained warnings about AIDS and other sexually transmitted diseases, uni remained a place of sexual experimentation. 'Boys and girls like to look at each other' at Monash, said one student, because the 'architecture doesn't offer much else to admire'.[49]

The desire to transgress old taboos has been a constant of student life for generations, and in the 1990s the boundaries of toleration and acceptance continued to expand. It was a decade in which the voices of gay, lesbian, bisexual and transgender students were heard more often. 'No longer do you have to suffer those high school indignities—the hiding, the fear that you were the only one', the Not Quite Straight Group assured new students in 1996. 'At Monash you are allowed to be yourself.'[50] Monash legislation now protected the right to express a sexual preference against prejudice or harassment. Gay and lesbian organisations flourished at most campuses.

The drug scene, once considered a feature of campus life, continued to attract a minority of students, although its connection to the campus was more tenuous. The appearance of a range of new recreational drugs linked to the clubbing and rave scenes also drew users away from the campus, although MAS offered a popular service in issuing free passes to downtown dance clubs. In the 1990s, as in the 1970s, marijuana was the illicit student drug of choice. The Mullers and Packers Union, formed in 1991 to lobby for the legalisation of cannabis, claimed to be one of the most active clubs on campus.[51]

While alcohol remained students' legal drug of choice, the long drinking sessions common in the 1960s may have decreased, if only because nobody in a drive-in university could afford to risk encountering a booze bus on the way home. While students in halls continued to frequent the Nott, it no longer appeared on the social map of most non-resident students. Until the mid-1990s, Clayton remained without a student bar and, more surprisingly, seemed in no hurry to get one. More than 60 per cent of voters in a 1988 referendum opposed one, and, even in 1991, when the 'yes' case was finally carried, some international students and women worried that it would be an unwelcoming environment 'inhabited mainly by Aussie blokes'.[52] The new bar finally opened in 1997, just as the Union Building was renamed the Campus Centre. The Gryph-Inn, a bar and bistro, had already opened at Caulfield in 1994, while Peninsula's popular Seahorse Tavern opened in 1995.

University authorities hoped that bars and bistros would encourage more 'civilised' drinking habits than those regularly displayed during Orientation Week or Green Week, the reincarnated version of the old Farm Week, so-called because of the colour of the cans the free Victoria Bitter came in. In 1994, Pro Vice-Chancellor Lauchlan Chipman declared war on Gippsland's own beerfest, known as Animal Comp. The campus's 'immature drinking culture' was 'inconsistent with a genuine international research university', he declared. Rather than beer-swilling contests, he urged his students to arrange wine-tastings and visits to local vineyards, pastimes more likely to overcome 'some of the negatives associated with their backgrounds'. Needless to say, his 'derogatory' reflections on the character of students from the La Trobe Valley did not endear him to the locals, although one student said he was prepared to reconsider if Chipman offered an invitation to his own wine cellars, said to be strategically located around the campus.[53]

The electronic university

'The electronic university is an attempt to take advantage of the community's acceptance of electronic communication in meeting educational needs', Logan declared in 1992.[54] Australians, judging by their rapid take-up of video cassette recorders, home computers and other devices, were comfortable with the new technologies: the electronic university was simply a response to their desires. Not everyone shared his utopian vision, however. Fellow vice-chancellor Don Aitkin anticipated, without much enthusiasm, that the 'ultimate utilitarian university degree, done entirely by computer, e-mail and video, without any face-to-face contact with university teachers, let alone fellow students, is not far away'.[55]

Nowhere was the arrival of the electronic university more apparent than in the traditional heart of the university, the Library. Monash would have to move quickly, Librarian Edward Lim warned in 1992, if it did not wish to be 'left behind or dragged screaming into the twenty-first century'.[56] In partnership with the Computer Centre, the Library was embracing a new paradigm, the parallel library, coupling electronic and print media. In the 1960s, photocopiers had brought a small but important shift in study habits, enabling readers to study library materials away from the library itself. With the digital revolution, the library would itself become a virtual study space accessible electronically not just on campus, or even in the student's home, but almost anywhere in the world.

Because we now know where that revolution was headed, we may be in danger of forgetting how slowly and haltingly it began. A 1994 survey of first-year students found that 42 per cent had not used computer-based learning materials at all in their courses. McCausland remembers being introduced to the internet when she began university in 1995, but it was 'mainly just for fun then'.[57] Even by 1999, when increasing numbers of households had home computers and internet use was growing rapidly, many students were still unfamiliar with the new technologies or used them only irregularly.[58] The university had its own internal digital divide between students with home computers and those without, those with private internet access and those who depended on computers being available in the library or labs. In 1995, the average price for a home-use computer was $3000, a sizeable outlay for the average undergraduate. Learning to use a computer, especially before the introduction of more intuitive, menu-driven software like Windows 95, was also a challenge for many students. Others, with the money or technical know-how, had equipment and software well in advance of what the university could provide.

Going places

Although the possibilities of the new technologies were yet to be fully realised, the information revolution expanded the university's vision of itself as an 'international' university. In 1991, Logan urged students to develop an 'international perspective' as part of their studies, to seek to understand other cultures and customs, economies and traditions.[59] An early manifestation of this vision was the provision of financial support for students to travel abroad as part of their degree. The program began by focusing on American universities, but by the end of the decade students could study in one of more than twenty countries throughout Asia, Europe, the United States, South America and the Pacific.

In offering an opportunity to study abroad, Logan was tapping a widely felt aspiration among Monash students. *Lot's Wife*, Berwick's *Ink* and other student publications regularly included articles on travel or excerpts from Lonely Planet travel guides. Leeyong Soo, who arrived at Clayton in 1993 to study Japanese, was not aware of Monash's claim to be an international university—she chose Monash because it was closest to her home. But she soon became aware of the possibilities for travel through Monash programs. In 1994, she went to Kanazawa in Japan for six weeks to do an intensive language course. In 1995–96, she travelled to Bonn in Germany, then on to Chiba University in Japan, to do research for her honours thesis. She and fellow Monash students were accommodated in home-stays and took classes with a Monash teacher in the morning, attending the university in the afternoon. Leeyong has 'fond memories' of her time at Clayton, but her memories of being overseas through Monash's programs made a stronger impression.[60] For local students who took advantage of Monash's exchange programs, the experience of being a Monash student was no longer geographically confined to Clayton, Victoria or Australia. Going to uni was taking them places, in a whole new way.

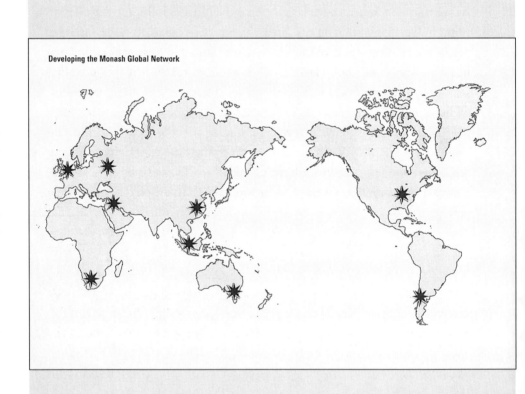

Developing the Monash Global Network

TEN
AT THE LIMIT?

Monash sees the world as a place where there should be no boundaries to, and the widest possible opportunities for, the pursuit of legitimate, high quality academic activity.

GLOBAL DEVELOPMENT FRAMEWORK, 2001

Memories of the vice-chancellorship of David Robinson are still refracted through the circumstances of his departure: in disgrace, following a plagiarism scandal that made national and international headlines. But the significance of his time at Monash extended well beyond the impact of this dramatic downfall. In his five and a half years in the job, Robinson steered Monash down paths it still follows today. A 'man in a hurry', canny, energetic and ambitious, Robinson positioned Monash favourably in the starkly competitive higher education landscape of the late 1990s. His bold program of international expansion took the university to the edge of this new frontier. But some of the costs of this success, combined with his apparent disregard for scholarly propriety, made Robinson a potent symbol of the threat to 'traditional' academic values.

David Robinson is a man easily demonised, both for what is known about him and what is unknown. His predecessor, Mal Logan, spoke openly about his childhood, his academic life and passions, his political and educational philosophies. Robinson does not appear to have spoken thus. In public speeches, he seldom used the personal voice. He has been described, even by some who worked closely with him, as the sort of man you don't easily get to know. He declined to be interviewed for this book.

Under Vice-Chancellor David Robinson, Monash aimed to plant its footprint on every continent except Antarctica by 2020.

The new broom

Logan's departure left a sense of uncertainty about the direction that the university should now take. Deputy Vice-Chancellor Ian Chubb had been appointed in 1993 with an eye to the succession. But the two big men clashed, and Chubb departed to become vice-chancellor of Flinders. In seeking a new leader, the university faced a number of unanswered questions. How were the several campuses to work together? Was Clayton too elitist? What balance was the university to find between collegiate and corporate identities? Was it time for consolidation, or sensible expansion? Should the university pull back from the bold entrepreneurialism of the Logan period?

The selection committee, chaired by Chancellor Bill Rogers, an influential Melbourne solicitor and businessman, agreed that the new vice-chancellor should be aged between forty and sixty, with a PhD and a traditional academic background. Some hoped for an academic of 'international standing'; others were content with 'bare academic credibility'. Above all, the appointee should be a 'leader, a person of stature', able to command respect, an accomplished manager and administrator who could 'see the big picture', ready to consolidate recent gains yet with an 'eye for opportunity', collegiate in temperament ('not an ego-seeker') yet capable of making firm decisions. It was a tall order.[1]

The committee was eager to make a clean break with the past. It agreed that an internal candidate was not desirable but decided it was politic to interview deputy vice-chancellors Robert Pargetter and Peter Darvall. Robinson was one of four external candidates, including one woman. Some others remained undeclared, including a 'dark horse' who was said to have indicated that he was interested, but only if tapped on the shoulder.

Robinson was frank with the committee: he didn't know what structural changes he would make, but he saw room for improvement. Monash was viewed as 'buccaneering' but was not clearly among the top five Australian universities. It should aspire to be number one. Bill Rogers thought him impressive. Others already knew something of Robinson's management style and strengths, either from experience or reliable reports. At the end of the interviews, he was ahead by a clear margin.

Robinson seemed the outstanding candidate, and the committee decided unanimously to appoint him.[2]

Robinson was one of the stars of the Dawkins era. He had overseen the early years of the new University of South Australia and its progression from band five to band one in the government's quality rankings. He became prominent as chief of the Australian Technology Network (linking the five former institutes of technology), vice-president of the Australian Higher Education Industrial Association and director of the Open Learning Agency. With his appointment at Monash, he became the first Englishman to have been successively appointed vice-chancellor at two Australian universities. His rise was hailed as 'meteoric'.[3]

It was a long way from Gomersal, the Yorkshire textile town where Robinson had been born fifty-four years earlier. His father, the manager of a spinning mill, died when David was nine, and he completed his schooling at the Royal Masonic School for Boys in Hertfordshire, an

A man in a hurry. Vice-Chancellor
Professor David Robinson, 1997.

independent boarding school for the needy sons of Freemasons. Later, at University College, Swansea, Robinson took a bachelor's degree in sociology and politics and a PhD in his chosen field, medical sociology. In 1971, he was appointed to a lectureship in the Addiction Research Unit of the Institute of Psychiatry in London. He was by then publishing prolifically, with no fewer than seven titles in four years. His sociological approach to alcoholism was attracting international, as well as national, interest. In 1981, he won a chair in health studies at the University of Hull, in his native Yorkshire, later becoming dean of social and political sciences and pro vice-chancellor (1989–91).[4]

According to the *Australian*, Robinson had a 'reputation for toughness leavened by a well-developed sense of fun and light-heartedness'.[5] The toughness was soon apparent. Even before his arrival, he ruffled feathers by requiring members of the Vice-Chancellor's Group (VCG) to inform him in writing why they should remain in their positions. Pargetter, outraged, refused to do so and returned to a chair in the Arts Faculty. Robinson went on to effect a shake-up of Monash's senior management, appointing Alan Lindsay of Macquarie as deputy vice-chancellor (academic and planning) and former Curtin vice-chancellor John Maloney deputy vice-chancellor (international and public affairs) five months before he arrived himself.

A man for the times

From the beginning, Robinson elicited passionate but contradictory responses from those around him. Some liked his forceful style, seeing him as admirably direct and decisive. But what some experienced as refreshing candour others perceived as ruthlessness.

Robinson was a man for the times, and by the late 1990s the times were changing. He arrived just as the election of the Howard government heralded a sharp decrease in funding for higher education. In 1996, the government reduced operating grants for universities and decided not to supplement them for expected salary increases. An effective 12–15 per cent funding cut for 1997–2000[6] was soon felt in job losses, heavier workloads and declining staff–student ratios.

Financial exigency bred an emphasis on 'self-reliance', a watchword of the Robinson years. Self-reliance meant generating external income from research and entrepreneurial activity, and attracting and retaining students, especially those who would pay up-front fees. Universities were allowed to charge fees for students enrolled beyond HECS quotas, up to a maximum of 25 per cent of students in a given course. From 1998, this included domestic as well as international students. Characteristically, Monash crested the wave of change. It was the first university after Melbourne to introduce full fees for domestic students. *Lot's Wife* referred darkly to a 'Monash Uni Grab for Cash™ (formerly known as education)'.[7]

The new climate fostered a shift towards a more managerial style of administration. The Academic Board became less a debating chamber than a stage for members of the VCG, deans and representatives of Monash's far-flung empire (present by conference phone or video-link) to report their latest triumphs to a largely passive academic community. The English Department's Jenny Strauss, who had served as a staff representative on many university bodies, found the new style 'profoundly hierarchical' and hostile to any criticism of those at the top.[8] Even those closest to the seat of power were discouraged from expressing dissenting views. 'Cabinet solidarity', informally observed under Logan, became an explicit policy of Robinson's VCG, now expected to 'speak with one voice'. There was rarely any divergence from 'Yes sir, no sir, three bags full sir', Darvall recalls.[9]

At its first meeting, Robinson announced that one of his early priorities was to update Logan's strategic plan. Words such as 'devolution', 'energy', 'engagement', 'enlightenment' and 'meaningful' should be inserted in the new plan, which would operate on a five-year rolling basis.[10] Recalling its soviet associations, *Lot's Wife* found the very idea of a five-year plan ridiculous. Robinson was either 'wholly ignorant of history or has a very grim sense of humour'.[11]

Leading the Way: The Monash Plan, 1998–2002 announced three 'defining themes': innovation, engagement and internationalisation. The university would escape the effects of government penury by embracing more fee-paying students, stronger links with industry and a more visible overseas presence. Learning and teaching would be more flexible, drawing on new educational technologies, and the curriculum would be internationalised, with 10 per cent of undergraduate students spending at least one semester in an overseas institution. Monash would be not only *international* but also *global*, with a significant presence in seven strategic locations by 2003.[12]

Copies of the plan were sent to Monash graduates. 'Monash University has sent me its new "vision" statement', reported former PhD student Don Watson. '"It is a vision", it says, "which will become more concrete and more detailed over time as the precise nature of external and internal change becomes known".' In a pro-forma letter, Robinson hoped that the recipient would find the vision 'inspiring'. 'I don't', Watson replied. 'On the contrary, I blame it and hundreds of documents like it for chronic headaches, neuralgia and bouts of dull-wittedness similar to a hangover.'[13] *The Monash Plan* was a fine specimen of the decay of public language that Watson later damned in his book *Death Sentence*.

Inside the university, however, anyone who wanted anything could not afford to ignore the plan. At a Christmas party, Science Faculty secretary Paul Rodan treated guests to an ironical rendition of 'Stand by Your Plan'. To accompany the master plan there was a raft of 'second-tier' plans: the Teaching and Learning Plan, the Research Management Plan, Campus Plans, Administrative Units Plans and Faculty Plans.

Robinson's embrace of comprehensive planning represented a step away from the more personal leadership exercised by his predecessors. Logan had begun as a planner but largely abandoned formal planning processes under the pressure of circumstances. Robinson had neither Logan's detailed inside knowledge of Monash nor his political finesse. Yet, in meeting the challenge of Logan's legacy—imposing a cohesive academic design and budgetary rationale on a disparate collection of academic enterprises—centralised planning may have been the most effective, if not the most inspiring, form of leadership for the times. Robinson had the strategic skill, resolute sense of purpose and eye for detail required to pilot a big ship in a difficult climate.

Global planning

Internationalisation was at the core of the university's long-range strategic vision statement *Leading the Way: Monash 2020*. From the beginning, Robinson signalled that he intended to continue down the international path forged by Logan. Having maintained its lead in the numbers of international students enrolled, and with a campus soon to open in

Malaysia, Monash was 'extremely well-placed to take advantage of the opportunities that exist elsewhere in the world'. Just as Britain had realised there was a world beyond Europe, so Australian institutions needed to discover there was a world outside Asia.[14]

Robinson was convinced that globalisation was now fundamental to the business of universities. Academic endeavour was increasingly 'multisite, multimodal, multilingual, multicultural, and multinational'.[15] Broad-based institutions that operated both nationally and globally would become the most successful.[16] In the eyes of its marketing team, Monash's brand—as instanced by the Southern Cross in its logo—was still too 'Australian'. Robinson foresaw the day when the university's headquarters might well not be in Melbourne or even in Australia.[17] 'Monash', he liked to say, 'is just six letters'.[18]

Monash 2020 envisaged a 'matrix of campuses which will be nodes in an educational network that spans the globe'. A map of the world showed stars in key locations on every continent bar Antarctica. Monash would become a university of 80 000 students by 2020, half of them outside Australia. They would be 'global citizens' entering a 'gateway to the world' through an internationalised curriculum, flexible delivery and international exchange.[19]

Robinson was the main instigator of the Monash Institute for the Study of Global Movements, a research initiative involving the faculties of Art and Design, Arts, Business and Economics, Education, and Law. The institute aimed to bridge the gap between the social sciences and business disciplines to pursue research themes related to the global movements of people, resources and ideas. Ambitiously, it pledged to address the tensions of globalism seen in events like the World Trade Center attacks of September 2001.[20] Robinson also encouraged plans for a Monash ePress that would make the university 'a prime node for the distribution of academic material in our region and beyond'.[21]

For Logan, internationalisation had been a means of breaking down the defensive walls of the traditional university. He had remained, however, a very Australian character with roots firmly sunk in the Labor tradition. Robinson also wanted to use external forces to transform the university's culture, but, as one of a new breed of globe-trotting vice-chancellors, his vision of the global university reflected his own more peripatetic experience. Not everyone shared his vision of global citizenship. 'I think he thought it is possible to have a view from nowhere', former dean of law Stephen Parker observes, 'whereas I think it is only possible to have a view from somewhere'.[22]

Monash Global was established in late 1998 to direct Monash's international activities. Its board included external members, the Hon. John Button and banker Will Bailey, as well as senior members of the university and its council, while Deputy Vice-Chancellor (International) John Maloney and Executive Director (International Affairs) Ian Porter managed day-to-day activities.[23] The Monash Global group spearheaded the 'scramble' for international opportunities. Its *Global Development Framework* (December 1999) outlined the principles underpinning Monash's international development activities and developed a fifteen-point 'Location and Partner Selection Matrix' for assessing offshore development opportunities. Any global initiative would have to be relevant and viable, with a controlled exit strategy.[24]

The *Global Development Framework* proposed one or two more campuses outside Australia by 2010, but the administration had more ambitious plans: campuses in three countries, including Indonesia and Thailand, by 2005 and a further two, including Chile, by 2010. Only in 2010, with major operations in Australia, Asia, North and South America, Africa, West Europe and the Middle East, would Monash 'be able to claim that it is truly a global University'.[25]

The Asian connection

While the university's ambitions ranged widely, they focused first on Asia. Indonesia was expected to be the first cab off the rank. Monash already had strong links in the country and had been involved in the establishment of a preparatory facility (Unisadhuguna) with the University of New South Wales in the mid-1990s.[26] After some initial enthusiasm, Logan had pulled back, but, under Robinson, the fragile Indonesian economic and political situation stemming from the currency collapse in July 1997 and the riots of May 1998 seemed to present a 'unique opportunity'. Plans were hatched for a staged development beginning with a 'soft entry' via a private Indonesian university called Monash University Centre, Jakarta, but were shelved after an unfavourable market assessment.[27]

The arrival of the long-expected Malaysian campus was also temporarily thwarted by the Asian economic crisis. Monash's partner Jeffrey Cheah's Sunway group very nearly went under. As the creditors closed in, Cheah instructed one of his senior executives, Elizabeth Lee, to place his precious educational activities in a trust beyond their reach.[28] The crisis left Malaysia with a depreciated currency and a Chinese middle class anxious for their children's future but no longer able to afford an overseas education.

On the evening of 23 February 1998, Robin Pollard, Director of undergraduate business courses at Caulfield and Frankston, arrived at the Sunway Lagoon Hotel. In the morning, picking up the copy of the *New Straits Times* slipped under his door, he read: 'MONASH BRANCH CAMPUS TO OPEN 1 JULY'. Parting the curtains, he gazed across the Sunway Lagoon theme park towards Sunway College, now topped by a 'Hollywood-style' sign: 'MONASH UNIVERSITY'. 'Well, no one told me anything about that!' he thought.[29]

Monash Sunway pioneers. From left to right, Robin Pollard, Lee Weng Keng, Cheong Sieuw Yoong, Jim Warren and Robin Alfredson, 1999.

For two years, negotiations over the branch campus had been stalled. Political friction between Malaysia and Australia, the Asian economic crisis and hesitation by each of the partners had contributed to the delay. Suddenly, the political logjam had been broken. Education Minister Najib Tun Abdul Razak, flanked by David Robinson and Australian diplomatic officials, made the official announcement.[30] Once again, Monash was racing against the clock on a new educational frontier. By agreeing to start immediately in makeshift accommodation at Sunway College, it stole a march on its competitors, including the University of Nottingham. 'Monash was very fast', Sunway executive director Lee Weng Keng recalls.[31]

A few months earlier, Monash veteran 66-year-old zoologist Jim Warren had received an unexpected phone call. Would he become pro vice-chancellor of a new Monash campus in Malaysia? It was not the first unexpected turn in Warren's life. As a graduate student at the University of California, Los Angeles, in the early 1960s, he had been sent by his supervisor to meet an Australian visitor at Los Angeles airport. He discovered the ebullient biologist Jock Marshall arguing with American customs officials over a suitcase full of Australian beer. Marshall had later offered him a lectureship at Monash, and in 1968 he had succeeded to Marshall's chair, becoming in turn a popular dean of science. Now, recently retired, he was being invited to start all over again. At first he hesitated. 'I said, "Look, if I was still here in the Professorial Board, I don't think I would be approving setting up a campus in Malaysia".' But after second thoughts he agreed: 'Here I was retired, no family, so maybe it was an interesting thing to do'.[32]

He was not the only doubter. Would the campus be expected to observe the ethnic quotas that governed entry to Malaysian public universities, asked Arts Dean Marian Quartly. As a private university, Monash was exempt from such requirements, Robinson assured her. Could academic staff be sure their teaching would not be subject to political censorship?[33] 'While Monash would operate as completely as possible under its own Act and policies, its operations must abide by the laws of the country in which its campuses were located', Robinson replied.[34] In practice, the partners worked overtime to avoid such conflicts. For example, the syllabus recommended by the Department of Education for the ethics course required under Malaysian law was politically and religiously loaded, so Monash simply ignored it. If Malaysian entry or course approval requirements clashed with Monash regulations, the university bent or even broke the rules of its Education Committee.[35] Everyone was looking, Asian style, for 'win-win' solutions.

Monash had promised to open in four months but had no idea how to achieve it. 'It was a complete leap into the dark', Warren recalls. 'We occupied a vacant annex of Sunway College with no offices, no chairs, no computer system, no functional laboratories [and] . . . no application forms for potential staff or students.' By March, he had been joined by two other Australians: Robin Pollard, the surprised witness at the birth of the new campus, who became head of a school of business and IT, and Robin Alfredson, a former associate dean of teaching in the Faculty of Engineering, who headed science and engineering. In Kuala Lumpur, the three Australians joined Dr Cheong Sieuw Yoong, a former dean of education at the University of Malaya, who became director of administration and registrar. Warren—the kind, diplomatic and culturally sensitive academic—set the academic tone of the campus, while Cheong—a forceful administrator with an unrivalled understanding of the Malaysian educational scene—became, as Warren generously acknowledges, its organisational linchpin.[36]

Their first challenge was finding high-quality academic staff. Academics in the Malaysian national system were obliged to retire at fifty-five, so Monash was able to attract some excellent experienced lecturers, as well as a number of able younger academics attracted to the freer academic environment of the new campus. Mahendhiran Nair, an econometrician, had studied and worked in Canada before returning to teach in a Malaysian public university. He missed the 'openness' of the Canadian university and was about to go back there when Monash offered him the chance to work close to home. Cathy Yule had completed a Monash PhD in freshwater ecology before accompanying her mining engineer husband to posts in Bougainville, Borneo and Kuala Lumpur. Seeing an announcement of Warren's appointment, she rang up: 'Hey, do you want anyone?' Warren hired her on the spot.[37]

Monash promised Malaysians an 'affordable but uncompromised world-class education'.[38] But could it be delivered at a price that Malaysian parents could afford? Sunway, which was responsible for the physical facilities, was still recovering from the crisis. 'Spend money as though it were your own', Jeffrey Cheah exhorted his employees. Pens and paper, even toilet rolls, were carefully rationed.[39] Rather than compromise quality, Robinson offered to guarantee a 1 million-ringgit bank loan for essential equipment. While only some of the funds were needed, the gesture strengthened the partnership.[40]

Teaching began with an array of courses selected mainly from the Gippsland distance learning syllabus. 'Here are the slides, now teach the course', was the academic order of the day. 'We were like jungle fighters waiting for the next consignment of rations to be dropped from the air', jokes Mahendhiran Nair.[41] The parachute drop wasn't just a way of saving time or costs. After Jim Warren finished his opening day address, a parent rose to ask the vital question: 'How can you guarantee that this campus will be the same as in Australia?' It would take the greater part of a decade for the campus to shed the assumption that Monash quality required an Australian-derived syllabus.

By beginning in makeshift accommodation, the partners had been able to minimise risk and test the market. As economic conditions improved, enrolments grew strongly, reaching 800 in less than two years, and 2000 by the end of Robinson's reign. Expectations rose too. In 2000, when IT academic Bob Bignall succeeded Jim Warren, he detected a 'credibility gap' between Monash's claims and what it delivered. It needed to improve the quality of its staff, boost research activity and revamp its marketing. Above all, it needed a campus of its own. Only when it had buildings in a style that reflected its own character would Monash be able to distinguish itself from its host.[42] For academic staff, working in cramped partitioned offices, the day could not come fast enough. Sunway had achieved its success by ruthlessly paring costs, but for the university to live up to its image the partner would have to loosen its purse strings. Monash wanted a campus almost twice as expensive as Sunway proposed. It insisted on an Australian architect whose ideas sometimes left the partner puzzled. Why would you provide outdoor seats and tables in a tropical climate where it rained half the time, Lee Weng Keng asked. But, in the end, Monash mostly got its way. The new campus, just a short walk from Sunway College, is airy, well planned, commodious, sociable. Robinson would not see the full realisation of the university's first overseas campus, but he boldly led the way towards it.

The European connection

Along with overseas campuses, Monash was pursuing a range of strategic alliances and partnerships on almost every continent. 'We will position ourselves as the Australian university which has the closest ties with Europe', Stephen Parker, Chair of the Europe Steering Group, declared in 2002.[43] A link established by Logan with the Menzies Centre for Australian Studies in London was boosted to a broader alliance with King's College, leading to the establishment of a Monash Centre on the Strand, opposite Australia House. The search for an American partner inspired a scheme for a similar office in Chicago to give the university a 'face' in the region. There were plans for twinning arrangements with a Chinese university and for links with other regions, such as Indonesia and Singapore, regarded as ripe for student recruitment. The whole university, Peter Darvall recalls, seemed infected with a 'crazy imperialism'.

One of Monash's most successful international ventures began not at the behest of a central committee checking boxes on a selection matrix, but through personal enthusiasm and local knowledge. Bill Kent was one of Monash's academic stars, a Footscray High boy who joined Monash as a tutor in the 1960s, returned after doctoral study in London and Florence, and became an inspiring teacher and researcher of Florentine history. As a regular visitor to I Tatti, the Harvard Center in Fiesole, Kent watched as American colleges established study centres in Europe. From the mid-1990s, he began to follow their example, by taking small groups of Monash students to study 'The Renaissance *in* Italy'. He had supported the vision of painter Arthur Boyd to establish a joint Australian centre in Italy. After that project foundered, he persuaded Monash to establish a Monash European studies centre in Italy. At first, there was some reluctance to back the brainchild of a 'wacky academic [who] wasn't very good administratively'.[44] In March 1998, Robinson met a visiting delegation from Tuscany, and soon afterwards the search began for a suitable location.

'We all hoped [it would be] in Florence', Kent recalled. When Prato, a textile town 19 kilometres from Florence, was first suggested, he was

Italian Renaissance historian Bill Kent, a Clayton pioneer in the early 1960s, inspired the creation of the university's first European centre in Prato, near Florence.

lukewarm. The proposed site, an industrial village on the outskirts of the town, was even less inspiring. 'Oh, here we go again', he thought, 'Monash 1960s, Footscray High 1954. Why am I always starting in these sorts of places?' Then someone suggested the Palazzo Vai, an eighteenth-century classical palace in the medieval centre of the town. The building had thirty-five rooms ranging from a large *salone* to smaller rooms suitable for studios and studies. Prato had many of the artistic and historic associations of Florence, but it was off the main tourist beat. The more he thought about it, the more Kent liked it. 'It was safer, it was cheaper and they [the local authorities] wanted us.'[45] In Prato, students would be encountering the real Tuscany, a historic region undergoing profound social change, with the largest Chinese population in Italy, not a static tourist landscape. Finally, in late 1999, the university secured the philanthropic support of a prominent Italian-Australian couple, Rino and Diana Grollo, and the project was launched.

For the next four years, Kent suspended his big research project, a life of the Florentine patron-politician Lorenzo de' Medici, to direct the new centre. He negotiated with local officials, oversaw renovations, organised courses, conferences and exhibitions, and shored up support from Monash's sometimes doubtful administrators. A product of the old, collegial Monash, Kent utilised the opportunities created by the university's global ambitions to gain a foothold for Monash, and Australia, in Europe. By the time Kent died, prematurely, in 2010, the Monash Prato Centre had welcomed more than 5000 visitors and was hosting courses, conferences and research projects in fields as diverse as international law, textile design, road safety and, of course, Renaissance history.

Into Africa

In January 2000, Monash became the first Australian university to be registered as a private higher education institution in South Africa, following the end of apartheid. The campus opened in 2001 in Ruimsig, Roodepoort ('Red Valley'), a former gold-mining area, now a rapidly expanding suburb 20 kilometres northwest of Johannesburg.

At first sight, there was no more unpromising place for Monash to plant a campus. In Malaysia, the university was well known through three generations of Monash alumni, but in South Africa it was known to almost nobody. Only an ambition to become truly global could explain such a marked departure from familiar paths. Was an English-born vice-chancellor perhaps more receptive to its attractions than an Australian one? At the University of South Australia, Robinson had overseen the development of a teacher training centre in South Africa,[46] and his interest was further aroused by a visit by South Africa's deputy minister of education.[47] Meanwhile, other Monash people, including Dean of Business and Economics John Rickard and Peter Cunliffe, Chief Executive Officer of Monash University Foundation Year, had visited the country, where they met with Australian High Commissioner Ian Porter. Here, they had decided, was a chance to 'take the lead in a country and indeed a continent well ahead of any other Australian or indeed quality international university'.[48]

In August 1997, a Monash delegation met the management of AdvTech Education Ltd, a private education provider in South Africa, and other potential partners. Robinson and John Maloney later met AdvTech chairman Brian Buckham, examined potential sites for the campus and held talks with South Africa's minister of education Professor Sibusiso Bengu.

Everyone believed that education would become the powerhouse of the New South Africa. Many of the old South African universities were tainted by the legacy of apartheid. Perhaps an Australian university, with no such baggage, could 'lead the way' in widening educational opportunity for South Africans, while getting in on the ground floor of what everyone hoped would be an educational bonanza. Institutional ambition, commercial advantage and political opportunism jostled with the desire to be 'engaged' (another Monash buzzword) in what everyone felt was one of the great liberating stories of the era.

By the end of 1997, Monash and its proposed partner AdvTech had outlined a plan to build the first international university in South Africa on a greenfields site somewhere in the northern suburbs of Johannesburg. Its degrees would be as good as those granted in Australia and better than those of its foreign competitors. Its fees would be high (around 30 000 rand, or A$7000), well beyond the means of all but the white minority. How the venture was to be reconciled with the South African government's desire to increase the representation of blacks in higher education was not explained.[49]

Monash soon adjusted its rhetoric to match emerging South African expectations. A concept brief presented to the minister for education in April 1998 began with a quotation from Nelson Mandela and related its goals to the government's 1997 White Paper *A Programme for the Transformation of Higher Education*. But the internal contradictions remained. The new university would be the closest to Soweto, would forge links with disadvantaged black universities like Mandela's own Fort Hare, would recruit 10 per cent of its students through bursaries and would reinvest any surpluses in the campus. But how many black people from Soweto could afford its steep fees, and how would it help redress the intractable racial inequalities of the nation?

The project soon faced more immediate problems. In July 1998, the deal with AdvTech fell through. The partner wanted more control over the joint venture than Monash would relinquish. In retrospect, this was a crucial decision point: without a local partner, Monash would be taking much greater financial and political risks. Yet Robinson assured the minister that Monash still intended to move ahead with its plans.[50]

It was now becoming clear that the promised educational bonanza would not materialise. The number of qualified school-leavers was barely half that forecast by the National Council on Higher Education. Black students were flooding the well-resourced public universities from which they had previously been barred, while the black universities and distance learning institutions languished. Monash would be left to compete with an increasing number of other private higher education institutions, many offering generous incentives to attract students.[51]

A further blow to Monash's plans came in June 1999 when Education Minister Bengu was replaced by Kader Asmal, a former academic and human rights expert. Asmal was hostile to the operations of foreign universities in South Africa, fearing that they would dominate the market, sucking resources from the public universities and contributing to 'brain drain' and dependence on the North.[52] In September, he warned that the government might not continue to look so kindly on Monash establishing a full-scale university in South Africa.[53]

Monash's Project Reference Group now began to wonder whether the South African venture was still a 'good idea', since registration was not assured, and a 'worst case loss' might amount to as much as $14 300 000.[54] Yet in September 1999, the Monash Council, meeting in Kuala Lumpur, resolved to proceed with the campus, with only one dissenting vote. Associate Professor Andrew Markus, a staff representative, had read the proposal on the plane (on principle, he had asked to fly economy class). To his mind, it just didn't add up. The margin for error seemed too small, and the projected maximum loss didn't take into account the potential cost to the reputation of the university if it failed. He couldn't see how the campus would attract sufficient students. Why would white parents send their children to an expensive local private university when paying a similar amount to a foreign university would give them a visa to live somewhere better? Markus was sceptical about claims that the campus would benefit South Africa. If Monash wanted to help people, why didn't it set up a campus in Alice Springs?[55]

That a vote was recorded at all is testament to Markus' determination. The new chancellor, Jerry Ellis, an ex–chief executive and chairman of BHP, brought, by his own admission, a 'corporatist view to the job of being Chancellor'. He preferred council to operate like the board of a public company, with decisions made by consensus rather than by a vote.[56] While other council members had doubts about the South Africa plan, they were reluctant to gainsay 'the experts', who had scored it highly on fourteen of the fifteen selection criteria.[57]

Robinson and those closest to the South Africa project were not about to let the opportunity go. The campus was a key part of the long-term plan for Monash to move outside its 'comfort zone' in Western Europe and Southeast Asia.[58] Robinson regarded it as 'the activity which is most defining of the Monash we are trying to create by 2020'.[59] In January 2000, Monash gained provisional registration to offer undergraduate courses in arts, business and commerce, business systems, computing, and IT. Beating a large field of Australian and foreign competitors steeled its resolve to proceed. But, as a 'provisionally' registered institution, its position remained precarious.[60] In September, the conditions of registration were amended to prevent Monash using the name 'university'. Ultimately, the operational name Monash South Africa (MSA) was accepted.

Construction of the 18 million-rand campus got under way in July 2000. Recruitment efforts ran into flak from rivals indignant about the newcomer's pushy style. Meanwhile, Monash staff and the National Tertiary Education Union protested that scarce resources were being diverted from hard-pressed local departments to an internationalisation program that might never turn a profit. Professor John Anderson, the affable former campus director at Berwick and Gippsland, became the founding pro vice-chancellor of MSA. Anderson relocated to South Africa in 2000 with his partner, Jan Houge, who was appointed director of Student and Administrative Services. They relished the opportunity to build a new campus from the ground up in a new democracy.

After optimistic early reports, the opening of the campus, with only fifty students, was disappointing, especially considering the target of 6000 required to break even at the end of the first decade.[61] But Anderson was confident. 'I still think you/we can build something worthwhile here', he assured Robinson in April 2001. 'Essentially, if the country works

The next frontier. Construction of the MSA campus, 2000.

the project will work.' The first cohort of students reported a positive experience, and from 2002 the political environment became less hostile.[62] But student numbers never reached the projected target. Robinson acknowledged the difficulties but insisted that Monash would persevere. It was now a matter of 'managing our way through'.[63] In July 2002, the campus was reported to be struggling financially, with expected losses of more than $20 million by 2003.[64] With hindsight, even Ellis conceded that 'we didn't listen well enough to that particular member of Council . . .'[65]

Disciplining the disciplines

Planning for the South Africa campus had begun just as the university announced it would face a $40 million budget shortfall by 2000, as a result of the cuts imposed in the 1996 federal budget. Two faculties, Science and Arts, faced cuts in student load, job losses and restructuring. They had low enrolments in some disciplines and had failed, it was said, to seize opportunities in the marketplace. Under the *Monash Plan*, some of the money that used to flow to the faculties was now taken 'off the top' and distributed in accordance with each faculty's success in winning money externally. This was a contest which the basic disciplines found hard to win.

'The University is determined to preserve its strength in fundamental research, which underpins its successes in applied research', *Monash 2020* asserted,[66] but, while the Arts and Science faculties had large student bodies, they found it difficult to attract full-fee-paying students, who instead favoured more vocational courses in Business, Economics, Law and IT. Over his five years at the helm, Robinson radically reshaped the university's profile, reducing enrolments in the discipline-based faculties, Arts (–12.5 per cent) and Science (–12.1) and increasing them in established professional faculties like Business and Economics (+11.1), Law (+18.1), Education (+8.8) and Engineering (+20.3), while rapidly expanding in new vocational faculties such as Art and Design (+34.3) and IT (+55.2). Medicine (+58.2) also grew spectacularly, partly through the acquisition of nursing, psychology and social work, as well as the creation of new courses in physiotherapy and occupational therapy.

Monash's founders had regarded the sciences and humanities as integral to the character of the university. In August 1997, hundreds of staff and students signed a form letter to the vice-chancellor insisting that the reputation of the university rested on its reputation in these disciplines. Their value to the community and culture could not be measured in financial terms.[67] The unions cited Monash as an 'extreme example' of a trend towards lavish overseas expenditure combined with frugality among the faculties.[68] The University Unlimited was stretched at home.

Since the early 1990s, the Science Faculty had struggled to address some entrenched problems. Robinson immediately identified its weaknesses. Its curriculum was 'competent but conventional', having failed to respond to the swing towards 'relevant' areas of applied science. As a result, it had suffered a reduction of over 9 per cent in students, particularly in mathematics, physics and chemistry.[69]

News broke in November 1997 that the Science budget was to be cut by 8 per cent, or $2.4 million—meaning a loss of at least fifty jobs over the next two years. Dean Ron Davies was convinced that his faculty, which had already suffered an 18 per cent reduction in staffing, had been unfairly targeted. Davies had come to Monash in 1996 from the University of Calgary, where he had served two five-year terms as head of biological sciences. Colleagues at Calgary described a forthright leader who called a spade a spade. But he was a man of 'considerable empathy' and honesty, and a passionate advocate for science.[70]

Science, Davies complained, would have to shoulder more than half of the total university reduction in government funding.[71] Three hundred staff and postgraduate students signed a petition protesting against the cuts. Hadn't anyone noticed that the faculty earned more than 30 per cent of the university's research income? There was a risk that its high-flyers would simply leave. 'Do you and your advisors wish to be remembered for decimating one of Australia's strongest and most prestigious Science Faculties?' a professor asked Robinson. 'It has taken 35 years to build up this reputation, it will take weeks to destroy it.'[72]

It was not the cuts alone but the lack of discussion that disturbed the faculty. Even the dean, it seemed, had been given little chance to discuss the issues with the senior leadership.[73] When a meeting was finally held to discuss the review of Science, Robinson dismissed it as 'the usual mixture of good sense, perception, enthusiasm, whingeing and lunacy that one expects from any group of university colleagues anywhere in the world!' Faculty members, he insisted, must abandon their 'mendicant mentality', always asking the university for help rather than innovating to keep up with the changing world.[74]

Robinson selected former senior Department of Employment, Education and Training official David Phillips and former Australian Research Council chairman Professor Max Brennan to work with the faculty executive. The report *Science at Monash* (March 1998) was '*not* a review of the Faculty of Science' but an attempt to view science and technology at Monash in its totality and 'search for . . . opportunities'. A number of other faculties (particularly Medicine, Pharmacy, Engineering and IT) were involved in teaching and research in science. While students were eschewing the 'non-vocational' areas of physical science, demand for psychology, biology, ecology, pharmacy, medical and 'human' sciences, IT and other areas was strong. The faculty's future depended on its ability to capitalise on this trend.

The failure of the faculty's curriculum to reflect the multi-disciplinarity of contemporary science and current directions in biological and biomedical science was blamed on historical divisions at Monash between the Faculty of Science and those departments in the Faculty of Medicine which taught science. The report drew attention to the tendency for faculties to discourage students from taking subjects in other faculties, calling for greater cross-faculty cooperation and a review of double degrees across the university. In Science, double degrees were to be developed and promoted along with multi-disciplinary programs in relevant, contemporary and vocational subjects such as environmental science. A revamped bachelor of science was introduced in 1999. Monash's traditional prerequisites for entry into science were dropped, in an attempt to reverse declining student numbers, and full-fee-paying programs were expanded.

When a third round of cuts was announced in November 1999, the breach between Robinson and Davies became unbridgeable. The two men, says Davies, had fundamentally different ideas about what a university should be. 'I remain strongly committed to the von Humboldt model while VC Robinson was committed to a financial profit model.' After a Committee of Deans meeting where the two clashed, Davies asked to see Robinson privately and pointed out some of their philosophical differences. 'After a lot of puffing and blowing . . . Robinson concluded that "we cannot work together". I agreed and asked the VC "so when are you leaving then?" This angered him and he said that we should meet in a week's time to discuss my future at Monash.' A week later, Robinson told Davies that he would support his continuing as dean only if he agreed to sack two (named) members of his faculty administration. Davies refused, and Robinson told him that he would like him to leave Monash.[75]

Davies summoned faculty office staff to advise them of his imminent departure. 'It was an immensely emotional occasion and within a short time, the majority of the staff were in tears', recalls Faculty Secretary Paul Rodan. 'Davies himself was too emotional to continue beyond a basic announcement.'[76] Having disagreed with his vice-chancellor, Davies had difficulty finding another position in Australia and eventually returned to Canada. Dean of Arts Homer Le Grand was appointed as interim dean and moved to implement a number of reforms, including new teaching initiatives and interdisciplinary programs.

In the Faculty of Arts, the experience of rationalisation and restructuring was similarly painful. Historian Marian Quartly was the first

Deans in distress. The Monash Plan *called for the expansion of applied studies but brought cuts and staff retrenchments to the traditional disciplines of science and arts. Deans Ron Davies (Science) and Marian Quartly (Arts) clashed with Robinson, the former resigning after only four years of his term.*

woman to head the faculty. She had arrived at Monash as a graduate student in the 1960s, returned in the early 1980s and became active among the feminist scholars reshaping the humanities curriculum. Her open, collegial style made her a popular choice as dean. She introduced new policies on assessment, created new scholarships, revived the Arts Students Society and established a coffee stall on the ground floor of the Menzies Building, which became a sociable gathering place. But she had come to the deanship late, with little senior administrative experience, only to confront a vice-chancellor bent on cutting the humanities down to size.

The *Monash Plan* required Arts to reduce its enrolments by 10 per cent over the following five years. Combined with unfunded salary increases, this necessitated seventy-five redundancies, about one in six academic positions. After years of budgetary cuts, any fat had long since disappeared: more pruning, Quartly estimated, would 'cut into flesh and bone'.[77] Classics and human relations, both small departments with low enrolments, were slated for closure at the end of 1997. To observers, the disappearance of classics, the historical fount of the humanities, only confirmed the philistinism of the post-Dawkins era.

The only path that seemed likely to achieve the savings while maintaining the integrity of the faculty was to identify and sack staff whose performance fell below expectations. But only if information on all facets of performance was gathered for every academic staff member could the faculty be confident of its actions withstanding appeal. This meant a lengthy process, but Quartly decided to proceed. 'The executive has committed itself to a process of pruning rather than slicing—of identifying staff right across the Faculty whose performance is less satisfactory than that of their fellows', she wrote to Robinson on 11 November 1997. 'What you are doing is in the University's strategic interest', he replied.[78]

Every academic would now be required to list his or her 'contributions to the faculty'.[79] But what if they simply refused to do so? On 14 May 1998, a special meeting of the faculty board staged a revolt. Respected senior figures condemned the central administration for its 'unjust and academically ill-considered' cuts and demanded that the dean and senior members of the faculty present its resolutions to the vice-chancellor.[80] Quartly, to the consternation of those who had reluctantly accepted the need for cuts, threw down her papers and declared: 'You're right, bugger them!'[81]

Robinson refused to meet the delegation. He was now convinced that Arts was incapable of downsizing itself. 'The high level of staff and student anxiety and uncertainty in your faculty indicates that the time for reflection is over', he wrote to Quartly. A review panel would be imposed to work with the dean to develop a 'clear strategy for future development'. David Phillips, Professor Merran Evans, Deputy Vice-Chancellor Alan Lindsay and five Arts academics were appointed to draw up a new 'blueprint' for the faculty.[82] Only then did Robinson agree to face the faculty. People wanted him to justify the cuts and receive representations, but his patience had been tried and he was in no mood for conciliation. Times had changed, he told them. The days when an academic could cycle in at ten, take off his bike clips, read the newspaper in the staffroom and cycle off again mid-afternoon were over. Around the room there were incredulous looks. Someone pointed out, respectfully, that most Arts academics were working sixty-hour weeks, but the plea drew no sympathy from the man at the top.

At the end of July, the National Tertiary Education Union called a stop work forum to protest the cuts. No university building should be used for the meeting, Robinson warned. Staff would have their pay docked unless they completed a form declaring that they had remained 'on duty'.[83] The meeting proceeded anyway. Former dean Emeritus Professor John Legge gave an 'urbane, pertinent and informative' talk on the history of the faculty.[84] Next day, he received a curt note from Robinson: 'It has been brought to my attention that you retired in 1986, but nevertheless continue to occupy space in the grossly-overcrowded Menzies Building'. He should quit the room within two weeks, after which 'no university space will be available to you'.[85]

Legge's senior colleagues were 'aghast'. Didn't the vice-chancellor know of Legge's long and distinguished service to Monash, his high reputation in the community and 'the vast amount of unpaid work' he still performed?[86] Legge estimated that he had saved the university \$50 000 by voluntarily running the Centre of Southeast Asian Studies. He knew that his eviction was not about space, because a colleague had warned him of Robinson's intention to act if he spoke at the forum. Robinson grudgingly backed down, although he could not resist a parting shot. While retired professors could have access to a room if it benefited the university, 'such staff [must] confine their interests and actions to focused academic effort and in no way abuse the hospitality of their host'.[87]

Word of the affair quickly spread across the campus and beyond, provoking a wave of indignation. Back in the 1960s, historian Don Watson noted, 'juvenile radicals like me were regularly told by academics like John Legge that we were entitled to dream any kind of revolution we fancied, but the university must remain a haven for free speech and the pursuit of knowledge'. It was a bitter irony that Legge should now be censured for defending the same liberal ideals not by student revolutionaries, but by the agent of a 'crude species of managerialism'.[88]

Through July and August, the review panel deliberated, receiving submissions, crunching numbers, pondering alternative structures. It had abandoned the attempt to secure redundancies by identifying low performers and was now concentrating its efforts on reconfiguring the twenty-five departments into ten schools, so as to identify areas for potential closure. In a four-hour meeting in council chambers, a two-thirds majority of the Arts Faculty Board reluctantly adopted the blueprint. Thirteen resolutions were passed in an effort to wrest back control over restructuring. These insisted that the cuts would make staff–student ratios 'significantly worse', weakening the faculty. They sought a commitment that students in threatened teaching areas could complete their majors and degrees.[89] Some hardheads worried that the review's recommendations were being eroded. 'I must confess to a measure of despondency as a result of what is unfolding at Fac. Bd.', geographer Chris Cocklin wrote to Quartly. 'I must also admit to a measure of despondency at the continuing refusal of the faculty to be led—or at least led by me', she replied. 'If I could resign I would. I am not the first to find that a consensual style of leadership is never very effective in deeply divided times.'[90]

Rational debate, though not necessarily rational decision-making, was the life-blood of faculties of arts; yet, by its insistence on actively participating in its own restructuring, the faculty may have prolonged the agony without improving the result. For Robinson, the planning process was as important as the bottom line. Receiving the report, he congratulated the review group on its work and approved an interest-free loan of up to $5 million over three years to tide the faculty over the process.[91]

Over the following months, the process of restructuring proceeded, with the departments being reshuffled into larger schools. In the end, the faculty achieved the necessary economies mainly through voluntary, rather than forced, redundancies. Some staff, close to retirement, left early, while others with good superannuation decided to take the money and run. Others feared, sometimes wrongly, that they would be forced out and preferred to go without shame. Some sought new pastures rather than endure the uncertainty any longer.

Quartly and her executive were accused of rolling over under pressure from the administration. A group of students occupied her office for around twenty-four hours, taking down radical texts from her shelves and inserting notes directing her to 're-read this'.[92] On 11 September, a valuable bronze bust of General Sir John Monash (the work of sculptor Paul Montford) was stolen from the Administration Building. A ransom note left in its place was addressed to Robinson from 'Sir John'. 'I can no longer bear to see my name used as a facade', it said. 'I will not be used as a justification for the destruction of decent higher education.' On 23 September, a small group of

Professor Homer Le Grand, Dean of the Faculty of Arts (1999–2006) and Interim Dean of Science (2000), with one of his Ford Mustangs.

students occupied the Administration Building, breaking down a door in the process. Police were called immediately: the Matheson days, in which the administration agonised over bringing police onto campus, were long over. Forty-three students were arrested and subsequently disciplined by the university.

Quartly served out the remainder of her term, but the crisis had eroded her authority. Robinson was determined that her successor would not have to learn on the job. Homer Le Grand, a philosopher of science, had already served a term as dean of arts at Melbourne. A graduate of the University of North Carolina, he drove a turquoise Ford Mustang and wore a belt buckle to match. Le Grand won the vice-chancellor's goodwill (and financial support for Arts) by doubling for a time as dean of science. The Arts Faculty, one wit observed, had lost classics and got Homer.

Downfall

As the new century dawned, Robinson's global vision was burning brightly. 'Things here at Monash are full of interest and excitement and appear to be going from strength to strength', he wrote to a former colleague at Hull. 'Over the past year we have opened a Centre inside King's College London, just opposite Australia House!'[93] The new centre was due to be opened officially by the Australian high commissioner on 11 July 2002, a moment the English-born vice-chancellor may well have anticipated with relish.

On 21 June, however, an article, 'Plagiarism Scandal Returns to Haunt V-C', appeared under the byline of Phil Baty in the *Times Higher Education Supplement*. It revealed that in 1983 David Robinson had admitted to 'a serious violation of scholarly standards' by plagiarising the work of another researcher in his contribution to the book *Drug Use and Misuse: Cultural Perspectives*. The *Supplement* had since discovered further evidence of plagiarism in his earlier book *Alcoholism Perspective*. These past misdemeanours cast doubt on his fitness for high university office. 'I find it unthinkable that he has major responsibility in [a] leading university', declared an unnamed English professor who had worked with Robinson.

The timing of the article, shortly before the opening of the London centre, was curious. Who had inspired it, and with what intent? 'Some information landed on my desk in a plain brown envelope, provided by a concerned individual', Baty later explained.[94] The unnamed professor and the 'concerned individual' were presumably one and the same. While Robinson was climbing the academic ladder in remote Australia, his old misdemeanours had apparently gone unnoticed. It was his expected reappearance in London that had evidently prompted an old enemy to denounce him.

The charges, Robinson responded, were stale news. The matter had been properly and publicly resolved in 1983, and neither the publisher nor his employer had taken further action. Chancellor Jerry Ellis assured Robinson that he continued to enjoy his full support and convinced the council to follow suit, which 'took a bit of doing . . . a lot of telephoning and talking'.[95]

For the moment, the issue seemed to have blown over. Robinson's opponents consoled themselves that the incident had at least embarrassed the vice-chancellor.[96] Bookshop manager Jim McGrath, at that point the anonymous author of the *Monash Gazette*—'the unofficial newsletter of Monash University'—published a spoof entitled 'Monash Bids for National Research Centre of Research Ethics', in which a spokesman, asked whether Monash had an original contribution to make, replied, 'Not exactly'. Thereafter, the *Gazette* referred to Robinson as 'David (Ditto) Robinson'.[97]

Then, on 6 July, the *Age* published details of a fresh case of plagiarism. Two days earlier, Professor John Bigelow, a mild-mannered Canadian-born philosopher, had had an hour or so between classes. He had heard from senior members of his faculty that Robinson had offered assurances that there were no more examples of plagiarism in his work. Looking out of his window in the Ming Wing towards the Law School, he wondered if this was true. On the shelves of the Law Library, Bigelow found a book by Robinson. There, next to it, was another author's book on the same topic. In the index of Robinson's book he found a reference to the other book. 'So I check this book and there's the bit that he quoted, but then he goes on quoting as though it's his own voice.' That night, reading while watching Wimbledon in bed, Bigelow found further 'convincing' examples of plagiarism in the book. The following day, he telephoned the chancellor to discuss what he had found. He sent a follow-up email:

> After our telephone conversation on Thursday afternoon I felt frankly terrified. I am no good at keeping secrets and I have been talking to lots of my friends, seeking advice, both before and after our conversation. You asked me why I had not gone to David Robinson with my concerns ... I replied that I thought he was in London, which was true, but I was not being candid. For me, David Robinson inspires fear but not respect ... In my opinion David Robinson does not have the confidence of the majority of my colleagues at Monash ...

Many people, Bigelow added, had not expressed their true opinions about Robinson for fear of ramifications. He, however, was going through a period of suffering in his personal life and felt 'reckless'.[98]

On 8 July, Robinson flew to London to launch the new Monash University centre. Back home, Ellis sent an email to all staff addressing the situation in light of the third instance of plagiarism. He copied in comments from Robinson, who acknowledged that in the works referred to he had reproduced text written by others without appropriate acknowledgement. He denied that this had been intentional. At the time, he said, he had been working on two other books, three book chapters and five journal articles. He referred to 'pressures to publish, to publish more and to publish more quickly'. While these omissions were 'sloppy', they were 'certainly inadvertent'. The man in a hurry had evidently been undone by haste.[99]

The response to this 'explanation' was swift. Professor Gary Bouma, Chair of Monash's Ethics Committee, informed Ellis that he had seen the instances of plagiarism that had come to light. Some of them could not be described as 'inadvertent' but appeared to be 'systematic and substantial'. Plagiarism, Bouma explained to Ellis, was a 'violation of a core value directly related to our core business as a university', comparable in gravity to the chief executive of a business being found to be a repeat embezzler.[100] Throughout the episode, Ellis had struggled to understand the significance academics accorded to what, from his vantage point, seemed 'a very minor sin'. He thought Robinson thoroughly professional, honest and hardworking, and admired his 'extraordinary energy and drive'. But, he concluded, 'it was for academics to judge'. He was particularly concerned about the views of Law Dean Stephen Parker. From the beginning, Parker's view had been clear-cut. 'I could not see as the Dean of Law that we could possibly countenance [Robinson's actions]. If the Law Faculty wasn't a university's conscience, then where was it?'[101]

Deputy Vice-Chancellor Peter Darvall had meanwhile directed Bouma to determine whether the alleged instances did in fact constitute plagiarism and academic misconduct. A panel of senior academics from across the university was asked to examine the material and give its assessment. As additional examples came to light, they were submitted to Bouma, who reported that the search had 'become a sport'. The investigation concluded that of the twelve examples contained in the works submitted, nine were clear cases of direct quotation without proper referencing. An additional instance—from a 1983 journal article—was also a straightforward case of plagiarism. The pattern did not appear to be accidental.[102]

Bouma's conclusions coincided with calls from the *Age* and the *Australian* for Robinson to stand down. These circumstances forced Ellis' hand. When Robinson arrived in London, a message from Ellis awaited him, instructing him to return at once. Deputy Chancellor June Hearn, who had travelled with him, was asked to stand in to open the London centre. Robinson was on the next plane home. On the morning of 11 July, Ellis and Robinson met for an hour. That afternoon, Ellis announced that the men had agreed that Robinson should leave the university. Robinson released a brief statement saying that he was 'obviously disappointed to be leaving Monash' but that he was confident the deans would continue with the 'enormous progress we have already made together'.[103]

Reactions to Robinson's departure were mixed. In some parts of the university, the corridors 'rang with laughter' and rejoicing.[104] Bookshop manager Jim McGrath was in the staff club when the news broke:

Monash forces its chief to quit

Misha Ketchell
Higher Education Reporter

The head of Australia's largest university has been forced to resign over claims that he is a repeat plagiarist.

David Robinson, the embattled vice-chancellor of Monash University, yesterday agreed to quit his job after chancellor Jerry Ellis summoned him home from a trip to London.

"He could see he was creating damage for the university. The only solution that he could see, and I could see, and we came to this together, was to leave," Mr Ellis said after an hour-long meeting with Professor Robinson.

David Robinson

Whistleblower: Professor Bigelow, above, and Professor Robinson, below

Job loss threat for accused plagiarist

Allegations of plagiarism against Vice-Chancellor David Robinson attracted national and international attention in July 2002, eventually forcing his resignation.

Homer [Le Grand]'s phone rang, and he answered it. After a moment he thanked the person on the other end, and rang off, and said 'It's done!' By this we understood that Ellis had sacked Robinson . . . and we clinked our glasses so hard that I still wonder that there weren't breakages. Then Homer got up and walked across to break the news to John Legge, who was at a nearby table. And when he came back he said 'John says to tell David that he can have a share of his office'.[105]

In the days following, a plaster copy of the missing bust of Sir John Monash was discovered in the Menzies Building. Glued to its reverse side was a newspaper article detailing Bigelow's role in Robinson's demise. Inscribed below were the words: 'The Sir John Monash Award for Academic Excellence. Awarded this 12th day of July 2002 to Professor John Bigelow for professional conduct of the highest order.' The original bronze bust has never been located. It was rumoured that the persons responsible for its removal, frightened by the possibility of criminal charges, threw it into a lake, where (in Bigelow's words) Sir John 'sleeps with the fishes'.[106]

Others were disappointed by Robinson's departure. 'There was very little dancing in the corridors here', Education Dean Sue Willis wrote to a colleague.[107] In an email to staff, she wrote:

I have worked under five Vice Chancellors and, through close colleagues, have considerable knowledge of quite a few others. I believe that he is one [of] a small number of the outstanding Vice Chancellors in Australia and possibly the best of our time. In my view, he presented us with an inspirational vision which did not try to emulate other universities but rather envisaged a university of its own making, to its core a university of quality but positioned differently from other universities . . . I am one who believes that his going is a loss to the University.[108]

Some worried that Monash had shown more concern for public relations than for Robinson's fair treatment.[109] Those who had uncovered and revealed further cases of plagiarism, it was said, had concealed motives and were engaged in a campaign to get rid of him. There was some truth in this. While Robinson had support among some deans, especially those he had appointed, his heavy-handed, authoritarian style and the neo-liberal bent of his vision for the university had elicited animosity, even hostility, among some staff. These sentiments did not cause his downfall, but they provided the momentum for it. Bigelow concedes that it 'wouldn't have happened if I hadn't been so keen to find more [examples], if the Dean hadn't been so keen to push the argument, if people . . . hadn't been keen to get it out to the newspapers'.[110]

Robinson himself never suggested he had been treated unfairly. He acted, in Ellis' view, with 'great honour'.[111] One may wonder what legal proceedings might have followed if he had refused to go. Robinson had not violated the terms of his contract, and he was not legally obliged to inform the university of past accusations of plagiarism.[112] He was appointed on the understanding that his role would be similar to that of a chief executive officer. His academic background, some argued, was not an important consideration: scholarly excellence and achievement had ceased to be critical criteria for the office. He had recently been reappointed for another five-year term, meaning that a substantial payout was to be expected. The sum was kept confidential but was rumoured to be about $1 million.

As the dust settled, Ellis' attention turned to the task of securing an interim vice-chancellor until a permanent appointment could be made. Peter Darvall was in no mood to be overlooked again. 'If you don't appoint me I'll leave', he told Ellis. But he wasn't interested in doing the long haul in the job he'd always wanted. He would do it until they found someone else. Council approved Darvall's appointment on 18 July.

The son of a prominent legal family, Peter Darvall had grown up in Eaglemont, attended Scotch College and the University of Melbourne. 'I was always expected to do law', he recalls, but neither his father nor his elder brother seemed to enjoy it much, so he chose engineering instead. After further studies at Ohio State and Princeton, and professional experience in Europe, he came to a lectureship in structural engineering at Monash in 1969. 'I think I got the job because I had this lovely mushroom-coloured linen suit which I picked up in a rummage sale in Princeton for fifty cents', he jokes. In a department that privileged research, Darvall was a popular and devoted teacher. As a staff representative on the university council and later president of the Staff Association, he was an energetic advocate for his fellow academics. When he became dean of engineering in 1988, he joked that the poacher had turned gamekeeper. His recitations of satirical verse honouring (and sending up) his colleagues became a highlight of faculty occasions. Even as deputy vice-chancellor (research), he had worn his authority lightly, often seeming as much the court jester as the prince. He personified many of the qualities he himself defined as quintessentially Monash—progressive, aggressive, vigorous, friendly, daring, a little rough around the edges.[113] As vice-chancellor, he pledged to re-emphasise teaching and research excellence, but would not back away from the international campuses. His appointment was welcomed as a safe choice that would bring a stabilising, civilising influence to Monash. Much reference was made to his area of expertise as an engineer: reinforced concrete.

The year that the Robinson scandal shook the university also saw the quiet death of Foundation Vice-Chancellor Louis Matheson. It was a sad year for Monash, but one that brought a healthy revival of debate about the role and meaning of the university. Few would have denied that the world had changed since Matheson's time, and it was imperative that universities kept pace. As Monash's retiring general manager Peter Wade observed in 1999, tertiary education had always been defined by

Peter Darvall as a young lecturer and staff representative on council, early 1970s, and in 1997 as deputy vice-chancellor (research).

dynamism and change. Criticisms of managerialism, which was 'seen by some to have replaced the collegiality of the past', implied a static environment in the past. This was a 'mirage'.[114] Nonetheless, Robinson's demise reintroduced the phrase 'academic values'—one that had been little used in the preceding years—into the public domain. The episode illustrated that a particular vision of the university—as a community of scholars committed to truth-seeking, collegiality and the life of the mind—retained considerable influence and power. It suggested that a balance might need to be struck between the corporate ethos that had come to dominate higher education and the intellectual values inherent to the historical concept of a university. The University Unlimited could not reach so far that it strained its core.

Under Robinson, Monash had grown and was materially better off. Critics claimed that this success had come at the expense of 'intellectual capital'. The 2001 Australian Research Council grants round produced dispiriting results, stirring a new wave of soul-searching on how to improve research performance.[115] But by other measures, the university was doing very well. In June 2001, it won approval as the site for the coveted $157 million Australian synchrotron. In 2002, construction began on the Monash Science Technology Research and Innovation Precinct (STRIP), and the new Monash Science Centre was opened. Prato and the London centre promised to become successful ventures. While South Africa's future was less clear, Robinson had made an indelible mark.

After leaving Monash, Robinson dabbled in consulting work and was for a time chair of VERNet Pty Ltd, a company responsible for the optical fibre infrastructure for the Victorian Education and Research Network. Some years after the scandal that ended his career, he asked to visit Monash's Prato Centre in Italy. After Director Bill Kent showed the former vice-chancellor and his partner around, Robinson was visibly affected. 'I don't think he was crying for his own fate', Kent reflected. 'He was moved by the fact that one of these initiatives was going forward.' The University Unlimited might have alienated some, but perhaps it mattered to David Robinson. He was, in Kent's words, 'a complicated sort of guy'.[116]

INTERLUDE: DEATH IN THE FAMILY

It was 21 October 2002, a sunny Monday in the spring swot vac. A few minutes after eleven o'clock, a dozen or so final-year honours students began taking their seats in a small classroom on the sixth floor of the Ming Wing. They were a tight-knit group, well known to each other and to their lecturers in econometrics, a field in which Monash enjoyed international renown. The lecturer, 44-year-old Lee Gordon-Brown, was writing a problem on the whiteboard for a revision session in his subject, Optimisation for Management. One or two students were still making their way back from an adjoining office where they had stopped off to pick up revision papers.

Suddenly, without warning, the room exploded in a volley of gunfire. Gordon-Brown turned around, felt an intense burning sensation in his thigh and collapsed on the floor. At the back of the class in his usual place, one of the students, 36-year-old Huang (Alan) Xiang, was standing, face impassive, arms outstretched, pointing a small dark object. 'You never understand me', he yelled. One of his classmates, William Woo, was slumped in his chair, unmoving, while another, Steven Chau, sprawled face down on the floor. As he attempted to get up, Gordon-Brown noticed that Xiang was fumbling with the zip of his parka. Only 2 or 3 metres separated the lecturer and the gunman. 'I just walked over and grabbed his hands', he recalled. Another student, Alistair Boast, seized Xiang from behind, and, together, they pinned him by the waist and shoulders. He made little resistance. 'Please do not kill me, Lee', he implored.[1]

Associate Professor Brett Inder had heard the shots and walked down the corridor to investigate. Quickly taking in the horrific scene, he rushed over to assist his colleague, now doubled up with pain. Under Xiang's jacket Inder and Boast felt the bulging outlines of more weapons: five loaded pistols, a knife and scissors. From time to time, their prisoner tried to loosen their hold. 'It was all I could do', he muttered, as though to explain

Following the 2002 shootings, staff and students left floral tributes to the victims in the breezeway of the Menzies Building. (Photograph: Simon Schluter/Fairfax Syndication)

the inexplicable. 'It's coming to an end, it's finishing.' His captors held on desperately, waiting for help to arrive. It took about twenty minutes for police to apprehend the gunman, though it seemed much longer to the occupants of Room 659E. Two of his victims, Woo and Chau, were dead, and five others were wounded, two—Lee Gordon-Brown and Laurie Brown—critically.

Liisa Williams was an administrative officer in the School of Historical Studies at the other end of the sixth floor. 'I had ducked over to the Union to buy a sandwich when it happened', she recounted. 'I had started walking back when a girl rushed in covered with blood on her way to the doctor.' An academic shouted that someone was shooting on the sixth floor and implored her to raise the alarm. 'I raced over to the information desk and told them. They rang Security [who] locked the doors, and there we waited, and waited and waited.' News of the incident spread quickly, and Monash telephones ran hot, overloading the Monash exchange and local mobile networks. Along with hundreds of others, Williams spent the next hour or so locked out of the Menzies Building, now surrounded by police cars with flashing red and blue lights, not knowing the fate of her colleagues and unable to be reached by worried family and friends.[2]

Inside the building, those who had heard the shots locked their doors and crouched behind their desks. On the stairs and escalators, there was pandemonium as rescuers struggled against the tide of occupants rushing to get out. Nobody knew exactly what was happening. In Building 3A, a VCG meeting was in progress when someone arrived with the frightening news. 'Is it terrorism?' was everyone's first thought. Memories of American campus shootings, fears of snipers hiding on the roof, mingled with more recent images of 9/11 and the Bali bombings. Less than a year earlier, as part of a risk assessment exercise commissioned by David Robinson, most of the VCG, including the new vice-chancellor, Peter Darvall, had rehearsed their response to a hypothetical emergency. Uncannily, the chosen scenario was a shooting at the Caulfield campus by a psychotic staff member. Darvall and his colleagues knew the steps of establishing a communications centre, putting on extra telephone lines, issuing press releases, arranging trauma counselling and the like. Over the following hours, as the university responded systematically to the emergency, few recalled the forethought of the departed vice-chancellor.[3]

At the Mount Waverley police station, police interviewing the gunman began to piece together his story. Xiang was born in the People's Republic of China in 1966, the second son of a well-educated couple who had been forced to undertake manual labour during Mao's Cultural Revolution. He was, by all accounts, a highly intelligent, obedient but lonely child, excelling in chess and mathematics. At school, he complained, the other children picked on him and laughed behind his back. He later completed a course in acupuncture but practised only briefly. Eventually, in 1996, he joined his mother and elder brother in Australia, studying English and business subjects at a Sydney TAFE before enrolling at Monash. He became a member of the Church of the Latter Day Saints and, more ominously, of the Sporting Shooters' Association. At the time of the fatal incident, he lived with his mother in a small flat in Wellington Road, just a stone's throw from the campus. Next door, Xiang's classmate 26-year-old William Woo, a clever, outgoing student from Hong Kong, lived with his girlfriend. Woo and Xiang were among the brightest in their class. Each was expected to progress to postgraduate study. Unwittingly, though, Woo had become the object of Xiang's paranoid suspicion and hatred. 'I finally ended WW's life', he wrote in a statement at the police station. A note later found in his flat was even darker: 'To kill WW is the responsibility defined in my destiny'.

In the days after the shooting, Xiang's teachers reviewed their encounters with the student for evidence of his murderous intentions. Everyone agreed that he was introverted, prickly and highly competitive. In a 'bizarre' email to Brett Inder, he had referred to his fellow students as 'animals'. In a class taken by Professor Alan Powell, he had called out: 'Those guys are killing me'. Powell had reassured him and reported the incident to Head of Department Keith McLaren. The consensus had been that Xiang, whose spoken English was poor, was anxious about his approaching seminar presentation, so a staff member volunteered to coach him beforehand. If anyone had serious concerns, it was for Xiang's welfare, not that of his classmates. Nobody anticipated the catastrophe, yet when it happened nobody was surprised that the silent, lonely man in the far corner of the room was the perpetrator.

All the evidence was that the shootings were a tragic aberration, the culmination of one man's personal disintegration. Yet, in the post-millennial atmosphere of October 2002, the event reverberated far beyond the campus. Only nine days earlier, eighty-nine young Australians had died in a terrorist attack in Bali. On the campus, a flag was still flying at half-mast in their memory. Even at five o'clock, when the ABC's *PM* program went to air, the spectre of terrorism lingered. The shooting felt like 'another invasion of the Australian idea of what's normal and what's right', said reporter Mark Colvin.[4] In assaulting people's sense of normality, the event had stirred other, more inchoate feelings of vulnerability, dread and loss.

When the Menzies Building was reopened, many people hesitated to re-enter, feeling that a safe, familiar place had been desecrated. Over the following days, a mound of floral tributes appeared in the breezeway on the northern threshold to the building. Emails flooded in from former students saluting the 'heroes' who had apprehended the gunman, offering prayers for the victims and messages of condolence to the 'university community'. 'Monash will never be quite the same place again', a 1981 arts graduate wrote. 'All the Monash community will be in our thoughts and prayers today', promised a 1970 science graduate. 'I think of Monash as my second home', confessed another. They remembered the Clayton campus as a 'carefree, peaceful and happy' place. Even the stark corridors of the Ming Wing had been 'a place of nurturing, growth and freewill'. In choosing words like 'community', 'family', 'home' and 'alma mater', the students were affirming that the university was something more than the sum of its increasingly diverse and far-flung parts.[5] 'Oh, it was so traumatic', Vice-Chancellor Peter Darvall recalls. 'Somebody you don't know has been killed by somebody else you don't know in a building on the other side of the campus, yet it's just so close, so close.'[6]

Few Monash people knew and loved the place better than Peter Darvall. In the aftermath of the shootings, he recognised the fragility of the university's morale and the need for healing and reassurance. On 25 October, at the end of a traumatic week, he addressed a 'Ceremony of Reflection and Respect for the Monash University Community' in Blackwood Hall. Politicians and relatives of the victims, some of whom had flown from Singapore and Hong Kong, were there. Representatives of Buddhist, Jewish, Muslim and Christian students offered readings and prayers. 'When you join Monash', Darvall declared, 'you join the Monash family. And when a tragic event like this occurs, the family rallies.' It was a while since a Monash vice-chancellor had used such words. For two decades, Monash had danced to the tune of the corporate managers and market realists. It had merged, downsized, upsized and restructured itself, pooh-poohed old-fashioned notions of collegiality and made sacrifices to the new gods of quality and efficiency. But a terrible tragedy, coming in the wake of other disgraces and disappointments, had elicited a sudden realisation that the university was not just an impersonal corporation, but also a community, even a family. To the mourners in Blackwood Hall, these were words of healing and hope. But for how long would the family remain united?

ELEVEN

STILL LEARNING

Monash University seeks to improve the human condition by advancing and transmitting knowledge through research and education and by a commitment to social justice, human rights and a sustainable environment.

EXCELLENCE AND DIVERSITY: STRATEGIC FRAMEWORK 2004–08

The events of 2002 induced a more reflective mood in the Monash community. It was time to stabilise the ship, check the health of the crew, take bearings and set a new course. Even if events within the university had not already inspired self-scrutiny, trends in higher education policy obliged it to do so. 'Quality assurance', 'risk assessment' and 'TQM' (total quality management) were the latest buzzwords to migrate from the world of big business to higher education. In March 2000, the Ministerial Council on Education, Training and Youth Affairs established a new independent authority, the Australian Universities Quality Agency, to audit the performance of higher education institutions. How they were rated would influence the distribution of government funding. Self-examination was not only good for the soul of an institution; it could affect its balance sheet as well.

Monash had resolved early in 2001 to conduct its own 'institutional self-review', using a similar methodology to the quality agency. A review team, led by Law Dean Stephen Parker and Graham Webb, Director of the Centre for Higher Education Quality, collected data, administered an online questionnaire, visited the campuses and interviewed staff and students. Their report struck a humble note. Invoking the university's motto, *ancora imparo*, it praised 'the willingness of a young and vigorous university to learn from its actions'. (It did not say 'mistakes', though

A classroom scene at the MSA campus.

perhaps that was implied.) 'We took as our starting point the bold, innovative and risk-taking nature of the institution', it began. The university's strategic plan, *Leading the Way*, was the team's 'core document'. Was Monash living up to its vision of a 'self-reliant, broad-based, global university'? Was it still leading, or had it lost its way?

While not questioning the university's objectives, the reviewers discovered that they were not always well understood or effectively followed. The concept of 'self-reliance', for example, was often mistaken for 'putting financial considerations ahead of educational ones'. Ten years after the mergers, there were still 'pockets of resentment' and 'continuing uncertainties about the role and future profile' of some campuses. While the themes of *Leading the Way*—innovation, engagement and internationalisation—had become an institutional mantra, the values that inspired them were unclear. The report was tabled in May 2002, just a month before the unexpected departure of David Robinson.[1] In the aftermath, when questions of scholarly integrity came to the fore, it was even more important to define and affirm the university's values. In August, Gary Bouma, former chair of the university's Ethics Committee, who had replaced Darvall as acting deputy vice-chancellor (research), proposed an expanded statement of both 'operational' values (transparency, collegiality, sustainability and diversity) and 'normative' ones (understanding, tolerance and improved quality of life).[2]

A new hand at the helm

The university had begun to clear the decks, but it could not really set its course until it had found a new captain. It approached the selection of the new vice-chancellor cautiously. Candidates signed a statement affirming that they were persons 'of the highest character' who had not previously engaged in activity 'which, if viewed objectively', would adversely impact on their own reputation or the university's.[3] To ensure that the academics had a voice in the decision, short-listed candidates met with expert panels selected to assess their credentials for leadership and vision, management and financial capacity, research leadership, communication and external relations. This 'beauty pageant' struck one candidate as 'bizarre and unprofessional', although others, including the successful one, found it informative and helpful.[4]

The new vice-chancellor would not only have to lead a large and complex organisation, but also restore confidence in its integrity. The selection committee reviewed a wide field of applicants, including several who became vice-chancellors elsewhere. In the end, the choice came down to two locals, one a lawyer, the other a doctor; one English-born, one Australian; one a Monash insider, the other from the University of Melbourne. Each represented a break with the immediate past, although in quite different ways.

Stephen Parker had come to Monash in 1999 as dean of law. Born into a middle-class family in Newcastle upon Tyne, he had attended the oldest boarding school in England, St Peter's School in York (founded in 627 AD). 'I guess I rebelled by the end of that period there', he recalls. He studied law at his hometown university, played in a rock band and, after graduation, worked as a legal aid lawyer in a 'run-down' part of town, often acting for victims of domestic violence. Later, as a PhD student at Cardiff, he defended anti-nuclear protestors and striking miners. Disillusioned with Thatcher's Britain, and now with a young family, he accepted a lectureship at ANU, later moving, as a foundation professor, to Griffith. Among his legal colleagues, he was an eager moderniser, interested in socio-legal issues and in fostering research. By 2002, his adroit chairmanship of Monash's self-review and uncompromising stance during the Robinson affair had won admirers beyond his own faculty. 'I was the people's friend who had stood up to Robinson', he wryly observes. As a forceful advocate for rethinking Monash's ad hoc campus structure, he offered a clear, but possibly turbulent, way ahead. At just fifty, however, he was still young for a vice-chancellor, came from a small faculty and had only limited university-wide administrative experience. 'It would have been a big stretch to appoint me at that level of experience', he admitted later.[5]

Richard Larkins, by contrast, was dean of the University of Melbourne's Faculty of Medicine, Dentistry and Health Sciences, a complex organisation with a budget larger than that of many universities. At sixty, he was at the zenith of a stellar career. Born into a family of doctors and lawyers, he had progressed with apparent ease from being dux of Melbourne Grammar to top graduate in medicine at the University of Melbourne, taking thirteen of the fifteen graduation prizes. By his early thirties, he had published two papers in *Nature*, the world's leading scientific journal; by his early forties, he was James Stewart Professor of Medicine at the Royal Melbourne Hospital, the plum clinical chair in Australia, and by his mid-fifties had become the 'universally admired' dean of the nation's leading medical faculty. Almost every accolade the profession could bestow, from chairmanship of the National Health and Medical Research Council to the presidency of the College of Physicians, had come his way.

Few of Larkins' contemporaries had seemed so clearly marked out for success, yet that is not how it seemed to the modest, almost shy, physician. 'My career followed a totally unpredicted and unplanned path', he liked to tell graduating students. From his family he had learned that success came only through intelligence and hard work, and often through adversity. His maternal grandmother, Joan Rosanove, daughter of a Jewish doctor in Ballarat, overcame male prejudice to become Victoria's first female barrister. 'I can never see why it is not considered the hallmark of success to have a brain like a woman', she once observed. His father, medical student Graeme Larkins, married Joan's daughter, Margaret (Peg) Rosanove, when both were just eighteen, against the wishes of their families—his nominally Protestant, and hers secular Jewish. They had two sons before Graeme graduated second in his class, in 1944. A quiet, gentle man, he practised in country Victoria and took further studies in London before returning to Melbourne to become a pioneer of geriatric medicine at Mount Royal Hospital.[6] 'He'd take us around on Christmas Day, and we'd see all the people there who obviously loved him', Richard recalls. In 1959, the 37-year-old physician suddenly collapsed with a subarachnoid haemorrhage. Sixteen-year-old Richard saw the ambulance depart. He was waiting at the top of the stairs when a visitor called and he overheard his mother say, 'They said that we were mad to get married when we did, but we had nineteen wonderful years' and realised the worst. Next day, he went back to school, carrying on as if nothing had happened, 'as you did in those days'. Now with the responsibility of rearing three teenage boys, Peg courageously followed her own mother's example, completing a law degree, going to the bar and, in 1976, becoming one of the first judges of the Family Court.[7]

Richard Larkins arrived at adulthood with a firm set of values: a strong work ethic, a love of learning, a belief in altruistic service, a

The healer. Physician Richard Larkins restored Monash's morale while giving its international strategy a philanthropic dimension.

hatred of religious and ethnic intolerance, and a deep integrity. When a schoolmaster ordered his class to buy Flanders poppies on Remembrance Day, the young Larkins objected, not because he doubted that the dead soldiers should be honoured, but because it was a matter for each boy's conscience. In a hierarchical profession, he was sometimes prepared to buck conventional expectations. In his mid-thirties, he resigned a prestigious appointment at the Royal Melbourne to set up a new endocrinology unit at the lowly Repatriation Hospital. His mentor, Sir John ('Jock') Frew, president of the hospital, was alarmed. 'If you ever wanted to be Professor of Medicine at Royal Melbourne Hospital, you've laid the way wide open for X', he remonstrated. 'Well, that's very good', Larkins mildly replied, 'because he'd be a very good Professor of Medicine'. Six years later, he was appointed to the chair anyway.

By 2002, Larkins had been a dean at Melbourne University for five years. He loved the job, had solved some difficult problems and was proud of how his faculty was working. He was less content with the direction of his university. Vice-Chancellor Alan Gilbert's plan to create Melbourne University Private struck him as 'a flawed concept'. And he was dismayed by the scheme to turn Universitas 21, a valuable network of like-minded universities, into a kind of cyber-university. When Gilbert unexpectedly invited him to become his senior deputy vice-chancellor, Larkins was obliged to consider his future. 'I was king of that domain [Medicine], and I couldn't see the attraction of going and being second in charge.' But, in declining Gilbert's invitation, he began to wonder whether he might prefer to be king of another university. Applications for the Monash vice-chancellorship had closed and interviews were about to begin, but, after meeting the head hunter and chancellor, Jerry Ellis, he threw his hat in the ring.[8]

Larkins initially believed that the differences between Melbourne and Monash were more superficial than real. His commitment was to high-quality education and research, not to a particular institution. He admired Monash's international vision and the commitment to 'social justice' he saw in its regional and outer-suburban campuses. This was music to the ears of a council seeking a leader of high intellect and integrity committed to the direction set by his predecessors. When the runner-up, Parker, was later appointed as Larkins' senior deputy, the university congratulated itself on having recruited a dream-team.

The personal style of the new vice-chancellor—courteous, deft, humane, earnest but not humourless—made a favourable impression. The role of a vice-chancellor, Larkins believed, was to lead, not just to manage, the university. He sought to personify, as well as articulate, its values, contributing to the intellectual life of the university where he could, writing a regular column, 'Ancora Imparo', in *Monash Memo*, and visiting the corners of his far-flung empire, often in company with his wife, Caroline, whose hospitable presence reminded old-timers of earlier vice-chancellors' wives. In graduation addresses, Larkins emphasised the value of education not just to the graduate, but also to humankind. 'Human history', he would say, quoting H.G. Wells, 'becomes more and more a race between education and catastrophe'. As Monash graduates, they were 'equipped not only for your professional calling but for a fairer, more peaceful, more tolerant world'.[9]

In Larkins' Monash, academic values were paramount. From the beginning, he signalled a departure from the corporate style of his predecessors. Since Matheson's day, vice-chancellors had chaired the senior academic body, now the Academic Board. Robinson had modified the tradition by delegating the chair to his senior deputy, although the senior management group continued to set the agenda. Larkins proposed that the chair should be elected by the board itself to 'encourage free and frank debate' and 'empower the academic community'.[10] Activity-based costing, the financial regime introduced by Deputy Vice-Chancellor Alison Crook, would be used to show where the money came from and how much activities cost, but not to determine how it should be spent. Faculties like Business and Economics, which generated large revenues from mass teaching operations in accounting and marketing, were expected to make a 'contribution' to the university's coffers in order to cross-subsidise academically valuable but less lucrative research and teaching in other faculties. Charity on this scale (Business and Economics was contributing more than $20 million a year by 2007) did not sit easily with a faculty that taught market principles and expected the university to follow them too.

Three months into the job, Larkins had revised his first impressions. The differences between Monash and Melbourne, he now decided, were much more than superficial. The wounds and divisions created by the Robinson era had still to be healed. Within the senior executive team there were tensions too. The mergers had changed Monash forever, but some people, especially at Clayton, were still reluctant to admit it. 'To seek to go back to the pre-1990 situation with a single campus at Clayton would be unrealistic and would be politically disastrous', Larkins warned. Monash still laboured under an exaggerated sense of its disadvantages: its suburban location, the 'millstone' of its regional campus, its far-flung international commitments. 'I can't understand this', he protested. 'I come from a university that is land-locked, where the real estate around it is so expensive that it is really locked in.' It would have been impossible for Melbourne to host the synchrotron or develop the STRIP. Its aspirations to become an international university would always run up against Australia's isolation from the great European and American centres of research. By waiting for the world to come to it—'the last stop before Antarctica'—Parkville was always going to be disappointed. By going out to meet the world, Monash had chosen the better path.[11]

But, while Monash should not retreat, nor could it advance until it had a clearer plan for its Victorian campuses. There would be 'no closure of any Australian campus, by sale or moth-balling', Stephen Parker acknowledged in September 2003, but this did not preclude a range of other possibilities. Deputy vice-chancellors Alison Crook and Alan Lindsay had already floated a corporate model in which each campus became an independent enterprise, with its own company board, range of programs and financial autonomy.[12] Parker, now in charge of campus planning, began with the university's vision and values and sought roles for each campus. Each should have its own distinctive mix of disciplines, functional relationships with other campuses, levels of study, teaching–research relationships and ethos. Not every campus could be a 'mini-Clayton' with the full array of disciplines, research intensity and teaching styles, but all could have at least some high-quality research. The smaller campuses, such as Gippsland and Berwick, could emphasise their regional links and 'community feeling', while Clayton and Caulfield could exploit their 'metropolitan feel'.[13]

By differentiating its campuses, but giving each at least a bit of research, Monash sought to hold on to its place in the Group of Eight research-intensive universities without differentiating its testamurs or de-merging campuses. Publicly, Larkins emphasised the 'strong public support' for the outer campuses. They brought Monash real benefits, he contended, apart from the political damage that would ensue if they were downgraded or abandoned. He urged state and federal politicians to translate their support into dollars.[14] 'We need specific funding for these [campuses] to be viable', the VCG acknowledged in November 2003.[15] Parker, however, continued to push for a more radical restructuring. As late as 2006, just before he left to become vice-chancellor of the University of Canberra, he floated the idea of dividing the university vertically between M1, a research-intensive university based at Clayton and Caulfield, and M2, an undergraduate university linked to Monash College and based on the outer campuses.[16] Wary of the insecurity such a scheme would arouse, Larkins wanted the issue resolved. 'You can't actually be half-hearted. You either have to say we're going to change it, or you say we're going to absolutely support it.' The die was cast, and it would not be recast, not on his watch, at any rate.[17]

The road to Johannesburg

A more pressing issue, from Larkins' viewpoint, was the mixed legacy of David Robinson's global vision. The brightest spot was the campus in Kuala Lumpur, soon to reach a new milestone with the opening of the Tan Sri Jeffrey Cheah School of Medicine and Health Sciences. No qualification is more prized in Malaysia than a medical degree, and Monash had long aspired to offer one offshore. But the sheer cost of the project, and the refusal of the Australian Medical Council to accredit the proposed degree in Australia, slowed its realisation. In 1994, a partnership with the proposed Asean medical school in Ipoh generated a lukewarm response from sections of the medical faculty.[18] Five years later, Dean Nick Saunders and Pro Vice-Chancellor Merilyn Liddell developed a new proposal for students to split their studies between the Monash Sunway campus and a new clinical school at Johor Bahru. While it won enthusiastic support from the Malaysian Ministry of Health, the first budgetary projections were discouraging.[19] Even strong supporters of the partnership like Lee Weng Keng doubted its viability. But Jeffrey Cheah was determined to proceed and agreed to underwrite the project himself.[20] The last hurdle was crossed when Larkins led a successful application to the accreditation committee of the Australian Medical Council, overturning the stance it had previously taken under his own chairmanship.[21] Larkins' stature and international connections helped Monash to attract an outstanding team of new medical academics headed by Professor Anwar Zaini, former vice-chancellor of the University of Malaya.

A more vexed issue was MSA, the university's financially strapped campus on the fringes of Johannesburg. Shortly after Larkins' arrival, an advisory group convened by Stephen Parker offered a blunt summary of the situation:

> Although extraordinary things have been achieved, the project is significantly off track. Some key premises in the Project Proposal have been abandoned, without adequate explanation. Student numbers are well below those projected. Costs are far higher

than in the original model. Break-even points are being pushed further away. The maximum capital exposure of the University is far greater than projected. Future growth scenarios seem to us to be little more than guesswork. The general supervision of the venture is in disarray. If events move further against us we face the largest loss that the University has ever shouldered on a project, and possibly the largest ever by an Australian university ... The only argument for pressing on regardless in a vigorous way is based upon the potentially calamitous consequences of an exit from South Africa.[22]

When Larkins had first heard of Monash's plans in South Africa, he had thought they seemed 'crazy'. In October 2003, as he prepared to go and see the campus for himself, he was 'probably more of the view that it would have to close'.[23] But the academics on the spot were confident. 'The best advertisement for the campus', said Head of Arts Kevin Foster, 'was the campus. Anybody who came and saw what we were doing would get behind it.' Foster, a literary critic, had studied in England and taught at Monash in Melbourne before taking up the appointment at MSA. 'The two years I spent there were the best two years I've had anywhere in any University', he enthuses.[24] It was 'the most informative and inspiring experience I've had as an academic', his successor, Simon Adams, agrees. 'If you talk about the grand challenges of our age ... the front line of those grand challenges is Africa, of every single one of them, whether it be poverty, disease, climate change, everything ... and the front line of Africa is South Africa.'[25]

As Foster anticipated, Larkins became a convert, returning home committed to the venture. The campus was beautiful, and he was there to witness MSA's first graduation ceremony. The twenty-one graduating students had clearly embraced 'Monash values' and had had a wonderful experience.

The students were inspiring, given those small numbers, and they'd made their commitment to Monash and our rhetoric. And I thought, well ... I certainly wouldn't have had the courage, or the initiative, or foolhardiness to establish a campus in South Africa. But once that's done, you've got to make it work ...[26]

*'The project is significantly off-track',
Deputy Vice-Chancellor Stephen Parker
warned after visiting MSA, 1999.*

The campus had made 'quite spectacular' progress in staff recruitment, educational programs and network-building, he told council. Yes, the original business plan had been 'unrealistic', but whether it had been a good idea to go into South Africa was now irrelevant. It would cost too much in both money and reputation to withdraw, while the benefits of staying were potentially 'immense'. 'The most damaging approach', he argued, 'would be to continue with the exercise in a half-hearted fashion'. The commitment had to be long-term and unequivocal.[27]

David Gilmour, a consultant hired to review all aspects of the operation, visited the campus and also 'caught the bug'.[28] Financially, he admitted, it was a bad investment, but Monash's recently adopted 'Statement of Purpose', emphasising its mission to 'improve the human condition' through a commitment to human rights and social justice, offered another way of looking at it. Making a profit in South Africa, where so many people lived in poverty, contradicted those values; but contributing to South Africa's development could bring indirect benefits to Monash staff and students through engagement with the problems of the continent. Philanthropy, however, would have its limits: Monash would not embark on new overseas campuses until both South Africa and Malaysia were self-sustaining.[29] With these assurances and only two dissenters, council agreed to continue support for the campus. The funds borrowed to establish it would now be regarded as a 'strategic' investment, attracting zero interest, so making the venture 'potentially financially viable'.[30] This was a tacit admission that the costs incurred so far were 'spilt milk' never to be recovered. Having gone to South Africa to make money, Monash resolved to stay in order to do good.

While its fate was being decided, the campus was actually becoming something quite different from Robinson's original conception. It was not the white enclave that many Monash players had expected (with some embarrassment) that it would be. While the staff profile was as yet 'too white', the majority of students were black, more of them from outside South Africa, particularly Botswana and Zimbabwe, than from within. And while the number of students on bursaries (16 per cent in 2000) was larger than originally planned, it strengthened Monash's claim to good intentions for South Africa.[31]

After a difficult start, when it was widely characterised as a colonial interloper, Monash was making efforts to become more South African. In 2005, it appointed Tyrone Pretorius, Deputy Vice-Chancellor of the University of Western Cape, a psychologist with an interest in youth violence and experience at Yale, as pro vice-chancellor in succession to John Anderson. Well connected to the African National Congress, and with a strong commitment to the new South Africa, Pretorius established a board of leading South Africans and made some significant symbolic innovations, including the singing of 'Nkosi Sikelel' iAfrika' at graduation ceremonies. The campus itself, once an outpost on the suburban fringe, was now surrounded by new housing estates, retail outlets, light industry and sporting facilities. But the students never came in the numbers expected: by 2008, there were still only 1636 on the campus (in 2012, there were close to 3000). MSA still lacks university status, a fact that many new students are shocked to discover when they arrive.

The rankings game

In the 1990s, Monash billed itself as 'Australia's international university'. It built on its long record of engagement in Southeast Asia to generate a strong flow of students from traditional markets in Malaysia, Singapore, Hong Kong and Indonesia. Going international seemed a smart move when the Howard government later reduced the proportion of university costs funded by government. Monash, along with other Australian universities, rapidly increased its enrolments of private fee-paying international students. In 1997, fewer than 10 per cent of students on the Clayton campus came from overseas, but by 2002 the proportion had grown to 15 per cent and by 2011 to around 20 per cent. At Caulfield, dominated by business and IT, it grew over the same period from 21.7 per cent to 37.3 per cent. Almost half (45 per cent) of the students at Berwick, a campus originally established to offer higher education to the suburban fringe, in 2011 came from overseas. Since international students paid more than locals, their contribution to the university's finances was proportionately greater.

By the beginning of the new century, however, the conditions that had favoured Monash in the Dawkins era were changing. Students now came from a much wider range of countries, including China, India and the Middle East as well as Southeast Asia. They were more discriminating, more swayed by international rankings than by the marketing campaigns that had proved successful in the past. The reforms introduced by Education Minister Brendan Nelson favoured institutions with a clear educational profile and a strong record of international research. Only a few Australian universities remained in the top rank. Those with 'mixed brands', like Monash, were most at risk.[32]

'I don't regard students as clients', Larkins observed.[33] He meant that they were more important than that. But the students increasingly saw themselves as clients, carefully assessing the costs and benefits offered by 'educational providers', as they came to be called, and demanding acceptable levels of service. In Australia, they read books like the *Good Universities Guide*, while international students checked the rankings produced by international academic ratings agencies like the Times Higher Education or the Shanghai Jiao Tong (now ARWU) indices. These scores were flawed and often skewed by how the various components—research publications, teaching, international engagement, numbers of Nobel laureates, and so on—were weighted. When the Times Higher Education index was first published, in 2003, Monash ranked at number thirty-three, partly because of its strong reputation for international engagement. It remained in the forties until 2010, when it suddenly plummeted to number sixty, largely because the index no longer weighted international engagement as highly. Meanwhile, its rank on the ARWU index, which emphasised high-level research, had risen from the 200–300 band to the 150–200 band. Academics understandably viewed these rankings sceptically, but their arrival had produced at least one important effect: after two decades of free-for-all competition, research performance had re-emerged as a primary determinant of academic reputation and success.[34]

Larkins publicly decried the public penury that made the universities so reliant on international student income. 'The vicious cycle of progressively decreasing public funding and extreme regulation preventing increased income from students must be broken', he declared in 2006.[35] It was like General Motors-Holden getting a subsidy to sell its cars to the Australian consumer below cost in the hope that it could make up the difference by selling them abroad for much more.[36] The risks of this policy became apparent in 2009 when the global financial crisis, combined with a high Australian dollar, a tightening of immigration policy and a series of attacks on Indian students in Melbourne sent shock waves through the international student market. Monash escaped the worst of the crisis, thanks to its academic reputation and its capacity to absorb students priced out of the Australian educational market on its Malaysian campus. But it was a salutary reminder of the hazards of hocking the university's future to an inherently volatile international student market.

Sooner or later, Monash began to realise, the countries supplying its international students would have strong universities and colleges of their own. In the long-term, selling undergraduate education, whether it was through a campus in Australia, or in Kuala Lumpur or Johannesburg, would become a dying industry. If Monash were to undertake another international adventure, Larkins argued, it would have to be in something that reinforced Monash's long-term interest in high-quality international research collaboration.

> If we wish to be a vibrant, exciting country participating in and contributing to the knowledge economy of the twenty-first century, we have to do better than selling our commodities and being a tourist destination . . . Our universities must develop a vibrant research culture by going out and engaging with the world . . . Other universities may regard overseas campuses as money-earning, teaching only enterprises, but for Monash University that would be missing the point. The real dividend will come when the campuses are fully mature, research-intensive and linked into the education and research networks of the host countries.[37]

Maturing the Malaysian and South African campuses into research hubs might take many years; in the meantime, new opportunities had emerged in the two fastest growing economies in the world, China and India. While it had no appetite for establishing more campuses, Monash continued to take a forward, rather than a fortress, approach to international collaboration. 'Our philosophy is based on the premise that if we wait for the world to come to us, it will be a long wait', Larkins declared in 2006. 'Instead, we have adopted the strategy of reaching out and engaging the world in a physical sense.'[38]

For almost twenty years, China had seemed the obvious new frontier. Already, many of Monash's students were ethnic Chinese. The country was growing rapidly, and many talented Chinese academics were returning to the homeland to join its universities' great leap forward. Through the 1990s, the numbers of visiting delegations and exchange agreements steadily grew, as Monash opened up research and teaching collaborations with Fudan, Nanjing, Shanghai and Beijing. But the university's stated ambition, to secure a physical presence in China, proved harder to realise.[39] In the wake of the South African debacle, the university favoured a 'focused, innovative and low-risk' strategy designed to bolster its research reputation and protect its income from Chinese student enrolments.[40] Yet larger visions continued to beckon. In 2006, Monash signed 'a comprehensive cooperative agreement' with Sichuan University, a well-ranked new university in western China. Monash, it was said, would develop a 'Sichuan flavour', while Sichuan would make Monash its 'no. 1' international partner.[41] Once again, it seemed, Monash was pioneering on a new academic frontier. But realising these aspirations proved difficult. The Chinese, as Deputy Vice-Chancellor (Global Engagement) Stephanie Fahey emphasises, are very pragmatic.[42] Academic partnerships may wax or wane according to the political priorities of local officials or the needs of the region. In May 2008, Sichuan was hit by a devastating earthquake. The university, along with the rest of the society, turned inwards, focusing its energies on the recovery effort, and the Monash partnership inevitably lost impetus. But China still looms large in Monash's global ambitions.

In India, Monash's ambitions bore fruit with breathtaking rapidity. In 2006, Larkins embarked on a 'voyage of discovery to India' accompanied by Engineering Dean Tam Sridhar, Deputy Vice-Chancellor (Research) Edwina Cornish, Science Dean Rob Norris and senior BHP executive Megan Clark. Sridhar, the tour leader, was an expatriate Indian who came to Monash as a PhD student from the Indian Institute of Science in Bangalore in 1974. He began on a $200-a-month scholarship, became a tutor, a lecturer and eventually a professor, winning election to two academies—science and technological science—along the way. Visiting his homeland, he noticed how many large international companies had moved their research and development labs to India. 'The geography of science is moving and we [in Australia] don't have a ready conduit to it', he realised. Talking to his former university friends now in influential positions in India, he began to think about how such a conduit could be created. It was important for Monash and Australia, but, as he admits, there was a sentimental reason as well: 'The opportunity to build a bridge between your country of birth and your adopted country was just too tempting to pass up'.[43]

The Monash team travelled hot on the heels of American journalist Thomas Friedman, author of the best-selling book *The World Is Flat* (2005). The book took its title from an observation by Nandan Nilekani, Chief Executive Officer of Infosys, the Indian-based IT company, whose meteoric growth from a US$250 start-up to a US$6 billion global corporation dramatised India's emergence as a new power in the 'flat' world of global communications. Larkins and his colleagues visited the Infosys research laboratories and General Electric's nearby John F. Welch Technology Center, state-of-the-art research centres sequestered from the noise and pollution of Bangalore in park-like compounds. They met the heads of India's main scientific organisations and the minister for science and technology, who welcomed Monash's interest. From these conversations, a bold plan emerged to establish a joint research academy between Monash and the Indian Institute of Technology Bombay in Mumbai.

The academy is essentially a PhD factory in which the most talented graduates of the institute, India's premier scientific and technological academy, will investigate problems in biotechnology, computational engineering, nanotechnology, clean energy and clean water. The academy will soon have its own building on the Indian Institute of Technology

The newest frontier. Left to right: Chancellor Alan Finkel, Engineering Dean Tam Sridhar, Vice-President (Finance) David Pitt, Vice-Chancellor Ed Byrne, Director of Business Strategy Loren Miller and Academy Executive Officer Anasuya Banerji at the site of the future Monash–IITB Research Academy, Mumbai, November 2010.

Bombay campus, supported by government and industry in both countries. Students are jointly supervised by academics in both institutions and spend time in Melbourne as well as Mumbai.[44]

The check-in campus

In the 1960s, when Monash was young, the Clayton campus still had the sparse, unfinished look of a suburban industrial estate. Its first buildings stood in the centre of a campus that was still more paddock than park, and on the edge of a city that had still to catch up. Over the next fifty years, it gradually filled up with offices, laboratories, classrooms, sports centres and multistorey car parks erected according to no discernible plan. It grew denser, messier and less legible, so that by the 1990s it was hard even to discern the logic of its original plan.

By then, in any case, architectural fashion was turning against the modernist philosophy that had inspired Osborn McCutcheon and his contemporaries. Architect Roland Black, engaged by Mal Logan to prepare a new landscape plan for the Clayton campus, challenged the 'false but cherished notion that campuses are parklands with isolated pavilions scattered between them'. This notion, derived from 'the Australian Suburban Model of low-density urban sprawl', was inappropriate to the needs of a university. Instead of planting buildings in a neutral space, the planner should focus on the spaces themselves, creating a series of 'outdoor rooms'. Rather than grand vistas, Black wanted density, variety, intimacy and surprise. Allan Powell's new Performing Arts Precinct between the Library and Blackwood Hall and his tilt-slab facade to the Union Building (soon to be renamed 'Campus Centre') aimed to create 'recessed and interesting courtyards'. At Caulfield, a crowded campus that was always more industrial estate than park, architects Denton Corker Marshall planned a 'central green', a 'union square' and a 'ceremonial walk'.[45] A series of 'urban plans' for each campus commissioned by Alison Crook in 2002–03 echoed the themes of the 'new urbanism': 'exciting', 'vibrant', 'pedestrian', 'access', 'intimate'. They captured the 'metropolitan feel', the anonymous, cosmopolitan, restless ethos of a 'just-in-time' university.[46]

Perhaps nothing evokes the changing ambience of the campus as well as the fortunes of the university staff club. It had begun in the early 1960s, when there was hardly a milk bar or pie shop within cooee of the campus, as a convivial retreat from what one of its founders described as 'the relentless proximity' of students.[47] By the 1970s, it had over 1500 members and was considering raising the fees (about $100) in order to stave off demand. On Fridays, lunchtime at the club stretched into the early evening as weary lecturers took refreshment, shared their gripes about colleagues and students, and set the world to rights. With the coming of the Dawkins era and heavier teaching loads, it entered a steady decline. In 1989, it was doing so badly that Vice-Chancellor Mal Logan had to bail it out. The slide continued through the 1990s, bottoming out at around 650 members in 2006. Dropping the membership fee to $20 produced a modest revival to around 1000 today. Why the long decline? 'How long have you got?' replies club manager Adam Kitto. 'The most common things we hear are "time poor", "working lunch", "cash strapped".'[48] There are other places to eat, too, closer to one's desk, or at it, accompanied by the ubiquitous beaker of caffe latte. Academics now spend more time working electronically from home, commuting between campuses, or flying to Kuala Lumpur or Johannesburg. They're as likely to bump into a colleague in the Qantas Club as in their own staff club.

For students, too, the campus has become a place to check in rather than hang out. By 2009, the average first-year student spent around ten hours a week studying, less than the fifteen hours or spent so in paid work. 'The days when being a student meant you could sit in the coffee bar . . . and discuss important issues [such as] Dostoyevsky and whether the Pope should remain a Catholic' are gone, says Student Ombudsman Rob Willis.[49] With little time for on-campus activities, their connection to it weakens. Many hang on to old school friends rather than make new university ones. They connect with the university through the electronic systems that schedule their classes, stream their lectures and post their results as much as through face-to-face relationships with professors and lecturers.

The 'electronic university' forecast by Logan in the 1990s finally arrived after 'Y2K'. The time spent by first-year students in online study increased from 4.2 hours a week in 2004 to 6.5 hours in 2009. Essay-writers could now download journal articles to their laptops to read at home or on the train, or listen to lectures online. But, while welcoming the range and accessibility of electronic resources, students did not necessarily abandon print or stop using the library. Visits to Monash libraries actually rose from 2.7 million in 2002 to 4.1 million in 2010. Two-thirds of the students surveyed visited the library at least two days a week. The library had replanned its interiors to provide more spaces where students could study in groups. There are signs, according to university librarian Cathrine Harboe-Ree, that students are becoming so bombarded with electronic distractions that they actually look to the library to provide a quiet space (a 'study bubble', as one called it) where they can concentrate for long periods of time. 'We are providing an increasing proportion of quiet study areas with ergonomically sound seating and we are resisting suggestions for creating café-like or funky environments', she adds.[50]

Politics was now often played out online rather than on campus, a shift that may account for waning interest in national party politics and a leaning towards 'global' or identity issues, such as climate change and gay marriage. A vigorous minority still nurtured ideals about the function of the university in society and fought for them sporadically. When Monash moved to increase HECS fees by 25 per cent in March 2004, in line with the Howard government's Nelson reforms, campus protests again made the headlines. One hundred students, unable to breach the security barriers of the Administration Building, forced entry into Robert Blackwood Hall. It was, said Larkins, 'Berkeley 101'. They threw marbles under police horses and trampled on security staff. A group occupying the former vice-chancellor's residence invited the vice-chancellor to meet. Since most university students came from higher socioeconomic homes and were supported by the taxes of people who couldn't go to university, 'it seemed only reasonable that the children of the rich should pay a bit more', Larkins argued. This impeccable socialist logic made no impression on the angry protestors. Standing in Louis Matheson's former home, Larkins felt a bond of sympathy with his embattled predecessor.

Coming to university was not quite the exciting, sometimes bewildering, experience it was in the 1960s. Well prepared by their schools, and with university-educated parents often in the background, most freshers settled into university life with relative ease. Expecting less of the experience, and investing less in it, they may have been more easily satisfied. Surveys of first-year students in the 1990s had picked up negative feelings, especially about the experience of teaching and learning. But the 2003 Monash Experience questionnaire found 92.5 per cent broadly satisfied with their university experience, and by 2007 satisfaction was higher still.[51]

Liz Porter, a member of the Monash Labor Club in the late 1960s, returned to Clayton in 2010 to view the new Monash through her daughter Alice's eyes. She lamented the hours her daughter had to spend in paid work compared with the freedom she had enjoyed, thanks to a government scholarship, to devote herself completely to university life. But she envied other aspects of Alice's university experience, such as the opportunity to 'lecture-shop', sampling different subjects, and to give feedback on her teachers' performance. While Liz had to stand in a queue to photocopy books and articles, and hunt down poor-quality tapes of lectures, her daughter simply downloaded them. Her own university experience was confined to the campus, while students now had the opportunity to study overseas, using the 'Monash Passport'. 'Suddenly, the radical heyday of the '70s seems narrow and parochial.' Her conclusion? 'Academically, I think it's better than 1970. I want to go back.'[52]

The revolutionary days of the early 1970s may be an unsatisfactory benchmark for the experience of the majority of students, then or since. Yet, in quieter ways, Monash still holds out the promise of personal and social transformation. Richard Scully came to Monash in 1999 from a 'desperately self-conscious' upper middle-class family, on the rebound after missing out on a place at Melbourne. From a distance, he thought, it looked like 'a breeding ground for "lefties" of the worst sort; a concrete wasteland of car park after car park and monuments to the failure of Modernism'. He enrolled in arts/law with an emphasis on law, but his arts subjects soon drew him into a new social circle, away from his school friends. 'We actually discussed things like politics, high and popular culture, and—shock, horror!—our studies!' he exclaims. The trip from Brighton on the 630 bus was 'more than just a geographical shift. It was a shift from the problematic certainties and staidness of my adolescent life, to the excitement and ever-shifting challenges of my adult life.' When Scully moved on to postgraduate work, he never considered another uni. 'Monash was everything to me.'[53]

The new academic frontier

Fifty years after its foundation, Monash continued to think of itself as a young university. As Clayton began to age, it rejuvenated itself by planting new campuses on the fringes of other cities, recapitulating its own pioneering era. Today, if you want to find Monash students living like the first generation at Clayton, studying full-time, hanging out on the campus from morning till evening, you must go to Sunway or Roodeport, islands of educational privilege in societies where higher education is still scarce, and more highly prized, than in Australia.

Almost everyone at Monash Sunway is a full-time student. Most live close by in one of the high-rise student residences, come to the campus around eight thirty in the morning and stay well into the evening. 'It's the students' home', Pro Vice-Chancellor Robin Pollard observes. 'I sometimes think you could run advertisements in Australia showing [prospective students] a campus just as their parents experienced it!'[54] Fees are high, so most students are from well-to-do families who have nevertheless often made sacrifices for them to come. Parents take a keen interest in their performance, even ringing up lecturers to check on their children's progress. Too much rides on the venture to mix study with paid work.

Diligent and grateful, Sunway students are a delight to teach, says lecturer Cathy Yule.[55] Coming through a Malaysian school system that stresses rote learning, they may seem less outspoken than Australians, Americans and Canadians, but everyone, including the students themselves, regards them as more 'liberated' than the products of other Malaysian institutions. 'It is different from my previous university', one student reported in 2003. 'Students are more open-minded.'[56]

'Liberated', of course, is a relative term, as students transferring from other Monash campuses have sometimes noticed. Australian–Malaysian student Dahlia Martin was discouraged from standing for election as president of the student council because, she was told, it was not a position for a woman.[57] At MSA, Petunia Mpoza's lecturers encouraged robust debate, but at Sunway, where she studied on exchange, her classmates seemed reluctant to ask questions. Sometimes, a student would present her with a list of questions to ask the teacher, 'because they realised I was brave enough'. She returned to South Africa more convinced than ever that culture is 'very, very important'.[58]

In keeping with its full-time, all-day character, Sunway has a thriving 'campus lifestyle'. Yvonne Yap first experienced Monash on Open Day and was instantly 'sold'. The campus was 'beautiful, vibrant, the people . . . very friendly'.[59] The move to the new campus had stimulated the growth of a wide array of sports clubs, religious organisations and faculty societies within a framework that explicitly endorsed tolerance and harmony (*muhibbah*). In 2009, new vice-chancellor Ed Byrne opened a multi-faith centre modelled on the Religious Centre at Clayton. Monash, he noted, had been founded as a secular institution, but the new centre was designed 'to acknowledge the multiple faiths of our staff and students'. As Pro Vice-Chancellor Pollard acknowledged, the centre emerged in response to occasional difficulties in reconciling the 'value systems' of staff and students. By providing a 'purpose-built facility for quiet reflection and religious activities', the university was reinforcing its code of conduct, forbidding religious activities that could 'reasonably cause offence' elsewhere on campus.[60] From MSA, the campus has borrowed the idea of a volunteer program, now involving over a hundred students. A speakers' corner encourages the free expression of ideas and develops confidence in public speaking, even if discussion of politics, sex and religion is banned.

The fifty students who enrolled on Monash's newest campus on the fringes of Johannesburg in 2001 called themselves 'pioneers', just like the first cohort of students at Clayton forty years earlier. Once again, Monash had opened a year before schedule, with the site still mud-bound and the students walking between classes on duckboards. Only twenty turned up for Orientation Day. 'We tried to do a team-building thing . . . rah, rah, let's all hold this rope together and sing kumbaya', Community Engagement Manager Craig Rowe recalls.[61] There was the same sense of camaraderie between students and staff, sharing the challenges and frustrations of frontier life. 'You knew the students by name, they knew us by name . . . we were like a close-knit family', says personal assistant to the pro vice-chancellor Charmain Caroto.[62]

Coming with no historical baggage, Monash brought a 'new culture', free of the antagonisms found on other campuses in the country.[63] The campus was secluded from the rest of the city in a tranquil, semi-rural location, guarded by tight but unobtrusive security. Those who didn't live in dormitories on campus came on Monash buses. Alcohol was banned. Inside its high fences, however, was an African cosmopolis, with black and white students from Botswana and Zimbabwe as well as South Africa, and exchange students from Malaysia and Australia. 'You can hear Zulu, Shino, Swahili, French . . . it was just like this swirling of languages and cultures and people', Simon Adams noted when he arrived in 2007.[64]

The sons and daughters of wealthy political and business leaders ('they're driving Audis and they're nineteen!') shared classes with bursary students who could scarcely afford to feed and clothe themselves.[65] 'Can you help me get some batteries for a torch?' one student asked Adams. 'Why?' 'Because I live in a shack and I don't have electricity at home and I need to study for my exams.'

Pro Vice-Chancellor Tyrone Pretorius nurtures a vision of MSA as a 'micro-cosmos of what South Africa could be like, where black and white, South African and Non-South African work and study together with little regard to ethnic and racist labels'.[66] It's not quite like that yet, of course. Cliques inevitably form. 'There was a Botswana group that very much stuck together, and the Zimbabwean group stuck together, and the Kenyan group stuck together or hung out with the Tanzanians as well', Will Moore, an Australian exchange student, noticed.[67] Students tend to vote along national lines in student elections.

Achieving Pretorius' ideal may require a level of literacy—linguistic, social and political—that the campus has yet to achieve. Many students, especially those from outside South Africa, arrive with only rudimentary English and poor study skills. Marianne Hicks, who taught international studies, recalls that many of her students came 'from very patriarchal backgrounds, so they're taught at any early age not to question, not to be engaged, not to be critical'.[68] The student culture of MSA is largely apolitical, focused around religion (as at Clayton in the 1960s, many of the most active student groups are faith-based), sport, partying and community service. Masters student Lennon Mhishi, who came from the University of Zimbabwe in 2008 when his studies were interrupted by the political crisis, noticed the reluctance of MSA students to engage in political discussion.[69]

At first sight, a beautiful foreign-owned campus situated behind high security fences on the edge of a complex, dangerous city may look more like a sanctuary from the problems of Africa than a launching pad for solving them. Yet, remarkably, under Richard Larkins' vice-chancellorship, community involvement came to redefine the campus. In 2008, Monash was approached by a non-government organisation seeking space for a Saturday program to assist the primary school at Zandspruit, an informal settlement just 5 kilometres from the campus, where 60 000 people live on

1 square kilometre of land. The school houses over a thousand children in converted shipping containers, sitting five or six to a desk. Monash students became involved in the program, effectively 'hijacking' it and, according to Simon Adams, took it 'in directions that we never had the vision and foresight to imagine'. Among the volunteers was Will Moore. Attracted to South Africa by the cheap beer, he was challenged by the massive gap between rich and poor. He recruited more volunteers, so that every weekend between fifty and seventy Monash students, most of them African, now work intensively with 150 schoolchildren in a program based on the high school curriculum, designed to boost pass rates and bridge the gap to tertiary study. After study is over, they share a barbeque lunch and play soccer. Some of the volunteers are themselves graduates of the program, now studying at MSA on bursaries.

Moore sees MSA as a hopeful place. Students who come from more privileged backgrounds destined to play leadership roles in Africa are becoming more socially aware, while those who have grown up in poverty or lost parents to AIDS see their lives literally transformed. In a way that Monash's founders could never have imagined, its founding vision has found fresh expression on one of the world's harshest frontiers. Nigerian IT student Joshua Vihishima decided to come to Monash after reading the words of Sir John Monash on the university's website: 'Adopt as your fundamental creed that you will equip yourself for life, not solely for your benefit alone, but for the benefit of the community'.[70] He is now among the students engaged in the campus's volunteer program. To these students, as Larkins noted, Monash's 'rhetoric' truly means something.

The University Unlimited

From its beginnings, Monash has been a 'university in a hurry'. Born on the suburban fringe, it has regularly set itself daunting timetables and renewed itself by the challenge of new frontiers of enterprise and opportunity. Reaching outwards, rather than gazing inwards, is its natural disposition. 'It is the reverse of an ivory tower', says the current vice-chancellor, Ed Byrne.[71] Older universities project a vision that balances ideas of continuity and change, celebrates face-to-face community and seeks to draw their students towards a nurturing centre. But Monash is a university that refuses to be circumscribed by geography or consoled by tradition. It is a university unlimited.

Market researchers confirm its reputation as Australia's biggest and most international university. Yet big does not mean impersonal: the same researchers found that Monash was considered friendlier, more approachable, adaptable, innovative, honest and engaged than its local rivals. It lacked the University of Melbourne's 'prestige' and 'tradition', but its teaching and research were on a par.[72] Perhaps it could appear to be all these things because, in fact, there is not one Monash, but several. Its internal diversity remains one of the university's main attractions, as well as a continuing source of tension. Will it remain one university, with common curricula and testamurs, or will campuses inevitably develop their own characters? Will it divide vertically between a research-intensive Clayton–Caulfield core and a periphery of community colleges? If so, what will make the several parts 'Monash'? To students and teachers in Kuala Lumpur and Johannesburg, as well as in Clayton and Gippsland, Monash is more than a brand or a logo; it stands for common standards and ideals.

Through its five decades, Monash has crested the waves of social and political change. In the 1960s, the age of Sputnik, it embraced the vision of 'an educated democracy' dedicated to liberal ideals of social opportunity, scientific advancement and humane learning. In the early 1970s, the Age of Aquarius, it became Australia's most radical campus, a host, and sometimes a hostage, to utopian dreams of a socialist paradise. By the 1980s, as market capitalism made a resounding comeback, Monash became the most striking Australian specimen of the 'enterprise university', embracing a corporate culture and leadership style, merging and acquiring campuses, seeking new educational markets in Asia and cyberspace. By the 1990s, as higher education began to globalise, Monash projected itself as 'Australia's international university'. Only with the coming of the new millennium, and a series of internal shocks, did the university pause to take its bearings and, after checking its moral compass, set sail again. Paradoxically, it was Monash's bravest experiment, the campus in South Africa, that defined both the prudential limits and the ethical potential of the University Unlimited.

In 2011, after almost five decades of service, the last escalator was removed from the Menzies Building. Over the years, thousands of freshers had ridden them up to their first tutorials on medieval history or Greek philosophy, macroeconomics or accounting. In an optimistic era, they were a vivid symbol of modernity and social mobility. Albert Langer and Pete Steedman, Peter Costello and Simon Crean, Michelle Grattan and Jane Turner, Don Watson and Damien Broderick: all began their rise to fame by stepping on the Monash escalators. By the 1990s, however, the escalators were wearing out, with whole flights out of action for weeks on end. There were even moments when the death of the escalators seemed likely to condemn the Ming Wing itself. Would it be blown up, like the Pruitt-Igoe apartment block in St Louis, whose spectacular 1972 demolition sounded the death-knell of architectural modernism? Or would it be turned into apartments for graduate students?

Against the odds, the Menzies Building, *sans* escalators, but with a new lift tower, café and jauntily postmodern decor, will survive into a new era. Students riding the lifts will catch a glimpse, in the photographs etched into their stainless-steel interiors, of the original Ming Wing. The modernism of the 1960s is now distant enough to evoke nostalgia. Perhaps, after fifty years of resisting tradition, the university has begun to acquire a lively sense of its history? One of the marks of maturity, in institutions as well as individuals, is an ability to learn from the past. Over its fifty years, Monash has sometimes been reluctant to look back or gaze inwards, lest it lose momentum or quench the thirst for change. But in recognising where we have come from, acknowledging setbacks as well as successes, keeping alive the memory of the men and women who made Monash, we are not only paying our debts to the past; we are honouring the university's founding ideal. We are still learning.

NOTES

Note on sources

The main archival source for this book is the Monash University Archives, which falls under the administration of the university's Records and Archives Services (see Monash University website, at <http://adm.monash.edu/records-archives>). The archives are located in the basement of Building 3D on the Clayton campus.
A general description of the archives and main record bodies is available on the website, but researchers are advised to contact the archives for more detailed information. In a small number of cases, we have also cited records still in the custody of faculties or the central administration and not accessioned by the central archives. To keep the scholarly apparatus of the book within reasonable limits, in citing archival sources we have used an abbreviated reference, based on a succinct description of the nature of the record together with a file or item number, but omitting detailed series information. Where not otherwise indicated, archival references are to these records. Other archival sources are indicated by their location in the Public Record Office of Victoria (PROV), University of Melbourne Archives (UMA), National Library of Australia (NLA) and Noel Butlin Archives Centre, Australian National University.

Prelude

1 James Adam Louis Matheson was generally known as Louis, pronounced 'Loo-iss' in the Scottish manner rather than 'Loo-ee' in the French style. The Matheson family were Scots, and Louis's father named him after the celebrated Scottish writer, Robert Louis Stevenson.
2 Interview with Lady Audrey Matheson, 23 February 2010.
3 Testimonial of Graham F. Mucklow, 1946, attached to Louis Matheson Curriculum Vitae, Louis Matheson Personnel File, 1951/636, UMA.
4 Interview with Lady Audrey Matheson, 23 February 2010.
5 Louis Matheson, 'Tribute to Robert Blackwood', in *Robert Rutherford Blackwood 1906–1982*, Monash University, 1982, p. 2.

6 Blackwood's early career at Dunlop is covered in Geoffrey Blainey, *Jumping over the Wheel*, Allen & Unwin, Sydney, 1993, pp. 171–80; Robert Blackwood to Registrar, University of Melbourne, 13 September 1946, Robert Blackwood Personnel File, 1947/109, UM 312, UMA; Ian D. Rae, 'Blackwood, Sir Robert Rutherford', in *Australian Dictionary of Biography*, vol. 17: 1981–90, Melbourne University Press, 2007, pp. 111–12.

7 Carolyn Rasmussen, *Increasing Momentum: Engineering at the University of Melbourne 1861–2004*, Melbourne University Press, 2004, pp. 132–47.

8 *Cranks and Nuts*, 1947, p. 4.

9 Patrick O'Farrell, *UNSW A Portrait: The University of New South Wales 1949–1999*, University of New South Wales Press, 1999, pp. 18, 58.

10 Institute of Technology, Faculty of Engineering, University of Melbourne, 29/7/49, CP 9/12, UMA; *Age*, 31 May 1950.

11 University of Melbourne Professorial Board Minutes, 22 March 1949, quoted in Anthony John Dare, 'The Movement to Establish a Higher Technological Institute in Victoria, 1940–1963', MEd Thesis, University of Melbourne, 1976, p. 158.

12 Louis Matheson, 'Engineering in the University', *University Gazette*, vol. 4, no. 2, 30 March 1948, p. 10, quoted in Dare, p. 155.

13 Institute of Technology, Faculty of Engineering, University of Melbourne, 29/7/49, CP 9/12, UMA.

14 Blackwood to Acting Vice-Chancellor, 12 September 1947, Robert Blackwood Personnel File, 1947/109, UMA.

15 Louis Matheson, Presidential Address to MUESC, quoted in *Cranks and Nuts*, 1948, p. 7.

16 Matheson to Registrar, 2 February 1950, Louis Matheson Personnel File, 1951/636, UMA.

17 Medley to Matheson, 7 March 1950, Louis Matheson Personnel File, 1951/636, UMA.

18 Louis Matheson, *Still Learning*, Macmillan, South Melbourne, 1980, p. 1.

Chapter 1

1 Barbara Barkdale Clowse, *Brainpower for the Cold War: The Sputnik Crisis and National Defense Education Act of 1958*, Greenwood Press, Westwood, Conn., 1981, p. 18; Robert A. Divine, *The Sputnik Challenge*, Oxford University Press, New York, 1993, pp. 13–15.

2 *Age*, 5, 6 October 1957.

3 ibid., 7 October 1957.

4 C.P. Snow, *The Two Cultures and a Second Look*, Cambridge University Press, 1965; see also Sir Eric Ashby, *Technology and the Academies: An Essay on the Universities and the Scientific Revolution*, Macmillan, London, 1959.

5 *Age*, 19 June 1958.

6 *Report to the Minister of Education the Hon. John Bloomfield, MLA by a Committee Appointed to Consider the Establishment of a University of Technology in Victoria*, Government Printer, Melbourne, 20 April 1956; Sir Robert Blackwood, *Monash University: The First Ten Years*, Hampden Hall, Melbourne, 1968, pp. 1–9.

7   A.J. Francis, 'An Institute of Technology in Victoria', *Royal Australian Chemical Institute Proceedings*, September 1956, p. 276; compare T.G. Hunter, 'Technological Education', ibid., October 1957, p. 564.

8   I.W. Wark, 'The Status and Emoluments of Chemists', *Royal Australian Chemical Institute Proceedings*, Supplement, November 1957, pp. 56–7.

9   John Rossiter, 'A University of Technology for Victoria', *Royal Australian Chemical Institute Proceedings*, September 1956, pp. 264–5.

10 *Age*, 26 August 1957.

11 D.S. Anderson, 'Access to Higher Education', in G.S. Harman and C. Selby Smith (eds), *Australian Higher Education: Problems of a Developing System*, Angus and Robertson, Sydney, 1972, p. 118.

12 Hugh Mackay, *Generations: Babyboomers, Their Parents and Their Children*, Macmillan, Sydney, 1997, p. 35.

13 W.D. Borrie, 'The Demography of Education', in Harman and Selby Smith (eds), *Australian Higher Education*, pp. 58–61.

14 *Age*, 4 June 1957.

15 A.W. Martin, *Robert Menzies: A Life*, vol. 2, 1944–78, Melbourne University Press, 1999, pp. 396–9.

16 The Committee on Australian Universities, The Future Development of University Education in Victoria (hereafter Murray Committee Report to Victoria), Report to the Honourable the Minister of Education, Victoria, 1958, VPRS 1163/ P0, Unit 1129, 58/353, PROV.

17 J.R. Poynter and Carolyn Rasmussen, *A Place Apart: The University of Melbourne: Decades of Challenge*, Melbourne University Press, 1996, p. 174.

18 Murray Committee Report to Victoria.

19 *Report of the Committee on Australian Universities, September 1957* (hereafter Murray Report), AGPS, Canberra, 1958, pp. 8–9. For Clunies Ross' views, see his 'The Responsibility of Science and the University in the Modern World' (1952) and 'The University and the Challenge of the Future' (1956), in Ian Clunies Ross, *Memoirs and Papers with Some Fragments of Autobiography*, Oxford University Press, Melbourne, 1961, pp. 171–86, 213–22; and compare Poynter and Rasmussen, *A Place Apart*, pp. 169–70.

20 *Parliamentary Debates*, House of Representatives, 28 November 1957, p. 2696.

21 *Royal Australian Chemical Institute Proceedings*, November 1956, pp. 253–4; John Swan, Personal Communication, 17 July 2009.

22 *Age*, 7, 14 December 1957, 19 March 1958.

23 ibid., 24 April 1958.

24 John Henry Newman, *The Idea of a University* (1852), Image Books, New York, 1959, p. 165.

25 Statement of the Prime Minister, 28 November 1957, copy in VPRS 1163/P0, Unit 1129, 58/353, PROV.

26 *Victorian Parliamentary Debates*, vol. CCLIV, 1956–58, 2 April 1958, pp. 3700, 4041 (Monash University Bill).

27 Blackwood, *Monash University*, p. 10.

28 *Age*, 6 December 1957.

29 John Bloomfield to Essington Lewis, 24 December 1957, VPRS 1163/P0, Unit 1129, 58/353, PROV.

30 Geoffrey Blainey and Ann Smith, 'Lewis, Essington', in *Australian Dictionary of Biography*, vol. 10: 1891–1939, Melbourne University Press, 1986, pp. 87–92.

31 Essington Lewis to John Bloomfield, 3 January 1958, VPRS 1163/P0, Unit 1129, 58/353, PROV.

32 C.B. Schedvin, 'Clunies Ross, Sir William Ian', in *Australian Dictionary of Biography*, vol. 13: 1940–80, Melbourne University Press, 1993, pp. 448–51; Margery Collard O'Dea, *Ian Clunies-Ross: A Biography*, Hyland House, Melbourne, 1997, pp. 336–7; Margorie Harper, 'Copland, Sir Douglas', in *Australian Dictionary of Biography*, vol. 13, 1940–80, Melbourne University Press, 1993, pp. 496–500. Anthony Clunies Ross, who was living at home during this time, has no recollection of his father being approached for the Monash job: Personal Communication, 19 May 2010.

33 Bloomfield to Bolte, 23 January 1958, VPRS 1163/ P0, Unit 1129, 58/353, PROV.

34 Blainey, *Jumping over the Wheel*, p. 187.

35 Bloomfield to Blackwood, 18 June 1958, VPRS 1163/P0, Unit 1129, 58/353, PROV.

36 Blackwood, *Monash University*, pp. 12–13.

37 *Age*, 23, 28, 30 May 1958; H.W. Arndt (Social Science Research Council) to Blackwood, 13 June 1958, AA/1 Pt 1 Interim Council-General; Blackwood, *Monash University*, p. 14.

38 H.W. Arndt (SSRC) to Blackwood, 13 June 1958, AA/1 Pt 1 Interim Council-General.

39 *Herald*, 11 December 1957.

40 ibid., 30 November, 2 December 1957.

41 See, for example, opinions of Clunies Ross as quoted in *Herald*, 29 November, 2, 11 December 1957.

42 *Herald*, 14, 16 December 1957.

43 ibid., 30 November, 14, 16 December 1957.

44 J.A. Dunn to Bloomfield, 2 December 1957, MA/0 Pt 2, Site: Suggestions to Interim Council.

45 Goldsbrough Mort to Bloomfield, 11 December 1957, MA/0 Pt 2.

46 Shire of Keilor to R.R. Rawson, MLC, 14 April 1958, MA/0 Pt 4.

47 Murray Valley Development League to Bolte, 4 February 1958, MA/0 Pt 2.

48 See correspondence in MA/0 Pt 2.

49 Interim Council Minutes, 4 July 1958.

50 Murray Report, p. 52.

51 *Melbourne and Metropolitan Planning Scheme 1954, Report*, Melbourne and Metropolitan Board of Works, Melbourne, 1954, p. 41.

52 Melbourne and Metropolitan Board of Works, Report Relative to the Selection of Site for Monash University, Council Papers, 11 August 1958.

53 Members of the public also suggested other racecourses at Williamstown and Moonee Valley for consideration as a university site.

54 *Sydney Morning Herald*, 31 January, 1 February 1951.

55 Harold Luth to Bloomfield, 4 January 1958, 58/P000056, PROV.

56 *Age*, 9 April 1958.

57 Melbourne and Metropolitan Board of Works, Report Relative to the Selection of Site for Monash University, Council Papers, 11 August 1958, pp. 13–14; compare Bloomfield to M. Butler, 15 April 1958, MA/0 Pt 3.
58 Interim Council Minutes, 11 August, 8 September 1958.
59 City of Caulfield Ratebook, East Ward 1954, VPRS 8354/0001, Unit 170, vol. 5, PROV.
60 F.L. Murdoch to Robert Blackwood, 5 August 1958, MA/0 Pt 4.
61 Robert Coleman, *Above Renown: The Biography of Sir Henry Winneke*, Macmillan, Melbourne, 1988, p. 213.
62 Lindsay Thompson, *I Remember*, Hyland House, Melbourne, 1989, pp. 106–8.
63 *Age*, 28 October 1958; *Herald*, 28 October 1958.
64 Interim Council Minutes, 15 November 1958.
65 ibid., 11 August 1958.
66 Blackwood, *Monash University*, p. 19.
67 Graeme Davison, *Car Wars: How the Car Won Our Hearts and Conquered Our Cities*, Allen & Unwin, Sydney, 2004, Chapter 1; David Dunstan, 'Henry Bolte: The Lucky Developer', in Brian Costar and Paul Strangio (eds), *The Victorian Premiers: 1856–2000*, Federation Press, Sydney, 2006, pp. 280–4.
68 Patrick Troy (ed.), *Technological Change and the City*, Federation Press, Sydney, 1995, pp. 1–15.
69 P.J. Rimmer, *Manufacturing in Melbourne*, Research School of Pacific Studies, ANU, Canberra, 1969, pp. 18, 104; Lyndsay Neilson, *Business Activity in Three Melbourne Suburbs*, Urban Research Unit, ANU, Canberra, 1972.
70 *Sydney Morning Herald*, 5 July 1951.
71 Geoffrey Blainey, *Johns and Waygood Limited 1856–1956*, Johns and Waygood, Melbourne, 1956, p. 63.
72 *Age*, 26 November 1957.
73 Ken Johnson, *People and Property in Clayton: Development and Change in an Outer Suburb of Melbourne, in the Nineteen Fifties and Sixties*, Urban Research Unit, RSSS, ANU, Canberra, 1979; Tony Dingle, 'People and Places in Postwar Melbourne', in Graeme Davison, Tony Dingle and Seamus O'Hanlon (eds), *The Cream Brick Frontier: Histories of Australian Suburbia*, Monash Publications in History 19, Monash University, 1995, pp. 27–40.
74 Johnson, *People and Property*, pp. 67–8, 75–6; compare *Melbourne Transportation Study*, vol. 3, Metropolitan Transportation Committee, Carlton, Vic., 1969, p. 17; Neilson, *Business Activity*, pp. 95–6.
75 Robin Boyd, *The Australian Ugliness*, Penguin, Ringwood, Vic., 1960, pp. 78–88.
76 Davison, *Car Wars*, Chapter 4.
77 Interim Council Minutes, 10 November 1958.
78 *Herald*, 13 November 1958.
79 *Age*, 14 November 1958. The Huntingdale–Rowville line was included among the proposals for new rail connections in the 1969 Melbourne Transportation Plan but not pursued; see *Melbourne Transportation Study*, vol. 3, p. 35.
80 Survey of Student Travel by Monash University Student Union, 28 August 1963, LE/1 Pt 1.
81 Blackwood, *Monash University*, p. 27.
82 *Herald*, 13 November 1958.
83 ibid.

Chapter 2

1 Murray Committee Report to Victoria.

2 Registrar Frank Johnson told the story to journalist Keith Dunstan, writing under the pseudonym 'Batman', in a profile of 'Melbourne's Other University' in the *Bulletin*, 2 May 1964; Blackwood also tells the story in *Monash University*, pp. 56–7. Interview with Jack McDonell, 23 June 2010.

3 This explanation may seem more obvious to us than it would have to contemporaries. We can imagine how it might happen in an office today: a page becomes detached from the original document and the rest are fed into the copier, which prints and staples the copies for the council, and nobody notices the missing page, especially when the document seems to end quite conclusively. But in 1958 there were no photocopiers, let alone document feeders. The standard method of circulating documents for meetings was typing them onto a stencil and running off copies on a duplicator. Two duplicated copies of the truncated document ending at the bottom of page 7 are filed in the Premier's Department Archives, 58/353, Unit 1129, VPRS 1163/P0, PROV. One of these copies is annotated 'Received from S/Edn Dept on 23/1/58'. On this date, Minister Bloomfield wrote to Premier Henry Bolte recommending the appointment of Robert Blackwood as chairman of the Interim Council of Monash University. It is probable, then, that from the beginning of his appointment, this incomplete version of Murray's report was the only one that Blackwood, and hence his council, knew. How did the document become truncated? It is possible, but unlikely, that the last page of the original document had fallen off before it was retyped onto a stencil and duplicated; however, if this is what happened, how can we explain that the retyped version ends exactly at the bottom of the seventh page? More likely, the document had already been retyped and the last stencil was lost or mislaid, presumably by staff in the Department of Education. A more intriguing possibility that cannot be entirely discounted is that the document was deliberately circulated in a truncated form, so as not to offer the council any respite from the sense of urgency that by then had seized the government.

4 Blackwood, *Monash University*, p. 34.

5 *Age*, 20 June 1958.

6 Interview with Sir Louis Matheson (hereafter Matheson Interview) conducted by Stuart Broadhead and others, January 1976. As a member of the University of Melbourne's Council, Blackwood would also have been aware that in its submission to the Murray Committee it had predicted that the crisis in enrolments would require a new university by 1962. (University of Melbourne, Council Minutes, 2 December 1957; University of Melbourne, Submission to Committee on Australian Universities, in Universities: Commonwealth Committee of Inquiry, 1957/1384, UMA.)

7 John Rickard, 'Monash: The University in a Hurry', in F.W. Kent and D.D. Cuthbert (eds), *Making Monash: A Twenty-Five Year History*, Monash University, Clayton, Vic., 1986, pp. 6–22.

8 Robin Boyd, 'New University Is a Big Challenge', *Herald*, 26 March 1958.

9 Interim Council Minutes, 8 December 1958; Building Committee Minutes, 22 December 1958.

10 Geoffrey Serle, *Robin Boyd: A Life*, Melbourne University Press, 1995, p. 66.

11   Philip Goad, *Bates Smart: 150 Years of Australian Architecture*, Thames & Hudson, Fishermans Bend, Vic., 2004, pp. 148–75.

12   Interim Council Minutes, 22 December 1958.

13   BSM, Progress Report of Architect-Planners (hereafter First Progress Report), 5 February 1959; BSM, Progress Report of Architect-Planners (hereafter Second Progress Report), 3 March 1959, both in MA7, Pt 1.

14   Second Progress Report, pp. 1, 14.

15   Gilman in Thomas Bender, 'The University and the City', in Thomas Bender, *The Unfinished City: New York and the Metropolitan Idea*, New York University Press, 2002, p. 151.

16   *Age*, 1 April 1961.

17   Second Progress Report, p. 15.

18   ibid., pp. 6, 15–18.

19   ibid., pp. 8, 10, 13.

20   Murray Report, pp. 53–7.

21   Paul Venable Turner, *Campus: An American Planning Tradition*, MIT Press, Cambridge, Mass., 1984, p. 160.

22   Second Progress Report, p. 16.

23   ibid., pp. 16–18.

24   Report of Staff Committee on Selection of Vice-Chancellor, 30 April 1959, in Louis Matheson Personnel File.

25   Louis Matheson Personnel File.

26   J.B. Cragg to A.J. Marshall, 5 February 1960, Marshall Papers, 5/38, NLA.

27   Lord Stopford to Louis Matheson, 9 May 1959, Matheson Papers, 1986/09/001.

28   Matheson Interview.

29   Blackwood to Matheson, 28 May 1959, 1986/09/001.

30   McCutcheon to Matheson, 12 June 1959, 1986/09/003.

31   Matheson to McCutcheon, 24 June 1959, 1986/09/003.

32   Blackwood to Bassett, 1 August 1959, MA7 Pt 1.

33   McCutcheon to Matheson, 12 June 1959, 1986/09/003.

34   Blackwood to Bassett, 1 August 1959, 1986/09/003.

35   Building Committee Report, Interim Council Minutes, 10 August 1959.

36   *Age*, 26 April 1959.

37   'Interview with Professor Ron Brown', Australian Academy of Science, 2008, <www.science.org.au/scientists/interviews/b/brown.html>; Ron Brown Personnel File.

38   Honeycombe to Matheson, 7 July 1959, Robert Street Personnel File.

39   'Interview with Professor Robert Street', Australian Academy of Science, 2005, <www.science.org.au/scientists/interviews/s/street.html>.

40   Bassett to Blackwood, 2 July 1959; J.D.G. Medley to Bassett, 17 June 1959; Hill Worner to Bassett, 19 June 1959; C.E. Moorhouse to Bassett, 17 June 1959, all in Kenneth Hunt Personnel File.

41   James Warren, 'Marshall, Alan John (Jock)', in *Australian Dictionary of Biography*, vol. 15, Melbourne University Press, 2000, pp. 304–6; Jane Marshall, 'Jock Marshall: One Armed Warrior', Australian Science Archives Project, 1998, <www.asap.unimelb.edu.au/bsparcs/exhib/marshall/marshall.htm>.

42   A.J. Marshall to Bibio and Pepe, 30 August 1959, Marshall Papers, NLA.

43   Blackwood to Bassett, 25 July 1959, 1986/09/002.

44 Matheson to Bassett, 24 August 1959, 1986/09/002.
45 Application for Librarianship of Monash University, 17 July 1959; Matheson to Blackwood, 21 January 1960, both in Ernest Clark Personnel File.
46 Frank Johnson Curriculum Vitae, Frank Johnson Personnel File.
47 Matheson Interview.
48 Confidential: Monash University Development, AUC Report to Monash University Council, 7 October 1959; Interim Council Minutes, 20 October 1959.
49 *Herald*, 16 October 1959.
50 Matheson Interview.
51 Blackwood, *Monash University*, p. 53.
52 Interim Council Minutes, 20, 28 October 1959.
53 McCutcheon Report to Council, 10 April 1959.
54 Matheson to Blackwood, 24 November 1959, 1986/09/002; Interview with Lady Audrey Matheson, 23 February 2010.
55 Walter Bassett to Robert Blackwood, 2 July 1959, 1986/09/03.
56 Interview with Lady Audrey Matheson, 23 February 2010.
57 Blackwood to Matheson, 5 October 1959; Lady Audrey Matheson, Personal Communication, 24 June 2010.
58 Louis Matheson to A.J. Marshall, 9 February 1960, Marshall Papers, 10/1, NLA.
59 McCutcheon to Marshall, 5 February 1960, Marshall Papers, 10/1, NLA; A.J. Marshall, On Helping to Build a University, p. 6, Marshall Papers, 16/6, NLA.
60 Marshall to Matheson, 22 February, 10 March 1960; Matheson to Marshall, 1, 18 March 1960, both in Marshall Papers, 10/1, NLA.
61 A.J. Marshall, On Helping to Build a University, Marshall Papers, 16/6, NLA.
62 Blackwood, *Monash University*, p. 70.
63 BSM, Discussions with Vice-Chancellor, 3 May 1960, MH/1/3.
64 Interim Council, Arts Sub-Committee, 4 November 1959.
65 Max Hartwell to Matheson, 3 May 1960; Matheson to Hartwell, 19 May 1960; Geoffrey Serle Personnel File; interview with John Legge, 12 February 2010.
66 John David Legge Curriculum Vitae; Fred Alexander to Frank Johnson, 31 May 1960; Matheson to J.A. La Nauze, 8 June 1960, all in John Legge Personnel File.
67 Keith Campbell, 'David Hector Monro (1911–2001)', obituary in *The Australian Academy of the Humanities Proceedings*, 2001, <www.humanities.org.au/Resources/Downloads/ . . . /DavidHectorMonro.pdf>; A.K. Stout to Registrar, August 1960; J.L. Mackie to Registrar, 31 August 1960; Matheson to R.T. Wallace, 20 October 1970, all in Hector Monro Personnel File.
68 Westfold to Matheson, 7 September 1960; Matheson to Westfold, 20 September 1960; Westfold to Matheson, 21 September 1960, all in Kevin Westfold Personnel File.
69 Marshall to Matheson, 10 October 1960, Marshall Papers, 10/1, NLA.
70 Based on *Monash University Calendar*, 1965.
71 Compare Serle, *Robin Boyd*, p. 61.
72 Marshall Berman, *All That Is Solid Melts into Air: The Experience of Modernity*, Verso, London, 1982, pp. 15–36.

73 BSM, Discussions with Vice-Chancellor, 20 April 1960, 5 January 1961, MH/1/3.
74 Klingender to architects Eggleston, Macdonald and Secomb, 17 January 1962, MM/100.1/0.
75 Louis Matheson, Proposed Changes in Layout in the Arts Area, 23 December 1960, MM/100.1/0; Matheson to McCutcheon, 24 October 1960, MA/7 Pt 1.
76 BSM, Discussions with Vice-Chancellor, 13 April 1961, MH/1/3; Bill Rachinger, Reminiscences, unpublished account, 19 May 2010.
77 *Chaos*, 19 March 1964, p. 9; Bill Rachinger, Reminiscences, unpublished account, 19 May 2010.
78 Doug Ellis in *Monash Reporter*, Supplement, 'The First XV Years', 1975, p. 2.
79 Matheson to McCutcheon, 24 October 1960; Louis Matheson, Notes on the State of Development Reached by September, 1960, Interim Council Minutes, 10 October 1960.
80 Matheson to McCutcheon, 24 October 1960, MH/1/3.
81 John Legge, Personal Communication, June 2010.
82 J.M. Swan to Naming of Buildings Committee, 30 November 1967, ME/9 Pt 1.
83 John Legge, Personal Communication, June 2010.
84 Matheson to McCutcheon, 24 October 1960; Buildings Committee Meeting, 17 November, 14 December 1960; Professorial Board Meeting, 14 December 1960; Buildings Committee Meeting, 4 January 1961, all in MA/7 Pt 1.
85 Blackwood, *Monash University*, p. 192.
86 BSM, 25 August 1960, MH/1/3.
87 Requirements for the Design of the Arts and Law Faculty Buildings at Monash University, November 1960, MM/100.1/0.
88 On Fordism, see Davison, *Car Wars*, pp. 82–5.
89 Requirements for the Design of the Arts and Law Faculty Buildings at Monash University, November 1960, MM/100.1/0, p. 6.
90 'Batman' (Keith Dunstan), 'Keeping Them Down on the Farm', *Bulletin*, 2 May 1964.
91 Donald Cochrane, A Note on Staff and Tutorial Rooms, 9 January 1961, MM/100.1/0.
92 Matheson to Sir Leslie Martin, 31 January 1961; compare Matheson to D. Dexter, 8 November 1960, both in MM/100.1/0.
93 Buildings Committee Meeting 48, 18 January 1961.
94 John Legge, 'Ming Wing Windows: Cupboards and Corridors: Status and Room Size in the Menzies Building', and David Bradley, 'Ming Wing: The Ming Wing's Salad Days', in *Ming Wing: Winds of Change*, a photographic exhibition commemorating the Menzies Building in the 1960s, Monash University, n.d.; see also David Bradley to Matheson, 2 February 1961, MM/100.1/0.
95 Marshall to Matheson, 10 September 1960 (copy), Marshall Papers, NLA.
96 Professorial Board Minutes, 10 January 1961. At the end of 1961, the Naming Committee did agree to the placement of a plaque in a prominent position to mark the premier's opening of the university.
97 University Council Meeting, 13 November 1961.

98 Report of the Committee on Naming, 9 November 1961; Matheson to Naming Committee, 7 December 1964; Hector Monro to Matheson, 10 December 1964; Marshall to Matheson, 11 December 1964, all in ME/9 Pt 1.
99 Serle to Matheson, 26 March 1963, ME/9 Pt 1.
100 Professorial Board Minutes, 29 March, 13 November 1961.
101 Grace Fraser for John Stevens to Director, Natural Resources Conservation League, 9 August 1960; Marshall to Matheson, 12 August 1960; John Stevens to Matheson, 16 August 1960, all in MC/0/1 Pt 1; Matheson to Stevens, Grounds Committee Minutes, 3 July 1961.
102 Matheson to Stevens, 12 August 1960; Stevens to Matheson, 16 August 1960, both in MC/0/1 Pt 1.
103 Louis Matheson, Note to Grounds Committee summarising report from Turner, 23 August 1961, MC/0/4 Pt 1.
104 Martin Canny, 'The Grounds: An Act of Faith', in Kent and Cuthbert (eds), *Making Monash*, pp. 25–33.
105 Marshall, 'Jock Marshall', Chapter 18.
106 Pryor to Matheson, 28 July 1966, Marshall Papers, 12/7, NLA.
107 Marshall to Matheson, 13 September 1966, Marshall Papers, 12/7, NLA.
108 Matheson to Marshall, 2 September 1966, Marshall Papers, 12/7, NLA; Gordon Ford to Matheson, 21 September 1966; Marshall to Matheson, 16 November 1966, both in MC/0/1 Pt 2.

Chapter 3

1 John Legge, 'Monash—The First XV Years', *Monash Reporter*, Supplement, 'The First XV Years', 1975, p. 4.
2 Bill Rachinger, Reminiscences, unpublished account, 19 May 2010; Paddy Armstrong in *Monash Reporter*, Supplement, 'The First XV Years', 1975, p. 3.
3 *Bulletin*, 2 May 1964, p. 27.
4 Group Interview with Former Members of the Science Faculty, 4 September 2009.
5 Interview with Bruce Holloway, 18 February 2010.
6 Interview with John Legge, 12 February 2010.
7 *Age*, 10 February 1961.
8 Marshall to Blackwood, 30 January 1960, Jock Marshall Personnel File.
9 *Age*, 20 January 1965.
10 ibid., 10 February 1961.
11 Interview with Lady Audrey Matheson, 23 February 2010.
12 Matheson, *Still Learning*, pp. 9–10.
13 Monash Commemoration Ceremony, 16 April 1972, 1986/41/002.
14 Louis Matheson, Graduation Address for Honorary Doctorate, 1975, 1986/41/002.
15 *Monash Reporter*, no. 1, 1964.
16 ibid., no. 2, 1964. For various papers relating to this association, see Hector Monro Papers.
17 Membership figures extracted from club records by Jan Getson, December 2010.
18 Serle to Matheson, The Sad Case of the God-Professor, 31 August 1962, A/1/0 Pt 1, later published in revised form as A.G. Serle, 'God Professors and Their

Juniors', *Vestes*, vol. 5, no. 1, March 1963, pp. 11–18. The published version is 'recast and toned-down' as a critique of the Australian system in general.

19 Matheson to Serle, 3 September 1962; Serle to Matheson, 13 September 1962, both in A/1/0 Pt 1.

20 Louis Matheson, Governing the University—Some Thoughts on Problems, December 1962, A/1/0 Pt 1.

21 Butchart to Matheson, 10 September 1962, A/1/0 Pt 1.

22 Committee on University Government—Progress Report, Professorial Board Minutes, 29 May 1963; Committee on University Government, Second Progress Report, 31 January 1964, both in AB/1/3.6.

23 *Age*, 25 March 1960.

24 Some Ideas on the Structure and Function of a University with Particular Reference to Monash, n.d., C/0/3.1.

25 Matheson, *Still Learning*, p. 9.

26 Arts Faculty Executive Committee, Humanities Courses for Science Students and Science Courses for Humanities Students, 17 July 1962, 1984/52/008.

27 Anthony Clunies Ross, A Suggestion on Special Science and Humanities Courses, 9 September 1963, Meeting of Faculty of Arts 4/63, 1984/52/004.

28 Matheson, *Still Learning*, p. 9.

29 Interim Council, Arts Sub-Committee, Minutes, 4 November 1959, 1980/03/001; Frank Johnson to W.E.G. Scott, 18 April 1963; Monash University Pre-requisites, 2 July 1965, both in 1984/52/011.

30 Matheson to Dean of Arts, 2 December 1963, 1984/52/011.

31 Minutes of the Inaugural Meeting of the Faculty of Science Executive, 15 December 1961; A.J. Marshall, Proposed Developments during the Next Triennium, 12 April 1962, Faculty of Science Meeting 1/62.

32 K.C. Westfold, Future Development of the Faculty of Science, 24 July 1962, Faculty of Science Meeting 2/62; Report by the Dean on New Chairs in the Faculty of Science, 30 January 1963, Appendix B, Executive Committee Meeting 1/63.

33 Ross Day, Psychology as a Subject in the Faculty of Science, 14 September 1964, Faculty of Science Meeting 3/64.

34 P.D. Finch, Requirements in the First Degree of the Pass Degree of B.Sc., Memorandum to Members of the Faculty Board, 24 February 1966, Faculty Board Meeting 2/66.

35 Executive Committee, Faculty of Science, Minutes of Meeting 15/64, 16 December 1964.

36 Asa Briggs, 'Drawing a New Map of Learning', in David Daiches (ed.), *The Idea of a New University: An Experiment in Sussex*, André Deutsche, London, 1964, p. 66.

37 Louis Matheson, 'Problems in Australian Universities', Deakin Lecture, 1968, p. 4.

38 Louis Matheson, 'The Making of a University', *Medical Journal of Australia*, April 1969, p. 798.

39 J.D. Legge, Structure of Courses, Faculty of Arts Executive Minutes, 6 July, 11 August, 14 November 1961.

40 John Legge, 'One Man's View', *Monash Reporter*, Supplement, 1975, p. 5.

41 Professorial Board Minutes, 8 November 1960; compare Briggs, 'Drawing a New Map of Learning', p. 65.
42 Report of the Committee Appointed to Investigate the Operation of the Tutorial System of Teaching within the Faculty of Science, 10 July 1962, CM/400/4.
43 University Statistics; University Calendars.
44 Donald Cochrane Personnel File; Interview with ECOPS Staff, 11 September 2009.
45 Gus Sinclair and Tony Dingle, Interview with ECOPS Staff, 11 September 2009.
46 Based on Edna Hocking, *Keith Frearson: A Monash Legend*, published privately, 2000, and tributes by Alan Gregory, *Monash Reporter*, February 2000, p. 3; Gus Sinclair, 'Tribute', unpublished, 2000; Geoff Harcourt, *Economic Record*, 1 September 2000, both courtesy of Gus Sinclair.
47 Donald Cochrane, 'The Faculty of Economics and Politics', *Monash Reporter*, November 1968, pp. 1–4.
48 Professorial Board Minutes, 14 February 1961.
49 Cochrane, 'The Faculty of Economics and Politics'; see also tributes by Rufus Davis and Joe Isaac, *Monash Reporter*, May, September 1983.
50 Group Interview with ECOPS Staff, 11 September 2009.
51 Cochrane, 'The Faculty of Economics and Politics'.
52 R. Andrew and M. Ewing, Notes on Plans for Medical School, Interim Council Meeting, 9 February 1959.
53 Minutes of Interim Council, 16 March 1959; R. Andrew, Recommendations for the Establishment of the Medical School of Monash University, Interim Council Meeting, 11 May 1959.
54 Graeme Schofield, Letter of Application, Graeme Schofield Personnel File.
55 Interview with David de Kretser, 8 June 2010.
56 Monash Medical Centre, Submission Material [for hospital brief], 30 November 1967.
57 R.R. Andrew, 'Health Centres and Community Health Needs', *Medical Journal of Australia*, vol. 1, 30 January 1971, pp. 237–9.
58 Roger Strasser, Personal Communication, June 2010.
59 Andrew and H.A.F. Dudley to Vice-Chancellor, Origins and Planning for the Monash Medical Centre, 16 September 1966, CF/320/MON Pt 1.
60 J.G. Butchart to J.F. Emerson, 14 September 1967, CF/320/MON Pt 1.
61 Interview with Members of the Faculty of Medicine, 11 December 2009.
62 Richard Ward to Matheson, 13 March 1972, CF/300/0 Pt 4.
63 Richard Ward, 'Open Letter to the Faculty of Medicine', *Lot's Wife*, 4 September 1972; Richard Ward, 'Medical Education', *Medical Journal of Australia*, 26 August 1972, pp. 512–13.
64 Matheson to Ward, 2 October, 16 October 1972, CF/300/0 Pt 4.
65 Matheson to Hon. R.J. Hamer, 2 April 1973; Matheson to medical professors, 12 April 1973, both in CF/320/MON/1 Pt 2.
66 Matheson, *Still Learning*, p. 39.
67 Zelman Cowen to Matheson, 13 May 1960, CF/230/0.
68 Matheson to Cowen, 24 May 1960, CF/230/0.
69 Professorial Board Minutes, 28 March 1962.

70 Zelman Cowen to Matheson, 13 May 1960, CF/230/0.

71 Cecily Close, 'Derham, Sir David Plumley', in *Australian Dictionary of Biography*, vol. 17: 1981–90, Melbourne University Press, 2007, pp. 313–14.

72 Interview with Louis Waller, 18 February 2010.

73 Plan for the Faculty of Law, August 1964, CF/230/0 Pt 2.

74 Interview with Louis Waller, 18 February 2010.

75 Plan for the Faculty of Law, August 1964, CF/230/0 Pt 2.

76 Peter Hanks, Clinical Legal Education Committee, Draft Proposal, 1973, GW/230/1.

77 Philip Slade to Professor D.E. Allan, 12 April 1973; see also G. Stewart to Johnson, 11 May 1973; Allan to Stewart, 29 May 1973, all in GW/230/1.

78 Jeff Giddings, 'It's Taken a Long Time, 25 Years to Get to That Model': The Monash Clinical Model, draft chapter for PhD thesis, Griffith University, 2010. We are grateful to Professor Giddings for permitting us to see this valuable overview of the Monash program.

79 K.H. Hunt, 'Preface', in *Engineering Faculty Handbook*, 1963, 1964, 1965.

80 Report of the Committee on Courses in Education, 3 July 1962, CF/162/0 Pt 2.

81 Matheson, *Still Learning*, p. 20.

82 Louis Matheson, Conversation with Professor Selby Smith, 22 August 1963, CF/162/0 Pt 2.

83 Richard Selby Smith Curriculum Vitae, Richard Selby Smith Personnel File; James Mitchell, *A Deepening Roar: Scotch College, Melbourne, 1851–2001*, Allen & Unwin, Sydney, 2001, pp. 173–5.

84 Richard Selby Smith, Notes on the Possible Development of the Faculty of Education at Monash, 28 October 1966, CF/162/0 Pt 2.

85 This vision was realised in 1968 when Monash High became the first school in Victoria with its own closed-circuit television facilities. See 'Excerpts from The Laurels 1966', Monash Secondary College, <www.monashsc.com/1966.htm>.

86 Newman, *The Idea of a University*, Image Books, p. 165.

87 Clark Kerr, *The Uses of the University*, Harvard University Press, Cambridge, Mass., 1963, p. 20.

88 Louis Matheson, FAUSA Seminar on University Government, 1 June 1965, 1984/60/001.

89 Brenda Niall, *Life Class: The Education of a Biographer*, Melbourne University Press, 2007, p. 103.

90 'The Condition of Our Universities', in *The Incarnation in the University— Proceedings of the 13th Annual Conference of the University Catholic Federation*, Newman College, Melbourne, 1955, p. 55, quoted in Peter Janssen, *Monash University Religious Centre*, Religious Centre, Monash University, Melbourne, 1984, p. 3.

91 Interim Council, Churches Sub-Committee, Minutes, 5 August 1959.

92 Chaplaincy Committee, 9 October 1963; Archbishop Frank Woods (Melbourne) to Matheson, 8 October 1963, both in AE/965/0.1; Memorandum to the Vice-Chancellor, March 1960, quoted in Janssen, *Monash University Religious Centre*, p. 11.

93 See letters from David McKenna, Douglas Hobson, Louis Matheson and David Armstrong, *Age*, 1, 2, 7 August 1961.

94 Professorial Board Minutes, 17 January 1961; Janssen, *Monash University Religious Centre*, pp. 11–17.
95 Vice-Chancellor's Report, Council Meeting, 4/1962.
96 *Monash University Gazette*, vol. V, no. 1, 1968.
97 Woods to Matheson, 8 October 1963, AE/965/0.1.
98 Chaplaincy Centre Committee, 9 October 1963, 5 June 1967, 23 April 1968, AE/965/0.1.
99 Talk by the Vice-Chancellor at the Laying of the Foundation Stone of the Religious Centre, 9 April 1967, PW/965/0.
100 Interview with Peter Fensham, 29 November 2010; Renate Howe, *A Century of Influence: The Australian Student Christian Movement 1896–1996*, University of New South Wales Press, Kensington, 2009, p. 351.
101 Louis Matheson, Address at the Opening of the Religious Centre, 9 June 1968, *Monash University Gazette*, November 1968.

Chapter 4

1   Matheson, *Still Learning*, p. 97.
2   *Age*, 1 April 1961.
3   *Chaos*, 13 April 1961.
4   *Monash Reporter*, October 1983; *Chaos*, 20 April 1961.
5   *Chaos*, April 1961.
6   *Age*, 1 April 1961.
7   Philip Mendes, *The New Left, the Jews and the Vietnam War, 1965–1972*, Lazare, North Caulfield, Vic., 1993, p. 25.
8   Kathy De La Rue submission.
9   *Chaos*, April 1961.
10 ibid., 22 June 1961.
11 Charles Taylor, *A Secular Age*, Harvard University Press, Cambridge, Mass., 2007, Chapter 13.
12 Donald Horne, *Time of Hope: Australia 1966–72*, Angus and Robertson, Sydney, 1980, p. 42.
13 See *Oxford English Dictionary* and *Australian National Dictionary* for a range of contemporary usages.
14 *The Australian National Dictionary*, Oxford University Press, 1988, pp. 697–8.
15 *Report of the Interim Council June 1958–July 1961*, Monash University, 1961; *Report of the Council 1962*, Monash University, 1962; Monash University Statistics.
16 Ian Gibson submission.
17 Interview with David Williamson, 18 June 2010.
18 Ann Smurthwaite, 'Entrants to Monash University and the University of Melbourne', *Australian University*, vol. 12, 1974, p. 190.
19 *Tertiary Education in Australia: Report of the Committee on the Future of Tertiary Education in Australia*, vol. 1, Government Printer, Canberra, 1964–65, p. 43.
20 Mark LaPirow submission.
21 Stephen Wilks submission.
22 Ian Gibson submission.
23 Smurthwaite, 'Entrants to Monash University', p. 183.
24 ibid., pp. 182–3.

25 *Orientation Handbook 1964.*

26 *Monash 66*, directed by Chris Maudson, 1966.

27 Laurie Duggan, 'The Monash Years, 1968–72', <austlit.com/a/duggan/d1monash-years.html>.

28 Pam Gibson submission.

29 Wendy Verhagen, *Report on Five Pilot Meetings of Second Year Students Selected at Random*, Monash University, 1973.

30 Ian Gibson submission.

31 Monash University Association, Report on Transition Conference, 30 June 1967, PT/0/1.

32 Bradley to Sweeney, 18 August 1975, 1982/05/051.

33 *Chaos*, 20 June 1962.

34 Louis Matheson, Address to the 'Industry, the University and Tomorrow' Conference, 1968, 1986/41/002.

35 *Report of the Council 1967.*

36 Butchart to Swan, 22 January 1975, 1982/05/56.

37 Graeme Sweeney, report based on discussions with groups of part-time students, 2 October 1974, 1982/05/56.

38 George Cally, Asian Students in Australia, 1966, 1982/05/123.

39 *Age*, 5 August 1964.

40 Matheson to Secretary, Transport Regulation Board, 25 July 1960; E.V. Field to Matheson, 27 July 1960; Interim Council Minutes, 10 October 1960, all in LE/1 Pt 1.

41 Sweeney to Sinclair, 4 February 1970, 1982/05/071.

42 Stephen Timewell submission.

43 Graeme Sweeney, Report on Public Transport, July 1972, 1982/05/71; Sweeney, Report to Residence Committee on Transport, 1966, LE/1 Pt 3; Sweeney, Report to Residence Committee on Transport, 1965, 1987/10/5; Sweeney to Matheson, 15 June 1967, LE/1 Pt 3.

44 Sweeney to Falk, 4 July 1967, 1982/05/122.

45 *Age*, 11 March 1961.

46 Smurthwaite, 'Entrants to Monash University', p. 177.

47 Student Housing Report, November 1964, 1987/10/33.

48 Mary Baldwin, Progress Report, 24 February 1964, April 1964, 1987/10/33.

49 Mary Baldwin, Staff/Student Housing Report, 1963, 1987/10/32.

50 Mary Baldwin, Student Housing, 19 April 1966, 1982/05/123.

51 *Herald*, 11 May 1966; *Orientation Handbook 1966.*

52 Interview with Ken Ward, 10 June 2010.

53 Interview with John (Jack) McDonell, 23 June 2010.

54 Matheson, *Still Learning*, p. 103; Residence Committee Meeting 2/63, 1987/10/32.

55 *Herald*, 11 May 1966.

56 Housing Committee Meeting, May 1963, 4/63, 1987/10/32.

57 McDonell to Halls of Residence Enquiry Committee, 5 November 1974, 1984/39/5.

58 *Alf*, 1971, n.p.

59 McDonell to S.A. Birch, 28 August 1973, 1987/10/36.

60 Student Housing Office, Report of Housing Officer, April 1965, 1987/10/34.

61 Interview with Marian Quartly, 8 December 2010.
62 Matheson, *Still Learning*, p. 105.
63 *Mannix College Handbook 1969*.
64 Fitzgerald to Sweeney, 22 May 1973, 1982/05/93.
65 Gabrielle L. McMullen, *Omnia Omnibus—All Things to All Collegians: The First Twenty-Five Years of Mannix College*, Aristoc Offset, Glen Waverley, Vic., 1993, p. 31; Correspondence between Sweeney and Fitzgerald, May 1973, 1982/05/93.
66 Housing Committee Report, November 1967, 1987/10/34.
67 Alan Wearne submission.
68 Stephen Wilks submission.
69 Matheson, *Still Learning*, p. 99; Sweeney to Johnson, 6 May 1964, 1982/05/159.
70 Pam Gibson submission.
71 *Orientation Handbook 1963*.
72 *Chaos*, 22 June 1961.
73 *Report of the Council 1962*.
74 *Orientation Handbook 1962*.
75 Clubs & Societies Council, *Thirty Years: A History of Clubs and Societies at Monash University, 1962–1992*, Clayton, Vic., 1992.
76 Judith Buckrich, unpublished memoir.
77 David Bradley, 'Theatre at Monash: A Personal View', in Kent and Cuthbert (eds), *Making Monash*, pp. 67–79.
78 *Orientation Handbook 1962*.
79 *Chaos*, 13 July 1961.
80 *Orientation Handbook 1963*.
81 Clubs & Societies Council, *Thirty Years*.
82 ibid.; *Chaos*, 26 June 1963.
83 *Apathy*, 4 March 1970.
84 Sweeney to Johnson, 6 May 1964, 1982/05/159.
85 *Chaos*, 18 July 1962, 22 April 1964.
86 *Report of the Council 1966*.
87 *Age*, 1 April 1961.
88 Clubs & Societies Council, *Thirty Years*.
89 *Chaos*, 22 June 1961.
90 *Lot's Wife*, 24 June 1964.
91 Damien Broderick, *Climbing Mount Implausible: The Evolution of a Science Fiction Writer*, Borgo Press, Rockville, MD, 2010; Damien Broderick, Personal Communication, 26 March 2011.
92 Broderick, *Climbing Mount Implausible*, p. 89.
93 Pam Gibson submission.
94 *Lot's Wife*, 15 June 1965.
95 'Fear And Loathing on the Vietnam War Trail: Looking Back at "Depraved" Lot's Wife', 10 February 2011, <littledarwin.blogspot.com/2011/02/fear-and-loathing-on-vietnam-war-trail.html>.
96 Graeme Sweeney, Speech at Monash 50th Anniversary Reunion, 25 February 2011.

97 Laurie Duggan, 'Graveney Marsh: Random Jottings on Poetry, Visual Culture, Local Oddities and the Weather', <graveneymarsh.blogspot.com.au/2008/03/mirabeau-goat-poems.html>.
98 Alan Wearne submission.
99 ibid.
100 *Age*, 7 August 1961.
101 ibid., 2 August 1961.
102 ibid., 30 July 1961.
103 *Orientation Handbook 1963*.
104 *Chaos*, 3 August 1961.
105 ibid., 20 July 1961.
106 Interview with David Bradley, 17 March 2010.
107 Ron Taft interviewed by Philip Mendes, 7 November 1990; Les Goldschlager interviewed by Philip Mendes, 18 December 1989, transcripts provided by Mendes.
108 Howe, *A Century of Influence*, pp. 294–5, 348, 366.
109 Bruce Wearne submission.
110 Howe, *A Century of Influence*, pp. 363–4.
111 Constitution of the Christian Radical Club, 1985/12/39; Bruce Wearne submission; Howe, *A Century of Influence*, p. 366.
112 Kathy De La Rue submission.
113 *Student Newspaper*, April 1961.
114 *Chaos*, 22 June 1961.
115 ibid., 6 July 1961.
116 ibid.
117 ibid., 20 July 1961, 20 June 1962, 12 June 1963.
118 Job to Sweeney, 2 December 1965, 1982/05/120.
119 *Lot's Wife*, 3 April 1969.
120 Interview with Gary Pollard, 25 June 2010.
121 Laurie Duggan submission; Pam Gibson submission.
122 Mark LaPirow submission.
123 *Chaos*, 12 June 1963.
124 *Monash Reporter*, Supplement, November 1975; Discussion with Former Students at Monash 50th Anniversary Reunion, 25 February 2011.
125 *Public Affairs Committee Research Bulletin*, vol. 2, no. 1, 1970.
126 Farm Week Committee of Enquiry Papers, 1995/20/5.
127 *Report of the Interim Council June 1958–July 1961*; *Monash Reporter*, Supplement, November 1975.
128 Union Board Catering Committee, 26 November 1965, 1991/03/18.
129 Paul Francis Perry, *The Rise and Fall of Practically Everybody: An Account of Student Political Activity at Monash University, 1965–72*, P.F. Perry, Balaclava, Vic., 1973, pp. 100–1.
130 Matheson, *Still Learning*, p. 99.
131 Interview with Ken Ward, 10 June 2010; Michael Headberry, quoted in John Elliott Report, 17 January 2011, <jdereport.com.au/monash-university-early-years-group-to-hold-50th-farm-anniversary/>.
132 Ross Fitzgerald, *My Name Is Ross: An Alcoholic's Journey*, University of New South Wales Press, Sydney, 2010.

133 Interview with David Williamson, 18 June 2010.
134 Peter Steedman, Speech at Monash 50th Anniversary Reunion, 25 February 2011.
135 *Lot's Wife*, 15 June 1965.
136 Simon Marginson, *Monash: Remaking the University*, Allen & Unwin, St Leonards, NSW, 2000, p. 46.
137 *Truth*, 10 September 1968.
138 *Orientation Handbook 1964*.
139 *Lot's Wife*, 7 August 1964; *Chaos*, 4 March 1964.
140 Fitzgerald, *My Name Is Ross*, pp. 24, 32.
141 Mark LaPirow submission.
142 *Orientation Handbook 1966*.
143 Pam Gibson submission.
144 *Sun*, 29 November 1967.
145 *Age*, 30 May 1968.
146 *Student Newspaper*, April 1961.
147 *Chaos*, 6 June 1962.
148 *Lot's Wife*, 13 July 1964.
149 Louis Matheson, Speech at First Graduation Ceremony, 8 April 1964, 1986/41/002.
150 *Chaos*, 10 March 1962.

Chapter 5

1 *Age*, 17 July 1968.
2 Two 'histories' were written by participants in the Monash student movement: Michael Hyde (ed.), *It Is Right to Rebel*, Diplomat, Canberra, 1972 (an account of the activities of the Monash Labor Club written by a group of key players), and *The Rise and Fall of Practically Everybody: An Account of Student Political Activity at Monash University, 1965–72*, self-published by moderate observer Paul Francis Perry, 1973.
3 Matheson, *Still Learning*, p. 109.
4 John Searle, 'The Anatomy of Student Revolt', *Monash Reporter*, June 1969.
5 Perry, *The Rise and Fall of Practically Everybody*, p. 4.
6 Sweeney to Griffiths, 1966, 1982/05/121.
7 Richard Gordon and Warren Osmond, 'An Overview of the Australian New Left', in Richard Gordon (ed.), *The Australian New Left*, W. Heinemann, Melbourne, 1970, pp. 16–24.
8 Peter Edwards, *A Nation at War: Australian Politics, Society and Diplomacy during the Vietnam War 1965–1975*, Allen & Unwin in assoc. with the Australian War Memorial, St Leonards, 1997, pp. 67–9.
9 *Lot's Wife*, August 1965.
10 *Sun*, 23 March 1967.
11 Hyde (ed.), *It Is Right to Rebel*, p. 115.
12 Warren Osmond, 'Universities: The Critical Weakness', *Analysis*, no. 2, 1968.
13 Interview with Dave Nadel, 12 February 2010.
14 ibid.
15 Matheson to members of Council, September 1969, 1986/41/05.

16 Michael Hyde, *All Along the Watchtower: Memoir of a Sixties Revolutionary*, Vulgar Press, Carlton North, Vic., 2010, pp. 22–3.

17 Duggan, 'Graveney Marsh'.

18 Alan Wearne submission.

19 Mendes, *The New Left, the Jews and the Vietnam War*, p. 66.

20 Facts about the Anti-LBJ Demonstration, November 1966, 1982/05/121.

21 Matheson, *Still Learning*, p. 125.

22 Alan Wearne submission.

23 Interview with John (Jack) McDonell, 23 June 2010.

24 Kent and Cuthbert (eds), *Making Monash*, p. 16.

25 Laurie Duggan submission.

26 Elliot Gingold submission.

27 Julie Ockenden, 'Anti-War Movement and the Student Revolt at Monash: An Examination of Contending Ideologies', history honours thesis, Monash University, 1985, p. 8.

28 Albert Langer, 'Universities and Student Rebels', *Analysis*, July 1968.

29 Gordon and Osmond, 'An Overview of the Australian New Left', pp. 32–3.

30 *Age*, 1 October 1988.

31 Laurie Duggan submission.

32 See, for example, Perry, *The Rise and Fall of Practically Everybody*, p. 6.

33 Mendes, *The New Left, the Jews and the Vietnam War*, p. 35.

34 Judith Buckrich, unpublished memoir.

35 *Age*, 7 August 1969; *Truth*, 20 September 1969.

36 Perry, *The Rise and Fall of Practically Everybody*, p. 15.

37 Hyde (ed.), *It Is Right to Rebel*, pp. 14–16.

38 ibid., p. 18; Interview with ECOPS Staff, 11 September 2009.

39 *Herald*, 24 July 1967.

40 Elliot Gingold submission.

41 Hyde, *All Along the Watchtower*, p. 53.

42 Hyde (ed.), *It Is Right to Rebel*, p. 67.

43 CUF broadsheet, 17 May 1968, 1982/05/122.

44 Sweeney to Griffiths, 1966, 1982/05/121.

45 *Print*, 17 May 1968, quoted in Hyde (ed.), *It Is Right to Rebel*, p. 69.

46 Monash Association of Students: A Description, 8 November 1968, 1982/05/145.

47 Hyde (ed.), *It Is Right to Rebel*, pp. 62–3.

48 Jim Falk, Personal Communication, 27 January 2010.

49 *Free Speech*, vol. 6, no. 6, 1971.

50 Grant Stinear and Keith Harvey to Chancellor and members of Council, 4 August 1971, A/0/4 Pt 3.

51 *Focus*, vol. 1, no. 7, 1969.

52 Interview with Dean Wells, 27 January 2010.

53 Louis Matheson, Student Activism at Monash, c. September 1969, 1986/41/05.

54 *Sun*, 7 March 1969.

55 Perry, *The Rise and Fall of Practically Everybody*, p. 33.

56 ibid., p. 33; Dave Nadel, Personal Communication, 6 October 2010.

57 Hyde (ed.), *It Is Right to Rebel*, pp. 84–5.

58 *Age*, 15 July 1969.

59 ibid., 7 August 1969.
60 Perry, *The Rise and Fall of Practically Everybody*, p. 39a.
61 Ockenden, 'Anti-War Movement', p. 94.
62 Interview with Louis Waller, 18 February 2010.
63 Hyde (ed.), *It Is Right to Rebel*, p. 112.
64 *Public Affairs Committee Research Bulletin*, vol. 2, no. 1, 1970, 1986/31/01. On Monash University Scientific and Industrial Community, see Matheson, *Still Learning*, pp. 148–51.
65 Hyde (ed.), *It Is Right to Rebel*, pp. 118–20.
66 Perry, *The Rise and Fall of Practically Everybody*, p. 79.
67 *Age*, 8 October 1970.
68 ibid., 10 October 1970.
69 Perry, *The Rise and Fall of Practically Everybody*, p. 149.
70 Hyde (ed.), *It Is Right to Rebel*, p. 149.
71 *Age*, 9 October 1970.
72 ibid., 19 October 1970.
73 Matheson, *Still Learning*, p. 139.
74 Legge, 'One Man's View'; see also *Monash University, 1961–1986: The First 25 Years*, Information Office, Clayton, Vic., 1986.
75 Smash the Exams Campaign pamphlet, 1971, 1988/15/90.
76 Why Re-Enrol in Economics Today?, 13 December 1972, 1988/15/96.
77 Tess Lee-Ack submission.
78 ibid.
79 *Australian*, 12 October 1974.
80 *Nation Review*, 23 September–3 October 1974.
81 *Herald*, 26 September 1975.
82 ibid., 14 October 1970.
83 See, for example, *Australian*, 30 September 1968.
84 *Monash Is Burning: Counter-Orientation Handbook 1971*.
85 *Australian*, 9 October 1970.
86 Interview with Dean Wells, 27 January 2010.
87 Ian Turner, The Nature of the University, and the Question of Protest and Discipline, 14 September 1970, Turner Papers, box 41, NLA.
88 Ian Turner, A Critique of Occupation, 1970, Turner Papers, box 36, NLA.
89 Bruce Holloway submission.
90 Elliot Gingold submission.
91 *Sun*, 29 June 1968.
92 Jim Falk, Personal Communication, 27 January 2010.
93 *Age*, 1 October 1988.
94 Vice-Chancellor's Report, in *Report of the Council 1971*.
95 Hyde (ed.), *It Is Right to Rebel*, p. 90.
96 Bruce Wearne submission.
97 Jim Falk, Personal Communication, 27 January 2010.
98 Legge to Shaw, 22 August 1969, John Legge Staff File, School of Philosophical, Historical and International Studies.
99 Hyde (ed.), *It Is Right to Rebel*, pp. 240–6.
100 Matheson, *Still Learning*, p. 172.
101 *Monash Reporter*, Supplement, 'The First XV Years', 1975.

102 Recommendations of the Commission on University Affairs, October 1969, 1984/40/2; John N. Crossley, Personal Communication, 29 December 2010.
103 Elliot Gingold submission.
104 Interview with Dave Nadel, 19 February 2010.
105 Louis Matheson, University Autonomy and Academic Freedom, August 1973, 1984/60/36, p. 4.
106 Louis Matheson, Address to Medico-Legal Society, 16 August 1969, 1984/60/36; Louis Matheson, Draft Letter to Students for 1971 Orientation Handbook, 23 November 1970, 1986/31/2.
107 Matheson, *Still Learning*, p. 173.
108 Louis Matheson, 'The University Challenge', Pleasant Sunday Afternoon Address, Wesley Church, 13 October 1971, 1984/60/36; Lady Audrey and Colin Matheson, Personal Communication, 20 July 2010.
109 Interview with Louis Waller, 18 February 2010.
110 Interview with Lady Audrey Matheson, 23 February 2010.

Interlude: A vanishing vice-chancellor

1 Andrew to Ian Langlands, 16 January 1975, 1994/07/099.
2 Profile for a Vice-Chancellor, 1975, 1994/07/099.
3 Robert Blake, 'Vaizey, John Ernest, Baron Vaizey (1929–1984)', *Oxford Dictionary of National Biography*, Oxford University Press, 2004–10, <www.oxforddnb.com.ezproxy.lib.monash.edu.au/view/article/31783?docPos=2>.
4 Geoffrey Harcourt to Ian Langlands, 16 April 1975, 1994/07/114.
5 Alan Bullock to Robert Porter, 10 April 1975, 1994/07/114.
6 Minutes of Sixth Meeting of Selection Committee (Vice-Chancellorship), 26 May 1975, 1994/07/114.
7 Vaizey to Johnson, 5 July 1975, 1994/07/114.
8 Vaizey to Johnson, Postscript, 26 June 1975, 1994/07/114.
9 Matheson to Richard Eggleston, 30 June 1975, 1992/05/009.
10 Notes of Chancellor for Briefing of Council, 11 August 1975, 1994/07/114.
11 Vaizey to Johnson (cable), 11 August 1975, 1994/07/114.
12 *Age*, 12 August 1975.
13 *Lot's Wife*, vol. XV, no. 18, 11 August 1975.
14 The adjectives are Vaizey's, as quoted in Richard Eggleston, Summary of Transactions in the Vaizey Affair, Chancellor's File, 1994/67/114.
15 Barry Jones, *A Thinking Reed*, Allen & Unwin, Sydney, 2006, pp. 234–5, attributes Vaizey's renunciation of the Monash vice-chancellorship to the impression of philistinism surrounding the Rowlinson debacle but appears unaware of Marina Vaizey's interest in the position.
16 Vaizey to Johnson (cable), 15 September 1975, 1994/07/114.
17 Vaizey to Johnson, 17 September 1975, 1994/07/115.
18 *Times Education Supplement*, 19 September 1975, copy in 1994/07/114.
19 'Appointment of Professor Vaizey: Statement by the Chancellor', *Sound*, 6 October 1975; Vaizey to Eggleston, 22 October 1975, 1994/07/115.
20 Vaizey to Porter, 15 December 1975 (copy), 1992/05/007.

Chapter 6

1 Vice-Chancellor Selection Committee, Agenda and Minutes, 9 October, 13 November 1975, 1994/07/100.
2 Interview with Ray Martin, 7 September 2010.
3 BWH [Hone], Handwritten Notes, 22 July 1976, Frank Johnson Notes, 1994/07/100.
4 Johnson to Martin, 19 August 1976, Ray Martin Personnel File.
5 'Interview with Professor Ray Martin', Australian Academy of Science, 2008, <www.science.org.au/scientists/interviews/m/rm.html>.
6 Marginson, *Monash*, p. 27.
7 Interview with Bob Porter, 19 March 2010.
8 *Monash Reporter*, July 1978.
9 Vice-Chancellor's Report, in *Report of the Council 1977*.
10 *This is Monash: A Visitor's Guide*, Monash University, 1980.
11 Seven Monash academics were members of the prestigious Academy of Science by 1980, and ten were members of other academies.
12 *Monash Reporter*, November 1986.
13 *Orientation Handbook 1977*.
14 *Monash Reporter*, March 1977.
15 ibid., July 1978.
16 ibid., June 1982.
17 ibid., March 1984.
18 Interview with Professor Maureen Brunt, 5 July 2010; Maureen Brunt, Occasional Address, Hon. DComm, University of Melbourne, 2000; Megan L. Richardson, 'Introduction', in Megan Richardson and Philip Williams (eds), *The Law and the Market*, Federation Press, Sydney, 1995, pp. 1–9.
19 Ray Over, 'Women Academics in Australian Universities', *The Australian Journal of Education*, vol. 25, no. 2, 1981, p. 168.
20 Jenny Strauss submission.
21 Gabrielle Baldwin, *Women at Monash University*, Monash University, 1985, pp. 10–12, 22.
22 ibid., pp. 93, 96.
23 ibid., p. 22.
24 John Legge, Southeast Asian Studies, [June 1964], Faculty of Arts, Dean's Correspondence, 1984/52/11.
25 Matheson to Scott, 26 May, 8 June 1964; Scott to Matheson, 4 June 1964, both in Faculty of Arts, Dean's Correspondence, 1984/52/11.
26 Bureau of Aboriginal Affairs, 27 April 1964; Colin Tatz to Matheson, 13 May 1964; Professorial Board Paper, 24 June 1964, all in CF/166/0 Pt 1.
27 Jemma Purdey, *From Vienna to Yogyakarta: The Life of Herb Feith*, University of New South Wales Press, Sydney, 2011, p. 83.
28 Michael Clyne, 'From Bilingual to Linguist', in Mary Besemeres and Anna Wierzbicka (eds), *Translating Lives: Living with Two Languages and Cultures*, University of Queensland Press, St Lucia, 2007, p. 13.
29 *Monash Reporter*, June 1980.
30 Bureau of Aboriginal Affairs, Professorial Board Paper, 24 June 1964, CF/160/0 Pt 1.

31 Interview with Colin Tatz, ABC Radio, August 2007, <www.abc.net.au/reslib/200708/r164834_609803.asx>.

32 Phillipa Weeks, 'Eggleston, Elizabeth Moulton', in *Australian Dictionary of Biography*, vol. 14, Melbourne University Press, 1996, pp. 84–5.

33 *Herald*, 27 September 1968.

34 *Monash Reporter*, May 1982.

35 Harry Kannegiesser, *Conception in the Test Tube: The IVF Story*, Macmillan, South Melbourne, 1988.

36 Proposal to Establish a Centre for Human Bioethics, Submission to Professorial Board, 10 September 1980, C306/80; *Monash Reporter*, March 1980; 'Celebrating 25 Years of the Centre for Human Bioethics', 4 June 2009, <arts.monash.edu.au/bioethics/history/index.php>.

37 Peter Singer and Helga Kuhse, '1980–2005: Bioethics Then and Now', *Monash Bioethics Review*, vol. 25, no. 1, 2006, p. 11.

38 Proposal for a Centre of Policy Studies, 23 September 1977, CF/210/0 Pt 1.

39 Press Release, 2 August 1979, CF/210/0 Pt 1.

40 *Australian*, 21 February 1987.

41 *Financial Review*, 18 February 1987.

42 *Monash Reporter*, June 1977, November 1978, March 1979.

43 Sarah Rood, *From Ferranti to Faculty: Information Technology at Monash University, 1960 to 1990*, Monash University ePress, Clayton, Vic., 2008.

44 *Monash Review*, no. 2, 1985.

45 *Monash Reporter*, November 1986.

46 Matheson, *Still Learning*, pp. 148–51.

47 *Report of the Council 1986*.

48 Interview with Bruce Holloway, 18 February 2010.

49 *Monash Review*, February 1986; Marginson, *Monash*, p. 37.

50 Ellis to Logan, 2 April 1987, A/1/0.1 Pt 2.

51 Information Office File, 1994/24/58.

52 *Monash Reporter*, August 1978.

53 ibid., November 1984.

54 *Age*, 3 July 2006; Celia Rosser submission.

55 Bruce Holloway, Personal Communication, 24 February 2010.

56 *Monash Reporter*, April 1986; Marginson, *Monash*, p. 190.

57 *Monash Reporter*, April 1985.

58 David Bradley, 'Theatre at Monash: A Personal View', in Kent and Cuthbert (eds), *Making Monash*, Monash University, 1986, pp. 67–78; Marginson, *Monash*, pp. 185–6, 190–3.

59 Ellis to Logan, 2 April 1987, A/1/0.1 Pt 2.

60 Marginson, *Monash*, p. 30; Baldwin, *Women at Monash University*, pp. 12–14.

61 *Monash Reporter*, November 1977; T. Hore and L.H.T. West (eds), *Mature Age Students in Australian Higher Education*, Higher Education Advisory and Research Unit, Monash University, 1980; Marginson, *Monash*, p. 30.

62 Higher Education Advisory and Research Unit, *The Early Leavers Scheme at Monash University, 1974–1977*, Monash University, 1977.

63 Interview with Bill Kent, 11 May 2010.

64 Marginson, *Monash*, p. 42.

65 *Sun*, 23 May 1984.

66 D.S. Anderson, R. Boven, P.J. Fensham and J.P. Powell, *Students in Australian Higher Education: A Study of Their Social Composition since the Abolition of Fees*, Australian Government Publishing Service, Canberra, 1980, p. 201.
67 Merle Ricklefs, Personal Communication, 13 November 2010.
68 *The Monash University Scheme for Aborigines: Prospectus*, Monash University, 1982; *Monash Reporter*, March 1984.
69 Merle Ricklefs, Personal Communication, 13 November 2010.
70 *Monash Reporter*, March 1984.
71 Deirdre F. Jordan, *Monash University Orientation Scheme for Aborigines: External Review*, Monash University, July 1987.
72 Merle Ricklefs, Personal Communication, 13 November 2010.
73 Stephen Wilks submission.
74 *Monash Resource Book 1980*.
75 Interview with Tim Costello, 17 December 2010.
76 Report to Martin, Information Office File, 1994/24/101; *Monash Reporter*, November 1984.
77 Interview with Peter Costello, 21 March 2011. Further quotations from Costello are from this interview.
78 Left Collective, Free Speech: A Radical Perspective, pamphlet, c. 1977, 1996/01/54; *Lot's Wife*, 27 June 1977.
79 *Orientation Handbook 1977*.
80 Tracey Aubin, *Peter Costello: A Biography*, HarperCollins, Pymble, NSW, 1999, Chapter 2.
81 *Monash Reporter*, November 1981.
82 Interview with Jon Faine, 5 September 2011. Further quotations from Faine are from this interview.
83 Performer and impersonator Campbell McComas, then a law student at Monash University, fooled hundreds of students and staff when he posed as leading English criminal law scholar Professor Glanville Williams, presenting a lecture on the laws governing rape. See 'A Tribute to Campbell McComas', *Law Matters*, March 2005, pp. 1–12, <www.law.monash.edu.au/alumni/law-matters/law-matters-march-05.pdf>.
84 'Interview with Professor Ray Martin', Australian Academy of Science, <www.science.org.au/scientists/interviews/m/rm.html>.
85 *Report of the Council 1986*.

Chapter 7

1 G.S. Harman (ed.), *Academia Becalmed: Australian Tertiary Education in the Aftermath of Expansion*, ANU Press, Canberra, 1980, p. 1.
2 Geoff Maslen, 'Education's Cyclone Belt', *Age*, 22 May 1989.
3 The following paragraphs draw on Malcolm I. Logan, 'Journeys through Time and Place', in Leslie J. King (ed.), *North American Explorations: Ten Memoirs of Geographers from Down Under*, Trafford Publishing, Victoria, BC, 2007, pp. 72–90, and Interview with Mal Logan, 16 December 2010.
4 Logan, 'Journeys', p. 80.
5 M.I. Logan, Address at Premier's Luncheon, 1 May 1987; Logan, 'Journeys', pp. 80–1.
6 Interview with Mal Logan, 16 December 2010.

7   Compare Marginson, *Monash*, pp. 48–51.
8   Report on the Top Administrative Structure (hereafter McNeill Report), August 1985, pp. 5, 16; Council Minutes, 12 August 1985.
9   Interview with Peter Wade, 2 March 2011.
10 ibid.
11 Committee of Vice-Chancellors and Principals, Report of the Steering Committee for Efficiency Studies in Universities, London, 1985, also quoted in the McNeill Report, Appendix 3.
12 Interview with Mal Logan, 16 December 2010.
13 McNeill Report, pp. 8, 25.
14 Daly to Lush, 4 September 1985; Legge to Lush, 25 July 1985, Mal Logan Personnel File; Vice-Chancellor Search Committee, 1984–85, AA/2/4.16.
15 Interview with Peter Darvall, 28 January 2011.
16 M.I. Logan to R.L. Martin, 17 April 1985, A/1/0.1.
17 M.I. Logan to P. Beilby and others, 22 April 1986; M.I. Logan, Longer Term Policies and Planning, n.d., A/1/0.1; Mal Logan, Address at Premier's Luncheon, 1 May 1987, Logan Speeches.
18 *The Monash Plan: A Strategy for the Future*, Monash University, 1 December 1987, p. 21.
19 Higher Education Advisory and Research Unit, Academic Staff Flow, 21 February 1986; Planning Working Group Meeting 3, 11 June 1987.
20 M.I. Logan, Planning at Monash—the Current Situation, 21 May 1987, Planning Working Group Papers, 1997/04/006.
21 Logan's thinking is outlined in a series of papers: Strategic Longer-Term Planning, 22 April 1986; Directions for the Future, 27 April 1987; Planning at Monash—The Current Situation, 21 May 1987; Monash University: A Strategy for the Future, 7 September 1987; and Confidential Introductory Note, 5 October 1987, all in AZ/5.
22 M.I. Logan to all professors, 13 August 1987, Planning Working Group Meeting 6, 25 August 1987, 1997/04/006.
23 Interview with Mal Logan, 16 December 2010.
24 Who was in the circle? Logan, his friend and fellow geographer Bob Smith of New England, Don Aitkin of ANU, and sometimes Don Watts of Western Australia Institute of Technology, later Bond University, are often mentioned. Journalists sometimes suggested there was also a 'Mauve Circle' of more conservative vice-chancellors headed by Melbourne's David Penington and including Michael Osborne of La Trobe, Don McNicol of Sydney and John Niland of the University of New South Wales. *Age*, 21 July 1988, 6 March 1993.
25 Interview with Mal Logan, 16 December 2010.
26 David Buckingham, Personal Communication, 28 June 2011.
27 *Higher Education: A Policy Discussion Paper* (hereafter Green Paper), Australian Government Publishing Service, Canberra, December 1987, p. 1.
28 *Australian*, 8 October 1987.
29 Editorial, *Age*, 23 September 1987; Greg Sheridan, *Australian*, 16 September 1987; Kenneth Randall, *Business Review Weekly*, 18 September 1987; Max Walsh, *Sydney Morning Herald*, 9 August 1987.
30 *Herald*, 21 September 1987.

31 Interview with Mal Logan, 16 December 2010.
32 M.I. Logan, New Approaches to Education: A Comment, November 1987, Logan Speeches.
33 See, for example, M.I. Logan, Vice-Chancellor's Speech to Staff on Clayton Campus, 1 July 1992, 1997/06/009.
34 M.I. Logan, The External Environment, 9 November 1987, 1994/24/020; *Australian*, 14 May 1986.
35 For Logan's thinking about comparative advantage, see M.I. Logan, Some General Observations, Address to Planning Working Party Meeting 4, 6 July 1987.
36 M.I. Logan, The External Environment, 9 November 1987, 1994/24/020.
37 Interview with Peter Wade, 2 March 2011.
38 In the following pages, we have drawn substantially on an unpublished detailed narrative by Arthur O'Neill, Under New Management: Monash University and the Amalgamations [1996]. With Dr O'Neill's permission, we have also consulted and occasionally quoted from the transcripts of the interviews he conducted with key participants.
39 Interview with Peter Darvall, 28 January 2011.
40 Committee of Deans, 3 February 1988.
41 Logan to Cullen, 12 February 1988, 1989/14/012.
42 Committee of Deans, 3 February 1988.
43 ibid., 1 December 1987.
44 ibid., 3 February 1988.
45 ibid., 11 February 1988.
46 ibid., 8 March 1988.
47 ibid., 8 March, 7 April 1988.
48 Arthur O'Neill, Interview with Mal Logan, 8 May 1996.
49 Committee of Deans, 8 March 1988.
50 ibid., 8 March, 10 May 1988.
51 ibid., 7 April 1988.
52 Gus Sinclair, Interview with ECOPS Former Staff, 11 September 2009.
53 Interview with Peter Darvall, 28 January 2011.
54 Committee of Deans, 8 March 1988.
55 Arthur O'Neill, Under New Management: Monash University and the Amalgamations, unpublished account, [1996], pp. 105–7.
56 Arthur O'Neill, Interview with John White, 3 April 1996.
57 Arthur O'Neill, Interviews with Geoff Vaughan, 24 October 1996, and Mal Logan, 16 December 2010.
58 Amalgamations: Selected Statistics and Comments, n.d., RMOT88/1255.
59 R.A. Jarvis to P. Darvall, 9 May 1988, RMOT88/1255.
60 Darvall to Logan, 13 May 1988, RMOT88/1255.
61 ibid.
62 W.A. Sinclair, Consequences of Amalgamation with Chisholm Institute of Technology, May 1988, RMOT88/1255.
63 ibid.; see also W.A. Sinclair, Response to Provisional Recommendations, 1 September 1989, RMOT89/1425.
64 Peter Chandler to M.D. Watson, 21 September 1989, RMOT89/1425.

65 Arthur O'Neill, Under New Management: Monash University and the Amalgamations, unpublished account, [1996], p. 113.

66 Committee of Deans, 12 July 1988.

67 Arthur O'Neill, Under New Management: Monash University and the Amalgamations, unpublished account, [1996], pp. 89–92; Arthur O'Neill, Interview with John White, 3 April 1996.

68 Arthur O'Neill, Interview with John Hay, 31 October 1997, quoted in O'Neill, Under New Management: Monash University and the Amalgamations, unpublished account, [1996], p. 95.

69 Proposal for a Faculty of Computing and Information Technology, 20 September 1989, RMOT89/1425.

70 Hugh Emy to J. Hay, 15 September 1989; see objections to the move in Sinclair to Hay, 19 September 1989, and David Kemp to Hay, 20 September 1989, all in RMOT89/1425.

71 Report to the Implementation Committee, September 1989, RMOT89/1425.

72 Dean's Advisory Committee on Academic and Administrative Structures, Draft Response to Recommendations of Working Party I, Faculty of Arts, n.d., RMOT89/1637.

73 W.A. Brown to M.I. Logan, 6 April 1989, RMOT89/0701.

74 Arthur O'Neill, Under New Management: Monash University and the Amalgamations, unpublished account, [1996], p. 129; Interview with Peter Darvall, 28 January 2011.

75 Academic Programs and Structures Working Party, Report, September 1989, RMOT89/1716.

76 Max L. King to M.I. Logan, 24 August 1989, RMOT89/1425.

77 Arthur O'Neill, Under New Management: Monash University and the Amalgamations, unpublished account, [1996], p. 132.

78 Vaughan to Logan, 14 December 1989, RMOT89/1637.

79 ibid.

80 Hay to Vaughan, 23 January 1990, RMOT89/1637.

81 Arthur O'Neill, Interview with Mal Logan, 8 May 1996.

82 ibid.; *Monash Reporter*, 22 March 1989.

83 V. Lynn Meek, *Brown Coal or Plato? A Study of the Gippsland Institute of Advanced Education*, ACER, Melbourne, 1984, pp. 68, 75; Neil Terrill in Group Discussion with Former Gippsland Staff, 26 November 2010.

84 Green Paper, p. 37.

85 Pritchard to Logan, 1 July 1988, RMOT88/1255.

86 Arthur O'Neill, Interview with Murray Homes, 18 October 1996.

87 Arthur O'Neill, Interviews with Tom Kennedy, 25 October 1996, and Murray Homes, 18 October 1996.

88 Arthur O'Neill, Interview with Tom Kennedy, 25 October 1996.

89 ibid.

90 Logan to Kennedy, 23 July 1990, RMOT89/1764.

91 Arthur O'Neill, Interview with John Hay, 31 October 1997.

92 Logan to Kennedy, 15 June 1990, RMOT89/1764.

93 Arthur O'Neill, Under New Management: Monash University and the Amalgamations, unpublished account, [1996], p. 96.

94 The view of some participants in Group Discussion with Former Gippsland Staff, 26 November 2010.
95 Arthur O'Neill, Under New Management: Monash University and the Amalgamations, unpublished account, [1996], p. 67.
96 *Age*, 21 February 1991.
97 A hierarchy of 20 areas of dissatisfaction, from notes made independently by John Bradshaw and John Cashion, n.d. [1991], Monaghan Papers, copies in Monash University Archives.
98 TRAG Membership List, TRAG, Monaghan Papers.
99 Interview with Joe Monaghan, 25 February 2011.
100 ibid.; Record of Interview between the TRAG Committee and the Vice-Chancellor, Prof. M. Logan, 10 May 1991, VC and Deans Ad Hoc, Monaghan Papers.
101 Robert Porter to Committee of Deans, Re Meeting of Ad Hoc Sub-Committee of Committee of Deans with Action Group, 31 May 1991, VC and Deans Ad Hoc, Monaghan Papers.
102 TRAG, Summary of the Protest Meeting, 3 June 1991, 2001/13/158; General Protest Meeting, 3 June 1991, TRAG, Monaghan Papers.
103 Interview with Mal Logan, 16 December 2010.
104 Research Review Committee, Minutes, 2/1991, 4 November 1991.
105 Research Review Committee, Report, April 1992; Academic Board Minutes, 4/92, pp. 533–57.
106 Research Review Committee, Minutes, 5/1991, 5 December 1991, p. 5; compare Logan to Waller, 4 November 1991, RMOT91/0881.
107 Interview with Mal Logan, 16 December 2010.
108 Janette Bomford, *Victorian College of Pharmacy: 125 Years of History, 1881–2006*, Victorian College of Pharmacy, Parkville, Vic., 2006.
109 Interview with Mal Logan, 16 December 2010.
110 Bomford, *Victorian College of Pharmacy*, p. 220.
111 T.R. Watson and L.R. Butcher to J.S. Dawkins, 4 September 1990, RMOT90/1634.
112 Logan to Pullen, 1 March 1991, RMOT90/2151.
113 Interview with Peter Wade, 2 March 2011.
114 Interview with Mal Logan, 16 December 2010.
115 ibid; M. Logan, Monash/Chisholm Links, Memorandum to the Professorial Board, 31 January 1989; Professorial Board Minutes, 8 February 1989.
116 Arthur O'Neill, Interviews with Tom Kennedy, 25 October, 8 November 1996.
117 Arthur O'Neill, Interview with Michael Watson, 26 October 1995.
118 Interview with Peter Darvall, 28 January 2011.
119 Arthur O'Neill, Interview with Mal Logan, 8 May 1996.
120 Grant Harman and Lynn Meek, 'Lessons from Recent Experience with Mergers', in G. Harman and L. Meek (eds), *Australian Higher Education Reconstructed? Analysis of the Proposals and Assumptions of the Dawkins Green Paper*, Department of Administrative and Higher Education Studies, UNE, Armidale, 1988, p. 120.
121 Interview with Joe Monaghan, 25 February 2011.
122 Interview with Mal Logan, 16 December 2010; compare Committee of Deans, 11 February 1988.

123 Jillian Maling and Bruce Keepes, 'Amalgamations and the Operation of Multi-Campus Institutions', in Harman and Meek (eds), *Australian Higher Education Reconstructed?*, p. 130.

Chapter 8

1 Mal Logan, Annual Report for Council, 1990; see also Proposals to Encompass the Establishment of Monash University College Gippsland within the Greater Monash, [1988], RMOT89/1764.
2 Peter Darvall, Speech at 25th Anniversary Medal Presentation, 28 October 1994.
3 Mission and Objectives of the Faculty of Medicine, 25 May 1989, 2000/28/521.
4 Robert Porter, Personal Communication, 18, 19 June 2011.
5 N.A. Saunders, Reorganising the Faculty of Medicine, 1 October 1999, RMO1998/0296.
6 A Preliminary Analysis of the Likely Growth in Demand for Higher Education in the Mornington Region of Melbourne, 25 November 1991; see also Department of Planning and Housing, Assessment of Proposed Higher Education Campus Melbourne's South-Eastern Suburbs, n.d., 1995/13/001.
7 Logan to G. Gallas, 19 September 1990, 1995/13/001.
8 Allen to Logan, 29 July, 26 August, 18 September 1991, 1995/13/001.
9 Logan to Allen, 9 October 1991, 1995/13/001.
10 Interview with John Bigelow, 21 January 2011.
11 Pargetter to Allen, 25 March 1992, RMOT92/0297.
12 *Berwick Journal*, 1 June 1992.
13 ibid., 21 September 1992.
14 Brian Costar and Nick Economou, 'The 1992 Election: Emphatically Ending the Labor Decade', *Current Affairs Bulletin*, vol. 69, no. 7, 1992, pp. 27–31.
15 Haddon to Logan, 3 December 1992, RMOT92/0934.
16 Higher Education Developments in the South Eastern Growth Area, Report of Joint Ministerial Working Party, July 1992, RMOT92/0297.
17 Logan to Allen, 28 September 1992, RMOT92/0934.
18 Logan to Allen, 8 September 1993; Michael Gallagher, Department of Employment, Education and Training, to Logan, 16 November 1993, both in RMOT92/0934.
19 Logan to Allen, 25 November 1993; [Lauchlan Chipman], Agreement between Monash University and Department of Education on Development of Berwick Campus, November 1993, both in RMOT92/0934.
20 Woods Bagot, Information Technology & Communications Building and Master Plan for Future Development (June 1994); Higher Education Developments in the South Eastern Growth Area, Report of Joint Ministerial Working Party, July 1992, both in RMOT92/0934.
21 'The Birth of Berwick: A New Campus for Monash University at Berwick, Melbourne, Victoria', n.d., <www.tefma.com/uploads/assets/conference_papers/1999/trembath.pdf>.
22 Cliff Bellamy to I. Chubb and J. White, Berwick and Educational Technology—Status Report, 7 October [1994], RMOT94/1185.
23 Monash University Library, Electronic Library Reserve System, Berwick Academic Group, 21 June 1994, RMOT95/0522.

24 Robert Pargetter to E. Lim, 10 August 1994, RMOT94/0934.

25 Ivan Gregory to Lauchlan Chipman, 1 December 1995, 95/1343.

26 Robert Pargetter to Marian Quartly, 30 November 1995, 95/1343.

27 Interview with Former Berwick Staff, 24 November 2010.

28 Ivan Gregory to Pargetter, 14 March 1995, RMOT95/0522.

29 Interview with Former Berwick Staff, 24 November 2010.

30 Interview with Mal Logan, 16 December 2010.

31 John White to Merran Evans, Berwick Directional Statement, 5 July 2000, RMO1998/0609.

32 Interview with Leon Piterman and Phil Steele, 20 May 2011.

33 John Dawkins, Budget Speech, 1992, p. 54, quoted in William Renner, 'The Open Learning Initiative: A Critical Analysis of Change in Australian Higher Education 1990–97', PhD thesis, Monash University, 2003, p. 85.

34 Compare Robert H.T. Smith, 'Reflections on a Peripatetic Career', in King (ed.), *North American Explorations*, pp. 163–79, and Logan, 'Journeys'; Anthony L. Pritchard, *Peering over the Balcony [A Life in Education]*, self-published, Melbourne, 2008, pp. 194–5.

35 Pritchard, *Peering over the Balcony*, p. 120.

36 *Age*, 19 April 1986.

37 A.L. Pritchard to Deans, 2 July 1990, RMOT90/0512.

38 Moodie to Pritchard, 11 October 1990, RMOT91/0104.

39 Moodie to Evans and others, 22 October 1990; Gary Neat to Rory Sutton, 16 October 1990, both in RMOT91/0104.

40 W.J. Howse to Jocelyn Calvert, 8 April 1991, RMOT91/0104.

41 See Brian Watt to Mal Logan, 20 May 1991, RMOT91/0104; John Chick to A.L. Pritchard, 31 May 1991; Chick to Moodie, 10 July 1991, both in RMOT91/0792.

42 Renner, 'The Open Learning Initiative', p. 93.

43 Pritchard to Brian Watt, n.d., RMOT91/0104; Pritchard, Open Learning Initiative, Report to Monash University Executive, 13 May 1992, RMOT92/0538.

44 Renner, 'The Open Learning Initiative', pp. 120–3.

45 ibid, pp. 124–5.

46 Mal Logan to Michael Gallagher, Laying the Foundations of an Electronic University, unpublished report, 14 December 1992, RMOT92/1243.

47 Mal Logan to W.A. Sinclair and J.A. Hay, 14 September 1987; Institute of Contemporary Asian Studies, [Objectives], n.d.; Faculty of Arts, Institute for Contemporary Asian Studies, Aims and Objectives, n.d.; Elaine McKay, Consultancy on Asian Studies, Final Report, 15 July 1988, all in RMOT88/0009.

48 G. Neustupny to R. Pargetter, 21 August 1989, RMOT89/0879.

49 Stewart E. Fraser, 'Australia and International Education: The Goldring and Jackson Reports—Mutual Aid or Uncommon Advantage?', *Vestes*, vol. 27, no. 2, 1984, pp. 15–29.

50 David Buckingham, Personal Communication, 28 June 2011.

51 Green Paper, p. 83.

52 Chin Yee Wah, 'The Evolution of Chinese Malaysian Entrepreneurship: From British Colonial Rule to Post-New Economic Policy', *Journal of the Chinese Overseas*, vol. 4, no. 2, November 2008, pp. 214–15.

53 Ross King, *Kuala Lumpur and Putrajaya: Negotiating Urban Space in Malaysia*, National University of Singapore Press, Singapore, 2008, pp. 66–7.

54 Katie Dyt, *Monash University Sunway: Building on a Vision*, Monash University, 2007, p. 6.

55 Pritchard to Logan, 11 September 1987, CA/6/7.

56 K.Y. Chin to Logan, 12 September 1987, CA/6/7.

57 *Australian*, 5 September 2007.

58 Interview with Phang Koon Tuck, 7 March 2011.

59 Undated advertisement from *New Straits Times*, filed in RMOT88/2470.

60 Pritchard to Logan, 16 September 1987, CA/6/7.

61 Pritchard to Ministry of Education, 26 February 1988, RMOT88/0448.

62 Pritchard to K.Y. Chin, 15 October 1987, RMOT88/0448.

63 Michael Yeoh to Peter Chandler, 20 September 1989, RMOT90/0605.

64 Logan to Vaughan, 27 September 1989, RMOT89/1637.

65 Pritchard to Logan, 14 March 1991, RMOT89/1173.

66 Dyt, *Monash University Sunway*, p. 11; *Australian*, 8 November 1991.

67 Pritchard to K.Y. Chin, 30 October 1991; Pritchard to Logan, 25 November 1991, both in RMOT91/0131.

68 M.I. Logan, Proposal Universiti Monash Malaysia (Confidential), 26 February 1992, 92/0590.

69 Pritchard to Logan, 9 March 1992, RMOT91/0131.

70 Dyt, *Monash University Sunway*, p. 15.

71 Memorandum of Understanding between Monash University and Sunway College to Establish a Branch Campus of Monash in Malaysia, 6 June 1994, RMOT94/0446.

72 Michael Yeoh to Geoffrey Vaughan, 11 October 1989, RMOT89/1610.

73 A Monash Campus in Malaysia, Extract from Meeting with Committee of Deans, 28 February 1995, 3/1995, RMOT92/1158.

74 A.L. Pritchard to Vice-Chancellor, A Malaysian-Monash Campus, 28 January 1992, p. 2, RMOT92/1158.

75 Minutes of Academic Board, 31 January 1996.

76 Logan to Jeffrey Cheah, 4 January 1996, RMOT96/0682.

77 Leo West to Michael Yeoh, 2 August 1995; Leo West to John Dawkins, 26 June 1995, both in RMOT96/0682; Dawkins to Logan, 13 September 1995; Dawkins to Razak, 13 September 1995; Logan to Dawkins, 18 September 1995; West to Logan, 27 September 1995, all in RMOT95/1073.

Chapter 9

1 *Making the Move: Transition Information for Secondary Students*, videorecording, produced by Amgad Louka, Prospective Students Office, Monash University, Clayton, Vic., 1999; *Orientation Handbook 1996*.

2 Peter Karmel, 'Public Policy and Higher Education', *Australian Journal of Management*, vol. 26, August 2001, pp. 127–8.

3 Ian R. Dobson, 'Overseas Students in Australian Higher Education: Trends to 1996', *People and Place*, vol. 5, no. 1, 1997, p. 26; Monash University Statistics.

4 Bob Birrell, Angelo Calderon, Ian R. Dobson and T. Fred Smith, 'Equity in Access to Higher Education Revisited', *People and Place*, vol. 8, no. 1, 2000, p. 50; Ian R. Dobson and Bob Birrell, 'Equity and University Entrance, a 1997 Update', *People and Place*, vol. 6, no. 3, 1997, pp. 83–7; Bob Birrell and Ian Dobson, 'Equity and University Attendance: The Monash Experience', *People and Place*, vol. 5, no. 2, 1997, pp. 51–2.
5 *Lot's Wife*, 19 February 1990.
6 *Ink*, vol. 3, 1999.
7 *Making the Move.*
8 Making the Transition: A Conference on the Transition from Secondary School to University, Monash University, Clayton, Vic., 1995.
9 *Orientation Handbook 1989.*
10 *Orientation Handbook 1990.*
11 *Counter Faculty Handbook 1989*; *Lot's Wife*, 19 February 1990.
12 *Lot's Wife*, 24 March 1992.
13 *Oxalian*, August 1994.
14 ibid., August 1992.
15 *Annual Report 1990.*
16 Clare McCausland submission.
17 *Academic Survival Guide 1992.*
18 Ruth Kweitel submission.
19 Letter dated 19 July 2001, RMO1997/1142.
20 History of MUISS, c. 1993, 1997/02/09.
21 *Network*, 1995.
22 Submission for Extension of the Overseas Students Lounge, c. 1991, 1997/02/09.
23 *Lot's Wife*, April 1997.
24 Report of Grievance Week Survey, September 1992, 1997/02/45.
25 Calvin Chow submission.
26 *Monash Reporter*, May 1990; Bob Birrell, Ian R. Dobson and T. Fred Smith, 'The New Youth Allowance and Access to Higher Education', *People and Place*, vol. 7, no. 3, 1999, p. 28.
27 Birrell and Dobson, 'Equity and University Attendance', p. 56; *Orientation Handbook 1992.*
28 Birrell, Calderon, Dobson and Smith, 'Equity in Access to Higher Education Revisited', p. 55.
29 Lenore Cox, *Students at Monash Gippsland: Healthy & Wise?*, Monash University College Gippsland, Churchill, Vic., 1992.
30 Birrell and Dobson, 'Equity and University Attendance', p. 56.
31 Michael Long and Martin Hayden, *Paying Their Way: A Survey of Australian Undergraduate University Student Finances*, Australian Vice-Chancellors' Committee, September 2001, p. 13, <www.universitiesaustralia.edu.au/resources/272/138>; Craig McInnis, Richard James and Robyn Hartle, *Trends in the First Year Experience in Australian Universities*, Australian Department of Education, Training and Youth Affairs, July 2000, pp. 38–9; Monash University Office of Planning and Academic Affairs, Student Profile: Past and Future.
32 Vikki Plant submission.
33 Clare McCausland submission.

34 Melissa McVeigh submission.
35 Pamela Dooley submission.
36 R.J.W. Selleck, *The Shop: The University of Melbourne 1850–1939*, Melbourne University Press, 2003, pp. 253–7.
37 *Orientation Handbook 1990*.
38 Tabatha Pettitt submission.
39 *Oxalian*, June 1994.
40 Pamela Dooley submission.
41 *Orientation Handbook 1990*.
42 Sasha Shtargot submission.
43 '"It's Time": Student Politics, 1996', <www.youtube.com/watch?v=-5gI9KhIBTU>.
44 *Lot's Wife*, 1 August 1995.
45 Student to Robinson, 10 July 2001, RMO1997/1142.
46 *Lot's Wife*, February 1997.
47 ibid., 25 April 1995.
48 *Otico*, vol. 3, no. 4, 1995.
49 *Orientation Handbook 1996*.
50 ibid.
51 *Lot's Wife*, 21 February 1995.
52 *Sun*, 1 July 1988; Representations to Licensed Student Entertainment Venue Sub-Committee, 1993, 2009/41/24.
53 *Oxalian*, June 1994.
54 Mal Logan to Michael Gallagher, Laying the Foundations of an Electronic University, attachment, 14 December 1992, RMOT92/1243.
55 Don Aitkin, 'The Astonishing Rise of Higher Education', *Quadrant*, January–February 1996, p. 81.
56 *Annual Report of the University Librarian 1992*.
57 Clare McCausland submission.
58 McInnis, James and Hartle, *Trends in the First Year Experience*, pp. 26–33.
59 *Orientation Handbook 1991*.
60 Leeyong Soo submission.

Chapter 10

1 Cordiner King Hever, Notes on Selection of Vice-Chancellor, c. 1995, 2002/09/02.
2 Interview with Bill Rogers, 17 March 2011; Interview with Marian Quartly, 8 December 2010.
3 *Times Higher Education Supplement*, 29 March 1996; *Australian*, 13 March 1996.
4 David Robinson, Curriculum Vitae, Hull University Archives.
5 *Australian*, 20 March 1996.
6 Simon Marginson, 'Competition and Contestability in Australian Higher Education, 1987–1997', *Australian Universities Review*, vol. 40, no. 1, 1997, p. 12.
7 *Lot's Wife*, August 1998.
8 Jennifer Strauss, 'Fumbling in a Greasy Till', in Paul James (ed.), *Burning Down the House: The Bonfire of the Universities*, Association for the Public University with Arena Publications, North Carlton, Vic., 2000, p. 53.
9 VCG Meeting 1/97, 2005/35/36; Interview with Peter Darvall, 28 January 2011.

10 VCG Meeting 1/97, 3/97, both in 2005/35/36.

11 *Lot's Wife*, August 1998.

12 *Leading the Way: The Monash Plan, 1998–2002*, 1997; *Leading the Way: The Monash Plan, 1999–2003*, Monash University, 1999.

13 Don Watson, 'Verbs on the Run—Verbiage', *Australian*, 9 February 2000.

14 *Times Higher Education Supplement*, 29 March 1996.

15 David Robinson, From International Relationships to a Global Presence: with Monash University as the Case Example, unpublished paper, January 1998, RMO1997/0672; see also David Robinson, The New Education for the Twenty-First Century—Higher Education in the Emerging Global Order, 16 November 1998, CF07/500.

16 *Leading the Way: Monash 2020*, 1999.

17 Global Marketing and Brand Management, RMO2001/0329; Ron Davies submission.

18 Interview with Stephen Parker, 22 June 2011.

19 *Leading the Way: Monash 2020*, 1999.

20 Institute for the Study of Global Movements, RMO2001/0993.

21 Graeme Davison to David Robinson, 24 March 1999, RMO1998/0350.

22 Interview with Stephen Parker, 22 June 2011.

23 Memorandum to Committee of Deans, Monash Global: The International Activities of Monash, 5 November 1998, RMO1999/0597; *Monash Memo*, February 1999.

24 *Leading the Way: Monash 2020*; see also *Global Development Framework*, December 1999, RMO2000/0343.

25 Monash University: International Priorities, August 1999, RMOR1999/065.

26 History of Monash University's Presence and Activity in Indonesia 1993 to 1999, c. 1999, RMO1999/0597.

27 Monash Global Board Paper: Indonesia Campus Project; Ian Porter and R.J. Cochrane, Indonesia—Campus Project, c. January 1999, both in RMO2000/1311.

28 Interview with Lee Weng Keng, 10 March 2011; Elizabeth Lee, Personal Communication, 10 March 2011.

29 Interview with Robin Pollard, 11 March 2011; *New Straits Times*, 24 February 1998.

30 Dyt, *Monash University Sunway*, pp. 17–18.

31 Interview with Lee Weng Keng, 10 March 2011.

32 Interview with James Warren, 18 May 2010.

33 Quartly to Robinson, 2 March 1998, RMO1997/0485.

34 Academic Board Meeting 3/98, 22 April 1998.

35 James Warren, Personal Communication, 15 July 2011.

36 ibid.

37 Interviews with Mahendhiran Nair, 8 March 2011, and Cathy Yule, 11 March 2011.

38 Vice-Chancellor to Academic Board Meeting 2/98.

39 Interview with Lily Leong, 7 March 2011.

40 Interview with Lee Weng Keng, 10 March 2011.

41 Interview with Mahendhiran Nair, 8 March 2011.

42 Interview with Bob Bignall, 10 March 2011.

43 S. Parker, Monash in Europe, Briefing Paper, Academic Board Meeting 1/2002.
44 Interview with Bill Kent, 11 May 2010.
45 ibid.; see also Bill Kent, 'Gaining a Foothold: Australian Cultural Institutions in Italy', in Bill Kent, Ros Pesman and Cynthia Troup (eds), *Australians in Italy*, Monash University Publishing, Clayton, Vic., 2010, pp. 39–53; see also Cynthia Troup with Jo-Anne Duggan, *A Site of Convergence: Celebrating 10 Years of the Monash University Prato Centre*, Monash University Publishing, 2011.
46 Interview with Ian Davey, 3 March 2011.
47 Maloney to Porter, 11 August 1997, RMO1997/0672.
48 John Rickard and Peter Cunliffe, Assessment of Market Potential for Education in South Africa, c. May 1997, RMO1997/0672.
49 Monash-South Africa. A Joint Venture between Monash University and the ADvTECH Group of Companies, September 1997, RMO1997/0672; Proposal for the Establishment of a Monash Campus in South Africa, c. November 1997; A Proposal for Monash University and ADvTECH Education Holdings Limited to Establish a Campus of Monash University in South Africa, April 1998, both in RMO 1999/1105.
50 Robinson to Bengu, 23 July 1998, RMOR1999/044.
51 *Sunday Times*, 17 December 2000.
52 *Campus Review*, 22 March 2000.
53 Asmal to Porter, 13 September 1999, RMOR1999/045.
54 Anthony Pollock, Questions for the Reference Group, with annotations, 6 August 1999; Status Report to Vice-Chancellor, with attachment, MUSA Worst Case Scenario, August 1999, both in RMOR1999/045.
55 Andrew Markus, Dissenting Paper, September 1999, 2000/10/01; Personal Communication.
56 Interview with Jerry Ellis, 19 May 2011.
57 Interview with Peter Darvall, 28 January 2011; Anthony Pollock, Monash University Southern Africa: Background to the Project, February 1998, RMOR1999/046.
58 Robinson to Council, Monash South Africa: Origins and Purpose, 30 July 2001, RMOR2001/050.
59 David Robinson, Monash South Africa: Key Issues, July 2001, Council Minutes 5/2001.
60 Asmal to Robinson, 12 June 2000, RMOR2000/043.
61 Robinson to T.D. Mseleku (Director General, Department of Education South Africa), 10 December 1999, RMOR1999/045.
62 John Anderson, Monash South Africa Project Report, 31 July 2001, Council Minutes 5/2001.
63 Robinson to Council, Monash South Africa: Origins and Purpose, 30 July 2001, RMOR2001/050.
64 *Age*, 30 July 2002.
65 Interview with Jerry Ellis, 19 May 2011.
66 *Leading the Way: Monash 2020*, p. 13.
67 Complaints Regarding Redundancies and Review, RMO1997/1002.
68 Julie Wells, National Tertiary Education Union, *7.30 Report*, ABC TV, 16 November 1998, <www.abc.net.au/7.30/stories/s66623.htm>.
69 *Science at Monash*, March 1998, RMO1997/0855.

70 Ronald Wallace Davies Personnel File.
71 Davies to Robinson, 13 November 1997, RMO1997/0855.
72 Professor in Department of Chemistry to Robinson, 20 November 1997, RMO1997/0855.
73 Dr John Beardall (on behalf of the Science Faculty Action Committee) to Robinson, 2 December 1997, RMO1997/0855.
74 Robinson to Davies and heads of Science departments, RMO1997/0855.
75 Ron Davies submission.
76 Paul Rodan, unpublished memoir, n.d.
77 Quartly to Arts Faculty, 12 May 1996, in personal files of Professor David Garrioch.
78 Quartly to Robinson, 11 November 1997, Arts Restructuring Process, Faculty of Arts.
79 Faculty of Arts, Contribution to the Faculty 1994–1997, n.d., [1998], Faculty of Arts Office.
80 Motions from a Meeting of the Faculty of Arts, 14 May 1998.
81 Professor David Garrioch, Personal Communication, 20 May 2011.
82 Robinson to Quartly, 5 June 1998; Quartly to Arts Faculty, Arts Faculty Restructuring, 25 June 1998.
83 Vice-Chancellor to Arts Faculty Staff, 23 July 1998.
84 Complaints Regarding Redundancies and Review, RMO1997/1002.
85 Robinson to Legge, 31 July 1998, RMO1998/2181.
86 B. Caine, G. Davison and B. Kent to Robinson, 4 August 1998, RMO1998/2181.
87 Robinson to Legge, 6 August 1998, RMO1998/2181.
88 Watson to Secretary, University Council, 11 September 1998, RMO1998/2181.
89 Unconfirmed Motions Passed, as Amended, by the Arts Board, Faculty of Arts, Meeting 5/98, 9 September 1998, Arts Restructuring, Arts Faculty; Faculty Board Minutes 5/98.
90 Cocklin to Quartly, 16 September 1998; Quartly to Cocklin, 20 September 1998, both in Arts Restructuring Process, Arts Faculty Restructuring, Faculty of Arts Office.
91 Robinson to Review Group, 1 September 1998, RMOR1998/070.
92 Interview with Marian Quartly, 8 December 2010.
93 Robinson to Sir William Taylor, 6 February 2001, RMO2000/0879.
94 Phil Baty, Personal Communication, 4 February 2011.
95 Interview with Jerry Ellis, 19 May 2011.
96 Paul Rodan, 'A Modest Victory for Academic Values: The Demise of David Robinson', *Australian Universities Review*, vol. 46, no. 2, 2004, pp. 19–20.
97 *Monash Gazette*, July 2002.
98 Bigelow to Ellis, 5 July 2002, 2003/50/01; Interview with John Bigelow, 21 January 2011.
99 Ellis to all staff, 8 July 2002, 2003/50/01.
100 Bouma to Ellis, 8 July 2002, 2003/50/01.
101 Interview with Stephen Parker, 22 June 2011.
102 Bouma to Ellis, 10 July 2002, 2003/50/01.
103 *Age*, 12 July 2002.
104 ibid., 13 July 2002.

105 Jim McGrath submission.
106 Interview with John Bigelow, 21 January 2011.
107 Willis to colleague, 29 August 2002, copy supplied by Professor Willis.
108 Willis to Faculty of Education, 11 July 2002, copy supplied by Professor Willis.
109 *Age*, 17 July 2002.
110 Interview with John Bigelow, 21 January 2011.
111 Interview with Jerry Ellis, 19 May 2011.
112 Kevin H. Bell QC, Memorandum of Advice, 15 July 2002, 2007/37/35.
113 Peter Darvall, Speech on Receiving his 25 Year Service Medal, 28 October 1994.
114 Peter Wade, Occasional Address to Graduation Ceremony, Faculty of Business and Economics, 6 October 1999.
115 *Age*, 20 July 2002; Council Meeting 7/2001.
116 Interview with Bill Kent, 11 May 2010.

Interlude: Death in the family

1 Narrative based on Testimony of Lee Gordon-Brown, Brett Inder and others at Committal Hearing of Huang Xiang, September 2003, 2010/23/005; [Meredith Jackson], Draft Briefing for Monash Council, Shooting Incident 21 October 2002; Meredith Jackson and Keith McLaren, Outline for the VCG, 6 November 2002; Draft Report to Council, The Incident of 21 October; RMOR2002/124.
2 Liisa Williams to David Garrioch, 21 October 2003, archived email, copy supplied by Liisa Williams.
3 Interview with Peter Darvall, 16 January 2011.
4 'Shooting Rocks Melbourne's Monash University', *PM*, ABC Radio, 21 October 2002, <www.abc.net.au/pm/stories/s706904.htm>.
5 Messages archived at <www.monash.edu.au/alumni/news/incident4.html>.
6 Interview with Peter Darvall, 16 January 2011.

Chapter 11

1 Still Learning: The Report of Our Self-Review, May 2002, p. 15; Quality Development Committee Minutes, 28 August 2002, 26 February 2003, RMO2003/0442.
2 Monash Values, Discussion Drafts, GDB, 22 January 2003, 1 April 2003, Academic Board Minutes 2/2003.
3 Candidates for the Position of Vice-Chancellor, Draft Declaration, 26 August 2002, Council Minutes 5/2002.
4 Selection of Vice-Chancellor and President, Draft Guidelines, 26 August 2002; Council Minutes, 5/2002; Interview with Stephen Parker, 22 June 2011.
5 Interview with Stephen Parker, 22 June 2011.
6 Isabel Carter, *Woman in a Wig: Joan Rosanove, QC*, Lansdowne Press, Melbourne, 1970, p. 102; Barbara Falk, 'Rosanove, Joan Mavis', *Australian Dictionary of Biography*, National Centre of Biography, ANU, <adb.anu.edu.au/biography/rosanove-joan-mavis-11560/text20631>; Graeme Larkins, Royal Australian College of Physicians, College Roll; 'Lusink (Peg), Margaret', in *Who's Who*, 2011; The University of Melbourne, Honorary Degree, Professor Richard Graeme Larkins, 21 December 2004.

7 Interview with Richard Larkins, 19 July 2011.
8 ibid; Richard Larkins, Personal Communication, 22 July 2011.
9 Richard Larkins, Occasional Addresses, 4 October, 16 December 2003; Richard Larkins, [Gippsland] Graduation Speech, n.d. [15 September 2003], all in Larkins Speeches. We are grateful to Kerrie Edwards for assistance in accessing the archive of Larkins' speeches.
10 Academic Board Minutes 5/2003, 1 October 2003.
11 Interview with Richard Larkins, 19 July 2011.
12 Draft Framework for University-Wide Planning, Committee of Deans Minutes, n.d., 6/2002.
13 Conceptual Framework for Campus Planning, Discussion Paper Version 2, 31 August 2003; Michelle King, Re-thinking Campus Planning Methodology, Discussion Paper 3, 7 June 2004; Stephen Parker, Re-thinking Campus Planning, Discussion Paper Version 4, 14 September 2003, all in 2006/02/19.
14 *Monash Memo*, 20 July 2005.
15 VCG Meeting, 10 September, 19 November 2003.
16 Stephen Parker, Being Positioned/Position Taking, powerpoint presentation, September 2005, copy supplied by Professor Parker.
17 Interview with Richard Larkins, 19 July 2011.
18 Robert Porter to medical professors and others, 17 February 1994, 2003/21/24.
19 N.A. Saunders to Robinson, 14 October 1999, 2010/48/7.
20 Interview with Lee Weng Keng, 10 March 2011.
21 Interview with Richard Larkins, 19 July 2011.
22 Report of Vice-Chancellor's Advisory Group Relating to the Risk Review of South Africa, 14 August 2003, 2006/02/08.
23 Interview with Richard Larkins, 19 July 2011.
24 Interview with Kevin Foster, 13 April 2010.
25 Interview with Simon Adams, 17 May 2010.
26 Interview with Richard Larkins, 19 July 2011.
27 Richard Larkins, Report on Visit to Monash South Africa, Council Minutes, 3 November 2003, 7/2003.
28 Interview with Kevin Foster, 13 April 2010.
29 Recommendations to Resources and Finance Committee and to Council Concerning Future Operations of Monash University in South Africa, 12 July 2004, Council Minutes 4/2004.
30 Interview with Richard Larkins, 19 July 2011.
31 Report of Vice-Chancellor's Advisory Group Relating to the Risk Review of South Africa, 14 August 2003, 2006/02/08.
32 Parker, Being Positioned/Position Taking.
33 Richard Larkins, *Four Corners*, interview, ABC TV, 27 June 2005.
34 'University Rankings 2010', <www.opq.monash.edu.au/research/external/leaguetables/rankings-influence-and-methodological-issues-2010-smte.pdf>.
35 Richard Larkins, Kincaid Smith Oration, 10 May 2006, Larkins Speeches.
36 Richard Larkins, Address to National Press Club, 18 March 2009.
37 Richard Larkins, Why Should Our Universities Engage Internationally?, 5 July 2006, Larkins Speeches.
38 Richard Larkins, 'The Asia Society', July 2006, <www.iitbmonash.org/>; *Monash Memo*, March 2006; Interview with Richard Larkins, 19 July 2011.

39 Draft Global Developments Paper, August 1999, RMOR1999/065.
40 Monash in China 2010—A Strategy Paper and an Update on Monash University's China Strategy, Council Minutes 3/2005.
41 'Monash Develops a Sichuan Flavour', *Monash Memo*, 13 December 2006.
42 Stephanie Fahey, Personal Communication, 23 September 2011.
43 Interview with Tam Sridhar, 1 July 2011.
44 Larkins, 'The Asia Society'.
45 Vice-Chancellor's Campus Planning Committee Minutes Meeting, 14, 15 June 1995, RMOT91/0051; Landscaping Proposal, 8 June 1995, RMOT93/0831.
46 Campus Urban Plans, 2003–04, 2006/02/18.
47 Frank Eastwood, The Beginnings of the Monash Faculty Club, unpublished memoir, 2011.
48 Statistics supplied by Jan Getson and Adam Kitto; Adam Kitto, Personal Communication, 29 July 2011.
49 Interview with Rob Willis, 18 July 2011.
50 Library User Statistics, courtesy Peter Mathews, 11 August 2011; Monash University Library Client Survey 2011; Cathrine Harboe-Ree, Personal Communication, 8 August 2011.
51 Office of Planning and Quality Monash University, The Monash Experience Questionnaire 2003, 2007, University and Campus Summaries.
52 *Age*, 31 August 2010.
53 Richard Scully submission.
54 Interview with Robin Pollard, 11 March 2011.
55 Interviews with Cathy Yule, 8, 11 March 2011.
56 Monash Experience Questionnaire 2003, Malaysian Campus, Part I: Summary Report, 2003.
57 Dahlia Martin submission.
58 Interview with Petunia Mpoza, 6 October 2010.
59 Interview with Sunway student leaders, 8 March 2011.
60 'Multi-Faith Centre to Foster Religious Understanding', Monash University, <www.monash.edu.my/advancement/marketing/2009/nov16-Multi-faith-Centre-To-Foster-Religious-Understanding.html>; and various documents at 'Venue Management: Multi-Faith Centre', Monash University, <www.monash.edu.my/facilities/venue-management/multi-faith.html>.
61 Interview with Craig Rowe, 6 October 2010.
62 Interview with Charmain Caroto, 8 October 2010.
63 John Anderson, Monash South Africa Project Report, 31 July 2001, Council Minutes 5/2001.
64 Interview with Simon Adams, 17 May 2010.
65 Interview with Marianne Hicks, 21 September 2010.
66 Tyrone Pretorius, Pro Vice-Chancellor's Report, 15 September 2005, Council Minutes 6/2005.
67 Interview with Will Moore, 8 October 2010.
68 Interview with Marianne Hicks, 21 September 2010.
69 Interview with Lennon Mhishi, 4 October 2010.
70 Joshua Vihishima, Personal Communication, 12 October 2010.
71 Interview with Ed Byrne, 5 August 2011.
72 Wallis Consulting, Brand Image Tracking Study, 2010, 2010/06/07.

INDEX

Note: Page numbers in *italics* denote illustrations.